AQA(B)

Learning R

PSYCHOLOGY
FOR AS

DONALD PENNINGTON
JULIE McLOUGHLIN

DYNAMIC LEARNING
Innovate • Motivate • Personalise
CD-ROM INSIDE

HODDER EDUCATION

Orders: please contact Bookpoint Ltd, 130 Milton Park, Abingdon, Oxon OX14 4SB. Telephone: (44) 01235 827720. Fax: (44) 01235 400454. Lines are open from 9.00–5.00, Monday to Saturday, with a 24-hour message answering service. You can also order through our website: www.hoddereducation.co.uk.

British Library Cataloguing in Publication Data
A catalogue record for this title is available from the British Library.

ISBN-13: 978 0 340 94702 9

First Published 2008
Impression number   10 9 8 7 6 5 4 3 2
Year   2012 2011 2010 2009 2008

Cover photo © Last Resort/Getty Images.
Typeset by Fakenham Photosetting Limited, Fakenham, Norfolk.
Printed in Italy for Hodder Education, part of Hachette Livre UK, 338 Euston Road, London NW1 3BH

Contents

This book has been designed for students and teachers following the GCE AS Level Psychology Specification B offered by the Assessment and Qualifications Alliance (AQA). There are ten chapters, which cover the topic areas in Unit 1 Introducing Psychology and Unit 2 Social Psychology, Cognitive Psychology and Individual Differences. Each chapter covers the specification content and includes descriptions of concepts, theories and studies, along with summary evaluation points.

'How Psychology Works'

At the end of each chapter there are activities to aid understanding of 'How Psychology Works'. These are essential classroom activities to enable students to 'think like a psychologist' and apply their knowledge of practical methods in psychology. The skills acquired through these activities will be tested fairly extensively in the examinations, where students are required to answer questions on research methods and data analysis. It is recommended that students keep a detailed record of these activities in a separate section of their classroom folder and use these as part of their examination preparation.

It is very important that students intending to do the Unit 2 examination before the Unit 1 examination cover the Experimental Methods section of Research Methods in Unit 1. This is because questions in Unit 2 will also assess knowledge and understanding of this aspect of practical psychology.

Further reading

There are suggestions for further reading at the end of each chapter. The introductory texts should be accessible for all students. The specialist texts are more demanding and perhaps more useful for teachers, although they will also be useful and interesting for the more ambitious student.

Dynamic Learning CD-ROM

The CD-ROM in the back of this book provides fantastic extra resources for students, including interactive drag-and-drop activities, multiple-choice questions, and additional further reading and website lists.

The authors would like to thank family, friends and colleagues for their support. Thanks also to Emma Woolf and Kate Short at Hodder Education for their guidance and advice. Particular thanks to Alison Thomas for her superb efficiency and attention to detail. Finally, a special mention is due to the many AS Level students who have unwittingly helped in the preparation of this book. Student response and feedback is the very best way to learn what works and what does not.

Donald Pennington and Julie McLoughlin

The authors and publishers would also like to thank the following for the use of photographs in this volume:

pp.1, 8, 13, 24 © Bettmann/Corbis; p.60 (top left) © Dennie Cody/Getty Images; p.60 (top right) © Barry Lewis/Corbis; p.72 © BW/TS/Keystone USA/Rex Features; pp.75, 297 © Bubbles Photolibrary/Alamy; p.89 © Paul Shearman/Alamy; p.108 © Monika Graff/The Image Works/Topfoto; p.125 (left) © Marmaduke St. John/Alamy; p.125 (right) © Flirt/Corbis/Photolibrary; p.129 © Lew Merrim/Science Photo Library; p.147 © Adams Picture Library t/a apl/Alamy; p.152 © Richard Pohle/Rex Features; p.158 © Richard Young/Rex Features; p.163 © David Giles/PA Archive/PA Photos; p.164 © From the film Obedience © 1968 by Stanley Milgram, © renewed 1993 by Alexandra Milgram, and distributed by Penn State; p.176 © Vidal/Sierakowski/Rex Features; p.184 © John Powell/ Rex Features; p.195 © Alessandra Schellnegger/zefa/Corbis; p.201 © Corbis; p.219 © Spencer Platt/Getty Images; p.232 © Time & Life Pictures/Getty Images; p.265 (Fig8.4d) © Organics image library/Alamy; p.268 © Laura Johansen/Beateworks/Corbis; p.274 © Galen Rowell/Corbis; p.276 (top) © Ray Doddy/Alamy; p.276 (middle, both) © 2007 Ron Williams/fotoLibra. All Rights Reserved; p.278 (left) © DIOMEDIA/Alamy; p.278 (right) © Matt Gray/Getty Images; p.290 © Lawrence Manning/Corbis; p.304 © Profimedia International s.r.o./Alamy; p.319 © Stephen Wiltshire – www.stephenwiltshire.co.uk; p.322 © Picture Press/Photolibrary.

What does 'the expert choice' mean for you?

We work with more examiners and experts than any other publisher

● Because we work with more experts and examiners than any other publisher, the very latest curriculum requirements are built into this course and there is a perfect match between your course and the resources that you need to succeed. We make it easier for you to gain the skills and knowledge that you need for the best results.

● We have chosen the best team of experts – including the people that mark the exams – to give you the very best chance of success; look out for their advice throughout this book: this is content that you can trust.

Welcome to Dynamic Learning

Dynamic Learning is a simple and powerful way of integrating this text with digital resources to help you succeed, by bringing learning to life. Whatever your learning style, Dynamic Learning will help boost your understanding. And our Dynamic Learning content is updated online so your book will never be out of date.

The CD in the back of the book can be used to increase your understanding of the material within the book. By navigating the menu panels on the left-hand side of the screen, you can gain access to a wealth of extra resources to help you in your studies.

● Boost your understanding through a wide variety of interactive activities, including fill-the-gap and matching activities, as well as PowerPoint presentations and worksheets

● Put your knowledge into practice using a broad range of multiple-choice questions, covering every AQA(B) Psychology topic

● View extensive additional resources, such as reading lists and links to useful websites, to further enhance your understanding

More direct contact with teachers and students than any other publisher

● We talk with more than 100 000 students every year through our student conferences, run by Philip Allan Updates. We hear at first hand what you need to make a success of your A-level studies and build what we learn into every new course. Learn more about our conferences at **www.philipallan.co.uk**

● Our new materials are trialled in classrooms as we develop them, and the feedback built into every new book or resource that we publish. You can be part of that. If you have comments that you would like to make about this book, please email us at: **feedback@hodder.co.uk**

More collaboration with Subject Associations than any other publisher

● Subject Associations sit at the heart of education. We work closely with more Associations than any other publisher. This means that our resources support the most creative teaching and learning, using the skills of the best teachers in their field to create resources for you.

More opportunities for your teachers to stay ahead than with any other publisher

● Through our Philip Allan Updates Conferences, we offer teachers access to Continuing Professional Development. Our focused and practical conferences ensure that your teachers have access to the best presenters, teaching materials and training resources. Our presenters include experienced teachers, Chief and Principal Examiners, leading educationalists, authors and consultants. This course is built on all of this expertise.

To start up Dynamic Learning now, make sure that your computer has an active broadband connection to the internet and insert the disk into your CD ROM drive. Dynamic Learning should run automatically if you have 'Auto Run' enabled. Full installation instructions are printed on the disk label.

Basic system requirements for your Student Edition: **PC** Windows 2000 (SP4), XP SP2 (Home & Pro), Vista; **PC (Server)** Windows 2000 and 2003; **Mac** Mac OS X 10.3 or 10.4; G4, G5 or Intel processor. Dynamic Learning is not currently Leopard-compatible: see the website for latest details. Up to 1.4Gb hard disc space per title. Minimum screen resolution 1024 x 768. Sound card. A fast processor (PC, 1GHz; Mac, 1.25 GHz) and good graphics card.

Copyright restrictions mean that some materials may not be accessible from within the Dynamic Learning edition. Full details of your single-user licence can be found on the disk under 'Contents'.

You can find out more at www.dynamic-learning.co.uk

Key approaches in psychology

1.1 Introduction

The word 'psychology' is derived from two Greek words: *psyche*, which literally means 'the mind or soul', and *logos*, which means 'the study of'. Hence, as a word, psychology means 'the study of mind or soul'. However, few definitions of psychology would restrict it to the study of mind alone. A more useful definition, and one which reflects what psychologists actually do, is as follows: **Psychology is the scientific study of human and animal behaviour and mental processes.**

This definition reflects the fact that psychology is concerned with mind (mental processes) and behaviour. It also emphasises that humans and animals are both legitimate objects of study, although with animals this tends to be limited to the study of behaviour. This is because we do not have the same insight into the mental processes of animals as we do with people. Humans can reflect and report on what they think and feel, whereas animals cannot. We could add to this definition that psychologists are interested in how behaviour and mind are affected by the organism's (person or animal) physical and mental state, and external environment.

Figure 1.1. The word 'psychology' derives from two Greek words: psyche *meaning 'mind', and* logos *meaning 'study of'.*

1.1.1 Psychology and other disciplines

The terms 'social sciences' or 'behavioural sciences' refer to a family or cluster of disciplines of which psychology is a member. The other disciplines are sociology, anthropology and biology. They are all interested in studying humans and animals – why they behave as they do.

Sociology is the study of groups and institutions within society. Sociology is concerned with groups such as the family, ethnic groups, subcultures (rappers or goths), religious institutions, the workplace and differences between societies. Sociologists are less interested in personality, interaction between two or more people, and social perception (how people think about other people). These are topics more suited to social psychologists. Sociology is concerned with larger groups and operates at a macro-level, while social psychology operates more at the micro-level of understanding human behaviour.

Anthropology is concerned with the different cultures that exist around the world and their historical origins and development. Anthropologists tend to work at a macro-level, concentrating on entire communities, tribes or society as a whole. Anthropologists are interested in how people lead their daily lives in different cultures, and usually live within a culture for a time in order to observe and study behaviour and traditions. The customs, practices and religions of a culture are all of interest. Anthropology is related to an area of psychology called cross-cultural psychology. Cross-cultural psychology is concerned with psychological differences (for example, personality, child development, social interaction) between cultures.

Biology is concerned with understanding how organisms (including human beings) are structured and how they function. Structures include muscles, the skeleton, organs, such as the heart and liver, and the nervous system. It is the study of the nervous system, particularly of humans, that relates biology to the biological approach in psychology (see Chapter 2). Figure 1.2 shows the relationships between psychology and these three other disciplines.

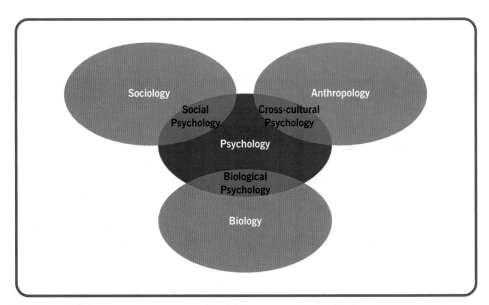

Figure 1.2. Relationship and overlap between psychology and other disciplines.

1.1.2 Psychology as science

The definition we considered at the beginning of this chapter emphasised that psychology is a scientific discipline. Karl Popper (1963), a famous philosopher of science, characterised science as the application of a scientific method to gather data or evidence. This evidence is then used to test a hypothesis, which is a prediction based on theory. If the evidence supports the hypothesis, then support is also provided for the theory. If the evidence does not support the hypothesis, the hypothesis is refuted. This may result in the theory being rejected.

Suppose a psychologist puts forward a theory that all people with blue eyes have an extrovert personality (someone who is outgoing, likes parties, and so on). From this theory, a hypothesis could be made that people with blue eyes will score as extroverts on a personality questionnaire. The psychologist gives this questionnaire to 1,000 people with blue eyes and finds that only 550 score as extroverts. This finding refutes the hypothesis, and in consequence casts doubt on (or refutes) the theory.

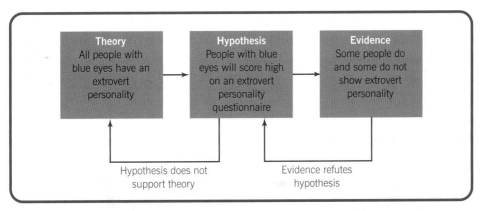

Figure 1.3. The scientific method of theory, hypothesis and evidence.

Evidence must be collected in an objective way and one which other scientists could replicate. Science uses an empirical method to collect evidence. This means that data is collected through observation and experiment. Observations must be objective, which means that more than one person would record them in the same way. Behaviour is observable and hence objective; how you think is not directly observable and can only be inferred. Many psychologists, especially behaviourists, place great emphasis on the need to focus on behaviour for psychology to be a science.

The use of the experimental method is also important in psychology. Experiments allow the psychologist to control conditions and then observe how people behave; they also allow cause-and-effect relationships to be established. Knowing what causes us to behave in certain ways allows hypotheses and theories to be tested.

3

Wundt and psychology as a science

Wilhelm Wundt (1832–1920), a philosopher, was the first scientist to set up a psychological laboratory, established in 1879 in Leipzig, Germany. Wundt stated in 1873 that he wanted to take psychology out of philosophy and establish it as a science in its own right. Wundt was interested in the areas of sensation, mental images, reaction times, perception and attention; he did not attempt to carry out research into personality and abnormal behaviour. For example, Wundt attempted to measure the speed of thought, and devised a device called a 'thought metre'.

One of Wundt's most commonly used research methods was that of **introspection**. Wundt would train his researchers to carefully analyse their own mental experiences – sensations, images and emotional reactions. Introspection would take place under controlled laboratory conditions. Once trained to introspect, Wundt's researchers took as long as 20 minutes to report on their inner experiences from a one-second experiment! Wundt claimed that trained introspectionists would produce reliable results which could be replicated by other introspectionists in different laboratories. However, it soon became apparent that reporting on inner experiences in this way was too subjective. Disagreement cannot be resolved since one person can never experience exactly what another person experiences.

1.2 The biological approach

The **biological approach** in psychology is concerned with how our physical structures – especially our genes and central nervous system – influence how we think and behave. Biological psychology investigates behaviour in both humans and other animals. It seeks to explain behaviour on the basis of anatomy, physiology and inheritance. Biological psychology includes the study of **behaviour genetics**, according to which human characteristics, such as intelligence and personality, result from our genetic make-up. It is fair to say that over the past 10 or 15 years the biological approach has gained in importance in psychology. This is largely to do with the detailed knowledge scientists have of our genetic make-up (the human genome) and advances in research techniques at a molecular level.

We will look in more detail at biopsychology in Chapter 2. Here, the basics are considered.

1.2.1 Basic assumptions and distinguishing features

The basic assumptions of the biological approach are as follows:

- Human behaviour is strongly influenced by our genetic make-up and our genetic inheritance.
- The central nervous system, especially the brain, is essential for thought and behaviour to take place. An understanding of brain structures and their functions can explain both behaviour and thought.
- Chemical processes in the brain are responsible for psychological functioning, and an imbalance of chemicals in the brain may cause certain types of mental disorders, for example bipolar mood disorder.
- The brain and the mind are the same. Some philosophers and psychologists have argued that the brain is physical and the mind mental, and hence they are qualitatively different.
- Humans have evolved biologically, through Darwinian evolution, and have much in common with other animals, especially those close to us on the 'evolutionary tree'.

The biological approach in psychology usually involves highly scientific and technological approaches to research. The functions of different structures in the brain are investigated using such techniques as electrode recording of the activity of neurons, external recording of brain activity by placing electrodes on the skull (electroencephalograms or EEG), and scanning techniques using advanced technology such as magnetic resonance imaging (MRI). Other research methods include:

- Using animals to investigate brain function, for example, by damaging specific areas of an animal's brain to determine its role in behaviour.

- Detailed case studies of people who have had brain damage, perhaps from a car accident, to understand the role a specific area of the brain has for personality, behaviour and perception.

- Selective breeding of animals, such as rats, to determine which behaviours and characteristics may have a genetic basis.

- Experimentation with chemicals known to have an effect on the brain, and subsequent investigation of the effects on human behaviour and thought, for example, drugs such as cannabis.

- The study of identical and non-identical human twins helps us to understand the genetic inheritance of human characteristics.

1.2.2 The influence of genes

To understand the influence of genes on human behaviour, a distinction needs to be made between genetics and heredity, as follows:

- **Genetics** is the study of the genetic make-up of organisms, and how genes influence physical and behavioural characteristics.

- **Heredity** is the traits, characteristics and behavioural tendencies inherited from one's parents and, in turn, their ancestors (Carlson and Buskist 1997).

It is also important to distinguish between **genotype** and **phenotype**. The genotype of a person is their actual genetic make-up, represented in the normal 23 pairs of chromosomes. Each person, apart from identical twins, has a unique genotype. The phenotype is the actual expression of the person's genetic make-up. This includes physical appearance (such as height and eye colour), behavioural and psychological characteristics. Some of the most well-researched human psychological characteristics that are thought to be influenced by genes are:

- intelligence (although this is controversial because of the debate about the relative importance of nature and nurture);

- certain aspects of personality, such as the trait of introversion-extroversion;

- certain psychological disorders such as schizophrenia, and mood disorders such as bipolar depression;

- male and female differences – for example, the claim that males are more aggressive than females may be explained by evolution and the difference in genetic make-up between males and females (again, the nature–nurture debate is important here since many psychologists argue that aggression is learnt and not genetic).

1.2.3 Biological structures

The most important biological structures for the biological approach in psychology are:

- the neuron or nerve cell – the basic unit of the brain and nervous system;

- the central nervous system – the spinal cord and the brain;

- the peripheral nervous system – the somatic and autonomic nervous systems;

- the endocrine system.

We will look at all these in much more detail in Chapter 2. What follows here is a short description of each biological structure.

The **neuron** is a specialised nerve cell which communicates either with other neurons in the central or peripheral nervous systems, or with muscles or organs in the body, such as the eyes or the heart. It is estimated that there are over 100 billion neurons or nerve cells in the average human nervous system; some are extremely small and others are more than a metre long.

The **central nervous system** is made up of the brain and the spinal cord. The brain has three major parts: the brain stem, the cerebellum and the cerebral hemispheres. The brain stem is the oldest part of the central nervous system in evolutionary terms, and the most primitive part of the brain. It controls basic functions such as breathing and heart rate. The cerebral hemispheres perform higher functions such as vision and memory. These hemispheres are what distinguish humans from other animals.

In the peripheral nervous system, the **somatic system** controls skeletal muscles and receives information from sensory receptors, such as in the eyes and the skin; the **autonomic nervous system** controls essential, life-maintaining processes, such as breathing, heartbeat and digestion. The autonomic nervous system is made up of two subsystems: the sympathetic nervous system and the parasympathetic nervous system. The latter deals with normal body functioning, while the former is activated when we are threatened or aroused.

The **endocrine system** secretes hormones into the body through a number of different endocrine glands located in different parts of the body. One of the most important endocrine glands is the **pituitary gland**. This is located in the middle of the brain and is regarded as the 'master gland', because it controls the greatest number of hormones and controls the other endocrine glands (such as the thyroid gland in the neck).

1.2.4 The evolution of behaviour

Charles Darwin published *On the Origin of Species* in 1859 and *The Descent of Man* in 1871, both of which detail his theory of evolution and the mechanism to explain how evolution works, that is, the concept of natural selection. Darwin argued that behavioural and physical changes to a species happen randomly. Some changes help the organism adapt better to its environment, while others are maladaptive and are not beneficial to the organism. The principle of natural selection ensures that adaptive characteristics are passed on to future generations, while maladaptive ones die out.

Darwin also stated that human beings are a product of evolution and are closely related to other primates, such as monkeys, chimpanzees and apes. Human beings have evolved over millions of years from the same primitive ancestors as have other mammals, such as dogs and cats.

Darwin published another book, in 1872, called *The Expression of the Emotions in Man and Animals*. In this book, Darwin produced evidence from his travels around the world that a limited number of facial expressions of emotion are shown in the same way in different cultures. These include happiness (smiling), hatred (glaring), displeasure (frowning) and surprise (raised eyebrows/eyes wide open). Furthermore, these expressions of emotion have resulted from evolution and are genetically 'wired in'.

Figure 1.4. Darwin's theory of evolution justified psychologists studying animal behaviour to help understand human behaviour.

Darwin also influenced the development of **evolutionary psychology**. Evolutionary psychologists (Buss 1995) try to explain behaviour in terms of how people adapt to a constantly changing environment. They claim that genes account for not only physical characteristics such as height, but also psychological characteristics such as personality traits and intelligence. They also claim that aggressiveness and musical ability result from genes passed down by parents (Plomin and DeFries 1998).

One specific aspect of human behaviour which has been studied extensively from an evolutionary perspective is aggression. For example, it is well known that many animal species defend their territory through aggression towards their own species. Territoriality means than an animal can have the resources necessary for survival, mating and care of offspring. Humans also show signs of being territorial and often resort to violence to defend what they regard as their territory. For example, neighbours may argue over land and the parking of cars in front of their house. War is often to do with fighting for the territory of a country. Men in some countries regard their wife or wives as territory that they have to protect. However, some psychologists regard the role of evolution in explaining aggression as limited, claiming that learning and environmental influences are more important.

Another aspect of human behaviour that has been explained from an evolutionary perspective is that of gender roles and sexual orientation (this is considered in more detail in Chapter 3). For example, homosexuality has been explained from an evolutionary and biological perspective, but other explanations associate it with environment and upbringing.

Evaluation of the biological approach

Strengths:

- The highly developed use of the scientific method and advanced techniques at a molecular level have led to great advances in understanding the biological basis of behaviour.
- The role of the brain in higher mental functions, such as memory, in humans is beginning to be understood.
- The approach has helped to develop drugs to treat mental disorders and the breakdown of brain functions, as in Parkinson's disease.
- The approach has shown us how evolution and genetics influence behaviour and play a role in child development.

Limitations:

- The biological approach is referred to as **reductionist** in that it attempts to reduce all aspects of human behaviour to physical processes and the activity of neurons.
- It ignores the influence of the environment on many behaviours, such as aggression. It is on the extreme nature side of the nature–nurture debate.
- It has difficulty explaining one of the most distinctive aspects of being human, that of consciousness and self-consciousness (self-awareness).
- The biological approach presents too simplistic a view of human behaviour because it does not fully recognise the importance of social factors – culture and society – in influencing human behaviour.

1.3 The behaviourist approach

One of the reasons why the behaviourist approach developed was in reaction to the subjectiveness of the introspective method of Wundt.

1.3.1 Basic assumptions and distinguishing features

The basic assumption of the **behaviourist approach** is that all behaviour is learned from the experiences a person has in their environment. This means that behaviourists are strongly on the side of nurture in the nature–nurture debate, and regard genetic influences on behaviour as minimal. The behaviourists argue further that all behaviour is learned through the reinforcement or punishment of behavioural responses. They claim that reinforcement – a reward – strengthens the link between a stimulus (something in the environment) and a behavioural response.

> The basic assumptions of the behaviourist approach are as follows:
> - All behaviour is learned from experience.
> - We are born a 'blank slate' for experience to write on.
> - All learning can be explained in terms of stimulus–response links.
> - Reinforcement strengthens a behaviour and punishment stops a behaviour.
> - Psychology should be scientific and objective. The only valid material to study is behaviour.
> - Internal mental processes cannot be studied scientifically. The experimental method is the only objective and scientific method to use.
> - It is valid to generalise from animal behaviour to human behaviour. Most research is conducted on animals such as rats, pigeons and monkeys.

The behaviourist approach also assumed that laws of human and animal behaviour could be developed. The general law proposed by Thorndike (1911), called the **law of effect**, states: 'the tendency of an organism to produce a behaviour depends on the effect the behaviour has on the environment' (Westen 1999).

If the effect is rewarding for the organism, then the behaviour will tend to be reproduced in the future. If the effect is punishing, the behaviour is not likely to be reproduced. The more occasions the behaviour has been rewarded, the more strongly it is 'stamped' into the organism and the more likely it is to be repeated. The law of effect also relates to another assumption of behaviourism: behaviour is determined by the environment and, as a consequence, people do not have free will. That is, behaviour is controlled by forces in the environment rather than by the will of the person.

1.3.2 Classical conditioning

Classical conditioning was developed by a Russian physiologist called Ivan Pavlov. He studied learning by association and used naturally occurring reflexes in animals. For example, when a hungry dog is shown food, the dog will naturally salivate. This behaviour of salivation is called a **reflex**. Pavlov conditioned a hungry dog which would salivate at the sight and smell of food, to salivate at the sound of a bell. In classical conditioning, the first step is to pair the two stimuli – here, food and the sound of a bell. Pavlov would ring a bell every time food was given to the dog.

In classical conditioning terms:

● the food is the **unconditioned stimulus;**

● the bell is the **conditioned stimulus;**

● the **unconditioned response** is the reflex of salivation.

After pairing food with the ring of a bell a number of times, Pavlov did not present the hungry dog with food, but only rung the bell. Pavlov found that this resulted in the dog salivating. The dog had learned that food and the bell were associated, and the sound of the bell on its own elicited the salivation reflex. The bell becomes the conditioned stimulus, and salivation at the sound of the bell, the conditioned response. This is summarised in Figure 1.5.

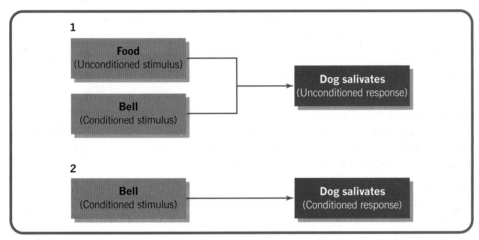

Figure 1.5. Classical conditioning.

Pavlov found that for association between two stimuli (here, food and the sound of a bell) to be learned, they had to be presented close together. The association forms best when the two stimuli are presented at the same time. Pavlov found:

● When there is a long time gap between the two stimuli, the association between the two is not learned.

● If the bell (conditioned stimulus) is repeatedly sounded without the food, salivation (conditioned response) slowly disappears. The behaviour is **extinguished.**

● The conditioned stimulus (the bell) could be changed in tone and volume and still elicit the conditioned response of salivation. This is called **stimulus generalisation.** A point is reached when the sound of the bell is so different that the conditioned response does not happen. This is called **stimulus discrimination.**

● If the conditioned response had been extinguished, then at a later time the dog would sometimes salivate at the sound of the bell. This is called **spontaneous recovery** of the conditioned behaviour.

One early application of classical conditioning to understanding and changing human behaviour was to do with how people acquire phobias (irrational fears, such as a fear of spiders). (We shall look at this in more detail in Chapter 9.) Classical conditioning can be used to understand how emotional responses may be learned. The most famous early experiment to show this was conducted by Watson and Rayner (1920).

Classic study

Watson and Rayner (1920) used a nine-month-old boy, Little Albert, to condition a fear of white rats which led to a phobia of white rats. Initially, Little Albert did not show a fear of white rats. Watson and Rayner had discovered that Little Albert showed fear when a hammer struck a metal bar behind his back (striking the metal bar is the unconditioned stimulus, and fear is the unconditioned response). Following this, Watson and Rayner placed a white rat (conditioned stimulus) in front of Little Albert, and at the same time made the loud noise with the metal bar. After a small number of pairings of the white rat with the loud noise, Little Albert showed fear, by crying and moving away from the rat. Watson and Rayner then presented the rat (conditioned stimulus) without the loud noise. Little Albert showed fear (conditioned response). Little Albert then developed a phobia for white rats and, more generally, small furry white objects. Watson and Rayner concluded that classical conditioning causes strong emotional behaviour such as that shown by somebody with a phobia. It is important to note that this study would not be allowed these days because it would not be regarded as ethical and would be in breach of the British Psychological Society's Code of Ethics and Conduct.

Classical conditioning may also be used to treat phobias by a technique called **systematic desensitisation**. To extinguish an irrational fear, the person has to confront the stimulus that causes the fear. So if a person has a fear of spiders, for example, the psychologist might first relax the person and then show them a picture of a spider. Slowly, the person would be exposed to a toy spider, and then a real spider in a jar. (We will look at this technique in more detail in Chapter 9.)

1.3.3 Operant conditioning

Burrhus Frederic Skinner (1904–90) developed the behaviourist approach called **radical behaviourism** (Skinner 1953, 1990). Radical behaviourism states that psychologists should use only scientific methods to investigate animal and human behaviour. Skinner claimed that all behaviour is learned from the consequences of behaviour. This he called **operant conditioning**. Operant conditioning is where behaviour becomes more or less likely as a result of its consequences. The consequences of behaviour are seen as either rewarding or punishing. Behaviours that receive a reward are more likely to be repeated on similar occasions in the future. Behaviours that receive punishment are less likely to be repeated in the future and may be extinguished entirely.

Although he did use humans at times, Skinner conducted most of his experiments on animals such as rats or pigeons. He used a device called a **Skinner box**. In this box, a hungry rat has to learn to press a lever to obtain the reward of food. Since pressing a lever is not a normal part of a rat's behaviour, it has to learn this operation. Only if the rat presses the lever does it get the reward of food. Hence, the rat has to operate on its environment to gain reinforcement. If the rat is reinforced every time it presses the

Figure 1.6. Skinner claimed that scientific study must be based only on observable and measurable behaviour.

lever (this is called **continuous reinforcement**), the behaviour of lever-pressing is learned, or becomes 'stamped in'. The process of operant conditioning is shown in Figure 1.7.

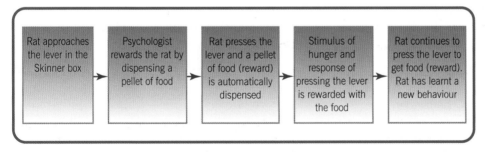

| Rat approaches the lever in the Skinner box | Psychologist rewards the rat by dispensing a pellet of food | Rat presses the lever and a pellet of food (reward) is automatically dispensed | Stimulus of hunger and response of pressing the lever is rewarded with the food | Rat continues to press the lever to get food (reward). Rat has learnt a new behaviour |

Figure 1.7. The process of operant conditioning. Note that the rat is first rewarded for approaching the lever. This is because the normal behaviour of a rat does not involve pressing levers. Pressing the lever has to be learned as a new behaviour.

We have said that the consequences of behaviour are of two basic types: rewarding (reinforcement) or punishing.

In operant conditioning the following further differences exist:

- **Positive reinforcement:** This is a positive or pleasant consequence, such as getting food, and increases the likelihood that a behaviour will be repeated in the future.

- **Negative reinforcement:** This is when a response removes an unpleasant consequence, such as an electric shock, and increases the likelihood that a behaviour will be repeated in future. This is often investigated by putting a rat in a box with two compartments, for example. The rat is placed in the first compartment, which has an electrified floor. The rat has to learn to press a lever to escape into the second compartment, which does not have an electrified floor. The reinforcing consequence of pressing the lever is the removal of a painful stimulus. This is sometimes referred to as **avoidance learning**.

- **Punishment:** This is different from negative reinforcement, since a punishing consequence of behaviour will result in the behaviour not being repeated in the future. The behaviour is extinguished. For example, if instead of food as a reward for pressing the lever, the rat receives an electric shock, the lever-pressing behaviour will be extinguished.

Most human behaviour does not rely on food or water as reinforcers (called **primary reinforcers**), but on what are known as **secondary reinforcers**. Secondary reinforcers are such things as money or tokens, praise, career success and status. A secondary reinforcer is not in itself rewarding; it is a neutral stimulus that acquires reinforcing properties because it can be linked with a primary reinforcer – for example, a token could be exchanged for sweets.

Evaluation of the behaviourist approach

Strengths:
- The approach is scientific and attempts to formulate laws of human behaviour.
- Animals other than humans can be used to study learning and do not raise ethical issues that would arise if such experiments were conducted on humans.
- The environment is seen as the sole determinant of behaviour. This means that new behaviours can be learned by people suffering from psychological problems, such as phobias.

Limitations:
- The behaviourist approach has been criticised because of its denial of free will, seeing human behaviour as mechanistic and determined by reinforcement and punishment.

- This approach also minimises the effect of genes on behaviour, and hence rejects the biological approach in psychology.
- Behaviourists assume that it is easy and straightforward to generalise findings from animal experiments to human behaviour.
- The assumption that all learning results from the consequences (reward or punishment) of a person's behaviour has been criticised and challenged by social learning theorists. Learning by observation is important.
- It ignores the importance of thinking and emotions.

1.4 The social learning theory approach

Social learning theory is based on observational learning. This approach states that behaviour is learned by watching other people behave and observing the consequences of the behaviour for the observed person. Hence, behaviour is not learned from direct reward and punishment for the individual, as with operant conditioning.

1.4.1 Basic assumptions and distinguishing features

Social learning theory assumes, as with the behaviourist approach, that all behaviour is learned from experience. This approach also assumes that mental processes are important in how people learn behaviour. This is because, when observing another person's behaviour and seeing the consequences of that behaviour, the observer must understand when behaviour is rewarded and when it is punished.

- Social learning theory assumes that people will tend to imitate or copy behaviour they have seen rewarded in other people, and not copy behaviour they have seen punished in other people.

- **Vicarious reinforcement** is a term used in social learning theory when the observer learns that a model's behaviour has been reinforced or rewarded. Vicarious reinforcement increases the likelihood that the observer will imitate the behaviour of the model.

A distinction is also made between learning behaviour and the performance of that behaviour. A person might learn a behaviour from observing someone receiving reward for behaving in a certain way. However, the person may not actually perform the behaviour themselves, either because it is not appropriate or because they choose not to. This is another way in which mental or cognitive processes are fundamental to the social learning theory approach.

The basic assumptions of the social learning theory approach are as follows:

- Much human behaviour is learned from observing other people's behaviour, that is, imitating the behaviour of others.
- Mental or cognitive processes are essential for learning to take place.
- Observational learning takes place as result of people with whom a person identifies acting as models.
- Reinforcement need not be direct, but can be what social learning theorists call vicarious reinforcement.

As with the behaviourist approach, social learning theory research has mostly employed the laboratory experiment to investigate observational learning. One distinguishing feature of this approach is that most of the research has been on people, rather than on animals such as rats and pigeons. Another feature is that much research has focused on aggression in people and has been interested in how children learn aggressive behaviour.

Social learning theory was initially developed by Albert Bandura (1977, 1986) and is often referred to as a cognitive social theory of learning. The key difference from behaviourism is the idea that mental processes (**mediating cognitive factors**) occur between stimulus and response.

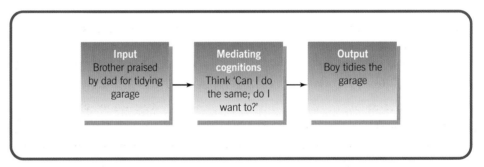

Figure 1.8. Social learning theory states that cognitions (expectations for reward or punishment) intervene between stimulus and response.

1.4.2 Modelling

Observational learning takes place as a result of one person watching another person and observing the consequences of behaviour for the other person. The consequences are either rewarding or punishing. Either way, the observer learns the behaviour from the other person, who is called the model. In performing the behaviour at a later time, the observer is said to be **modelling** their behaviour on that of the model they have observed.

Further research by Bandura (1965), using a similar experimental set-up, showed that the extent to which aggressive behaviour is imitated depends on the consequences for the model. Children were found to imitate aggression more if the model was seen to be rewarded for being aggressive. When the model was seen to be punished for being aggressive, children showed a low level of aggressive behaviour themselves. Bandura demonstrates that children learn a model's behaviour regardless of the consequences for the model. Different consequences for the model serve either to increase or decrease the likelihood of imitation of the aggressive behaviour.

Study

Aim In a classic study, Bandura et al. (1961) conducted an experiment with young children to demonstrate observational or imitative learning.

Method Children from one group were put into a room, one at a time, with an adult who behaved in an aggressive way towards a bobo doll (a lifelike, inflatable doll). The adult hit the doll with a hammer and shouted abuse at it. Children from a second group, again one at a time, were put in a room with an adult behaving in a subdued and non-aggressive way.

Each child was then put in a playroom which contained toys, along with a bobo doll and a hammer. The researchers recorded the number of aggressive behaviours each child made towards the doll.

Results The children who had observed an adult behaving aggressively behaved much more aggressively themselves than those who had observed the non-aggressive model. They also found that boys generally behaved more aggressively than girls.

Conclusion Mere exposure to a model behaving aggressively results in observational learning and aggressive behaviour.

Obviously we do not imitate every person's behaviour that we observe. Social learning theory has investigated what characteristics of the model and the observer are most likely to result in behaviour being imitated. Characteristics of the model most likely to influence the observer are:

- models that we see as most like ourselves, for example, same sex, same age, similar style of dress;

- the likeability and attractiveness of the model;

- high-status or famous people, such as pop stars or famous footballers.

A key characteristic of the observer is self-esteem. Self-esteem is how highly you value yourself in terms of ability, self-confidence, self-like, and so on. People with low self-esteem (feelings of low self-worth) are more likely to imitate a model's behaviour than people with high self-esteem.

1.4.3 Mediating cognitive factors

Bandura (1977) viewed observational learning as a four-stage process in which four types of mediating cognitive factors are necessary. These intervene between stimulus and behavioural response.

● Stage 1 **Attention**: the observer may not be interested in observing the model and will pay little attention to the model's behaviour, and so learn little.

● Stage 2 **Memory**: how well the observer remembers and can recall the behaviour of the model and its consequences.

● Stage 3 **Assessment of own ability**: for example, if you are observing an international-level tennis player perform a difficult shot and you are not good at tennis, you will think it very difficult for you to imitate the behaviour.

● Stage 4 **Observed consequences**: positive (rewarding) or negative (punishing) for the model.

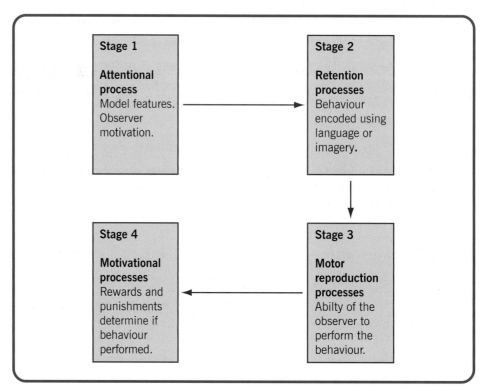

Figure 1.9. The four mediating cognitive factors in observational learning.

Evaluation of social learning theory

Strengths:

- Social learning theory has used the scientific method or experimentation to study learning in people. The theory has been applied to understanding media violence, health psychology and treatment of mental disorders.
- Social learning theory takes a less mechanistic view of human behaviour than behaviourism, and has the strength that cognitive processes (how we think) are taken into account.

Limitations:

- While much focus has been placed on aggression, social learning theory does not take into account sufficiently the role of biology and genetics in aggression.
- The laboratory experiments, using bobo dolls, seem highly artificial and it is therefore difficult to generalise the findings to people's everyday lives.
- The approach ignores personality differences such as introversion and extroversion.

1.5 The cognitive approach

Cognitive psychology, which is concerned with many different aspects of how we think, is the dominant approach in modern psychology. Cognitive psychology is concerned with mental processes such as language, attention, memory, reasoning and problem solving, and decision making. Cognitive psychology has also tried to take into account how emotions affect how we think, for example, being very upset may have a negative effect on our ability to recall from memory.

1.5.1 Basic assumptions and distinguishing features

Cognitive psychology assumes that only by studying mental processes can we understand why people behave as they do. This approach also assumes that mental processes can be studied in an objective and scientific way, and uses the experiment as its main method of investigation.

Other basic assumptions of the cognitive approach are as follows:

- The human mind actively processes information that comes in through different senses (sight, hearing, smell, touch, taste).
- Human information processing is similar to that of a computer, with the computer being used as an analogy for the mind. The computer has information inputs, it stores and retrieves information, and it has various programmes that determine the response.
- Mental processes can be studied scientifically using carefully controlled experiments, usually in a laboratory.
- Cognitive or mental processes mediate between stimulus and response.

The cognitive approach is distinguished by three main types of enquiry:

- experimental cognitive psychology;
- cognitive science;
- cognitive neuropsychology.

Cognitive neuropsychology typically studies cognitive processes in people who have suffered different types of brain damage. For example, in 1895 Paul Broca discovered that a particular area of the brain was concerned with speech production. He found that damage to this area resulted in a person having difficulty in speaking, although this did not affect how well the person could understand what other people were saying. Modern research looks at how damage to different areas of the brain affects different cognitive processes.

Cognitive science is largely to do with theories and theoretical development. For example, an important debate in cognitive science is whether or not we process information one piece at a time, in a linear fashion (called serial processing), or whether the human brain can process more than one piece of information at the same time (called parallel processing).

Experimental cognitive psychology is the main area that we are interested in because it investigates all types of mental processes in normal, healthy people, in controlled experimental and laboratory conditions.

Cognitive psychology is also distinguished by the range of areas of human thought and behaviour that it studies. These include the cognitive development of the child, changes to cognitive processes that take place as a result of ageing, and cognitive processes that are involved in our social and emotional lives. As such, cognitive psychology covers the full spectrum of human thought and behaviour.

1.5.2 The study of internal mental processes

Classic study

The first experimental study of internal mental processes dates back to Ebbinghaus (1885). Ebbinghaus wanted to measure loss of information in memory. To do this, he used nonsense words such as 'bok', 'waf' and 'ged'. He memorised long lists of nonsense words and tested himself for memory or retention of these words numerous times over a period of weeks. He found that forgetting was greatest soon after learning and that this levelled off after just two days. This basic method of giving people lists of words (or pictures or sounds) and subsequently testing recall memory has been used by cognitive psychologists ever since.

The point of mentioning this first study of memory is that cognitive psychologists study internal mental processes by measuring some kind of behaviour (usually verbal or written responses). This objective measurement of behaviour allows cognitive psychologists to create theories about what might be going on inside our minds. Obviously we cannot see a person's memory or thought processes, but we can measure them through behavioural responses. Behavioural responses can then be used to make inferences about mental processes.

Using some clever experiments, cognitive psychologists have studied how we evaluate arguments and beliefs, that is, how we reason. A classic study of deductive reasoning (drawing a logical conclusion from a set of statements) was conducted by Wason (1968).

Study

Aim Wason (1968) conducted an experiment to show how people reason and how this might not be entirely logical.

Method Participants were shown four cards and told that each card had a letter on one side and a number on the other side. They were also told that all the cards conform to the following rule: 'If a card has an A on one side, then it has a 3 on the other side.' Participants were shown four cards, showing A, B, 3 and 2. They were then asked to turn over only those cards necessary to discover if the rule was true or false.

Results Most participants correctly turned over the card with the A on it (a number other than 3 would prove the rule to be false). However, very few turned over the card with 2 showing. It is necessary to turn over this card since if there was an A on the other side it would prove the rule to be false.

Conclusion The logical way to prove or disprove the rule is to turn over the cards with A and 2 showing. Since most participants did not do this, the experiment shows that pure logical thinking may be difficult for people. This experiment also shows how cognitive psychologists use experiments to study internal mental processes.

The cognitive approach generally uses experiments such as those described above to study and better understand internal mental processes. However, you might wonder why we cannot ask people to report on their thoughts to explain why they behave as they do. Nisbett and Wilson (1977) claimed that people have very little access to their cognitive processes. This means that we cannot study mental processes scientifically in this way. Not all cognitive psychologists believe this to be the case, however, and some do make use of introspective reports of people's own conscious thought processes.

1.5.3 The use of models to explain processes

The primary model used by cognitive psychologists to explain mental processes is that of the computer.

- The computer is an information processor, and mental processes, such as memory, are seen to operate in a similar way.

- The computer model allows mental processes to be thought of in terms of inputting information, processing, storing and retrieving information. In human terms, infor-mation is input through our senses – sight, hearing, taste, smell and touch. Information is stored in memory and can be retrieved from memory through either recall or recognition.

Clearly there is a difference between the computer and the mind, and the mind as the brain, which is a living organism. Also, computers do not have their processes affected by emotions (at least not yet!) in the way that humans do. The computer model for mental processes is useful up to a point, but it does have its limitations.

While the computer provides a model at a general level, the cognitive approach also uses models for particular aspects of mental processes. A good example is memory, where a standard model of memory distinguishes between short-term memory and long-term memory.

- Short-term memory is our memory for information held for a short time in con-sciousness.

- Long-term memory is an enormous store of information that we are not continu-ously aware of, but can retrieve when required.

Any model of memory has to take account of forgetting and the loss of information, which can happen in both short-term and long-term memory. Finally, a model of memory has to show data input from our senses. A standard model of memory is shown in Figure 1.10.

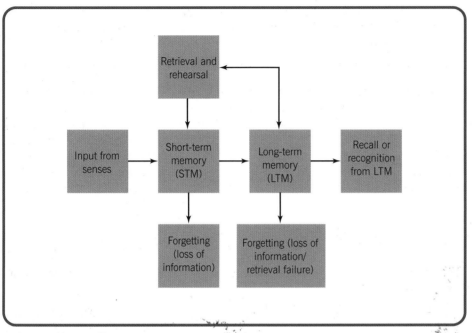

Figure 1.10 A standard model of memory.

Evaluation of the cognitive approach

Strengths:

- It adopts scientific procedures to develop and test theories using experimental techniques. This approach is also the dominant approach in modern psychology.
- The use of models, such as the computer, helps us understand mental processes (although these also have their limitations).
- The approach shows that experiments can be used to understand mental processes that are not directly observable.

Limitations:

- The cognitive approach tends to ignore biology and the influence of genes. It has also tended to ignore individual and personality differences between people.
- The approach is often seen as providing a mechanistic view of human

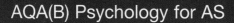

thought, and has not taken sufficient account of emotions and how they interact with mental processes.
- Some psychologists, for example humanistic psychologists, question the value of a purely scientific approach to understanding how people think, feel and behave.

1.6 The psychodynamic approach

Sigmund Freud (1856–1939), a qualified medical doctor, developed a theory of mental life called **psychoanalysis**. Psychologists who adopt this approach emphasise the **psychodynamics** of the mind. This means that different forces operate in the mind, and at times cause inner mental conflict that may be painful to the person. Psychoanalysis as a therapy was developed by Freud to help people come to terms with their inner conflicts, many of which are said to have their origin in early childhood.

1.6.1 Basic assumptions and distinguishing features

Freud (1933) assumed that a large part of our mental life operates at an unconscious level. By this, he meant that we have thoughts and ideas that we are not directly aware of. Freud believed that slips of the tongue and accidents have an unconscious explanation. For example, if you were to knock a vase off a shelf and then claim it was an accident, Freud would not accept this. Freud would have wanted to

Figure 1.11. Sigmund Freud claimed that the mind was largely unconscious and that human motives are largely determined by the sex instinct.

know more about the vase: who bought it, whether it had sentimental value, and so on. For Freud, the destruction of the vase might represent a symbolic act of harming the person who bought the vase. Freud assumed that these thoughts were held in the unconscious by a defence mechanism called repression.

Other assumptions of the psychodynamic approach are as follows:

- Behaviour is determined by unconscious mental processes.
- Early childhood experiences are important in the development of the adult personality.
- Childhood development, up to teenage years, takes place though psychosexual stages.
- The personality has three components – the id, ego and superego.
- The ego uses defence mechanisms to protect itself from harm and from unpleasant unconscious thoughts.
- Psychoanalysis as a therapy can uncover unconscious thoughts, particularly through the analysis of dreams.
- The typical method of research is through individual case studies, which are then used to make generalisations about our mental life. The focus of case studies has been on people suffering from a variety of mental disorders, rather than on normal, well-adjusted people.
- Unconscious mental processes are the most important for understanding how we think, feel and behave.
- Very early childhood experiences, especially those between birth and three years of age, are of vital importance for mental functioning as an adult.

1.6.2 The role of the unconscious

The psychodynamic approach likens the mind to an iceberg. By this it is meant that the thoughts of which we are conscious at any one time represent only a very small proportion of our mental activity. The vast majority of our mental processes take place at an unconscious level and are not easily accessible to consciousness. Freud distinguished between three levels of consciousness: the unconscious, the preconscious and the conscious. The preconscious is seen as those thoughts that are capable of becoming conscious, but at any one time are not. The preconscious represents most of what we would refer to as stored in long-term memory. For example, until you read this you were probably not thinking about your home address. Now this has been raised you can recall it easily, and then it will pass out of consciousness again. Memories of our experiences are stored in our preconscious and can be retrieved through both recall and recognition.

The unconscious contains instincts (biological in origin), drives and desires that we are not aware of, but which have a strong influence on behaviour. The unconscious also contains memories from early childhood, before we had language for memories, some of which are traumatic or upsetting. These are kept unconscious through the defence mechanism of repression, so as not to upset or cause mental disturbance to the individual.

The role of the unconscious is thus twofold:

- It is a reservoir for disturbing memories from childhood that are kept from con-sciousness in order to allow the adult to function in their everyday life.

- It is a reservoir for biological instincts and drives, which largely result from the sex instinct, many of which would be disturbing to the individual if they were to become conscious.

By claiming that much of our mental life and behaviour is unconscious, the psychody-namic approach paints a picture of the human condition as being irrational and at the mercy of uncontrollable unconscious processes.

1.6.3 Psychosexual stages

Freud claimed that development took place through four main stages of psychosexual development: the oral, anal, phallic and genital stages (the last following a latent period after the phallic stage). These stages are the result of two basic instincts, the sex instinct (life instinct) and the death instinct (aggressive instinct). Freud likened the sex instinct to a basic desire for pleasure, and the psychosexual stages relate to different areas of the body that give pleasure or gratification to the child. Normal development for the child is to pass through one stage and on to the next one. However, some children get 'stuck' or **fixated** at a particular stage, and this has consequences for the adult personality and behaviour.

- The **oral stage** starts immediately after birth because the mouth is the first area of the body to be associated with pleasure and gratification. This is because of feeding (breast or bottle). Within this stage there are two sub-stages: the oral-passive fol-lowed by the oral-aggressive. Someone who is fixated at the oral-aggressive stage may have a biting wit and be verbally very critical of everyone. Nail biting and pen chewing are also examples.

- The **anal stage** is where pleasure or gratification moves to the anal region of the body. Gratification comes from expelling and withholding faeces. The anal stage occurs around the time the child becomes toilet trained. Fixation at this stage may result in what is commonly called an 'anal personality'. This is someone who is obses-sively tidy, organised and concerned about body cleanliness.

- The **phallic stage** occurs between the ages of three and six years and is where pleasure is gained from the genital (penis or clitoris) area of the body. The most important aspect of the phallic stage is the **Oedipus complex**. Here Freud claimed that the boy has sexual desires for his mother. This is not acceptable and is resolved by the boy identifying with his father and taking on the male role in society. Fixation at this stage may result in an adult always looking to find a mother figure in his relation-ships. According to Freud, fixation may also result in the person becoming homosexual. The girl desires the father, but out of fear of what the mother might say, she gives up her father and identifies with her mother and the female role in society.

- The **latent stage** is a period of relative mental calm after the preceding three stages.

- Finally, as a young teenager, the **genital stage** is entered and here sexual desires become conscious, with the onset of puberty.

The oral, anal and phallic stages of psychosexual development are characterised by emotional and psychological conflict. According to the psychodynamic approach, this all happens at an unconscious level, so that the child, and later the adult, is not aware that these conflicts have taken place. These conflicts are kept in the unconscious by a key defence mechanism called **repression**. We shall look at defence mechanisms shortly.

1.6.4 The structure of personality

Freud's most important assumption was that the primary driving force in a person's mental life, which also affects behaviour, is the sexual instinct. This operates at an unconscious level in a part of the personality which Freud called the id.

- The **id** is the primitive and instinctual part of the personality that is inherited and a product of evolution. The id operates according to the pleasure principle and demands immediate satisfaction. The id operates entirely at an unconscious level.

- It is the task of another part of the personality, the **ego**, to satisfy, as best it can, the demands of the id. The ego operates according to the reality principle and has to judge what is possible in order to satisfy the id.

- A third part of the personality is the **superego**. This represents the person's conscience (sense of guilt) and ideal self. The superego normally represents the values and moral standards of the child's parents.

The id and the superego are opposing forces, and it is the task of the ego to try to reduce conflict between these two forces, as depicted in Figure 1.12.

As we have seen, the psychodynamic approach likens the mind to an iceberg, where the vast majority is unconscious. The id is entirely unconscious and primitive, while the ego and superego operate at both conscious and unconscious levels.

Dreams arise from the unconscious and, according to the psychodynamic approach, usually originate from early childhood conflicts. These conflicts come primarily from the oral, anal and phallic stages of psychosexual development. Freud (1900) saw dreams as the 'royal road to the unconscious'. By this he meant that dreams could be interpreted to find out what is in a person's unconscious. The main technique used to analyse dreams is **free association**. This requires a person to think about a part of the dream and say whatever comes to mind. It is then for the psychoanalyst to help the person interpret the dreams from these free associations.

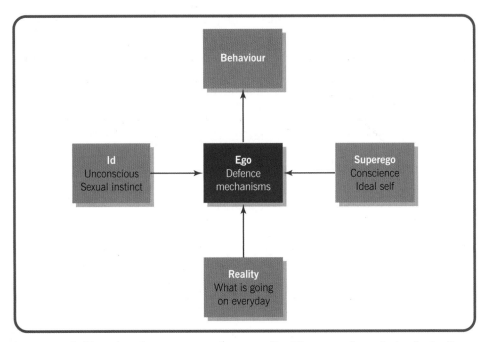

Figure 1.12. The tripartite structure of personality. The ego attempts to deal with the demands of the id and superego, and tries to find a response that is practical and acceptable to society.

1.6.5 Defence mechanisms

A number of different defence mechanisms are used by the ego to prevent painful, upsetting or disturbing unconscious thoughts and conflicts becoming conscious or entering into awareness. The most important and constantly used defence mechanism is that of repression. The ego represses id demands and unrealistic superego demands by not allowing them to become conscious. Repression may be described as unconscious, motivated forgetting. In other words, the ego tries to forget, and not allow thoughts and desires that would harm the individual to become conscious. Repression is to be distinguished from suppression. Suppression is the conscious attempt to forget or not think about certain things. The most important childhood memories that are repressed by the ego are those resulting from the Oedipal complex and associated Oedipal conflicts. The ego has to use up mental energy to keep thoughts repressed. If the thoughts and desires are potentially extremely disturbing, the individual may not be able to function in everyday life because all their mental energy will be consumed.

The ego employs a range of other defence mechanisms, as summarised in Figure 1.13.

A person with a strong ego will be able to cope with the competing demands of the id and superego, and will be able to use defence mechanisms effectively. A person with an overly strong id and/or superego and a weak ego will not be able to function well or adjust to the demands of everyday life. In such circumstances, a person may exhibit psychological disorders such as obsessive–compulsive behaviours. (This is considered in more detail in Chapter 9.)

Defence mechanism	Description	Example
Reaction formation	Behaving in ways directly opposite to unconscious impulses, feelings.	Behaving in a friendly way to someone you dislike.
Displacement	Transferring impulses and feelings to an originally neutral or innocent target.	Scapegoating where a social group is wrongly blamed, e.g. the Jews.
Projection	Attributing one's own unacceptable impulse to another person.	Saying somebody else is frightened of the dark when, actually, you are.
Rationalisation	Also known as intellectualisation. Remove the emotional content of an idea or event by logical analysis.	Coping with the death of someone close to you by intellectual analysis.
Denial	Refuses to acknowledge involved 'in denial'.	Denies liking someone by saying 'not interested'.
Sublimation	Redirection of threatening impulses to something socially acceptable.	Use of aggressive impulses in a sport such as boxing.

Figure 1.13. Examples of defence mechanisms used by the ego.

Evaluation of the psychodynamic approach

Strengths:
- The psychodynamic approach identifies the importance of childhood psychological experiences for the adult personality and how the adult functions in life.
- This approach recognises the complexity of human thought and behaviour, and that dreams and accidental behaviour may be of importance to understanding the person.
- Freud developed psychoanalytic therapy for the treatment of many types of mental disorder, and so started the development of psychological therapies.
- The approach demonstrated the value of individual and detailed case studies for highlighting psychological ideas.

Limitations:

- The psychodynamic approach is not scientific, and its theories and concepts are difficult to investigate in a scientific way. The theory is not falsifiable.
- The claim that much of our mental life operates at an unconscious level cannot be investigated scientifically. For example, the defence mechanism of repression is very difficult to subject to scientific analysis and experiments.
- While case studies provide valuable insight, the psychodynamic approach wrongly used them to generalise to all people.
- The approach places too much emphasis on the sexual instinct in childhood, when it is more realistic to regard this instinct as one of many.
- The approach is male-oriented and regards the female as inferior because she is seen to have a weak ego compared to the male.
- It is pessimistic in that the person is seen as always having to overcome childhood conflicts and repressed memories. It is backward-looking.

1.7 The humanistic approach

The humanistic approach emerged in the USA in the 1960s and was called the 'third force' in psychology (the other two forces being behaviourism and the psychodynamic approach). Humanistic psychologists, such as Abraham Maslow (1970) and Carl Rogers (1961), thought that the other two approaches neglected essential aspects of what it is to be human.

1.7.1 Basic assumptions and distinguishing features

The humanistic approach assumes that each person is unique and that psychology should focus on the subjective feelings and thoughts of the person. This is called an **idiographic** approach, since the emphasis is on understanding the uniqueness of a person rather than in formulating laws of behaviour or common aspects of personality. The humanistic approach also assumes that people have **free will**, and that their behaviour is not determined by unconscious forces (psychodynamic) or stimulus-response sequences (behaviourism). A further assumption is that people must be looked at from a **holistic perspective**, rather than trying to reduce thought and behaviour to smaller elements. The humanistic approach holds the view that breaking down behaviour into small elements results in the whole person being lost in this reductionist process.

Other assumptions of the humanistic approach are as follows:

- People are essentially good and will grow psychologically if given positive regard at all times.
- People strive to realise their full potential in life – called self-actualisation.
- People are motivated by a hierarchy of needs, with basic needs at the bottom of the hierarchy and self-actualisation needs at the top.
- Psychological therapies should be client-centred and involve warmth, empathy and genuineness.
- Psychological problems are due to a difference between a person's perceived self and their ideal self.
- The scientific method is not appropriate to help our understanding of people. The focus must be on subjective experience, known by the term phenomenology, which is to do with the person's own experience of the here and now.
- It is concerned with things that have meaning and value for people.
- The self and self-concept are fundamental, and conscious experience is all that counts.

1.7.2 Free will

The humanistic approach holds the view that the person is an active agent who is able to change and decide his or her own development. Seeing people as active agents means that they can both control and change the environment in which they live. This means that people are responsible for their actions and for their own personal growth. In contrast, the behaviourist approach characterises humans as passively responding to stimuli in the environment.

In terms of humanistic psychotherapy, people are encouraged to understand how free will may be constrained. People cannot go around doing whatever they want all the time. What other people want, the morals and laws of society, and family values, for example, may all constrain free will. In order to function effectively in society, the person has to understand these constraints and learn to live with them at times.

1.7.3 Concepts of self and self-actualisation

Carl Rogers (1980) said that the concept of **self** develops and emerges during childhood, and that the child develops an awareness of the self and 'I' or 'me' experiences. As the child grows older, they become aware of their own identity, personality characteristics, likes and dislikes, and so on. The self includes all aspects of personal experience and a sense of 'being'. Through the feeling of the self develops the **self-concept**. The most important aspect of this is the **ideal self**. This is what the person aspires to be, together with the values and morals which guide thought and behaviour towards other people. If there is a significant difference between a person's self-concept (based on experience) and a person's ideal self, then a state of discomfort or **incongruence** is said to exist. One aim of humanistic psychotherapy is to help a person to lessen the difference between their self-concept and their ideal self, and bring about a state of congruence.

Both Carl Rogers and Abraham Maslow believed that every person has an innate tendency to realise their full potential, or self-actualise. **Self-actualisation** may be achieved in different ways by different people. Some may achieve it through religious devotion, others through cooking, and others through writing poetry, for example. Maslow (1970) believed that people seek fulfilment and change through personal growth. The motives of a person are concerned with meeting certain needs, which are organised as a **hierarchy of needs**. Maslow said that there are five types of needs and that these are arranged in a certain order. The five needs are: physiological needs, safety needs, belonging and love needs, self-esteem needs and self-actualisation needs. These are shown in Figure 1.14.

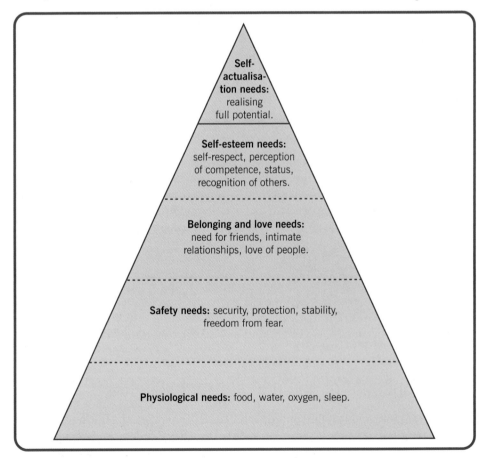

Figure 1.14. Maslow's hierarchy of needs.

As each need is satisfied, the person may go up the hierarchy and attempt to satisfy the next need. People who suffer extreme poverty or privation may spend all their time trying to satisfy the basic physiological and safety needs, and may never achieve the higher needs.

The first four needs are deficiency needs (trying to make or achieve what is essential to live), while the fifth need, self-actualisation, is a growth need. This is the innate need to grow and develop and realise one's full potential. According to Maslow, self-actualisation can only take place when the four deficiency needs have been satisfied. Maslow (1970) defined self-actualisers as people who are 'fulfilling themselves and doing the best they are capable of'. Maslow said that there are three main preconditions for a person to be able to self-actualise:

- no restraints imposed by others on what you can do;

- little or no distraction from deficiency needs;

- an ability to know yourself very well.

> **Key characteristics of people who self-actualise (Maslow 1970):**
> - accurate perceptions of the world;
> - acceptance of other people;
> - creative;
> - good sense of humour;
> - detached and needing privacy.

Maslow described the experience of self-actualisation as having a 'peak experience'. A peak experience involves feelings of ecstasy, which are very strongly felt and transcend reality and time. Some people may regard the peak experience of self-actualisation as a deeply religious or mystical experience that is of great significance in their life. Moments of self-actualisation do not often occur in life and some people may never achieve this.

1.7.4 Conditions of worth

Rogers (1980) said that we all need a kind of love from other people, which he called **unconditional positive regard**. This is where a person is loved, valued and accepted for what they are, without any conditions being attached. There is no evaluation, reservation or possessiveness by one person to another. Humanistic therapists accept a client without evaluations, reservations or conditions.

For Rogers, unconditional positive regard is the ideal way in which others should interact with us, and how we should be with other people. For example, if a child does something wrong, the ideal response by the parent is to make the child feel wanted and loved. However, Rogers says that all too often the response is for the parent to tell the child off and withhold love. This is called **conditions of worth** and is defined by Rogers (1959) as follows: 'A condition of worth arises when the positive regard of a significant other is conditional, when the individual feels that in some respects he is prized and in others he is not.'

Because it is so important for us to be accepted by others, we will generally meet the conditions that others impose on us in order to receive their love, respect and positive regard. This is also sometimes called **conditional positive regard**. The child is not truly loved and valued as a person in his or her own right. Instead, the child is loved and valued to the extent that the behaviour is approved by parents and/or significant others. As adults, this results in seeking approval from others and acting in ways others want us to. For Rogers, this represents a denial of the person, since conditions of worth do not allow the individual to fully understand and explore their likes and dislikes.

Earlier we introduced the idea of incongruence. This is when there is a difference between a person's self-concept (which is based on experience and conditions of worth) and the person's ideal self (how the person would really like to be). This results in the person having low self-esteem. Conditions of worth prevent the person from realising their ideal self and may prevent them from achieving self-actualisation. When there is a very large degree of incongruence between self-concept and ideal self, psychological stagnation may result. Here the individual is prevented from any personal growth and may become vulnerable to psychological disorders such as anxiety and feeling of threat.

The **client-centred therapy** that Rogers developed is based on the principle that the therapist must show the client unconditional positive regard at all times. The therapist must not impose any conditions of worth and must be genuine. The purpose of humanistic psychotherapy is to achieve personal growth in the client and reduce the degree of incongruence.

Evaluation of the humanistic approach

Strengths:

- The humanistic approach is optimistic about people, since it recognises the importance of personal experience and looks to the future in terms of personal growth.
- Client-centred therapy has been shown to be effective in the treatment of relatively mild rather than severe psychological disorders. (See Chapter 9 for more on this.)
- The humanistic approach, as the third force, made psychologists think carefully about what the subject matter of psychology should be, and recognise the importance of conscious experience, and what people think and feel.
- It recognises as a fundamental principle that people are responsible for their own behaviour and are not controlled by environmental forces (behaviourism) or inner unconscious conflicts (psychodynamics).

Limitations:

- The focus on subjective experience (the 'here and now' and conscious thoughts) means that the approach ignores mental processes that do not take place at a conscious level.
- The approach rejects the scientific method of understanding and explaining human behaviour and thought. As a result of this, theories, concepts and claims cannot be investigated properly.
- Roger's concepts and ideas have been criticised for being culture-bound. For example, self-actualisation is all about the individual in a western culture and does not deal with group achievements that may be more important in eastern cultures.
- By focusing entirely on the individual, the approach does not look at personality characteristics common to all people.

1.8 Summary of key approaches in psychology

Figure 1.15 summarises the basic assumptions, methods of research, areas of study and typical applications of each approach that we have considered in this chapter.

Approach	Basic assumption	Research methods	Areas of study	Application
Biological	Biology and genetics influence behaviour	Scientific, laboratory	Basic biological processes	Psychological disorders – drugs
Behaviourist	All behaviour is learned	Scientific, animals	Observable behaviour	Therapies, eg. systematic desensitisation
Social learning theory	Other people influence behaviour	Experiments with humans	Observational learning from models	Modelling to change behaviour
Cognitive	Mental processes can be studied scientifically	Laboratory experiment	Mental processes	Computer models of thought, e.g. face recognition programs
Psychody-namic	Unconscious mental processes are important	Case studies	Unconscious conflicts	Psychoanalysis of unconscious conflicts
Humanistic	Subjective experience is most important	One-to-one or small-group therapy	Subjective human experience	Person-centred therapy

Figure 1.15. Summary of key approaches in psychology.

How Psychology Works

A study of the effects of positive verbal reinforcement

You are going to investigate whether a person's choice can be conditioned by the use of positive verbal reinforcement. Skinner's theory of operant conditioning would state that any response that is positively reinforced would be likely to be repeated in the future, and any response that does not receive positive reinforcement is less likely to be repeated in the future.

- Decide on a very simple, repeat-choice task. For example, you could use a tray of 100 coloured beads with equal amounts of each colour. The task is to pick up one bead at a time and transfer it to another tray or box. Let's say the beads are red, yellow, blue and green. Before the task begins, you need to decide that you will give positive verbal reinforcement for one of the colours (the target colour) and not the others. For example, each time the person picks up a red bead you might say something like 'good', 'yes' or 'mmm'. You will say nothing for any of the other colours. You should find that after a few instances of reinforcement, the person starts to pick up more of the reinforced colour. Stop the procedure when exactly half the beads have been transferred.
- Decide on your task and assemble your materials.
- Write a suitable brief – what you will say to people when you approach them to ask if they will take part. Remember, it is important not to tell them the full purpose of the study at this point, as it would affect the outcome.
- Write a set of standardised instructions, clearly explaining the purpose of the task. Remember, these must be able to be understood by anyone, so do not use technical language. Make it as person-friendly as possible.
- There will be two conditions: the experimental condition, receiving reinforcement, as explained above, and the control condition, receiving no reinforcement at all.
- Write a suitable hypothesis. Remember that you would expect more of the 'target colour' beads to be chosen in the reinforcement condition.
- State the IV and DV for this study.
- Note any extraneous variables that are to be controlled.
- This study is an independent design. What does that mean and why is it important to use an independent design in this case?
- Try out your study with two friends, one in each condition. Do your results support the experimental hypothesis and agree with Skinner's theory?

How Psychology Works

Planning an observation of adult role model behaviour

Social learning theorists state that children learn through observation and imitation of role models. You are going to plan an observation study that could be used to see whether adults are more likely to exhibit socially desirable behaviour in the presence of young children than when young children are not present.

- Decide on a suitable context for the observation and what behaviour you would observe. Some examples are: rule-breaking behaviour at a pedestrian crossing – adults without young children might be more likely to break the rules at a pedestrian crossing than adults with young children; polite greeting behaviour – adults with young children might be more likely to use polite greetings than adults without young children.
- Design a tally chart to record the results of the study. Your tally chart should include all possible variations of the target behaviour that might occur. For example, if you are studying rule breaking at a pedestrian crossing, there are several different behaviours that might be considered rule-breaking. Your tally chart should accommodate all of these.
- Once you have decided on the categories of behaviour, you should formulate a suitable hypothesis.
- Now think about the sample. An opportunity sample would obviously be the sample to use in an observation in a natural setting. However, should certain people be excluded – perhaps those with more than one child or more than one adult? Why might that matter?
- Now specify the timescale and location for the observation. What would be the total observation time? Would it be sensible to do all the observations at once, or would it be better to do some on one day and some on another? Should they be in the same location or in different locations?
- What special ethical considerations might be important when carrying out observations? Write a short paragraph discussing ethical issues in relation to the observation study you have planned.
- Observers often work in pairs and check to see that they get the same results (showing inter-observer reliability). Explain why this is important in psychological research.

Further reading

Introductory texts

Baker, M. (2003) *Introductory Psychology: History, Themes and Perspectives*, Exeter: Learning Matters.

Glassman, W.E. and Hadad, M. (2006) *Approaches to Psychology*, Milton Keynes: Open University Press.

Gross, R. (2005) *Psychology: The Science of Mind and Behaviour*, 5th edn, London: Hodder Education.

Pennington, D.C. (2003) *Essential Personality*, London: Hodder Education.

Specialist sources

Fancher, R.E. (1996) *Pioneers of Psychology*, Hove: Lawrence Erlbaum.

Nye, R.E. (2000) *Three Psychologies: Perspectives from Freud, Skinner and Rogers*, 6th edn, Belmont, LA: Wadsworth.

Biopsychology

2.1 Introduction

Imagine that you have been involved in a car accident; while you have only sustained minor cuts and bruises, you were knocked unconscious for a couple of hours. You wake up in a hospital bed, look around and try to explain to yourself what you are doing in hospital! You cannot remember how you came to be there, nor can you remember the events of the previous day. A nurse comes up to talk to you and asks your name – you think and think but cannot remember it. Over the next few days, your memory comes back and you can remember your name and the car accident. What this example demonstrates, perhaps alarmingly, is that physical damage to your head (being knocked out) affects your brain, which in turn causes memory loss.

In Chapter 1 we considered the basic assumptions and distinguishing features of the biopsychological approach. In this chapter we will look in more detail at physiological psychology and the genetic basis of behaviour.

2.2 Physiological psychology

Physiology is the scientific study of living organisms and is concerned with functions and processes that sustain life. In contrast, anatomy is the study of the structure of living organisms. Psychologists are interested in the physiology of animals, especially human beings. This is because of the importance of our nervous system, particularly the brain, and because of its role in how we behave, think and sense the world around us. Physiological psychologists are also interested in the interaction of the physical body and mind. The body can affect the mind, as shown by the effects of alcohol. In turn, the mind can affect the body, for example, extreme stress may cause tiredness and lethargy. Biopsychologists generally regard the brain and the mind to be the same thing. Others regard mental life as not physical, and hence different to brain functions. This is known as the **mind–body problem** and was first raised by the French philosopher René Descartes (1596–1650).

2.2.1 Neurons and synaptic transmission

It is estimated that there are about 100 billion neurons or nerve cells in the average human nervous system. Neurons vary in size and shape; some are extremely small and others are more than a metre long. The neuron is specialised for communication, whether between other neurons, to and from muscles, or with other organs in the body, such as the heart or stomach.

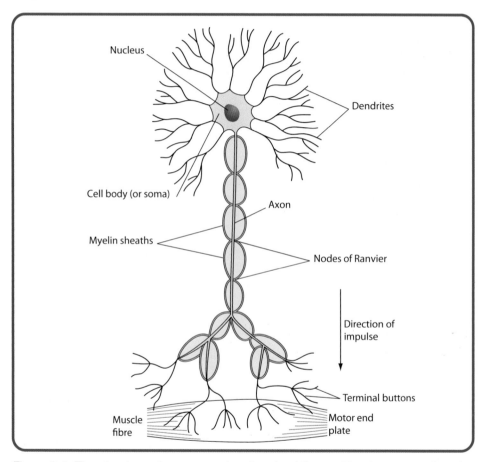

Figure 2.1. The structure of a neuron, showing dendrites, cell body, axon and nucleus.

Figure 2.1 depicts a neuron. Although no two neurons are exactly alike, their cellular structure is basically the same. Each neuron has a cell body, axon, terminal buttons and dendrites. The cell body, or soma, includes a nucleus which contains the genetic material (chromosomes) of the cell. Surrounding the nucleus are other components that are essential for the functioning of the whole neuron. The axon is a long extension from the cell body, which may be nearly a metre in length in some neurons. The axon usually has two or more branches, called **collateral branches**. Nearly all axons in the human nervous system are covered with a myelin sheath. The myelin sheath insulates or protects the axon from external influences that might affect the transmission of the nerve impulse down the axon. The myelin sheath is what gives the brain its white appearance (the 'white matter'), while cell bodies give a grey colour (the 'grey matter') to the brain. The myelin sheath also helps to increase the speed of transmission of the nerve impulse down the axon.

At the end of the axon are what are called terminal buttons. Terminal buttons of one axon send signals to an adjacent cell (another neuron, muscle cell, and so on). If the adjacent cell is another neuron, it is the dendrites (and cell bodies) that receive the nerve impulse or signal from the adjacent neuron. In this way, information is passed between neurons through electrical signals.

When a neuron is at rest there is a negative electrical charge inside the cell and a positive charge outside the cell. An electrical impulse moves down the neuron and along the axon. This is called an **action potential**. The action potential occurs as a result of a chemical process that affects the electric charge both inside and outside the neuron. The electrical charge inside and outside the cell reverses when the cell 'fires', or when a nerve impulse (action potential) passes down the cell to the synapse.

The connection between neurons is at the **synapse**. Neurons do not actually touch at the synapse; the electrical impulse 'jumps' between cells at what is called the **synaptic cleft**.

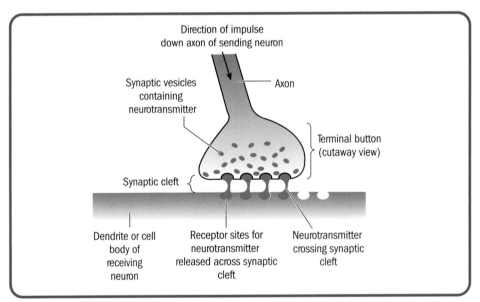

Figure 2.2. A typical synapse between two neurons. The nerve impulse travels from the pre-synaptic neuron, across the synaptic cleft, to the post-synaptic neuron.

Figure 2.2 depicts a typical synapse. The terminal buttons, sometimes called synaptic knobs, at the end of the axon contain small structures called synaptic vesicles. These contain certain chemicals called **neurotransmitters**. Neurotransmitters can either increase or decrease the firing (signal transmission between neurons) of the neuron and the transmission of the electrical impulse from one cell to another. Where a neurotransmitter increases the firing of a cell it is called an **excitatory synapse**, and where it decreases the firing of the cell it is called an **inhibitory synapse**. The function of the neuron is to pass and receive electrical information, or nerve impulses, either from other neurons or from other cells (such as muscle cells or heart cells).

There are basically three types of neurons, which function as follows:

- **Sensory neurons** receive messages from the outside world through our different senses (sight, hearing, smell, touch, taste). These messages are then sent to the central nervous system.

- **Motor neurons** carry information, or nerve impulses, from the central nervous system to a muscle, causing the muscle to contract. For example, if you touch something very hot, a withdrawal action happens automatically (called a reflex). Here, the motor neuron carries a message to the muscle. This goes from the central nervous system to the muscle, and you withdraw your hand from the hot object.

- **Interneurons,** or connecting neurons, are found only in the central nervous system and connect neurons to other neurons, including sensory and motor neurons. Interneurons represent over 95 per cent of all neurons in the nervous system, with most located in the brain.

The neurotransmitters found in the synaptic vesicles are known to have effects on behaviour and mental processes. More than 75 chemicals have been identified as neurotransmitters. For example, acetylcholine (ACH) is a neurotransmitter present at all synapses where a motor neuron is adjacent to a muscle cell. Drugs that block the release of ACH, such as curare, can cause fatal muscle paralysis. Nerve gas, used in warfare, works in the opposite way and aids the release of ACH. This results in death through prolonged contraction of all the muscles in the body. Other neurotransmitters include dopamine, serotonin and endorphins.

- **Dopamine** affects the nervous system in a number of ways, including emotional arousal, pleasure and voluntary movement. It is a chemical involved in the degenerative disease called Parkinson's disease.

- **Serotonin** regulates sleep and wakefulness and aggressive behaviour, and is involved in pain. For example, low levels of serotonin have been associated with aggressive behaviour in males (Cleare and Bond 1997). It is also important in obsessive–compulsive disorders. (See Chapter 9.). The hallucinogenic drug LSD is similar to serotonin. LSD causes neurons to fire in the absence of nerve impulses from sense organs. Hence the person taking LSD hears and sees things that are not in the outside world – hallucinations.

- **Endorphins** are a collection of neurotransmitters that affect mood and reduce feelings of pain. They are the body's natural 'painkiller' chemical.

2.2.2 The divisions of the nervous system

The purpose of the nervous system is to collect, process and respond to information. It also coordinates the workings of different organs and cells in the body. Simple organisms, such as earthworms and jellyfish, have simple, rudimentary nervous systems. However, mammals, especially humans, have extremely complex and highly developed nervous systems. The nervous system in humans is divided into the central nervous system and the peripheral nervous system. Each of these is subdivided into subsystems, as shown in Figure 2.3.

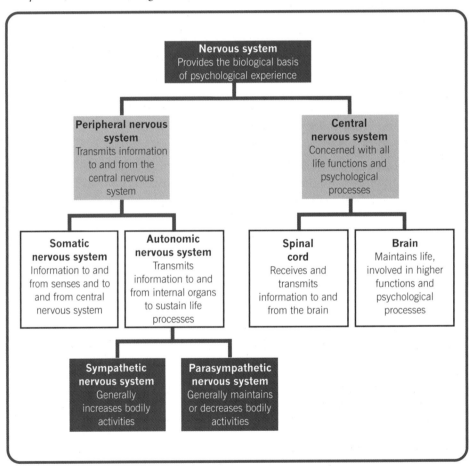

Figure 2.3. Divisions of the nervous system, with an indication of the function of each division.

The **central nervous system** is made up of the brain and spinal cord. The human brain has three major parts: the brain stem, the cerebellum and the cerebral hemispheres.

The **brain stem** is the oldest (in evolutionary terms) and one of the most primitive parts of the human brain. It controls basic functions such as sleeping and waking, and bodily functions such as breathing and heart rate.

The **cerebellum** is involved in regulating movement and sense of balance. The cerebellum coordinates the muscles so that movement and delicate hand coordination are smooth and precise. Damage to the cerebellum would result in a person being clumsy, awkward and poorly coordinated. Skills such as riding a bicycle, writing with a pen and threading a needle would all be severely affected. Fiez (1996) also claims that the cerebellum is involved in mental tasks such as problem solving and word generation.

The **cerebral hemispheres** perform higher functions, concerned with hearing, vision and memory, for example. We will look at the functions of different parts of the brain in more detail in the next section.

The **spinal cord** is really an extension of the brain, and runs from the base of the brain, down the centre of the back. The spinal cord is responsible for certain reflex or automatic behaviours, such as pulling your hand away from a very hot object. The spinal cord receives and passes messages to and from the brain,

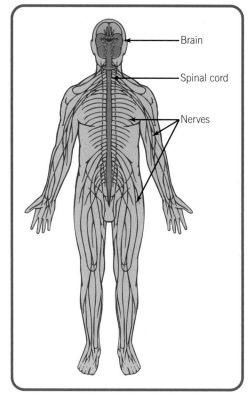

Figure 2.4. The central and peripheral nervous systems, including the brain and spinal cord.

and connects to nerves in the peripheral nervous system. A person who has an accident and has their spinal cord severed at the neck will be paralysed and without any feeling below the neck.

The **peripheral nervous system** is made up of neurons that transmit messages or information to and from the central nervous system. The peripheral nervous system has two subsystems: the somatic and autonomic nervous systems (as shown in Figure 2.3).

The **somatic nervous system** transmits information from our senses (eyes, ears, skin, nose, tongue), through receptors, to the central nervous system. It also receives information from the central nervous system that instructs muscles to act, resulting in walking or running, for example.

The **autonomic nervous system** consists of two subsystems, the sympathetic and parasympathetic nervous systems. The autonomic nervous system transmits information to and from internal bodily organs. This allows life processes such as breathing, digestion and sexual arousal to take place. We will look in more detail at this system later in this chapter.

2.2.3 Localisation of function

The human brain, as well as the brains of closely related primates, such as the chimpanzee or gorilla, have two cerebral hemispheres that make up the largest part of the brain. These hemispheres are the most recently evolved sections of the brain and are involved in higher cognitive functions such as vision, memory and thought. The left and right hemispheres are symmetrical in shape and are divided into two separate halves that are joined by a bundle of fibres called the **corpus callosum**. The corpus callosum allows the two hemispheres to communicate with or transfer information between each other. As a general rule, the right hemisphere is concerned with the left-hand side of the body, and the left hemisphere with the right-hand side of the body. If you stub your right toe and cause pain, this information will go to the left hemisphere of your cerebral cortex. The two hemispheres also perform different functions, as we shall see a little later.

Study

Aim Krupa et al. (1993) conducted a series of experiments on rabbits to investigate the role of the cerebellum in memory.

Method Rabbits were conditioned to blink their eyes in response to a certain sound. Once the rabbit had been conditioned to make this response, a drug was administered which temporarily stopped the action of the cerebellum.

Results The rabbits failed to blink to the sound that had been conditioned while the drug was active; however, as the drug wore off, the conditioned response returned.

Conclusions The results show that the cerebellum is involved in simple memory tasks.

The cerebral cortex is divided up into what are called frontal, parietal, temporal and occipital lobes, as shown in Figure 2.5. The occipital lobe is at the back of the brain, the parietal lobe at the top, and the temporal lobe at the lower side of the brain. Each lobe has different functions, as given below, but they also communicate with each other to perform more complex psychological processes.

- **Frontal lobe:** motor processing (body movement); higher thought processes such as abstract reasoning.
- **Parietal lobe:** processing of sensations from the skin and muscles of the body.

- **Temporal lobe**: mainly involved in processing auditory information; sometimes called the auditory cortex.

- **Occipital lobe**: mainly responsible for processing visual information; sometimes called the visual cortex.

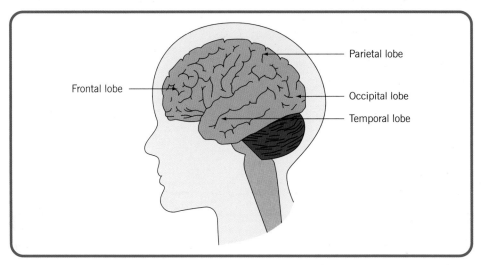

Figure 2.5. The location of the frontal, parietal, temporal and occipital lobes of the brain.

The idea that different parts of the brain perform different tasks and are involved with different parts of the body is known as **localisation of function**. The idea that the brain has specialised areas of function dates back to Joseph Gall (1758–1828). Gall was an anatomist who thought that different areas of the brain related to different aspects of personality. Gall created the pseudo-science of **phrenology**, which claimed that the 'bumps' or contours of the skull revealed different psychological characteristics of the person.

Gall was wrong about phrenology, but the underlying concept of localisation of function was correct. While the four lobes have the general functions that are listed above, certain areas of the brain have more specific localisation of function, as shown in Figure 2.6.

Localisation of aspects of language

An area of the left frontal lobe called **Broca's area** is responsible for the function of speech. To produce meaningful speech, the brain needs to convert memories and thoughts into spoken language. This is operated through the vocal cords. Damage to Broca's area causes a particular type of language disorder or **aphasia**. Here, speech is typically slow, laborious and lacking in fluency. However, further research has shown that damage to Broca's area alone will not cause this type of disorder. The damage has to be to the immediately surrounding area also (Naesar et al. 1989).

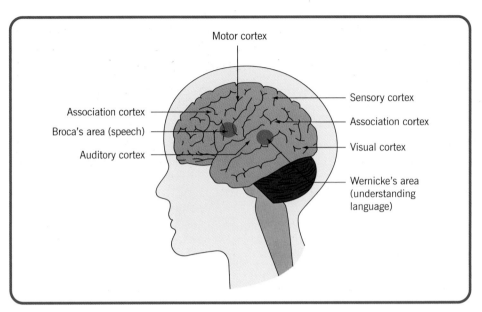

Figure 2.6. Localisation of cortical function.

An area of the left temporal lobe is responsible for speech comprehension, or recognition of spoken words. This is called **Wernicke's area**. Damage to this area causes a different type of disorder. Here, a person has difficulty understanding what another person says, and produces speech which is meaningless. In contrast to Broca's aphasia, speech is fluent and without hesitation, but it is ungrammatical and does not make a lot of sense. Notice that Wernicke's area is part of the auditory cortex, so it is not surprising that hearing what another person says is affected. Also notice that both Broca's area and Wernicke's area are located in the left hemisphere. Generally, the left hemisphere is responsible for most aspects of language.

Study

Aim Petersen et al. (1988) conducted a study to demonstrate different levels of activity in the brain resulting from different types of language tasks.

Method A specialised scanner was used to measure different levels of brain activity in the left hemisphere of the cerebral cortex. Participants were asked, on three separate occasions, to (a) listen passively to a list of nouns on a tape recorder; (b) think of verbs to attach to a noun (for example, 'to eat a cake'); and (c) silently read the list of nouns.

Results The scans showed that different parts of the left hemisphere were active according to the task the people were engaged with. In (a) Wernicke's area is activated from listening passively to nouns. In (b) thinking of verbs to attach to a noun activated Broca's area and other parts of the brain. In (c) Broca's area is activated by silently repeating the nouns.

Conclusions The scan demonstrated that certain areas of the brain are involved with different aspects of language. The brain scans also showed that other areas of the brain were involved, especially when people were asked to link nouns and verbs together.

Figure 2.7 shows a map of the different parts of the body associated with different parts of your brain. This is the sensory cortex of the parietal lobe, which receives information from various senses. Notice in Figure 2.7 that the relative size of different parts of the body relate to the density or number of neurons associated with each part. The face, tongue and hands have many more neurons than the trunk and legs.

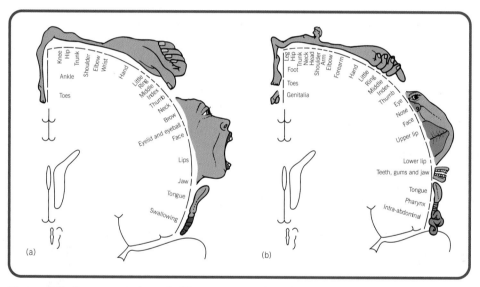

Figure 2.7. Representation of different parts of the human body on the sensory cortex. Notice that the face and hands take up more than half of the cortex.

Lateralisation of function

Localisation of function of different aspects of language (Broca's and Wernicke's areas) is located in the left hemisphere. The two hemispheres have different functions, and this is called **lateralisation of function** or **hemispheric specialisation**. While no one hemisphere has sole responsibility for a function, it is generally accepted that for right-handed people:

- the left hemisphere is dominant for language; it is also regarded as dominant for logical thought, complex motor behaviour and analytic thought;

- the right hemisphere is dominant for non-linguistic functions, such as the recognition of faces, music and non-logical thought such as emotion and intuition.

For left-handed people, the right hemisphere is dominant for language, and the left hemisphere dominant for, e.g,. music.

Gannon et al. (1998) showed lateralisation of function to be the same with macaque monkeys with respect to vocal sounds that they make. Cerebral lateralisation has typically been studied using what are called split-brain patients. These are people who, for some reason, have had their corpus callosum surgically cut, hence stopping communication between the two hemispheres. In a sense, split-brain people have two minds, where each hemisphere operates independently of the other. Sperry (1984) and Gazzaniga (1967) conducted a series of experiments using people with split brains and showed that for visual tasks, each hemisphere does see different things.

Evaluation

- Where are thoughts and memories stored in the brain? Those who support the idea of localisation of function try to identify specific areas of the brain for memory. However, others claim that information is stored across the brain as well. Lashley (1950) conducted research on rats' brains to try to find specific areas for memory. After 25 years of research, he was not able to find any one area of the rat's brain that specifically remembered how to run around a maze. He concluded that learned information is stored in every part of the cortex. This is called a **holistic theory** of brain function.
- One advantage of the holistic theory is that it is able to explain what is called **brain plasticity**. People with damage to certain parts of the brain, as a result of a stroke or accident, may recover some or much of the function that has been lost. Recovery may be over months or years. A head injury may damage a part of the motor cortex so that the person is unable to walk, yet after a period of physiotherapy the ability may be regained. It seems that while a specific area of the normal brain may have a specific function, another part of the brain may take this over. This may take months or years to happen. Some people do recover certain functions, but others do not.

2.2.4 Methods used to identify cortical specialisation

A range of methods is used to measure functions of the brain and cortical specialisation. These include neurosurgery, post-mortem examinations, electroencephalogram (EEG), electrical stimulation and scans.

Neurosurgery

Neurosurgery is where an area of the brain is deliberately destroyed or operated on in some way. In humans, neurosurgery is commonly used to operate on and remove brain tumours. In the 1940s and 1950s, a technique called **lobotomy** was commonly used to treat certain psychological disorders, especially for personality disorders and extreme aggressive behaviour. It is estimated that about 50,000 people in the United States had a lobotomy (Johnson 2005). The most common form of lobotomy was on the frontal lobes of the brain. Here the neurosurgeon severed the frontal lobes from the brain. This resulted in a person becoming passive and unresponsive, with low intelligence and lack of emotion. The frontal lobes are involved in higher mental functions in humans, and to cut them from the brain has dramatic and permanently damaging consequences for the individual. Psychosurgery these days is a very rare procedure and used only as a last resort in very severe cases of obsessive–compulsive disorders (Kim et al. 2003).

Neurosurgery is used in non-human animal experimentation, especially on rats and mice. Here an area of the brain is deliberately removed or destroyed, and psychological functions, such as ability to learn and aggressive behaviour, are investigated. Such methods allow the experimenter a high degree of precision over what area of the brain is removed. However, the damage is irreversible, and there are problems when attempting to generalise findings from animal studies to humans. Of course, ethical issues also arise concerning whether or not we should subject animals to such irreversible brain damage.

Post-mortem examinations

Techniques that relate behaviour to damaged brains make use of naturally occurring events, such as brain damage resulting from a car accident, or damage resulting from strokes or tumours of the brain. The disadvantage of exploring naturally or accidentally occurring events is that the degree of damage to an area of the brain cannot be controlled. Also, it is not really possible to compare how a person behaved before brain damage and afterwards.

Paul Broca (1824–80) pioneered the idea of localisation of function in the brain, as we have seen earlier in this chapter. Broca used post-mortem examinations of the brain to compare symptoms a person showed when alive to damaged areas of the brain found immediately after the person had died. Broca would write a case history of a person when they were alive and then dissect the brain on death. This is how he discovered that the function of speech was located in a particular area of the brain that is now called Broca's area.

Electroencephalograms

Electroencephalograms (EEG) are recordings made from electrodes that are attached to various points on the head. The EEG records the electrical activity of a certain part of the brain, or all of the brain if electrodes are placed all over the scalp. The EEG records brainwave patterns that come from the action of millions of neurons, not individual neuron activity. In general, two types of brainwave patterns are obtained:

- **rhythmic** brainwave patterns – these are typical of a healthy functioning brain;

- **arrhythmic** brainwave patterns – these are found when a person is having an epileptic fit, for example.

EEG is a safe and painless way of measuring brain activity. It is often used as a diagnostic tool when looking at epilepsy or sleep disorders, and to determine brain death. An EEG cannot tell us what a person is thinking, but it can tell us that a person *is* thinking, and whether the brain is normal, abnormal or dead.

EEGs give a global picture of brain activity and have been used to study differences between the left and right hemispheres of the brain. Traditionally, just eight electrodes have been placed on the scalp to get an EEG recording. Recently, more sophisticated use of computers has allowed many more electrodes to be used (up to 128 electrodes). This has produced better measures of specific areas of the brain and more detailed investigation of localisation of function.

Electrical stimulation

There are two main electrical stimulation techniques. These can be used on both normal and damaged brains, and can be used to measure cortical specialisation.

One technique is recording activity at the **level of the neuron**. Here, microelectrodes are inserted into a single neuron, and then the neuron is artificially stimulated with electricity. This technique was used by Hubel and Wiesel (1979) to investigate the role of different neurons in the visual cortex with respect to vision. This is a very accurate technique, but one that requires high levels of training and the use of expensive equipment. The technique is invasive in that an area of the skull has to be removed to expose the brain so that electrodes can be inserted. For this reason, it is used on animals and not humans, but raises ethical issues about whether we should be doing it to animals at all.

The second type of stimulation technique is when an **area of the brain** rather than a single neuron is stimulated. Figure 2.7 (see page 49) depicts the different parts of the sensory cortex and the areas of the body that are represented. Penfield and Rasmussen (1950) stimulated the exposed cortex of a person and asked the person to report what he felt. The areas of the brain shown in Figure 2.7, when stimulated, resulted in feeling in those parts of the body. Penfield and Jasper (1954) used brain stimulation techniques to treat areas of the brain associated with epileptic seizures. This gave some patients a reduction in the frequency and intensity of epileptic attacks. Electrical brain stimulation has also been used in humans to reduce severe, chronic pain. Here, electrodes are implanted in the grey matter of the brain and a mild electrical current is applied (Kumar et al. 1990). The stimulation of the grey matter results in the release of endorphins, which are chemicals released by the brain to reduce feelings of pain.

Scans

There are a number of different types of scanning techniques which are used to measure the activity of the brain, and cortical activity in particular. One is called **positron emission tomography (PET)**. A radioactive chemical, such as glucose, is injected into the bloodstream of an individual. The head is put into the scanning machine and the emission of radioactivity from different parts of the brain is measured. A computer then determines how much radioactivity is coming from different areas of the brain. The areas with the most radioactivity are the areas with the greatest blood flow and therefore the greatest brain activity. The PET scan can be used to determine which parts of the brain are active when a person is engaged in a particular task, for example attempting to solve mental-arithmetic problems.

PET scans are expensive and the results are not that easy to interpret. A standard experiment is to get a person to do a task, such as reading a book, and then compare brain activity when the person is not doing the task. The problem is that the brain is always active, so it is difficult to say that reading occurs only in certain areas of the brain. PET scans on different individuals doing the same task, playing chess, for example, have shown that different areas of the brain are activated in different people. This may be because very experienced chess players rely on memory more than logical reasoning.

Evaluation

No one method is best for investigating the function of the brain. Each has advantages and disadvantages, as indicated above. However, the use of PET scans to produce 3D pictures on a computer has greatly complemented these methods.

2.2.5 The autonomic nervous system

The autonomic nervous system controls the functions of blood vessels, glands and the internal organs of the body (bladder, stomach, heart, and so on). As shown in Figure 2.3 (see page 44), the autonomic nervous system is part of the **peripheral nervous system**, and transmits information to and from the central nervous system (spinal cord and the brain). It is given the name 'autonomic' because most of the system works automatically and without conscious control. For example, if you have just been to see a scary movie, you may have felt your heart pound and your hands get sweaty. This is the effect of the action of the autonomic nervous system.

While the autonomic nervous system operates largely beyond the conscious control of a person, use of biofeedback can result in someone gaining a degree of control. Biofeedback is where monitoring devices are attached to a person's body to provide information such as body temperature, blood pressure and heart rate. Using biofeedback, some people are able to exert voluntary, conscious control over these bodily functions. In India, yogis are trained to control their bodily systems, and some can make their body temperature stay warm when in a cold environment. However, this requires a lot of training, and most people have little conscious control over their autonomic nervous system.

Sympathetic and parasympathetic systems

The autonomic nervous system is subdivided into the sympathetic and parasympathetic nervous systems. These two systems operate at the same time, but in opposition to each other.

The **sympathetic nervous system** basically prepares the body for action in situations where a person is threatened. For example, if you are walking home alone on a dark night, an unusual noise may scare you. The autonomic nervous system prepares you for flight (run away) or fight (stay and confront what is there). It does this by diverting blood from the stomach to the muscles, increasing heart rate, dilating the pupils of the eyes and making the hairs on your body stand on end. However, the sympathetic nervous system may also affect performance in an adverse way. For example, when giving a speech to an audience or a presentation to your class, you may feel anxious and uptight. The sympathetic nervous system causes a dry mouth, sweating and shaking, all of which may make your speech hesitant and unclear to those listening. At the extreme, panic attacks, which are very debilitating, are the result of the action of the sympathetic nervous system.

The **parasympathetic nervous system** supports normal body activity, conserving and storing bodily energy. It also acts as a brake and reduces the activities of the body that have been increased by the sympathetic nervous system. Figure 2.8 summarises the key functions of each of these systems.

The interaction and interdependence of these two systems is highlighted by considering the physical effects of the body during sexual activity.

- In males, the parasympathetic nervous system controls the flow of blood to the penis and is therefore responsible for causing an erection. However, ejaculation is an effect of the sympathetic nervous system.

- In females, the parasympathetic system causes the emission of lubricating liquid in the vagina, while an orgasm is the effect of the action of the sympathetic system.

- If a person is anxious about sex, the parasympathetic nervous system will be inhibited and sexual performance will be affected adversely.

Sympathetic nervous system	Parasympathetic nervous system
Dilates pupils	Contracts pupils
Inhibits saliva production	Stimulates saliva production
Increases rate of breathing	Decreases rate of breathing
Inhibits digestion	Stimulates digestion
Relaxes the bladder (increases urination)	Contracts the bladder (decreases urination)
Increases heart rate	Decreases heart rate
Stimulates ejaculation in males and orgasm in females	Stimulates sexual arousal
Increases actions of adrenal glands	Decreases actions of adrenal glands
Generally, prepares the body to expend energy for fight or flight	Generally, maintains and conserves body energy and functions

Figure 2.8. The opposing actions of the sympathetic and parasympathetic nervous systems.

The endocrine system: The adrenal glands

The **endocrine system** is made up of a number of glands that secrete chemicals, called **hormones**, into the bloodstream. Hormones travel through the bloodstream and affect different body organs. The endocrine system provides a means of communication to the nervous system. The chemical structure of hormones is very similar to that of the neurotransmitters found in the synaptic vesicles of neurons. For example, the hormone **adrenalin** is chemically the same as the neurotransmitter epinephrine. Much of the time, the endocrine system and the autonomic nervous system send the same messages to the body. For example, in a threatening situation, the sympathetic nervous system acts as in Figure 2.8. At the same time, the endocrine system sends hormones through the bloodstream. People feel anxious or jittery for some time after the threat has gone away because the hormones take time to disappear from the bloodstream.

The main glands of the endocrine system are shown in Figure 2.9.

The **pituitary gland** is located deep in the middle of the brain and is often called the 'master gland'. This is because some of the hormones it releases also regulate and stimulate other glands to secrete hormones. The interaction between the endocrine system and the central nervous system occurs in a small structure in the brain called the **hypothalamus**. The hypothalamus controls the pituitary gland and hence the whole of the endocrine system.

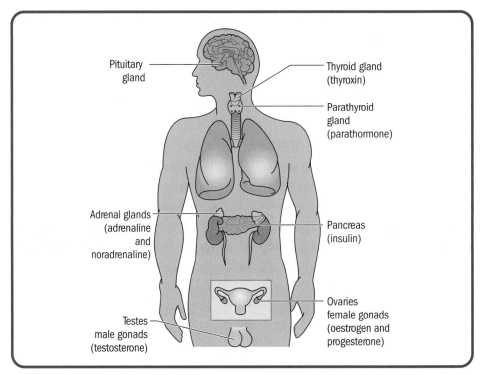

Figure 2.9. The endocrine system, showing the major glands in the human body.

Other glands are as follows:

- The thyroid gland releases hormones that affect general metabolism, energy levels of the organism, and mood.

- The testes in the male release the male hormone testosterone, and the ovaries in the female release the female hormones oestrogen and progesterone.

- The adrenal glands are located immediately above the kidneys and secrete a number of hormones. The most important psychologically is adrenalin. As we have seen, adrenalin is very similar to epinephrine. Both chemicals prepare the body in an emergency for flight or fight.

Adrenalin has been linked to stress reactions shown by individuals and has sometimes been called the 'stress hormone'. Events are said to be stressful if they have an arousing effect on both our bodily and central nervous system functions (Sapolsky 1992). A wide variety of quite different events can cause us to become stressed (taking examinations, break-up of an intimate relationship, death of someone we love, moving house, losing a job). When the brain perceives a stressful event, two separate chemical actions take place – one fast and one slow.

- The fast chemical response is where the brain stimulates the sympathetic nervous system, which in turn instructs the adrenal gland to release the hormone adrenalin.

This is the so-called 'adrenalin rush' that is experienced in moments of stress or high anxiety.

- The slow chemical response is where the hypothalamus stimulates the pituitary gland. This then instructs the adrenal gland to release a hormone called cortisol into the brain. Cortisol inhibits reproductive functions and allows glucose to be released into the bloodstream, thus creating energy.

Under normal circumstances, stressors are short-lived (a presentation to a class is soon over and you can relax). However, stress prolonged over days or weeks causes hormones to remain in the bloodstream and the stress response to be maintained. This is both physically damaging and mentally exhausting for the person.

2.3 The genetic basis of behaviour

Genetics and heredity may be distinguished as follows:

- **Genetics** is the study of the genetic make-up of organisms and how this influences physical and behavioural characteristics.

- **Heredity** is the traits, tendencies and characteristics inherited from a person's parents and their ancestors (Carlson and Buskist 1997).

We can see from these definitions that genetics and heredity are similar. Heredity concentrates on what we inherit from our parents. Genetics, by contrast, is less concerned with inheritance and more interested in how genes determine the physical and psychological characteristics of a person.

Darwin's theory of evolution states that human beings have evolved over millions of years. Evolution has taken place from very simple creatures that lived in water, through to animals and on to the most complex animal – human beings. What have evolved over this time are genes. **Genes** are units of inheritance that are passed on to future generations through sexual reproduction. Genes are found in the nucleus of each cell in the body and exist as pairs located on pairs of **chromosomes**. Chromosomes are made up of many genes. In humans there are 46 chromosomes, arranged into 23 pairs. Genes are the unit of inheritance that determines the colour of our eyes, for example. Biological psychologists claim that psychological characteristics such as intelligence and personality are determined by our genetic inheritance. It is also claimed that some psychological disorders, such as schizophrenia and bipolar depression, are a result of our genes. Genes, then, not only determine human physical characteristics, but might also determine numerous psychological ones as well.

It is important to realise that there are no genes for behaviour as such. This is because one of the main functions of genes is to make proteins. Chromosomes are made up of DNA (deoxyribonucleic acid), which has a structure that looks like a twisted ladder.

Genes are bits of DNA that make up a chromosome and direct the synthesis of proteins. It is the protein that then sets off certain physiological responses which result in behaviour. This is shown in Figure 2.10.

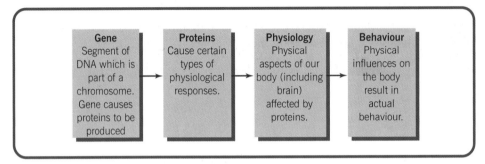

Figure 2.10. The action of genes in causing behaviour.

2.3.1 Genotype and phenotype

The **genotype** of a person is their actual genetic make-up, as represented in the 23 pairs of chromosomes. Each person, apart from identical twins, has a unique genotype. Identical twins have exactly the same genetic make-up. The genotype of brother and sister shares more genetic similarity (50 per cent) than exists between you and your best friend (assuming your best friend is not a relation).

The **phenotype** is the actual expression of a person's genetic make-up. The phenotype is a person's physical appearance, behavioural characteristics and psychological characteristics that result from heredity. Identical twins, for example, have exactly the same genotype. However, if for some reason they were separated at birth and one twin was fed a better diet than the other, the twin fed a better diet is likely to be taller and physically stronger. Each twin would exhibit a different phenotype.

In humans, each of the 23 chromosome pairs contains many pairs of genes; one gene in each pair comes from each of the parents. Each of the pair of genes may be a **dominant** gene or a **recessive** gene.

- A dominant gene controls the expression of a physical or behavioural characteristic, when either both gene pairs are dominant, or one is dominant and one is recessive.

- A recessive gene does not influence the expression of a physical characteristic or behaviour unless both genes of the pair are recessive. Figure 2.11 shows some physical characteristics that are the result (phenotype) of dominant and recessive genes.

The genetic make-up, or genotype, of an individual can interact with environmental factors to result in the genotype. An example of this is a rare genetic disorder called **phenylketonuria (PKU)**. This results from a double recessive gene pair, which causes severe learning difficulties for the individual. Children born with PKU are unable to metabolise an amine called phenylalanine. If not diagnosed at birth, the build-up of this amine in the bloodstream causes brain damage and intellectual impairment. However, if the baby is put on a special diet, free of this amine, it will grow and develop normally, with no adverse effect on intellectual development.

Dominant gene characteristics	Recessive gene characteristics
Brown eyes	Blue eyes
Dark hair	Blond/red hair
Curly hair	Straight hair
Normal colour vision	Colour blindness
Normal sight	Night blindness
Normal blood	Haemophilia
Normal hearing	Congenital deafness

Figure 2.11. Some examples of human physical characteristics resulting from dominant or recessive genes.

Evaluation

- We have seen with PKU that our genotype can be influenced by environmental factors. This example highlights the nature–nurture debate in psychology, and suggests that neither one on its own is sufficient to explain human behaviour.
- The interaction of genetic and environmental factors is important, especially for psychological characteristics such as schizophrenia and intelligence (see later in this chapter).

2.3.2 Types of twins

The use of twins to estimate heritability of behaviour or psychological characteristics is a commonly used method. There are two types of twins:

- **Monozygotic twins** share exactly the same genetic make-up because they develop from one fertilised egg that divides into two separate embryos. Monozygotic twins have exactly the same genotype.

- **Dizygotic twins,** or fraternal twins, develop from two separate eggs that are fertilised by different sperm. Dizygotic twins have 50 per cent of their genes in common. Dizygotic twins are no more alike genetically than any two siblings.

Obviously, identical twins are the same sex, while dizygotic twins may be the same or different sexes.

Figure 2.12. Some identical twins not only look alike but dress the same, both as children and as adults.

2.3.3 Twin studies

Research using twin studies looks for the degree of similarity (called **concordance**) between identical and dizygotic or fraternal twins.

● Twins are concordant for a trait if both or neither of the twins exhibits the trait.

● Twins are said to be disconcordant for a trait if one shows it and the other does not.

Identical twins have exactly the same genetic make-up, and fraternal twins have just 50 per cent of genes in common. Because of this, psychologists argue that if identical twins show a higher degree of similarity than fraternal twins for a particular trait, then this is evidence for heritability of the trait. Figure 2.13 shows concordance rates between identical and fraternal twins for a number of characteristics.

Trait	Concordance	
	Identical twins	**Fraternal twins**
Blood types	100%	66%
Eye colour	99%	28%
Learning difficulties	97%	37%
Epilepsy	72%	15%
Diabetes	65%	18%
Allergies	59%	5%
Tuberculosis	57%	23%

Figure 2.13. Concordance rates of identical and fraternal twins for a number of traits.

It might be expected that a higher degree of similarity or concordance for psychological characteristics would exist between identical twins than between fraternal twins. This is because identical twins not only share the same genes, but are also often treated the same. That is, the environmental experiences are more alike for identical twins than for fraternal twins. Identical twins are often dressed the same, have the same hairstyle, and so on. People often confuse one twin for the other – including their parents!

To get round this criticism, psychologists have studied identical twins who were separated at birth, or very early in life, and brought up separately. Of particular interest to psychologists is when each twin is raised in a very different environment. If identical twins show high levels of concordance for a trait such as intelligence or personality, having been brought up in different environments, then heritability can be said to play a major role in that trait.

Twin studies and the genetic basis of intelligence

The idea that intelligence results from the influences of both nature (inheritance) and nurture (experience or environment) is widely accepted in psychology (Sternberg 2001). Psychologists in favour of the heritability of intelligence date back to the 1860s, with the publication of a book by Sir Francis Galton (a relative of Darwin) called *Hereditary Genius*. Galton (1869) studied eminent people in society and looked at how successful their children were. A high correlation, Galton argued, meant that intelligence is genetic. What he forgot to take into account was that such people were often born into privileged positions in society – inheritance of status, not intelligence.

Research investigating the heritability of intelligence has used twin studies and measured intelligence through the use of standardised tests of intelligence (so-called IQ tests). Measures of intelligence of identical and fraternal twins are then compared to see how alike they are. The comparison is made using a correlation statistic (see Chapter 4), where a score of 1.0 indicates total similarity, and a score of 0 indicates no similarity. Henderson (1982) summarised findings from a number of studies that looked at varying degrees of relatedness (including brothers/sisters and adoptive parent and child) and similarity of intelligence. This is summarised in Figure 2.14. You can see that the correlation for identical twins reared together is high (0.86), indicating a strong genetic role in intelligence. For dizygotic or fraternal twins, the correlation is lower, and for parent/child, lower still. Notice the correlation for the same individual at 0.87. This is determined by giving the same intelligence test to the same person at different times. The correlation is not perfect (1.0) because the individual performs slightly differently on each occasion. The correlation is nearly the same as that for identical twins.

Relationship	Reared	% genetic similarity	Correlation
Same individual	–	100	0.87
Identical twins	Together	100	0.86
Fraternal twins	Together	50	0.62
Siblings brother/sister	Together	50	0.41
Parent–child	Together	50	0.35
Adoptive parent–child	Together	0(?)	0.16

Figure 2.14. Intelligence correlations between people of different genetic relatedness.

Study

Aim The Minnesota Twin Study started in 1986, with the aim of trying to determine the genetic and environmental influences on intelligence and other psychological traits. This research was conducted by Bouchard et al. (1990).

Method A longitudinal method was used to study twins, both identical and fraternal, some reared together and some raised apart. Twins were sent intelligence tests to complete. The Minnesota Twin Study has access to all twins born in Minnesota between 1961 and 1964.

Results Bouchard et al. found that identical twins had a greater similarity in intelligence test scores than fraternal twins. This was found to be the case for identical twins brought up together and for those reared apart.

Conclusion Intelligence as measured by standardised intelligence tests has a strong genetic basis.

Evaluation

- Great caution needs to be taken when attempting to interpret the results of twin studies and the heritability of intelligence. Intelligence tests only measure a certain kind of intelligence; they do not usually measure creativity, for example.
- Environmental influences, such as parental level of education and whether or not the person goes to university, are said to have a greater influence on how well people do on intelligence tests than genetic inheritance.
- Fraternal twins brought up together may not share the same environment to the same extent as identical twins. This is because identical twins are often

treated the same, while fraternal twins are not. Identical twins identify with each other much more closely than fraternal twins do. These considerations argue more for environment than genetics to explain intelligence.

Twin studies and the genetic basis of schizophrenia

Schizophrenia is a serious mental disorder characterised by hallucinations (visual and auditory), delusions, thought disturbance and emotional and social withdrawal. The most common hallucination consists of hearing voices, and the belief that one's thoughts are controlled by other people or external forces. It is a psychotic disorder, with typical onset in the late teens and twenties. It affects just under 1 per cent of the adult population. Of people diagnosed as schizophrenic, about one-third recover, one-third improve significantly, and the remainder do not improve.

There are many theories of the cause of schizophrenia. A biological or genetic explanation has received considerable empirical support. The heritability or genetic view has been studied through research on relatives of people with schizophrenia, twin studies, adoption studies and what is called 'chromosomal mapping'.

Gottesman (1991) and Kendler and Diehl (1993) have produced clear evidence that schizophrenia is more common in relatives of people with the disorder. The greater the genetic similarity between people, the greater the incidence of schizophrenia. This is shown in Figure 2.15, where it can be seen that the concordance for schizophrenia with identical twins is 48 per cent. In contrast, with fraternal twins it is only 17 per cent, and ordinary siblings just 9 per cent. If both parents are schizophrenic, the chances are nearly 50:50 (46 per cent) that their child will also develop schizophrenia.

Relationship to person with schizophrenia	Percentage concordance
Identical twin	48%
Offspring of two schizophrenic parents	46%
Fraternal twins	17%
Offspring of one schizophrenic parent	13%
Sibling (brother or sister)	9%
Parent	6%
Grandchild	5%
Nephew/niece	4%
Uncle/aunt	2%
General population	1%

Figure 2.15. Percentage of people with schizophrenia in relation to biological relatedness. (Adapted from Gottesman 1991)

The finding that concordance between identical twins is 48 per cent shows that schizophrenia is not solely determined by inheritance or genetic factors. To be solely genetic, this figure would need to be 100 per cent. Environmental influences also play an important role. The most widely accepted theory of schizophrenia is called the **diathesis–stress theory**. This states that certain people have a genetic predisposition to develop schizophrenia, but that this is only triggered by stressful environmental experiences. This theory implies that some people have a 'schizophrenic gene', but do not become schizophrenic.

Study

Aim Gottesman and Bertelsen (1989) conducted a study to test the diathesis–stress theory of schizophrenia by looking at the children of twins who were discordant for schizophrenia (that is, one twin had schizophrenia and the other did not).

Method The children of discordant monozygotic and dizygotic twins were looked at to see which children, if any, were schizophrenic.

Results For children of discordant monozygotic twins, the percentage diagnosed as schizophrenic was almost identical, at 17 per cent. For children of dizygotic twins, 17 per cent were schizophrenic where the parent twin was schizophrenic. However, where the parent twin was not schizophrenic, this dropped to 2 per cent.

Conclusion These results provide good evidence that schizophrenia is heritable. However, this does not mean that someone will go on to become schizophrenic.

Evaluation

- Some twin studies have investigated concordance for schizophrenia in identical twins reared apart. Findings have shown a high degree of concordance. The main criticism has been that the identical twins often had contact with each other, and were raised apart but by different members of the same family and in close proximity.
- Identical twins reared together share the same environment and are usually treated as if they are the same person. This may explain better than genetics the high concordance for schizophrenia.
- Some identical twins do not both develop schizophrenia and this is difficult to explain if the disorder is seen as solely genetic in origin.

Evaluation of twin studies

Twin studies have been used extensively in an attempt to separate out the genetic and environmental contributions to psychological traits and disorders. Generally, the outcome is that both must be taken into account and that genetics alone is not sufficient to provide an explanation.

Strengths:
- Identical and fraternal twins present researchers with naturally occurring experiments. Twins, both identical and fraternal, who have been separated and brought up apart due to unfortunate circumstances, also present another type of naturally occurring experiment. These naturally occurring experiments have been used to determine the contribution of genetics and environment to psychological traits, characteristics and disorders.
- It is not always easy to distinguish between identical and fraternal twins from physical characteristics. Modern scientific techniques can accurately determine whether or not twins are identical through comparing DNA.

Limitations:
- Identical twins brought up together share the same environment, are often treated the same and identify with each other very strongly. Fraternal twins experience more differences in their environment, are not treated as the 'same person' and do not identify with each other so strongly. This means that the environments of each type of twin are different, and this complicates the genetic approach.
- Twins reared apart, whether identical or fraternal, are often not reared apart in an absolute sense. It is rare for twins to be separated at birth. Only under exceptional circumstances are twins separated and reared in different families. It is often found that so-called 'twins reared apart' have been brought up by different members of the family who live close together. This has meant that the twins have been together at school and at play.

2.3.4 Family and adoption studies

Adoption studies are another method used to investigate heritability. This involves comparing a trait or characteristic of adopted children with their biological parents and adoptive parents. Biological parents pass on their genes to their children, while adoptive parents provide their adopted children with the same environment but none of their genes. However, sometimes it is possible to look at families with both adopted and biological children. This has the added advantage of all children sharing a similar environment. If a trait or psychological characteristic is genetic or heritable, then the biological children should show greater similarity for that characteristic with their biological parents than with their adopted parents. An adoption study conducted in Sweden by Cloniger (1987) reported that sons of alcoholic biological parents were more likely to become alcoholic than boys reared by adoptive parents who were alcoholic. Often, it is found that the heritability coefficient for adopted children is higher with their natural parents than with their adoptive parents.

Adoption studies also provide support for the heritability of schizophrenia. Such studies look at adults diagnosed as schizophrenic who were adopted when young, and compare them with both their biological and adoptive parents. If schizophrenia is higher in the biological parents, this is evidence for a genetic influence.

Study

Aim Kety (1988) conducted an adoption study in Denmark over a 20-year period to investigate the incidence of schizophrenia in children of adoptive and biological parents.

Method Over 5,000 adults who were adopted in early life were contacted and the incidence of schizophrenia noted. The biological and adoptive parents of these adults were also found, and levels of schizophrenia noted.

Results Of the 5,000 adults, 33 were found to have schizophrenia. Of their biological parents, 14 per cent were found to have schizophrenia, compared to 2.7 per cent of the adoptive parents.

Conclusion The findings provide strong evidence for a genetic factor in schizophrenia, since biological parents showed a much higher incidence of schizophrenia than adoptive parents or the level of incidence in the general population.

Adoption studies examining the importance of genetics in determining intelligence compare the degree of similarity in intelligence between adopted children with both their biological and their adoptive parents.

Study

Aim Scarr and Weinberg (1978) compared specific intellectual abilities, such as arithmetic, vocabulary and picture arrangement, of parents and their adopted and biological children.

Method A standardised intelligence test, called the Wechsler Adult Intelligence Scale (WAIS), which measures different aspects of intelligence, was given to parents and their adopted and biological children.

Results Correlations for the different aspects of intelligence were higher between parents and their biological children than between parents and adopted children.

Conclusion This shows that genetic factors play a more significant role in determining intelligence than environmental influences.

Evaluation of adoption studies

- Plomin (1988) argues that much of the research using adoption studies underestimates the importance of environmental influences. This is because the environment for siblings in a family is different for each one. No two children are treated exactly the same – for example, differences in appearance may affect how each is treated.
- Birth order has been identified as a factor in intelligence (Zajonc 1983). Children may go to different schools and study different subjects as teenagers. Once children leave home, the environment of each is often quite different. It may be wrong to assume that because siblings are brought up in the same family they are exposed to the same environmental influences.
- Ideally, adoption studies need to compare adopted children reared by non-biological parents to children reared by their biological parents, both in identical environments. This is not really achievable, since no two environments are exactly the same, not even for identical twins. Hence, criteria have to be developed to clarify to what extent the two environments are the same. Only when the two environments can be shown to be highly similar can differences between adopted siblings and siblings living with their biological parents be attributed to heritability.

2.3.5 Evaluation of the biological approach

We will now consider four limitations of the biological approach: reductionism; neglect of environmental factors; the mind–body problem; and genetics and ethical issues.

The biological approach is a **reductionist** approach in that it attempts to reduce human (and animal) psychological processes to physical processes. Physical processes, such as the nervous system, are then reduced to smaller component parts. Some psychologists claim that this loses sight of the person as a whole, and fails to reflect experience and everyday interaction with other people.

The biological approach tends to come down on the nature side of the **nature–nurture debate**. As such, the importance of environmental factors is often ignored. For example, one of the defining features of being human is that we are social creatures – we seek and enjoy the company of other people. How we relate to and interact with others strongly influences our behaviour. The biological approach tends to take the person out of social context and study only physical processes within the body.

The biological approach focuses on the body, that is, on physical processes, and in particular the structure and function of the central nervous system. Consciousness and conscious thought is a mental process which appears qualitatively different from physical processes. The **mind–body debate** in philosophy and psychology is about how the physical and the mental interact and come together in one person. Since the biological approach focuses on the physical, it does not have an answer to the mind–body problem. In many respects, it does not concern itself with the issue.

The final limitation is to do with the **ethical issues** which the biological approach raises. The Human Genome Project is mapping the entire genetic make-up of people. This involves determining the location of genes on specific chromosomes and then looking to discover the function of each gene. In time, this may allow genetic manipulation and selective breeding in future generations of people. This raises the question, should scientists tamper with human genetic make-up? While there may be many benefits, for example, discovering the genes that give an individual a predisposition to develop schizophrenia, there are many dangers as well. Some scientists may be unethical in their use of these scientific advances.

To end on a positive note, the biological approach does have great strengths and advantages:

- It provides an understanding of how psychological processes occur in the brain.

- It has useful applications in respect of the use of drugs to treat disorders such as schizophrenia, depression and anxiety. These drugs act on the nervous system; many affect neurotransmitters at the synapse.

The strengths and weaknesses of the biological approach in psychology can only be fully appreciated by comparison to other approaches, such as humanistic, psychodynamic and behaviourist (see Chapter 1).

How Psychology Works

A correlation study to investigate the relationship between age and reaction time

Biopsychologists have found that reaction time generally increases with age. With your class, decide on a test of reaction time. Every class member should collect at least one set of data from a family member or friend. The aim is to see whether the data from the class shows a positive correlation between reaction time and age.

- Decide on a task to test reaction time. If you do not have a reaction timer, a good way to test this is using a home-made one.

Make your own reaction timer
- Cut a piece of thick, heavy card, 20cm long and 5cm wide. This is your ruler timer.
- Using a ruler, mark the following distances (centimetres) from the bottom of the ruler: 0.4, 1.1, 2.8, 4.5, 6.0, 7.6, 9.6, 12.3, 17.5.
- Next to these distances, mark the following times (milliseconds): 40, 60, 80, 100, 120, 140, 160, 180, 200.
- To test a person's reaction time, hold the ruler at the top and get the person to line their finger and thumb up with the bottom edge, but not touching it. Tell the person you are going to drop the ruler and they will have to grab it between finger and thumb, keeping their hand, arm and body still. Drop the ruler without warning. Measure their time on the scale, taking the measurement from above the finger and thumb.
- As a group, try to test people of varying ages, ranging between 16 and 65.
- For each person, ask their age and test their reaction time five times. Then calculate their average time in milliseconds by taking their total time and dividing it by five.
- Collate the data in class and then plot a scattergram, with age in years on one axis and reaction time in milliseconds on the other.
- Give your scattergram a full title that includes reference to either 'correlation' or 'relationship' and both the variables.
- Write a brief paragraph to say whether or not the scattergram shows a correlation. If there is a correlation, identify what type of correlation it is and what this means in terms of the relationship between reaction time and age.
- Although you may have found a relationship between age and reaction time, we cannot say that increasing age causes reaction time to increase, or vice versa. One important limitation of correlation studies is that they can only tell us there is a relationship; they do not tell us about cause and effect.

How Psychology Works

An investigation into the genetic theory of handedness

Ninety per cent of people are strongly right-handed. They prefer to use their right hand for things like writing and throwing or catching a ball. Of the other 10 per cent, some are strongly left-handed, but the majority are ambidextrous, using the left hand for some things and the right for others. Whether a person is right-handed or left-handed has long been thought to be determined genetically, but the genetic influence is not straightforward. Some left-handed parents have a right-handed child, and sometimes (though very rarely) right-handed parents will have a left-handed child.

Support for the genetic theory of handedness comes from the observation that handedness is related to the direction of a person's hair whorl. A hair whorl is the radial swirl of hair from a central point at the back of the head. Look down on a friend's head and you will see that the whorl goes either clockwise or anticlockwise. The direction of the whorl is thought to be inherited. It stays the same throughout life, in spite of what you do to your hair! Klar (2003) found that more than 90 per cent of right-handers have a clockwise hair whorl and non-right-handers show an even split of clockwise and anticlockwise hair whorls.

- The aim of your investigation is to support or refute Klar's hypothesis about an association between handedness and direction of hair whorl.
- State an alternative hypothesis by finishing this sentence: *More right-handed people will have a*:
- State a corresponding null hypothesis by finishing this sentence: *There will be no difference in the number of right-handed people and the number of...*
- Each person in the class should survey as many people as possible. Note each person's handedness by asking them to write down what day of the week it is – see which hand they use. Then inspect their head to note the direction of the hair whorl – clockwise or anticlockwise.
- Collate the class data into a frequency table like the one below.
- Convert the frequencies to percentages and write a couple of sentences describing your results.
- Write a brief conclusion, relating your results to previous research.

Direction of hair whorl	Right-handers	Left-handers (or non-right-handers)
Clockwise		
Anticlockwise		

Further reading

Introductory texts

Gross, R. (2005) *Psychology: The Science of Mind and Behaviour*, 5th edn, London: Hodder Education.

Kolb, B. and Whishaw, I.Q. (2001) *An Introduction to Brain and Behaviour*, New York: Worth Publishers.

Smith, E., Nolan-Hoeksema, S. and Frederickson, B. (2002) *Atkinson and Hilgard's Introduction to Psychology*, 14th edn, Fort Worth, TX: Harcourt College Publishers.

Wagner, H. and Silber, K. (2004) *Physiological Psychology: Instant Notes*, London: Taylor & Francis.

Specialist sources

Kalat, J.W. (2007) *Biological Psychology*, United Kingdom: Thomson Wadsworth.

Toates, F. (2007) *Biological Psychology*, 2nd edn, London: Prentice Hall.

Gender development

The first thing that we usually notice about someone is whether they are male or female. On the odd occasion when we meet someone who is not clearly identifiable as either male or female it can be quite unnerving, so knowing a person's sex is obviously important to our understanding of other people. Similarly, our understanding of self is very much influenced by our own sex and our view of what it is to be either male or female. Psychologists have long been interested in sex differences in behaviour and the cause of these differences. If there are any differences, are they due to differences in biology, or are they due to the different social expectations of males and females? In this chapter we shall look at psychological notions of gender, gender research and theories that have been used to explain gender development.

3.1 Concepts

3.1.1 Sex and gender

> The term **sex** refers to biological status as either male or female. It is defined by our chromosomes, hormones and anatomical differences.
>
> The term **gender** is psychosocial and refers to notions about the expected roles, behaviours and attitudes of males and females within a given society.

Some writers prefer to use the terms sex and gender interchangeably, so different text-books can be confusing. In addition, we must remember that concepts are just ideas, they are not fixed. Thus the concept of gender may change over time and can vary both within and between cultures. The concept of gender is therefore a **social construction**, meaning it is invented by society, so different societies will understand gender differently.

The adjectives **masculine** and **feminine** are sometimes used to describe roles, behaviours and attitudes that are deemed to be appropriate for males and females respectively. An example of a masculine role would be that of father: traditionally, a father might be expected to be the financial provider for the family, to be responsible for practical jobs, to make important decisions. An example of a feminine role might be that of mother: traditionally, a mother might be expected to take the lead in caring for children, to manage the household, to take care of sick relatives.

Early attempts to measure masculinity and femininity assumed that a person could not be a bit of both, but had to be distinctly one or the other. Indeed, not so long ago in western society, anyone in one category having characteristics associated with a person in another category was regarded as deviant: a man who took an interest in his appearance and liked cooking might have been referred to as a 'sissy', or worse. More recently, it has been recognised that a person might be masculine in some ways, but can also show more typically feminine characteristics in other ways. So a man could be tough and aggressive (typically male traits) in the course of his work, and at the same time could be tender and gentle.

Figure 3.1. A man can be tough and aggressive and at the same time tender and gentle.

3.1.2 Androgyny

The word **androgyny** derives from a combination of the Greek work for 'man', *andro*, and the Greek word for 'woman', *gyne*. The term **androgynous**, therefore, describes people whose characteristics are a balanced mixture of masculine and feminine traits. In 1974 Sandra Bem developed the Bem Sex Role Inventory (BSRI) to measure androgyny. She suggested that androgenous people, who showed a mixture of masculine and feminine characteristics, were more psychologically healthy than people who showed only masculine or only feminine traits.

The BSRI is a way of measuring a person's androgyny. To develop the scale, 100 judges were asked to give ratings on a seven-point scale to 200 personality traits. The scale asked them to determine how desirable each trait was for either men or women. On the basis of these ratings, Bem chose 20 traits that the judges had rated as more desirable for males than for females, and 20 traits that they had rated as more desirable for females than for males. A further 20 neutral traits that had not been identified as particularly desirable for one sex but not the other were also chosen for the scale. A selection of some of these characteristics is shown below:

- **Masculine:** forceful; aggressive; independent.
- **Feminine:** warm; affectionate; gentle.
- **Neutral:** friendly; loyal, theatrical.

Respondents are asked to give themselves a rating for each trait on a seven-point scale, where 1 = never or almost never true of me, and 7 = always or almost always true of me. After completing the inventory, respondents receive an overall masculinity score and an overall femininity score, somewhere between 20 and 140. These two scores can then be plotted on the two dimensions, as shown in Figure 3.2.

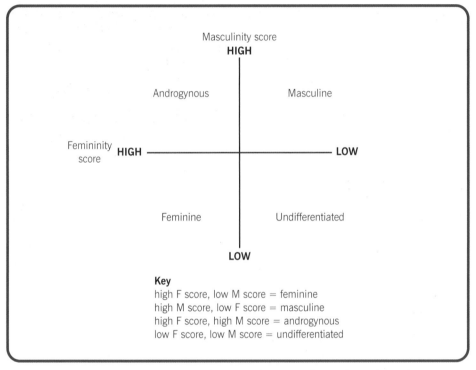

Figure 3.2. Diagram showing masculine and feminine dimensions. Note how a person who scores highly on both dimensions is classified as androgynous.

Evaluation

- Bem's scale has been found to have good test-retest reliability, producing similar results if used on more than one occasion with the same sample.
- Bem (1974) suggested that people with high androgyny scores are psychologically healthier than people who show more conventionally differentiated male or female traits. However, other researchers have suggested that it is the high masculinity score which is important for psychological wellbeing (Whitely 1983).

- Reducing the concepts of masculinity and femininity to a single score may be an oversimplification. More recent approaches also measure various aspects of gender-related behaviour, such as interests and abilities, rather than just personality traits (Golombok and Fivush 1994).
- The inventory is based on what American students assessed as desirable traits for men and women in the 1970s. Thus the BSRI has limited validity as a measure of masculinity and femininity in all societies and at all times.

3.1.3 Sex-role or gender stereotypes

A sex-role stereotype is an organised belief about the behaviour, attitudes and characteristics expected of males or females. Stereotypes cause us to overemphasise similarities between individual members of the same group; for example, we tend to believe that all males are ambitious. At the same time, stereotypes cause us to overestimate the differences between different groups; for example, if we believe that females are caring, we tend to believe that males are not caring (see Chapter 6).

The existence of gender stereotypes and the effect of stereotypes on our behaviour and attitudes has been investigated in a number of ways. We shall consider studies illustrating the following:

- adult gender stereotypes about infants;

- children's gender stereotypes;

- gender stereotypes in the media.

Adult gender stereotypes about infants

Many studies show that adults treat male and female children differently, perhaps suggesting that they have different expectations of the sexes in the form of stereotypes. The problem here is that maybe male and female children really do behave differently and this is what causes the difference in adult behaviour. To get round this problem, psychologists conduct what are known as 'Baby X' studies. In a Baby X study, adults are told that a baby is either male or female, and then observed interacting with the child. As the baby is actually the same baby, the researchers can then infer that any differences in the behaviour of the adults towards the child is due not to the child's behaviour, but to the gender expectations of the adult.

Many Baby X studies have shown that adults perceive and react towards babies in gender-stereotypical ways.

In a review of 23 such studies, Stern and Karraker (1989) investigated the effects on:

- adults' descriptions of the baby;

- adults' behaviours towards the baby;

- toy choices made by adults for the baby.

They found that how the baby was labelled strongly affected the adults' behaviour towards the child and the toy choices they made, but did not have the same effect on the way that the adults described the child's personality. These differences in findings between actual behaviour and what people say suggest that it is important how we measure stereotyping: self-reported measures (what adults say they think about the baby) may not always correspond with behavioural measures (how they treat the baby).

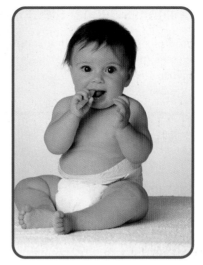

Figure 3.3. The mysterious Baby X. Boy or girl? Adults react differently towards a baby depending on whether it is labelled male or female.

Study

Aim Seavey et al. (1975) carried out the first Baby X study to see whether the gender label attached to a baby affected adult responses.

Method A three-month-old infant was dressed in a yellow babysuit. One-third of the participants were told that the infant was male, another third were told that the child was female, and another third were not given a gender label. Participants were left to interact with the child for three minutes. Also in the room were some toys: a ball (typically a male toy), a rag doll (typically a female toy) and a plastic ring (a gender-neutral toy).

Results When the baby was labelled as female, participants were more likely to use the doll when playing with the child. When the baby was labelled as male, participants tended to use the gender-neutral toy. When they were told nothing about the child's gender, female participants interacted freely with the child while male participants did not.

Conclusion Adults will interact differently with infants depending on whether they believe they are male or female.

Children's gender stereotypes

Studies show that children soon become aware of gender stereotypes, and that their ideas about gender are particularly fixed between three and five years (Golombok and Fivush 1994).

> ### Study
>
> **Aim** Urberg (1982) set out to investigate the content of gender stereotypes in children aged between three and seven years.
>
> **Method** Children aged three, five and seven years were told stories illustrating gender-stereotyped traits like bravery and caring. The bravery story went as follows: 'Some people are brave. If a house was on fire they would go inside to rescue people.' The children were then shown two pictures, one of a male and one of a female. The researcher then asked, 'Who are the brave people? Are they women, men, both women and men, or nobody?' For some stories the pictures were of adults and for others they were of children.
>
> **Results** All age groups chose according to cultural stereotypes. The five-year-old children were especially rigid in their choices, whereas the seven-year-olds were more flexible about whether the expected behaviour was typically male or female. Interestingly, the responses were more stereotyped when the pictures used were of children rather than adults.
>
> **Conclusion** Young children have clear expectations about the types of behaviours that are typical of each sex.

Whereas preschool children make predictions about people's gender-related behaviour based solely on their sex, older children's gender stereotypes become less fixed: they still use gender to predict behaviour, but they will use other information as well. Martin (1989) told children aged between four and ten years stories about male and female characters. These characters were described as playing with either gender-consistent or gender-inconsistent toys. When later asked to choose what other toys the characters might like to play with, very young children chose on the basis of the character's sex alone, despite what the character might have been playing with in the story. For example, a young child hearing about a girl playing with a toy car would still choose a typically girls' toy like a doll. Older children, however, took account of the fact that the character might already have been seen to prefer gender-inconsistent toys and therefore might like other gender-inconsistent toys. It seems that for very young children making this decision, information about the character's sex overrides any other available information.

Gender stereotypes in the media

The way in which the sexes are represented in children's books has changed enormously since the 1960s, when females were under-represented and were often shown in passive and needy roles. For example, a typical children's storybook would present a picture of boys making decisions, taking the lead, performing brave actions, and girls following, worrying and needing help.

As the content of storybooks has become much less stereotyped since the 1970s, it might be assumed that children are no longer getting stereotyped messages. However, a study by DeLoache et al. (1987) suggests that the effects may be more subtle.

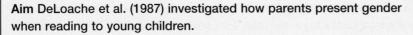

Study

Aim DeLoache et al. (1987) investigated how parents present gender when reading to young children.

Method The researchers used a special storybook of 'the three bears', in which all the bear characters were of indeterminate gender. In other words, they were not clearly identified as either male or female. Mothers were observed reading the storybook to their children.

Results The mothers spontaneously labelled 62 per cent of the bears as male, and only 16 per cent of the bears as female. Female labelling occurred only where a big bear was shown in a picture with a little bear.

Conclusion Even where the gender of characters is not given, adult readers will present characters as male except where the character could be seen to be involved in caring for young.

A great deal of television research has shown that males and females are presented differently on television. A review by Davis (1990) showed that females on television are:

● outnumbered 2 to 1 by males;

● younger than males;

● four times more likely than males to be dressed provocatively.

3.1.4 Cultural variations in gender-related behaviour

One of the earliest and most well-known studies of cultural differences in gender-related behaviour was carried out by the anthropologist Margaret Mead in 1935.

Study

Aim Mead carried out cross-cultural research to see whether there were differences in gender roles in three different societies.

Method For six months she lived with and observed three separate tribal communities on the island of New Guinea: the Arapesh, the Mundugamor and the Tchambuli. Mead recorded the behaviours shown by males and females in each group.

Results Both males and females in the Arapesh community showed personality traits and behaviours which are stereotypically feminine in western society. They were gentle and cooperative. Both males and females in the Mundugamor society were described as fierce and aggressive, traits which would traditionally be seen as masculine in the West. The Tchambuli people showed distinct gender roles for males and females, but these were a reversal of traditional western sex roles: men were sentimental and emotional, while women took decisions and were the providers.

Conclusion Different cultures show differences in gender-related behaviour.

Evaluation

- Mead's methods have been challenged as being unscientific.
- Even before her research, Mead had strong beliefs that the environment was responsible for shaping gender behaviour. This might have led to researcher bias in her observations.
- Errington and Gewertz (1989) revisited the Tchambuli and carried out an analysis of Mead's original records. They concluded that the women did not dominate the men, or vice versa.
- Some years later, Mead significantly changed her views about cultural influences, stating that women were 'naturally' better at childcare than men.

More recent research confirms that there are cross-cultural differences in gender.

> **Study**
>
> **Aim** La Fromboise et al. (1990) investigated gender roles in Native American cultures.
>
> **Method** They studied the Cheyenne, Blackfeet and Pawnee American Indian tribes of North America, using both observation and interviews.
>
> **Results** Gender roles were found to be different from those in traditional western societies. Women took an active part in conflict and were known as 'warrior women'.
>
> **Conclusion** Men are not exclusively the aggressors in all societies.

Mead perhaps exaggerated cultural differences in gender-related behaviour; most writers would now agree that there is broad similarity across cultures in relation to much of our gender-related behaviour. Wade and Tavris (1998) point out that in most cultures men have higher status and engage more in warfare, while women look after the children and perform household tasks. However, they also point out that there are several cultural variations in gender-related behaviour.

- Status – Women are of highest status in Scandinavian countries and of lowest status in Bangladesh.

- Occupation – The view of occupations as 'men's work' and 'women's work' varies. For example, dentistry and medicine have traditionally been seen as male occupations in the West, but are seen as female occupations in other countries, where they are much lower paid.

Mead's (1935) findings suggested that biological sex does not determine gender role and that culture is a greater influence than biology on gender-related behaviour. Despite the problems with Mead's research, the findings stimulated interest in the importance of nature and nurture in defining gender roles.

3.1.5 Nature and nurture

The nature–nurture debate is a debate about the extent to which our behaviour is governed by the forces of biology and experiences/environment.

The **extreme nature view** would suggest that gender-related behaviour is entirely controlled by hormonal and genetic factors. This view assumes that women are biologically programmed to be nurturers and carers, while men are biologically programmed to be providers and protectors.

The **extreme nurture view** would suggest that gender-related behaviour is entirely determined by social and cultural factors – our experiences and the environment in which we live.

In reality, most psychologists would take a more moderate **interactionist** view: some of our gender-related behaviour is governed by our biological make-up, but any innate predisposition can be modified by the environment and developmental experiences.

Theoretical explanations of gender vary in the extent to which they fall on the nature or nurture side of the debate.

Explanation	Position re: the nature–nurture debate
Biological	Pro-nature
Social learning theory	Pro-nurture
Cognitive approach	Development of understanding depends on biological maturation (nature), but is also influenced by experience (nurture)
Psychodynamic	Depends on a combination of instinctive biological forces (nature) and childhood experience (nurture)

Figure 3.4. The nature–nurture debate and explanations of gender development.

3.2 Explaining gender

3.2.1 Biological explanations

Biological theories assume that any differences between the sexes are attributable to biological differences and the action of hormones. Biopsychologists would seek to explain gender differences in terms of chromosomal differences, differences in brain structure and function, and differences in hormonal activity.

Typical sex chromosome patterns

The normal human body contains 23 pairs of chromosomes. Each pair of chromosomes carries genes that control different characteristics. Biological sex is determined by the 23rd chromosome pair. If the pairing for chromosome 23 is XX, the person is female, and if it is XY, the person is male.

Atypical sex-chromosome patterns

Any combination of sex chromosomes other than XX and XY is atypical. Klinefelter's syndrome and Turner's syndrome are examples of conditions which are the result of atypical sex chromosome combinations.

Klinefelter's syndrome, XXY:

- caused by the presence of an extra X chromosome;
- biological male with the physical appearance of male;
- affects between 1 in 500 and 1 in 1,000 males;
- psychological effects: poor language skills affecting reading ability; passive temperament;
- physical effects: less body hair than normal male; underdeveloped genitals; long legs in relation to torso; infertile.

Turner's syndrome, XO:

- caused by the absence of an X chromosome;
- biological female with female external appearance;
- affects one in 2,500 females;
- psychological effects: higher than average reading ability; lower than average spatial ability, visual memory and mathematical skills; difficulty in social adjustment;
- physical effects: ovaries fail to develop; short, squat body with webbed neck.

Studying people with atypical sex-chromosome combinations allows us to draw some conclusions about how much our biological make-up might be responsible for gender-related behaviour. We shall now consider evidence in relation to the biological explanation. Some unusual case studies seem to show that our combination of sex chromosomes has a more powerful influence on gender than our experiences.

Study

Aim Imperato-McGinley et al. (1979) reported the case of 38 boys from 23 families in the Dominican Republic – the Batista boys. The researchers aimed to investigate how well the boys adopted their biological male identity when they had been brought up as females.

Method The Batista boys had a rare genetic abnormality, which meant that although they were born with male sex chromosomes (XY), they appeared female at birth. At puberty, changes in testosterone levels caused them to change physically into males. (In normal males these changes take place in the womb before the child is born, but because of their genetic abnormality this had not happened, and they had been born with the physical appearance of girls.) Interviews with the boys and their families confirmed that for the first part of their childhood they had been brought up and treated as girls, and socialised as females.

Results Despite having been raised as girls, the boys had no problems adapting well to their new male identity. Most went on to marry local girls and raise a family as a traditional male.

Conclusion This case illustrates the importance of biological factors in gender development. It seems that having a Y chromosome and being biologically male can override the effects of years of socialisation as a female.

Money and Erhardt (1972) studied children born with ambiguous genitalia. These children are sometimes referred to as intersex children because their external appearance is not clear as one gender or the other. In such cases, it is usual to perform surgery to assign the child to a sex as either male or female. Thus a child who is born with a very small penis might be surgically reassigned as a girl and brought up as a girl. Money and Erhardt suggested at the time that biological factors have little effect on gender identity. They proposed the **theory of neutrality**, stating that children are born gender-neutral, and suggested that gender reassignment will be successful if carried out before the child is three years old. However, one famous case showed how socialisation cannot overcome biology.

Study

Aim Money and Erhardt (1972) studied a child whose sex had been reassigned to see whether he could be successfully socialised as a female.

Method Bruce was a healthy seven-month-old twin boy, who was accidentally castrated during a routine operation. Money advised Bruce's parents that the best solution would be to raise him as a girl and use plastic surgery to create a female external appearance. At adolescence the child was given the female hormone, oestrogen. Progress was monitored until early adolescence, when the family ceased contact with the researchers. Many years later, Bruce made his identity public. He had discontinued oestrogen treatment at the age of 12 years and had later had surgery to reverse the effects of previous plastic surgery. He was married and living as a man. Despite his parents' efforts to treat him as a girl, he said he had hated wearing dresses and remembered preferring boys' toys.

Results Money initially reported that the case was a success and that the child had assumed a traditional female identity. Money took this as evidence for his theory of neutrality. The later revelations suggest that gender reassignment was not successful.

Conclusion The final outcome suggests that biological influences are more important than socialisation. Bruce was always a biological male with XY chromosomes; treating him as a girl for many years appeared not to have affected his identity as a male.

Diamond (1982) supports the biological explanation. He challenged Money's theory of neutrality, stating that there are hard-wired brain differences between males and females and it is these differences that are responsible for gender behaviours. Diamond was referring to the work of Gorski et al. (1978), who discovered a structural difference in the brains of male and female rats. This region of the hypothalamus is known as the **sexually dimorphic nucleus**, and is larger in males than in females. Gorski attributed this difference to prenatal exposure to the male hormone testosterone.

Hormonal influences – androgens (including testosterone) and oestrogens

Hormones are chemical substances secreted by glands in the body. Men and women have the same sex hormones, but in different amounts. Male hormones are collectively known as androgens, and the most well-known of these is testosterone. While male and female hormones have obvious physical effects, psychologists are mainly interested in the effects of sex hormones on behaviour. Different levels of aggression have consistently been found between males and females. As a consequence, much research into the effects of hormones on behaviour has focused on the role of testosterone in aggression.

Testosterone is a predominantly male hormone that affects development and behaviour both before and after birth. In the fifth month of foetal development, the male gonads secrete testosterone, causing the male foetus to develop external sex organs. The psychological effects of testosterone can be seen in a condition known as **congenital adrenal hyperplasia** (CAH). It is a rare condition which can affect both males and females. It causes heightened levels of male hormones. Genetic females (XX) with the condition are often described as tomboys, have higher levels of aggression than other girls, prefer male toys and show superior ability in spatial tasks (Berenbaum and Hines

1992). However, studies of aggression in girls with CAH have so far yielded inconsistent results. Hines (2004) reports a number of studies comparing aggression levels between CAH girls, CAH males and controls, using various measures of aggression. Some of these studies show significant effects, while others show no differences. Most CAH research involves small samples. **Laboratory studies with animals** tend to show that testosterone does lead to increased aggression (Silber and Wagner 2004).

- Male rats show more aggression than female rats.
- Castrated males show reduced aggression.
- Male–male aggression begins at puberty when male hormones are secreted.
- Aggression increases with injections of testosterone. Van de Poll et al. (1988) found that injecting female rats with testosterone led to increases in aggression.

Studies with men taking bodybuilding androgenic steroids show that they have higher than normal aggression scores on questionnaires. For example, Midgley et al. (2001) found that 60 per cent of those taking steroids had raised anger scores on the State Trait Anger Expression Inventory. However, it is impossible to determine cause and effect in such studies. Midgley et al. found that these men also tended to be employed in 'aggressive' occupations, for example, as security staff or bouncers. Perhaps their line of work necessitated or caused higher than normal aggression levels. **Research with prison populations** has also been used to determine a link between testosterone and offending (and presumably aggression).

Study

Aim Dabbs et al. (1995) investigated the link between testosterone levels, prisoners' behaviour and the type of crime committed.

Method The amount of testosterone was analysed, using saliva samples from 692 male prisoners. These results were then related to prison records. Two types of information were taken from the records: type of crime committed and incidents of broken prison rules.

Results High-testosterone men were more likely to have committed crimes involving sex and violence than men with lower testosterone levels. Lower-testosterone men were more likely to have committed crimes such as burglary and drug offences. Prison rule breaking was also found to be more common in high-testosterone men.

Conclusion Testosterone can be linked to aggressive behaviour.

Most naturally occurring studies, such as the steroid research and prison research, are unable to demonstrate a cause-and-effect relationship between the level of testosterone and aggression. Just because bodybuilders and prisoners have high testosterone levels and show high levels of aggression, we cannot assume that the testosterone causes aggression. To determine cause and effect and eliminate the effects of confounding variables, it is necessary to carry out carefully controlled experimental studies. In one such study, Tricker et al. (1996) showed that administering testosterone had no significant effect on multiple measures of anger.

Study

Aim Tricker et al. (1996) carried out an experimental study to compare the effects of testosterone and a placebo on aggression.

Method In a double-blind study, 43 males between 19 and 40 years received either 600mg per week of testosterone enanthate or a placebo. As it was a double-blind study, neither the participants nor the researchers administering the substance knew who was receiving testosterone and who was receiving the placebo. The study lasted for ten weeks. Participants were tested before, during and after treatment on two anger questionnaires. Parents, spouses or live-in partners were also asked to rate the participants on aggressive behaviour and mood.

Results No significant differences between the experimental group and the control group were found on any of the measures over the ten-week period.

Conclusion The researchers concluded that high doses of testosterone have no effect on the aggressive behaviour or attitudes of adult males.

Evaluation of testosterone research

- Increased levels of testosterone may be a consequence of aggressive behaviour rather than the cause.
- It might not be appropriate to generalise from animal research findings to human behaviour.
- Explaining aggression purely in terms of chemical activity is perhaps an oversimplification.
- Environmental factors like family background also influence how people respond to frustrating situations. Most males manage to control their behaviour and behave in socially acceptable and non-violent ways.

- The effect of testosterone may be indirect: males with high testosterone might have more muscular bodies, which might lead others to treat them as if they are aggressive. Perhaps it is the way other people respond to them that leads them to become aggressive – the **self-fulfilling prophecy**.

Oestrogen is a female hormone, responsible for the development of female sexual characteristics and menstruation. In addition to physical changes which occur in the body due to oestrogen, some psychological and behavioural effects have been reported. In some women, these effects can be seen as premenstrual syndrome (PMS) or premenstrual tension (PMT). PMT may lead to increased emotionality, irritability and aggression. It has also been suggested that it could be responsible for momentary lapses in self-control or attention, leading to antisocial behaviours, such as committing criminal acts. Occasionally, hormonal activity has been used as a defence in court for women accused of shoplifting and even murder. In some instances this defence has been accepted (Easteal 1991).

Golombok and Fivush (1994) summarise the results of investigations into the effects of oestrogen on psychiatric symptoms in the premenstrual period and during the menopause. They conclude that there is no consistent evidence that changes in oestrogen levels are responsible for the depression, anxiety and irritability that many women report. They suggest that where these symptoms are carefully measured, for example using daily records, they are found to be less evident than when reported retrospectively.

Evaluation

- Some evidence supports the view that biological differences between males and females affect behaviour.
- Other evidence is less convincing.
- Even if biology has a role, it is also important to consider environmental factors.
- Social learning theorists would argue that gender is socially constructed rather than biological.

3.2.2 Social learning theory (SLT)

According to social learning theory (Bandura 1986), most behaviour, including gender-related behaviour, is learned as a result of observation. Whether or not an observed behaviour is demonstrated depends on a number of factors, including the person's perception of their own ability and their understanding of the likely consequences. Social learning theory differs from traditional learning theory in that it does not automatically assume that a behaviour will be performed as a result of association between stimulus and response (see Chapter 1). Social learning theory acknowledges the role of the social context and key individuals like parents in the development of gender-related behaviour.

The following key concepts are used by social learning theorists to explain the acquisition of gender-related behaviour:

- imitation;
- reinforcement;
- identification;
- modelling.

Imitation

Imitation is copying behaviour and is the most efficient way of learning complex behaviours. Imitation does not imply any special relationship between the imitator and the person being imitated. Simple observation of the behaviour can sometimes be sufficient for learning to take place.

Reinforcement

Observed behaviour is more likely to be imitated if it is seen to be rewarding. The reward may be in the form of direct **positive reinforcement**; for example, a boy is rewarded with praise by a football coach for copying the successful actions of another footballer. Alternatively, the reward may be indirect, in the form of **vicarious reinforcement**; for example, a girl may see her sister being praised for helping to make the dinner. In the case of vicarious reinforcement, learning occurs through observation of the consequences of actions for other people.

Mischel (1966) argued that sex-typed behaviour occurs as a result of differential reinforcement of males and females. Certainly, many studies show that there are differences in the types of behaviours that are reinforced for boys and girls. Parents are especially influential, but teachers and peers are also instrumental in shaping the behaviour of young children.

Study

Aim Fagot (1978) wanted to see whether parents treated male and female toddlers differently when they were playing at home.

Method She observed 24 toddlers aged 20–24 months, playing at home in the presence of parents. She recorded instances of reinforcement (verbal encouragement) and punishment ('telling off' or critical comment). Various toys were available during the observation.

Results Girls were reinforced for dressing up, asking for help and staying near the parent. They were discouraged from playing roughly, jumping and climbing. Boys were reinforced for playing with sex-appropriate toys like bricks and discouraged from playing with dolls.

Conclusion Parents respond differently to the behaviour of male and female toddlers, encouraging them to behave in ways that are seen to be gender-appropriate.

Study

Aim Dweck et al. (1978) observed teachers' use of negative and positive feedback in the classroom.

Method A total of 79 young children were observed in the classroom twice a week for five weeks. The observers were blind to the purpose of the study. The type of teacher feedback to boys and girls was recorded as follows:

- whether the feedback was related to work or behaviour;
- whether it was positive or negative;
- whether it was related to content or presentation (e.g. neatness).

Results Boys tended to receive positive reinforcement for content, while girls tended to receive positive reinforcement for neatness. This pattern was reversed for negative comments.

Conclusion This study demonstrated that teachers respond in different ways to boys and girls.

Identification

Identification is the process whereby a child sees him or herself as somehow similar to a specific person who is seen as possessing attractive qualities, or qualities that are seen to be rewarding. The child experiences a form of attachment to this person and aspires to be like them. Unlike imitation, identification implies some form of relationship between the imitator and the imitated.

Modelling

Modelling refers to the process of copying the behaviours of a chosen person, a model. This model acts as an example, as in the term 'role model'. In acquiring gender-related behaviour, boys may model themselves on their father, brother or a famous footballer, for example. Girls may model themselves on their mother, sister or a member of a girl band. A child will probably have several models whose behaviour they try to imitate. Maccoby and Jacklin (1974) referred to this process as **self-socialisation**, because the learning does not depend on the need for direct reinforcement from other people.

According to classic social learning theory, children observe and imitate the behaviour of those around them and are most likely to copy the behaviour of same-sex models. However, it was later recognised that this copying is not indiscriminate and that there are several reasons why children choose to copy some people and not others. This understanding that a child actively chooses whether or not to model behaviour led to interest in the role of **cognitive factors** in social learning and the circumstances that are most likely to lead to modelling, as shown in Figure 3.6 overleaf.

Figure 3.5. Boys may model the behaviour of a famous footballer.

Study

Aim Perry and Bussey (1979) investigated children's preferences for imitation of same-sex models.

Method Children saw four male and four female models choosing between two items, for example, a banana or an apple. All the female models chose one item and all the male models chose the other. After observing the adult choices, the children were asked which of the two items they liked the best.

Results Children clearly preferred the item that had been chosen by all the adults of their own sex.

Conclusion Children will copy the behaviour of their own sex.

It is now thought that the appropriateness of the model's behaviour is a more important factor in modelling than whether the model is the same sex as the child (Golombok and Fivush 1994). The effect of sex-appropriateness on modelling was demonstrated in a study by Masters et al. (1979).

Similarity	Models who are seen to be similar (e.g. in age or sex) are more likely to be copied
Status	High-status models like older brothers are more likely to be copied than low-status models
Attractive	Glamorous, successful, heroic models are more likely to be copied than unattractive models
Behaviour is appropriate	Behaviour seen as appropriate for the role is more likely to be copied
Reward and punishment	The model is more likely to be copied if they are seen to be rewarded

Figure 3.6. Factors affecting the likelihood of a child copying the behaviour of a model.

Study

Aim Masters et al. (1979) set out to investigate if knowing about whether a behaviour was sex-appropriate or sex-inappropriate would affect the likelihood of a child imitating the behaviour.

Method Children aged four to five years were shown gender-neutral toys like a balloon and a xylophone, and told that some of these toys were appropriate for girls and some for boys. The children then watched a video of a girl model or a boy model playing with the toys. After the video, the children were given the opportunity to play with the toys and asked which they liked the best.

Results Girls were more likely to play with the toy they had been told was appropriate for girls than the toy they had seen the girl model play with. Boys were more likely to play with the toy they had been told was appropriate for boys than the toy that they had seen the boy model play with. If the label attached to the toy and the model's sex corresponded, children showed even stronger preferences.

Conclusion Perceived appropriateness of a behaviour appears to be more important for imitation than whether the model is the same sex.

Evaluation of social learning theory

- SLT does not account for changes in the development of gender understanding with age. In fact, it assumes that there is no process of gradual development in understanding.
- Many studies of modelling are unrealistic; they use adult models playing with toys or pretending in one context or another.
- If behaviour always arises as a result of imitation, it does not easily explain the emergence of new trends in gender-related behaviour, such as 'the new man', who is happy to change nappies and prepare the dinner.
- The theory does not easily explain gender differences which exist between same-sex siblings. Two sisters have been raised in the same household by the same parents, but one may be exceptionally more feminine than the other.
- SLT does not explain why children at a certain age (usually around four to five years) often have more rigid views about sex-typed behaviour than their parents.
- SLT neglects the role of biological factors in gender development.
- There is ample evidence that boys and girls are reinforced differently and that children do model the behaviour of others.
- SLT emphasises the role of cognitive factors in learning, acting as a bridge between traditional learning and cognitive theory. Golombok and Fivush (1994) suggest that the gap between social learning and cognitive explanations of gender is now so narrow that it no longer makes sense to separate the two.
- Cross-cultural studies support the view that gender is learned.

3.2.3 The cognitive approach to gender

The cognitive approach to explaining gender focuses on how the child understands gender, on the mental processes that enable a child to learn the appropriate sex-role. According to cognitive psychologists, our knowledge of the world is actively constructed and this happens through a process of gradually developing understanding. The first person to suggest a cognitive account of gender development was Lawrence Kohlberg (1966).

Kohlberg's cognitive developmental theory

Kohlberg's theory of gender is based on the ideas of the famous developmental psychologist, Piaget. According to Piaget's theory of cognitive development, a child's thinking and understanding of the physical world change with age. Piaget was a stage theorist in that he suggested that thinking developed in age-related stages. Similarly, Kohlberg suggested that understanding of the social world develops in a series of stages. At each stage, the child's understanding becomes increasingly sophisticated. Kohlberg's stages of gender development are outlined below.

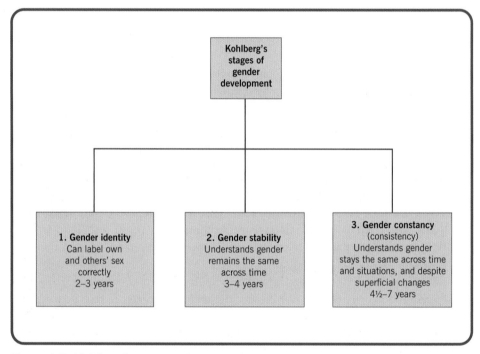

Figure 3.7. Kohlberg's stages of gender development.

1 Gender identity or gender labelling

At around two to three years old, a child slowly begins to understand that they are either male or female. They start to be able to label their own sex correctly, and also start to recognise other people as either male or female. They are able to apply gender labels such as 'boy', 'girl', 'mummy' and 'daddy' correctly. At this stage understanding is based very much on external physical characteristics such as hair length and clothes. Children at this age do not understand that sex is consistent across time.

2 Gender stability

At about three to four years old, a child's understanding of gender becomes more complex. Children realise that sex remains stable over time. For example, a boy in the gender-stability stage will recognise that he is male now, was male in the past and will remain male in the future. A little girl who has not yet achieved gender stability knows that she is a girl at the moment, but might not realise that she was a baby girl when she was tiny, and might think that she will 'be a daddy' when she grows up. Although children who have reached the stability stage have a fuller understanding of gender, their thinking about gender is still limited in two ways:

- They do not understand that gender stays the same across situations. For example, children in the gender-stability stage who see a boy playing with dolls might think that he has changed into a girl.
- They still rely heavily on external appearances. Changing a person's superficial appearance by changing their clothes or hair might cause a child in this stage to think that the person has changed sex. McConaghy (1979) showed that children in this stage judged the sex of a doll on the basis of the doll's clothing rather than on the basis of its genitals (which were visible).

3 Gender constancy or gender consistency

A complete understanding of gender is acquired between the ages of four and a half and seven years, when the child realises that gender remains the same across time, across different situations and despite superficial changes in appearance. For example, a child who has developed gender constancy would understand that even though a woman might crop her hair, wear men's clothes and drive a heavy lorry, she is still a woman and hasn't changed into a man. Only when a child reaches this stage of development can they be said to fully understand gender. According to Bem (1989), children's understanding of gender constancy is related to knowledge of biological differences between males and females.

Study

Aim To test Kohlberg's stage theory of gender development, Slaby and Frey (1975) carried out the Gender Concept Interview. (See Figure 3.8 on page 94.)

Method Young children were asked a series of questions. Gender identity was tested by showing the child dolls or photographs of adults, then asking whether the doll or the person in the photograph was male or female. Gender stability was tested by asking the child what they were when they were little, and what they would be when they grew up. Gender constancy was tested by asking children whether or not they would be a girl or a boy if they wore opposite-sex clothes or played with opposite-sex toys.

Results Slaby and Frey found that children's responses to these questions reflected the stages proposed by Kohlberg.

Conclusion The findings seem to confirm that understanding of gender develops in a sequence of age-related stages.

Identity question	Stimulus – a girl doll Q: Is this a girl or a boy?
Identity question	Stimulus – a photo of a man Q: Is this a woman or a man?
Stability question	Q: When you were a little baby, were you a little girl or a little boy?
Stability question	Q: When you grow up, will you be a mummy or a daddy?
Constancy question	To a boy Q: If you wore girls' clothes, would you be a girl or a boy?

Figure 3.8. Questions from the Gender Concept Interview used by Slaby and Frey (1975).

Research using other methods has confirmed that the understanding of gender changes with age.

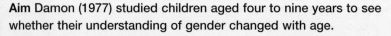

Study

Aim Damon (1977) studied children aged four to nine years to see whether their understanding of gender changed with age.

Method The children heard a story about a boy called George. George liked playing with dolls, but his parents tried to discourage him. They told him that only girls played with dolls. Damon then asked the children questions about whether George's parents were right to try to stop him playing with dolls, and whether George should be able to play with dolls if he wanted to.

Results The children's responses varied according to their age. The four-year-olds tended to say that it was all right for George to play with dolls. Six-year-olds had a very fixed view that it was quite wrong and should not be allowed. The older children thought that George could play with dolls if he really wanted to, although they recognised that this was unusual and maybe not such a good idea.

Conclusion Children's understanding of gender-appropriate behaviour changes with age and reflects their cognitive development.

Figure 3.9. George likes playing with dolls. Should George be allowed to play with dolls?

Gender schema theory

A **gender schema** is an organised unit of knowledge about the characteristics and behaviours associated with a specific gender. According to gender schema theory (Martin and Halverson 1981), as soon as children can label their own sex, at around two years, they actively search their environment for information to increase their understanding of maleness or femaleness. Gender schemas are used to interpret information in the environment and decide how to behave as a boy or a girl. A gender schema contains various components of information associated with a specific sex: behaviour, roles, occupations, hobbies and personality characteristics. Once we have identified a person as male or female, our gender schema is triggered for the relevant sex.

To start with, a child will identify activities and toys that are appropriate for his or her sex. The child then focuses on finding out more about behaviours and activities seen as appropriate for their sex and largely ignores behaviours and activities that are not usually associated with their own sex. Any information that conflicts with the child's gender schema is disregarded, forgotten or misremembered. According to Martin and Halverson (1981), gender schemas are built up gradually in three stages, as the child experiences the social world:

- **Stage 1**: Child learns what things are associated with each sex (e.g. girls play with dolls).

- **Stage 2**: Child begins to make links between different components of the schema, so that knowing what someone likes to play with will allow the child to predict other things about them. For example, someone who plays with dolls is likely to wear dresses and have long hair. In Stage 2, a child can only make these links for their own sex.

- **Stage 3**: Child can now use linked components for both sexes.

In support of gender schema theory, there is evidence to show that young children seem to have a better understanding of activities typically associated with their own sex than those typically associated with the opposite sex.

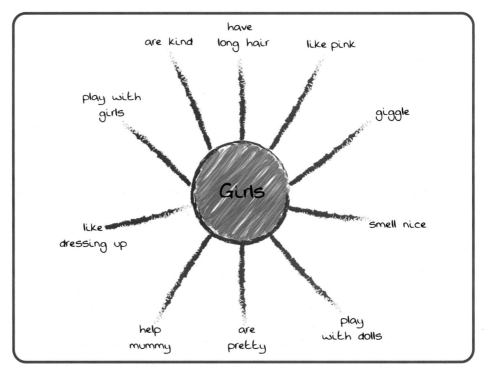

Figure 3.10. Three-year-old Maria's gender schema of 'girls'.

Study

Aim Boston and Levy (1991) wanted to see whether knowledge about stereotypically male and female activities differed between boys and girls.

Method Boys and girls between the ages of three and six years were asked to put sequences of four pictures in the correct order. Each set of four pictures described an activity, e.g. cooking the dinner (typically female activity) and building a birdhouse (typically male activity).

Results Both boys and girls were found to be able to put the picture sequences in the correct order more accurately for their own-gender activity than for the opposite-gender activity. This effect was particularly noticeable for boys.

Conclusion Since the task required detailed knowledge of an activity, boys and girls must have more knowledge of own-gender activities than of opposite-gender activities. The findings were interpreted as consistent with gender schema theory.

Research has also shown that children reject information that is inconsistent with their gender schema, and misremember information that is inconsistent with what they already know about gender. Cordua et al. (1979) showed that five- and six-year-old children's memory for videos can be influenced by their gender schema. In some of the videos, the occupations were stereotypical, for example, male doctors and female nurses. In others, the occupations were non-stereotypical, for example, female doctors and male nurses. It was found that children remembered the stereotypical video content quite accurately, but made errors when recalling the content of the non-stereotypical videos. For example, they would 'recall' that the doctor was a man even though the doctor in the video was female.

Evaluation of the cognitive developmental approach

- Cognitive developmental theory does not explain why males have a more fixed understanding of their gender than females. Many studies show that boys show more extreme gender-typed behaviour and a greater resistance to opposite-sex activities than girls.
- Cognitive developmental theory states that gender understanding begins around two years old. However, even before they can correctly label their

own sex, children will choose same-sex playmates, as if they are already unconsciously aware of the difference.

- Cognitive developmental theory focuses on development within the individual as if the child is passively absorbing the relevant information. It takes no account of the role of social interaction in developing understanding. However, taken together with social learning theory, it can provide a comprehensive account of gender development.
- Gender schema theory explains why children are more likely to model behaviour that is seen to be appropriate for their gender than automatically copy a same-sex model.
- Summarising the approach, Durkin (1995) states that it is 'currently the most influential approach to understanding gender'.

3.2.4 The psychodynamic approach
Freud's psychoanalytic theory of gender

Freud's explanation for gender development is part of his stage theory of psychosexual development (see Chapter 1). According to this theory, children pass through a series of stages of development, experiencing an unconscious conflict at each stage. According to Freud, during the first two stages, the oral stage and the anal stage, the child is essentially bisexual; gender identity does not exist and there is no differentiation between the behaviour of males and females. The key stage in relation to gender development is the phallic stage. In the **phallic stage**, at about five years, the child's attention is focused on the genital area. It is at this time that gender identity develops through the resolution of either the **Oedipus complex** (boys) or the **Electra complex** (girls) (Freud 1933).

The Oedipus complex

Sexual energy (Freud refers to this as libido) is directed into the phallus (penis), and a boy develops a sexual interest in his mother. Although this is very exciting, the boy is also afraid because he recognises his father as a powerful rival. The boy realises that not everyone has a penis and he wonders whether he might lose his penis. This leads to the fear that his father might castrate him if he discovered the boy's desire for his mother. This is known as **castration anxiety**. To resolve the conflict between the love for his mother and the fear of castration, the boy gives up the love for his mother and identifies with his father. This is referred to as **identifying with the aggressor**. It is this process of **identification** with the father that results in the boy adopting the male identity and assuming male characteristics. A boy who has resolved his Oedipus complex has a strong sense of male identity. Freud would therefore predict that a boy who has not satisfactorily resolved his Oedipus complex, perhaps because of the absence of a father, will be confused about his sexual identity.

The Electra complex

Freud believed that in the phallic stage the girl is becoming aware that she does not have a penis and believes she has already been castrated. Seeing that the mother also has no penis, the girl blames the mother for her lack of a penis. She sees both herself and her mother as powerless. The girl desires a penis, the symbol of male power. This **penis envy** leads her to desire the father because he possesses what she wants. As the girl cannot have a penis of her own, she converts her penis envy into a desire for a baby, the 'penis-baby' project. Having resolved the conflict, the girl identifies with the mother. It is the process of **identification** that results in the girl adopting the female identity and assuming female characteristics. According to Freud's explanation, female identification is not as strong as male identification because the girl thinks she has already been castrated and therefore is not as fearful as the boy. This means that the girl does not identify with the mother as strongly as the boy identifies with the father. Freud believed that women are sexually inferior to men; he viewed male development as the norm, and female development as deviant.

Through the Oedipus complex, the boy actively identifies with the father, whereas in the Electra complex, the girl passively identifies with the mother. Gender roles develop along the same lines: the boy leaves behind the passivity of his bisexual phase, becoming active and dominant; the girl assumes the passivity of the bisexual stage, becoming quiet and submissive.

One study that is often cited as evidence for the existence of the Oedipus complex is the case of Little Hans.

The Case of Little Hans

Hans was the son of a friend of Freud. He had developed a phobia of horses at the age of four and three-quarters. Hans's father wrote to Freud with details about his child. Hans was especially afraid of large white horses with black blinkers and black around the mouth. He was terrified that a horse might bite him. Freud interpreted the child's anxiety as expressing his unconscious fear of his father who had a full dark beard. The horse was merely a symbol of the father, and the fact that Hans feared being bitten by the horse symbolised his fear of castration by the father.

Figure 3.11. The case of Little Hans.

In fact, the case of Little Hans is better seen as an explanation for Hans's phobia than as support for Freud's theory of gender acquisition. Note that Freud had already decided that the Oedipus complex existed, and then tried to fit the details of the case to this theory. There is also a much more plausible account for the child's phobia in terms of classical conditioning: that the phobia had developed as a result of a frightening incident with a horse that the child had witnessed in the street.

One test of Freud's theory of gender development would be to consider cases where children grow up in households without two parents in the traditional mother and father roles. Freud's account of the Oedipus and Electra complexes depends on the presence of a mother and father who have a continuing relationship with each other. Perhaps children growing up in a household without a father and a mother would not be able to identify satisfactorily as either male or female, and would therefore have confused sexual identity. Several studies have shown that children growing up in non-traditional households are no more likely than other children to show gender confusion.

Study

Aim Green (1978) set out to study sexual identity in children living in atypical households.

Method The study involved 37 children, aged between 3 and 20 years. They were from households where the parents were either homosexual or transsexual. Various measures of the children's gender identity were used: toys and clothing preferences, occupational preferences and roles assumed in role plays.

Results All except one of the children showed typical gender preferences and roles.

Conclusion The development of secure gender identity does not seem to depend on the presence of two parents acting in the traditional 'mother' and 'father' roles.

Evaluation of Freud's psychoanalytic theory

- The Oedipus and Electra complexes are very controversial; many people find the notion of childhood sexuality difficult to accept.
- The theory would predict that gender identity arises at approximately four or five years of age, following either the Oedipus or Electra complex. Most evidence suggests that children have some understanding of gender identity long before this and that gender identity develops gradually.

- There is little or no empirical support for the theory and some evidence to contradict it.
- Freud himself was unhappy with the Electra complex, claiming that women were 'a great mystery'.
- The Oedipus complex arose from his self-analysis (Masson 1985) and, as a result, is not the product of objective scientific research.
- Golombok and Fivush (1994) note that most gender researchers 'do not consider Freud's ideas ... to have serious scientific merit'.

Other psychodynamic theories

Various neo-Freudians (new Freudians) have reinterpreted aspects of Freud's theory about gender development.

Karen Horney (1933/1967) offers an alternative interpretation of penis envy. She argues that girls are not envious of the penis itself, but instead are envious of the male position in society. The penis is desired because it is a symbol of male dominance, and females desire the power and control that males possess.

Erikson (1968/1974) questions Freud's assumption that males are superior to females. He argues that far from experiencing penis envy, females are very positive and secure about their own bodies. He even suggests that males suffer from womb envy, desiring women's ability to create. This is why, according to Erikson, men channel their energies into active pursuits, making things and getting involved in creative enterprises like business. Women, on the other hand, are more content to be inner-directed and focus on relationships.

Nancy Chodorow (1978) argues that gender begins in infancy and focuses on the early mother–child relationship as the basis for gender identity. She says that because the mother is female, she identifies more strongly with her daughter than with her son. Whereas the mother sees herself and her daughter as similar, she sees her son as different. This leads the mother to behave towards her daughter in ways that encourage mutuality and closeness. At the same time, she behaves towards her son in ways that encourage his individuality, and lead him to be even more separate. Female identification with the mother continues as the daughter grows older, and leads to the child developing a self-concept that includes ideas of mutual caring and responsibility. As males grow older they distance their own identity further from that of the mother, rejecting all things feminine and thereby establishing a separate male identity.

Golombok and Fivush (1994) point out that there is little evidence to support Chodorow's theory of a difference in the bonds between mother and daughter and mother and son. However, they also note that there is plenty of evidence to show that females are more relationship-oriented and males are more autonomous and independent, which is just what Chodorow's theory would predict.

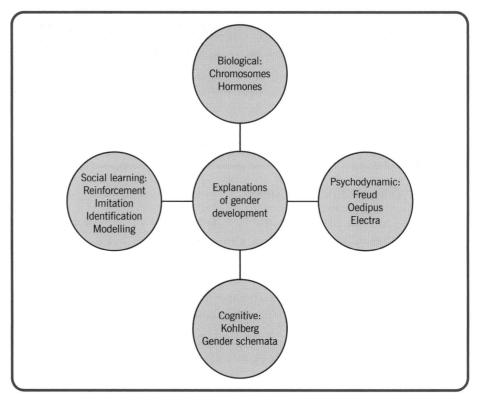

Figure 3.12. Explanations for gender: A summary.

How Psychology Works

A content analysis of gender representation in television adverts

- Your aim is to determine whether there are differences in the way males and females are represented in TV adverts. Previous studies have shown that there are differences.
- Make a video or DVD recording of a selection of TV adverts.
- In class, decide on the categories you should use to analyse the content of the recorded adverts. You might like to include some of the following: sex of the main character in the advert; product being advertised (e.g. body product, motoring, food); context in which the character appears (e.g. home, work, outdoors).
- Now devise a record table on which you can tally the frequency of the different categories of behaviour as they occur. For example:
- Working with a partner, decide exactly how you will interpret each of the categories you have put on your record sheet.

	Male	Female
Home context		
Work context		

- Watch the recording and tally the frequencies, without discussing it with your partner.
- Total the frequencies and compare your results with those of your partner to check whether or not you have similar frequencies. If so, you can say you have good **inter-observer reliability**.
- Now display your results in the form of a frequency table or bar graph. Write a short summary of what you have found. This should link back to the aim at the beginning of this list.
- Write a couple of sentences to explain why inter-observer reliability is important in a study like this.

How Psychology Works

An investigation into gender schema in teenagers

- Read about gender schema (see page 95) before you begin this activity.
- You are going to interview one male and one female teenager about their understanding of the concepts 'male' and 'female'.
- Decide on what questions you will ask. Remember, it is important that you do not impose your ideas on the person you are interviewing. Ideally, the interview should have as little interviewer input as possible.
- The data will be collected in the form of a spider diagram (see Figure 3.10 on page 96). Decide whether you should draw the spider diagram as the participant talks, or whether you should let the participants do the drawing.
- Explain to your participants what you would like them to do.
- To elicit as much information as you can, you might decide to use gentle verbal prompts, such as, 'Is there anything else about being male you can think of?'
- When they have finished, you should thank them and explain briefly about gender schema to debrief them.
- Now you need to analyse the gender schema diagrams by looking for the following components: behaviour, roles, occupations, personality characteristics, likes/dislikes, hobbies/activities. Use different-coloured highlighters to make each component stand out.

- As we get older, gender schemas become quite complex and we make links between and within components. Look to see whether the diagram shows any links within or between different components; for example, if the role 'mother' appears, are there separate behaviours like 'caring' attached to it? This would be a **between-components** link. If the hobby 'playing football' appears and is linked to 'playing cricket', this would be a **within-components** link.
- Now compare the diagrams of males and females. Are there any differences?

How Psychology Works

A Baby X study, using teenagers as participants

- Read about Baby X studies (page 74) before you start this activity.
- Decide how you are going to present Baby X to your participants. You could use a picture of a child from a baby-clothes catalogue, or you might produce a digital baby on the computer.
- Next, decide how you are going to label the baby's sex. If you are using a computer image you could dress the baby in either pink or blue, or if you are using a photo you could put a male or female name above the picture.
- Now think about how you are going to measure whether the participants are stereotyping the baby. You could ask them to indicate what sorts of toys the child might prefer, or ask them about the baby's personality characteristics. If you ask about personality characteristics, you will need to decide whether to offer them a checklist or some kind of rating scale; for example: On a scale of 1–10, how adventurous do you think the baby is (where 1 = Not at all adventurous and 10 = Very adventurous)?
- Once you have decided exactly how you are going to measure the variables in your study, you can write a precise, testable hypothesis.
- Now write some instructions for your participants, telling them what you would like them to do. You will also need a debrief to explain fully the purpose of the study at the end.
- Decide what experimental design is appropriate here and why.
- Carry out your study using a couple of friends for the male baby condition and a couple for the female baby condition.
- Check how your results relate to other Baby X research. Do your findings support your hypothesis or go against it?
- In an experimental study like this one, it is important to control extraneous variables that might have an effect on the dependent variable (DV). What extraneous variables have you controlled in this study? Are there any others that you did not control that you ought to have done?

Further reading

Introductory texts

Gross, R. (2005) *Psychology: The Science of Mind and Behaviour*, 5th edn, London: Hodder Education.

Schaffer, H.R. (1996) *Social Development*, Oxford: Blackwell.

Smith, P. K., Cowie, H. and Blades, M. (2003) *Understanding Children's Development*, 4th edn, Oxford: Blackwell.

Specialist sources

Archer, J. and Lloyd, B. (2002) *Sex and Gender*, 2nd edn, Cambridge: Cambridge University Press.

Bem, S.L. (1994) *The Lenses of Gender*, London: Yale University Press.

Burr, V. (1998) *Gender and Social Psychology*, London: Routledge.

Durkin, K. (1995) *Developmental Social Psychology*, Oxford: Blackwell.

Golombok, S. and Fivush, R. (1994) *Gender Development*, Cambridge: Cambridge University Press.

Hines, M. (2004) *Brain Gender*, Oxford: Oxford University Press.

Maccoby, E.E. and Jacklin, C.N. (1974) *Psychology of Sex Difference*, Stanford, CA: Stanford University Press.

Turner, P. (1995) *Sex, Gender and Identity*, Leicester: BPS Books.

Research methods

4 Chapter

4.1 Methods of research

4.1.1 Planning research

Psychologists study human behaviour using a variety of different research methods. The method used for any investigation depends on what is being studied. Some behaviours, like memory, are more suited to experimental, laboratory-based research. Other types of behaviour, for example, children's social behaviour, are more suited to non-laboratory methods, such as naturalistic observation. In some situations, it might not be appropriate to study behaviour directly, but might be more sensible to ask people to report on their own behaviour and attitudes, using interviews or questionnaires; such methods are known as **self-report methods**.

Part of the planning process often involves the use of a **pilot study**. This is a small-scale study carried out before the full investigation, to see whether or not the method is appropriate and to highlight any problems with the design. This allows the researcher to modify the design of the study and sort out any problems before the data are gathered.

Qualitative and quantitative research

Qualitative research usually focuses on a participant's thoughts and feelings about an aspect of their life or a particular experience. An example might be an in-depth interview about childhood experiences, where the researcher records the conversation and then writes up case notes, summarising what has been said. Qualitative data is often described as more meaningful information, since it is true to its original source and reflects behaviour in a real-life context.

Quantitative research involves measuring behaviour in a numerical way. An example might be the score out of 20 on a memory test. Quantitative data is sometimes described as less meaningful since it usually involves narrow focus on a very specific aspect of behaviour, and the measurement often takes place out of the context in which that behaviour usually occurs.

As a general rule, unstructured interviews, case studies, open questionnaires and some observational studies involve the collection of qualitative data, whereas experiments, correlation studies, structured observations, structured interviews and closed questionnaires lead to quantitative data.

Quite often, researchers gather data using a qualitative method and then convert the information into quantitative data for the purpose of analysis. As an example, having recorded an in-depth interview about childhood experiences, a researcher might analyse the recording to see how many times certain themes occur, for example, sibling rivalry, discipline methods used by parents, peer influences, and so on.

Type of research	Strengths	Limitations
Qualitative (non-numerical data)	Rich and detailed Meaningful High validity	Difficult to replicate Difficult to analyse Low reliability (very personal, subjective account)
Quantitative (numerical data)	Easy to analyse Can replicate More objective	Less meaningful Low in ecological validity

Figure 4.1. Strengths and limitations of qualitative and quantitative research.

Formulating research questions – aims and hypotheses

Ideas for research usually come from reading about studies that other researchers have carried out. Some investigations are focused on validating a psychological theory, either to support the theory or to refute it. Other investigations are carried out for applied purposes, enabling psychologists to make some practical contribution to an applied area of psychology, such as health, occupational or forensic psychology. Frequently, the initial idea for research is in the form of a vague query; for example: *Does the way that people are given instructions have anything to do with their ability to learn a new task?*

Taking a vague idea for research, the researcher then narrows the focus by stating a clear aim. In the example above, the aim might clarify the ideas about how 'people are given instructions' and 'ability to learn a new task' as follows: *The aim of the investigation is to see whether organised instructions lead to improved learning of how to operate a coffee machine.*

From this general aim, the researcher then has to formulate a precise hypothesis. A hypothesis is a testable statement that should clarify exactly what is being tested and make a prediction about the relationship between two variables. To take the example above, the researcher must define the variables 'organised instructions' and 'improved learning'. This could lead to the following hypothesis: *People given instructions in a five-*

step sequence will take less time (in minutes) to make a cup of coffee using a coffee machine than people who do not have five-step instructions.

So, the process of formulating research questions moves from **vague idea** to **clear aim** to **precise, testable hypothesis.**

A hypothesis like the one above is known as a **research** or **alternative hypothesis.** If the method used to investigate the hypothesis is experimental, it would also be called an **experimental hypothesis.** For every research/alternative hypothesis (**H1**) there is a corresponding **null hypothesis (H0).** The null hypothesis predicts that the expected effect will not occur. In this case, the null hypothesis would state that: *There will be no difference in time taken to make a cup of coffee using a coffee machine whether people have five-step instructions or not.*

Note that the null hypothesis is not the opposite of the research hypothesis, but simply states that there will be no difference. Strictly speaking, it is the null hypothesis that is being tested in the research. According to the outcome of the study, the researcher will accept the H0 and reject the H1 (the results show that there is no effect), or reject the H0 and accept the H1 (the results show that there is an effect).

To write a clear, testable hypothesis, the researcher needs to identify the key variables in the research investigation. In the example above, one variable is the use of five-step instructions or not, and the other variable is the time taken to make a cup of coffee using a coffee machine (in minutes). This precise definition of exactly how variables will be realised in a study is known as **operationalisation.** We shall look at this again when we consider variables in more detail for the experimental method later in this chapter.

Populations and sampling

Research involves establishing theories of human behaviour which can be used to understand and predict how people will behave in different situations. However, although we might want to understand and predict the behaviour of people in general, for practical reasons we can only study a limited number of people. The group of people we study in an investigation is known as the **sample.** The individuals in a sample are known as **participants** because they participate in the research. This limited group is chosen from a larger group of people whose behaviour we are interested in studying. This larger group is known as the **target population.**

Figure 4.2. Are you representative of the population?

Ideally, the characteristics of the sample should reflect the characteristics of the population from which the sample is drawn. For example, if the target population comprises male and female university students aged 18 to 30 years, then ideally we should have a sample of university students, both males and females, whose ages vary from 18 to 30 years. This would then allow the researcher to generalise the findings of the research from the sample to the wider population. **Sampling bias** occurs if a specific section of the target population is over-represented in the sample. For example, if a sample of 50 primary school children consisted of 40 girls and 10 boys, girls would appear to be over-represented in the sample. Examples of target populations in psychological research might be AS level students in a sixth-form college, employees of a chain of supermarkets or people taking part in activities at a sports club. Once the target population has been identified, a technique for obtaining a sample must be used.

4.1.2 Sampling techniques
Opportunity

An opportunity sample consists of people who are available to take part and accessible to the researcher. Because the participants are selected by the researcher this can be a biased sample: all the participants may be similar to the researcher in terms of age or background. Worse still, they may all be friends or associates of the researcher, and therefore might behave in an especially cooperative way, seeking to help the researcher in the investigation. As such, an opportunity sample may not always be representative of a target population. Nevertheless, it is a quick and easy way to obtain participants for a study.

Random

A random sample is one where every member of the target population has an equal chance of being chosen for the sample. If the target population is relatively small, the most usual way to do this is to draw names from a hat. With a larger target population, it is better to give everyone in the population a number, say between 1 and 5,000. A computer programme is then used to generate a set of 50 numbers at random. The people with these 50 numbers would then be the sample. The researcher has no control over who is chosen, so there is no possibility of researcher or selector bias, but a randomly selected sample may still not be representative of the target population. Simply by chance, it could happen that there are far more males in the sample than females, or far more young people than old people.

Stratified

A stratified sample involves the researcher first identifying the different subgroups (strata means layers) of people in the population and then drawing participants from each of these subgroups. For example, in the staff of a nationwide chain of supermarkets there may be several different subgroups: store managers, till operators, security staff, lorry drivers, administration staff, and so on. Each of these subgroups should be represented in the sample in proportion to their existence in the target population as a whole. Thus, if the population consists of 20 per cent administration staff and 30 per cent till operators, then 20 per cent of the sample should be administration staff and 30 per cent should be till operators. The participants should be selected at random from each subgroup. Although it is quite a time-consuming method of sampling, stratified sampling should lead to a sample that represents the target population fairly.

Sampling method	College example	Strengths	Limitations
Opportunity – anyone who is available	Asking people you bump into at college	Quick and easy	Unlikely to be representative due to researcher/ selector bias
Random – everyone in the target population has an equal chance of being chosen	Put every student's name into a hat and choose 40 names	More likely to be representative	Time-consuming
Stratified – identify subgroups, then choose randomly from each in proportion	Identify different groups of students, find out the proportion of each group, randomly sample each group	All subgroups are represented, therefore representative	Very time-consuming
Systematic – every nth person	Ask every 5th person who walks through the college refectory at break	Fairly simple procedure and avoids researcher bias	Sample may not be representative

Figure 4.3. Summary of different sampling techniques, with strengths and limitations.

Systematic

A systematic sample is one where every nth member of the target population is chosen, for example every 5th house on a street or every 10th person on a register. Here the researcher cannot choose who should be in the sample, so there is no researcher bias. Note that this method is very often confused with random sampling.

4.1.3 Experimental methods

One of the most frequently used methods in psychological research is the experiment. An experiment exists when the researcher manipulates or changes one variable to see how this affects another variable. For example, a researcher might investigate the time it takes to complete a set of anagrams, either in silence or listening to music. Here the researcher will manipulate the conditions – silence or listening to music – and see how this affects the time taken to complete the anagrams. The variable the researcher changes or manipulates is known as the **independent variable (IV)**, and the variable the researcher measures is known as the **dependent variable (DV)**. The DV is always some aspect of behaviour. A key feature of the experiment is that all other variables, apart from the IV, should be kept constant, or controlled. Thus, if there is a change in behaviour as a result of the manipulation of the IV, the researcher can infer a cause-and-effect relationship between the IV and the DV. To take the example above, we would be able to say whether or not the noise condition affects the time it takes to complete the anagrams.

Laboratory experiment

A laboratory experiment is conducted in a carefully controlled environment, which does not actually have to be a laboratory. Students often use this method by conducting their experiment in a specific place, for example a quiet study room. Using the same environment for every participant means that external factors such as noise levels and lighting are controlled, so that they are the same for all participants in the study.

Issue of ecological validity

A major problem with the laboratory experiment is that once people are given precise instructions about what they have to do, the behaviour they produce is often very different from the behaviour they would normally exhibit. In other words, once a participant knows they are taking part in an experiment, their behaviour becomes quite artificial. A further problem arises in experiments because the task that participants are asked to perform is often a very artificial task. For this reason, experiments are often said to lack **ecological validity**, meaning that the behaviour is being tested in a way in which it would not normally occur in everyday life. For example, doing anagrams either in complete silence or listening to music is not how people solve everyday problems in real life.

Field experiment

A field experiment is an experiment that takes place in a natural environment rather than in an artificial laboratory environment. Bickman's study of compliance (1974) involved researchers dressed casually or in uniforms, asking people passing by on the street to pick up litter or give a coin to a stranger. Although it was a natural setting and the participants did not know they were taking part in any research, there was an experimental manipulation because the dress of the researcher was changed to see whether or not this affected the response. Field experiments have greater ecological validity as they normally involve testing a real-life behaviour in a situation in which the behaviour usually occurs.

Quasi-experiment

A quasi-experiment occurs in cases where there is no random allocation to conditions and thus no directly controlled manipulation of the IV by the researcher. A very common example would be an experiment investigating sex differences in behaviour. Using sex as the IV means that the researcher would compare a group of males and a group of females on some behaviour or ability. However, in this case, there is no direct manipulation of the sex of the participants; they are simply assigned to one group or the other, depending on whether they are male or female. Here the IV (sex of participant) is a pre-existing variable. Other examples of pre-existing variables might be age, IQ, position in family and social background. All these could be employed as IVs in an experiment, but none of them can be influenced directly by the researcher. Where the IV is a pre-existing variable, the researcher cannot be as confident in drawing conclusions about cause and effect as in a true experiment, where there is direct manipulation of the IV. Another common example of a quasi-experiment is where a researcher might take before-and-after measures of participants' behaviour, for example, when looking at the effects of a therapy.

Experiment	Strengths	Limitations
Laboratory	High control Can infer cause and effect Ethical – participants know they are taking part	Artificial situation Less ecological validity
Field	Natural behaviour and environment Great ecological validity	Less ethical – participants may not know they are taking part
Quasi	Allow for investigation using pre-existing variables, e.g. sex	No random allocation/direct manipulation, so less confidence inferring cause and effect

Figure 4.4. Strengths and limitations of different types of experiment.

Independent and dependent variables

As noted previously, every experiment involves an independent variable and a dependent variable.

The independent variable (IV) is the variable the researcher manipulates.

The dependent variable (DV) is the variable the researcher measures.

To take the example of research into solving anagrams in silence or while listening to music, the researcher manipulates the noise conditions and measures the time it takes participants to solve the anagrams. In this case, listening to music or being in silence would be the IV, and the time taken to solve the anagrams would be the DV. Here, the IV is directly manipulated by the researcher, who would make sure that conditions were absolutely silent in the 'silence' condition, and play music at a predetermined volume in the 'music' condition. In other studies, the researcher might use a pre-existing IV such as age or sex, contrasting the anagram-solving ability of 18-year-olds with that of 30-year-olds. Here, age is the IV, even though the researcher has not directly manipulated the ages of the participants, but simply used people from two different age groups.

If you have difficulty identifying the IV and DV in a study, identify the DV first – think what it is that the researcher is measuring. Once you have sorted that out, the IV is the other thing which changes.

Here are some more examples of IVs and DVs in different experiments.

An experiment to see whether people react faster to a light stimulus or a noise stimulus.

IV: Whether the stimulus is a light or a buzzer.

DV: Reaction time in milliseconds.

An experiment to see whether children who go to nursery have a wider vocabulary than children who do not go to nursery.

IV: Whether children attend nursery daily or not at all.

DV: The total number of words a child understands in a vocabulary test.

An experiment to see whether athletes run faster when training with another athlete than when training alone.

IV: Whether training alongside one other athlete or training alone.

DV: Time in seconds taken to run a full circuit of the track.

When we discussed hypotheses at the start of this chapter, we noted that a good hypothesis should include clearly operationalised variables. In other words, the variables need to be defined in practical terms. In the examples above, you will see that the variables in each case are clearly defined, indicating exactly what is being manipulated and exactly what is being measured in the experiment.

Extraneous and confounding variables – control

An **extraneous variable** is a variable other than the IV that might affect the dependent variable if it is not controlled. If an extraneous variable is not controlled and then goes on to affect the results of the study, we say that it has confounded (spoiled) the outcome. In such a case, it would be referred to as a **confounding variable**. Careful design of an experiment includes finding ways of controlling extraneous variables so that they do not affect the DV.

To return to the example of solving anagrams in silence or when listening to music, we would need to determine what factors other than the noise conditions might affect the participants' ability to solve anagrams. Possible problems could include the following:

- The difficulty of the anagrams used. *Solution*: Make sure that all the anagrams are of five-letter words.

- Time allowed. *Solution*: Allow a fixed time limit for each participant.

- Presence of other people in the room. *Solution*: Each participant should perform the task in the presence of the researcher and no one else.

Different types of confounding variables can be identified: participant variables, situational variables and experimenter variables.

Participant variables occur where individual characteristics of participants affect their behaviour in an experiment. For example, in a study investigating differences in reaction time to a light or a buzzer, several participant variables could act to confound the results of the study. If all the participants in the light stimulus condition happen to be aged below 20 years, and all the participants in the buzzer stimulus condition happen to be aged over 50 years, the difference in reaction time may well be due to age differences rather than the type of stimulus. In this case, the age of participants would be a confounding variable. This problem could easily be controlled by ensuring that all participants are of a similar age.

Situational variables may also affect the behaviour of participants in an experiment. For example, in an experiment to see whether athletes run faster when training alongside another athlete than when training on their own, it would be important to keep the environmental conditions the same for each experimental condition. If athletes training on their own are tested on a dry day and athletes running alongside another athlete are tested on a wet day, it would not be sensible to compare results. Any difference in running times is likely to be affected not just by the presence of another athlete, but also by the weather conditions. In this case, the weather conditions would be a confounding variable. To control for situational variables, the researcher should ensure that participants in each group undertake the task in the same situational conditions.

Experimenter variables occur where the experimenter treats some participants differently to others. For example, if the experimenter smiles while giving instructions to one group of participants and does not smile with another group, this might affect how the two groups behave. Any difference in results might be due to **experimenter bias** and not to the IV. In this case, the experimenter's behaviour would be a confounding variable. Note that experimenters can be biased quite unconsciously, and might not realise that they are smiling more with one group than the other. To control for this, it is often better to provide participants with written instructions, so each person has exactly the same instructions and is not affected by the experimenters' expression, tone of voice, gestures, and so on. One way to control for an experimenter effect is to carry out what is known as **double-blind research**. In this case, the researcher dealing with the participants is not aware of the purpose of the study.

Figure 4.5. In double-blind research neither the participant nor the researcher is aware of the purpose of the study.

At the end of an experiment, it is essential that the researcher is confident that it was the manipulation of the IV which caused the DV to change, and not anything else.

Experimental designs

The term 'experimental design' refers to how participants are used in an experiment. There are three main experimental designs in psychological research: repeated measures, independent groups and matched pairs.

In a **repeated** or **related measures design,** the same people are used in both conditions of the experiment and their performances in the two conditions are compared. For example, the same people would be tested for their reaction time to a light stimulus and a buzzer stimulus.

Strengths:

● Participant variables are eliminated.

● Each participant is tested in each condition, so fewer participants are needed overall.

Limitations:

● **Order effects** may occur, where a participant's performance in the second condition may be affected by having already performed in the first condition. There are two possible problems here. First, performance in the second condition might be better because the participants have had some practice (**practice effect**). Alternatively, performance in the second condition may be worse because the participants are tired or bored (**fatigue effect**). Order effects can be controlled for using a technique known as **counterbalancing.** In counterbalancing, half the participants do Condition A followed by Condition B, and the other half do Condition B followed by Condition A. This means that the effects of the order of conditions are balanced out between the two conditions.

● Using a repeated design means that participants may figure out the aim of the study, even if they have not been told what it is. This means that they may behave differently because they are not naive and have an idea of what the researcher expects to find.

● In some studies it is necessary to have two different sets of materials. For example, in the problem-solving study using anagrams, different anagrams would be needed for the music condition and for the silence condition. The researcher would have to find two sets of anagrams of equal difficulty.

In an **independent groups design,** different people take part in each condition and their performances are compared. In some cases this is the only design that can be used, for example, where the IV is sex or age. In other studies, where the researcher divides the sample into two groups, the participants should be randomly allocated to conditions to prevent researcher bias. Random allocation can be carried out by giving everyone in the sample a number, putting the numbers into a hat, and then drawing out the first ten numbers. These ten people take part in one condition and the remainder take part in the other condition. Random allocation means that each person has an equal chance of being in either condition, and this is an important aspect of control in an independent design experiment.

Strengths:

- There are no order effects, such as practice or fatigue, as people participate in only one condition.

- Participants taking part in only one condition will not be able to figure out the aim of the study; they are naive, so should behave more naturally.

- There is no need to find two sets of materials, as in the case of the anagram study above, because people take part in only one condition.

Limitations:

- Participant variables could confound the results because the people in one condition are not the same as those in the other condition.

- More participants are needed to get the same amount of data, as each participant is tested only once.

> In a **matched pairs design,** different people take part in each condition, but they are matched in ways that matter for the experiment. Matching the two groups for variables such as age, sex and IQ means that participant variables are less likely to affect the results. In practical terms, the researcher must ensure that for each participant in one condition there is a matching participant, or 'twin', in the other condition. Real twins, especially identical twins, are often considered to be ideal for psychological research because they are ready-matched for age and social background.

Strengths:

- Participant variables are minimised by the matching process.

- There are no order effects because each participant performs in only one condition. Each participant performs only once and so can remain naive to the aim of the experiment.

- There is no need to find two sets of materials because people only take part in one condition.

Limitations:

- Matching is very difficult and time-consuming.

- Participant variables are not eliminated altogether, as no two people are exactly alike.

Repeated measures	Independent groups	Matched pairs
Same people in each condition	Different people in each condition	Different people in each condition, but for each person in one condition there is a matching person in the other condition

Figure 4.6. The three experimental designs.

Evaluation of the experimental method

Strengths:
- A high degree of control over the variables means that a cause-and-effect relationship can be established.
- Precise operationalisation of variables means that the results can be clearly measured and verified, meaning that they are objective.
- Because the procedure is carefully controlled and clearly specified, the study can be replicated to check whether the findings are reliable.
- Participants are usually aware that they are taking part in research, and in this way experiments could be said to be ethical.

Limitations:
- The artificial nature of some experimental tasks may mean that behaviour is being tested in a way in which it would not normally occur in real life. In this case, experiments may be said to lack **ecological validity**.
- When participants know they are taking part in an experiment, they sometimes look for clues as to the aim of the research and then 'act up' accordingly. This is known as responding to **demand characteristics**. Some participants behave in ways that they think will be helpful, resulting in 'the please-you effect'. Other participants might try to sabotage the study, resulting in 'the screw-you effect' (Masling 1966).

4.1.4 Non-experimental methods
Self-report methods

Any method where the participant reports on their own behaviour or feelings is known as a self-report measure. Unlike experiments, self-report measures are subjective in that the results are often just the participant's opinion. An example might be a questionnaire where participants report on their level of stress on a scale of 1–10. Here the stress is measured as a number, but this is really just the participant's opinion. An objective measure of stress, on the other hand, might be something like heart rate, which can be recorded on a monitor and verified, or checked, by anyone who looks at it.

Questionnaires

Questionnaires are often used in surveys to find out about people's behaviour or opinions, and they are especially useful for studying behaviours and opinions that cannot be observed directly. For example, it would be very difficult to observe people's TV-watching habits directly or to carry out experiments to investigate people's attitudes to their peer group. In designing a questionnaire it is important that all the items are clear and unambiguous. Certain things should be avoided, such as double-barrelled questions, double negatives and emotive language. It is also important that questions are possible to answer. Look at the questionnaire items below and see whether you can tell what is wrong with them.

> How many times did you eat sweets per week when you were ten years old?
>
> It is not acceptable that children are not allowed to play outside with friends. *Agree/Disagree*
>
> Fox hunting is a ridiculously cruel sport for upper-class toffs. *Agree/Disagree*
>
> Divorce is very bad for children and morally unacceptable. *Agree/Disagree*

> **Closed questions** are ones where there is a fixed number of optional answers and the respondent has to choose one of the options. Here are some examples:
>
> Approximately how many hours a week do you spend on the Internet?
>
> *1 hour or less / 2–3 hours / 4–5 hours / More than 5 hours*
>
> How would you describe your ability to socialise?
>
> *Below average / About average / Above average*
>
> Who in your household is mostly responsible for household chores?
>
> *Mother / Father / Neither*

Closed questions produce quantitative data that are easy to summarise, allowing for straightforward comparison across different groups of respondents. However, there is little depth or richness to the data. People do not have the chance to explain their answers, so the data may have less validity. Closed questions can also result in frustration when there is no suitable option, and, as such, they are not very participant-friendly.

Open questions are ones where the respondent can answer any way they like, as in the examples below:

What things are most important for choice of university?

How well do you get on with your brothers and sisters?

Who has been the biggest influence on your career choice?

Using open questions, people's responses are more likely to be the true response, giving the data greater validity. Open questions produce qualitative, in-depth and more meaningful information. They are less restrictive as people put their own answer forward, rather than being forced to choose from a set of fixed options. This means they are more participant-friendly, as there is less chance of frustration because none of the answers is appropriate. However, it is difficult to analyse the responses and look for patterns across all participants as everyone's answer is unique. In the end, it might be necessary to analyse the raw responses by putting them into categories and recording the frequencies, for example recording how many people mention 'nightlife' when asked what they like about university.

Evaluation of the questionnaire method

Strengths:
- Large amounts of data can be collected quite quickly.
- Questionnaires can be highly replicable.
- Questionnaires using closed questions are easy to score.
- Questionnaires using open questions give richer and more valid data.
- Usually no ethical problems since participants know they are taking part in research.

Limitations:
- Questionnaires are a self-report method, so are subjective (based on opinion).
- Respondents may not give a true answer as they want to present themselves as socially desirable. This means the data may not be valid.

- Respondents have a natural tendency to acquiesce or say they agree with items, even when they really do not.
- Response set may occur, where respondents tend to reply in the same way by failing to read the questions properly and ticking all 'yes' or all 'no' answers.

Interviews

Interviews can be face to face or carried out over the telephone. The interview method is often used in conjunction with a questionnaire. Most interviews involve one researcher and one participant. The researcher may make notes at the time, make notes after the interview, or record the interview and analyse the information later. If the researcher is interviewing a number of people, it is helpful to standardise or structure the interview procedure, asking the same questions for each participant. This enables data from several participants to be combined to look for patterns.

A **structured interview** is one where the interviewer has a pre-prepared set of questions that are asked in a fixed order. There is no chance to ask extra questions. A fully structured interview is one where there are pre-prepared questions and fixed option answers for the interviewee (the person being asked the questions) to choose from.

Using the same questions for each participant has the advantage that the data can be summarised easily and analysed statistically, usually in the form of percentages. It also means that the focus of the interview will be maintained throughout, with less chance that the interview will go off the point. Having fixed questions also makes it possible to repeat or replicate a study and check that the results are reliable. However, it can be quite frustrating, for both the interviewer and the interviewee, if interesting or unexpected issues arise. Ideally, the researcher would like to ask a supplementary follow-up question, but the structured method does not allow for this. A structured interview is more formal and therefore may be less comfortable for the participant.

An **unstructured interview** is where the interviewer starts off with an aim and the interviewee is invited to discuss a specific topic. There are no predetermined questions.

The interviewer listens and makes comments, prompting the interviewee to expand on interesting or relevant points, and moves the interview forward. The interviewer must be sensitive to the content as the interview proceeds, and adjust to the interviewee's answers as they occur. Such interviews are often used by clinical psychologists as part of a case study. The main advantage of an unstructured interview is that the data is qualitative, detailed and unprocessed, which means it has greater validity. This type of information allows behaviour to be understood in a meaningful context which is personal to the interviewee. If interesting responses arise they can be probed further with follow-up questions. As each interview is personally tailored to the individual, participants tend to feel valued and are less intimidated by the process. The greatest problem with an unstructured interview is the difficulty of analysing the data. Usually researchers will record or make notes in the interview and analyse the data for themes at some later date. Due to the informal nature of an unstructured interview, there may be a lack of focus; a skilled interviewer is required, to prevent the interview from going off the point.

Evaluation of the interview method

Strengths:
- Interviews allow for the study of thoughts and opinions that cannot be observed directly.
- Interviews usually produce large amounts of data.
- Structured interviews are replicable and produce data that is easy to analyse.
- Unstructured interviews produce detailed and more valid data.

Limitations:
- Interviews are a self-report method, so the data are subjective (opinion-based).
- Interviews do not tell us about the causes of behaviour.
- Structured interviews are formal and restricted, resulting in less valid responses.
- Unstructured interviews are not replicable and are difficult to analyse.

Correlation studies

Correlation is not actually a research technique. It is a statistical technique for analysing data where two sets of numerical scores can be obtained for each participant. Correlations enable us to measure a relationship between the two sets of data or variables. Correlation data is normally represented in a scattergram (see Figure 4.7). Here are some examples of questions that can be answered using a correlation technique:

> Are people who have long journeys to work likely to be more stressed?
>
> Is there a relationship between the number of hours of sleep and success?
>
> Is there a relationship between self-esteem and the number of pets a person owns?

Figure 4.7a shows a **positive correlation**. In a positive correlation, as one variable increases, the other variable increases. In this example, the further a person travels to work, the higher their stress score.

Figure 4.7b shows a **negative correlation**. In a negative correlation, as one variable increases, the other variable decreases. In this example, the fewer hours of sleep a person has, the more successful they are.

Both positive and negative correlations show there is a relationship between the two variables. Knowing that there is either a positive or a negative correlation allows us to use one variable to make predictions about the other variable. For example, if we know that people who sleep less tend to be more successful (negative correlation), we can predict that someone who sleeps five hours per night will be more successful than someone who sleeps ten hours per night. Similarly, if we know that there is a positive correlation between the distance travelled to work and stress scores, we can predict that someone who travels 50 miles to work will be more stressed than someone who travels 1 mile to work.

Figure 4.7c shows a **zero correlation**. A zero correlation means that there is no relationship between the two variables, either positive or negative. In this example, there is no relationship between the number of pets a person owns and their self-esteem score. In this case, even if we know a person's score on one of these variables, we can make no predictions about how they would score on the other variable.

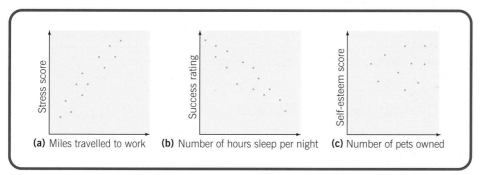

Figure 4.7. Scattergrams illustrating the three types of correlation: a) Positive correlation; b) Negative correlation; c) Zero correlation.

Evaluation of the correlation method

Strengths:
- Correlations allow us to see if two variables are related in some way.
- Once we know there is a relationship, other types of study can be carried out to investigate this relationship further.

Limitations:
Correlations show that there is a relationship, but they do not tell us that one variable causes another. In the example above, knowing that there is a

relationship between length of journey to work and stress does not mean that long journeys cause stress. It may be that there are other important factors that contribute to this relationship. For example, travelling is costly, so perhaps people who travel greater distances to work have more money worries and this is what makes them feel stressed. Or perhaps people who travel greater distances to work do so because a job worth travelling for is a more important job, and having an important job is the cause of the stress.

- Correlation does not show cause and effect; only an experiment can establish cause-and-effect relationships. A research hypothesis for a correlation study does not predict that one variable will affect another; it simply predicts that there will be a relationship.
- Correlation involves measurement of the two variables being investigated, without control of extraneous variables.

Experiment	Correlation
Shows cause and effect	Does not show cause and effect
Extraneous variables are controlled	No control of extraneous variables

Figure 4.8. Differences between an experiment and a correlation study.

4.1.5 Observational studies

Observational studies are especially useful for studying certain types of behaviour and certain groups of participants. For example, social behaviours such as crowd interaction and play can really only be studied sensibly in the environment where the behaviour normally takes place. Similarly, particular groups of people are more likely to behave normally if they do not know that they are being studied. For example, children are quite likely to be intimidated by more formal experimental research, and therefore, perhaps, they are better studied using observation. Sometimes researchers combine the use of the observational method with other research techniques. For example, it is possible to manipulate the natural play environment by changing the types of toys available to see what effect this has on play behaviour. In this instance, the behaviour is still natural behaviour, but the researcher has manipulated the environment, in effect creating an experiment.

Natural and laboratory settings

In a natural observation, participants are observed in the setting where the target behaviour normally occurs. For example, observing aggression in young children in a school playground, or greeting behaviour at an airport. Here there is no control over extraneous variables, but there is high validity because the behaviour is real behaviour in a real setting. As there is a lack of control, it is unlikely that a study carried out in a natural setting could be replicated.

Controlled observations are carried out in fully controlled laboratory conditions, although this does not actually have to be a laboratory. Very often, controlled observations take place in special viewing rooms, where observers can see into the room through one-way glass, without disturbing the action. The control of all extraneous variables enables the study to be replicated, but means that participants' behaviour is less likely to reflect the way they would behave in real life. In this way, the study could be said to lack validity.

Figure 4.9. Observations can take place in both laboratory and natural settings.

Participant and non-participant observation

A **participant observation** is one where the researcher takes part in the action, joining in with those being observed. This allows for close observation and enables the observer to note the precise context in which the behaviour is taking place, seeing what events lead up to a specific action. For example, an observer sitting with children playing at the finger-painting table will know that Jilly smacked Katie because Katie said something horrid about Jilly's painting. A problem with participant observations arises when an observer becomes so involved in the group's activity that the ability to make objective scientific recordings is lost. A further problem is the chance that the presence and actions of the observer will change the course of events, making the results less valid.

A **non-participant observation** is one where the observer does not take part in the action, but instead avoids involvement, watching from a distance. In this way, the observer can remain objective, but observations cannot be contextualised in the same way as in a participant observation. To use the example above, a non-participating observer will simply note that Jilly smacked Katie, and will not know why.

Covert and overt observations

A **covert observation** is one where the observer's presence is not obvious or apparent to those being observed. This is sensible in that it means that people's behaviour will be more natural, as they are unaware that they are being observed. This prevents what is known as the **observer effect** occurring, where people behave differently simply because they know they are being observed. Covert observation might involve the observer viewing the action from some unseen vantage point, for example, an upstairs window, or might involve the use of a one-way mirror. While covert observations may lead to greater validity, they could be considered unethical because people are unaware that they are being studied.

An **overt observation** is one where the observer's presence is obvious to those being observed. For example, an observer might stand in a playground making written observations, in full view of the children being observed. Although this is rather more ethical and 'up-front' than a covert observation, it does mean that the behaviours observed are less likely to be natural, due to our tendency to behave differently once we know that we are being watched. To lessen this observer effect, several visits could be made beforehand so that the observer becomes very familiar to those being observed and therefore less noticeable.

Data recording techniques in observational studies

One way to quantify behaviour in observations is to use a **category system**. For example, if the target behaviour is 'greeting behaviour at airports', the following behavioural categories might be used: kissing, hugging, back-slapping, giving flowers.

For a category system to be useful, it should accommodate all examples of the target behaviour that are likely to occur. A pilot study can be carried out beforehand to show what sorts of behaviours are likely to occur, to enable a useful category system to be devised. It should also be very clear whether a behaviour belongs in one category or another. Once a category system has been agreed, the observer can tally observations on a chart, like the one in Figure 4.10.

Kissing	Hugging	Back-slapping	Twirling	Flowers
JHĦ JHĦ III	JHĦ JHĦ JHĦ II	JHĦ IIII	II	I

Figure 4.10. A tally chart for use in an observation of greeting behaviour at airports.

Unfortunately, **observer bias** can occur due to the researcher's expectations. For example, a researcher who believes that northerners are more romantic than southerners might be more likely to interpret an action as a kiss at Manchester airport than at Heathrow airport. To ensure reliability and prevent observer bias, it is important that two researchers observe side by side. They should first discuss their behavioural categories and agree on the meaning of each term. For example, they should agree on exactly what constitutes a 'hug' and what constitutes a 'back slap'. They then observe the same people at the same time, but without consulting each other, and with each observer making separate recordings. At the end of the observation, they should find that the two sets of recordings are the same or very similar. This means that they have **inter-observer reliability**.

The method of recording observations may differ depending on what is being observed. In **continuous recording**, all instances of target behaviour are recorded. This method is suitable for behaviours that occur at an instant, like aggressive acts or greetings, but is not suitable for behaviours that go on for a long time, like play. For such behaviours, **time sampling** is a more useful technique. In time sampling, the observation time is split up into time intervals, for example every 20 seconds. At each 20-second interval, the observer notes the behaviour that is taking place. This means that over a 10-minute observation period, an observer would make a total of 30 observations.

Evaluation of the observational method

Strengths:
- Natural observations produce data that have high ecological validity.
- Observations are the most sensible way to study social and group behaviours.
- Observational studies tend to provide a more holistic view of a person's behaviour than the narrowly defined behaviour tested in experimental studies.

Limitations:
- Well-organised observations are difficult and time-consuming, and it is usually not possible to observe large numbers of people.
- In observations where there is a single observer, there is a chance that observer bias may occur.
- If people know they are being observed, there is a danger that the observer effect will occur; people will respond to the demands of the situation and behave artificially.
- Unless the observation involves some kind of experimental manipulation, observation studies do not enable us to draw conclusions about the causes of behaviour.

- Observations are often conducted without the knowledge of those being observed. This means that people are not asked for their consent and are not given the right to withdraw. Another ethical consideration is privacy; observations should only take place in public places where people might normally expect to be observed by others.

4.1.6 Content analysis

Content analysis is a systematic method used to quantify the content of any form of media, for example, books, TV programmes and even graffiti on the walls of public toilets. It is very similar to the observational method, but does not involve direct observation of people; instead, the researcher analyses a person's communication. The units analysed may be individual words, ideas, characters, images or the amount of time/space devoted to a particular issue. It is also possible to analyse what is not there, for example if there are no female characters in a children's story.

Data are usually collected using a coding or category system, recording the frequency with which each unit occurs. For example, a researcher might analyse the speeches of famous politicians to see how often they refer to 'family', 'religion' and 'national pride'. Alternatively, researchers might use a rating system, for example rating the characters in a children's story on a scale of 1–10 for confidence.

Evaluation of content analysis

Strengths:
- Enables the analysis of a wide range of materials.
- No ethical problems because people are not being dealt with directly.

Limitations:
- The findings are limited by the researcher's expectations as categories are decided beforehand.
- Although researchers are trained, their interpretations of material may still be subjective.
- Behaviour may be taken out of context. It is important to recognise that any media communication is most meaningful in the context in which it is produced, and for the audience for which it was originally intended.

4.1.7 The role of case studies in psychology

A case study is an in-depth study of a single individual or a small group. Case studies are generally carried out by professional psychologists working in a clinical or therapeutic context, and they often take place over a long period of time. For example, an educational psychologist might carry out a case study with a child who is behaving badly at school. Less frequently, case studies are used to study people who are of interest because of their unusual circumstances. Examples here might be a child who has been brought up in very deprived circumstances, or a man who, after a lifetime of being blind, has an operation to restore his sight. Although they often involve single cases, case studies can be used to support or refute a theory.

Data can be gathered from a wide variety of sources, including formal records, interviews with the individual and with people who know them, psychological tests and observations. A case study might include some or all of the following types of information:

- biographical information about the person's past;

- current-state observations;

- relevant current events;

- medical history;

- school reports;

- psychological test results;

- records of any treatment.

The researcher will write up a descriptive account of the case and then interpret the information in light of scientific theory. In

Figure 4.11. An educational psychologist might carry out a case study with a child who is behaving badly at school.

making this interpretation, the researcher may decide to emphasise certain information and omit other information. As a result, the account may be highly subjective. It should therefore be made quite clear which information is factual and which is the opinion of the researcher.

Evaluation of the case study method

Strengths:
- Case studies are useful where a long-term view of a person's behaviour is of interest.
- The data are detailed, qualitative and meaningful.
- As the case study is a real account of a person's real life, it has high validity.
- A single case study which goes against a theory is enough to cause that theory to be altered to take account of the new evidence.

129

Limitations:

- Each case study is unique and therefore the findings cannot be generalised to a wider population.
- Case studies cannot really be replicated.
- Since some of the data are retrospective, involving the recall of past events, there is a question about reliability.
- The case study may be affected by **researcher bias**, where the researcher's beliefs and expectations affect their interpretation of the data.
- The case study method needs careful ethical consideration, as such cases usually involve people who are vulnerable. The usual ethical considerations of consent, right to withdraw, protection from harm and confidentiality should be taken into account carefully, and dealt with in the best interests of the person being studied.

4.2 Representing data and descriptive statistics

The individual pieces of data that are collected directly from a participant or other source are known as raw data. To help understand the results and see any patterns in the data, it is important to summarise these raw data and convert them into a usable form. This involves calculating descriptive statistics, for example averages, and perhaps displaying the results in a table or graph. This enables someone looking at the results to see immediately the overall outcome of a study.

4.2.1 Descriptive statistics
Measures of central tendency

A measure of central tendency is a single value that can be used to describe a set of scores, more generally known as an 'average'. The following are all measures of central tendency:

- the mean;

- the median;

- the mode.

Each of these will be illustrated using data from a study investigating the number of errors made by males and females in a driving simulator. The raw data from the study are shown in Figure 4.12.

Males	Females
4	5
5	8
4	6
5	7
3	7
6	9

Figure 4.12. Raw data from a study to investigate the number of errors made by males and females in a driving simulator.

The **mean** (statistical symbol $\bar{x}$) is calculated by adding together all the values in a set of scores and then dividing by the number of values. To calculate the mean for the male participants:

$4 + 5 + 4 + 5 + 3 + 6 = 27$ (total number of errors for male participants)

$27 \div 6 = 4.5$ (mean number of errors for male participants)

The mean takes account of all the scores and is therefore the most sensitive measure of central tendency. However, if one of the values is particularly high or low (an **anomalous score**), this extreme value will distort the mean. In the example above, if one of the male participants had made an exceptionally high number of errors, this would have the effect of increasing the mean for the group, making it much less representative of the male participants' performances as a whole. This distortion effect can be seen below:

4, 5, 4, 5, 3, 19 (anomalous score)

Here the mean would be 6.7, higher than all the scores except for the anomalous score, and therefore not typical of the set of scores as a whole.

The **median** is calculated by putting the scores in order, from lowest to highest, and taking the middle score. If there is no middle score because there is an even number of scores, then take the numerical midpoint between the two middle scores. This can be found by adding the two middle values together and dividing by two. Using the male data from the driving simulator study:

4, 5, 4, 5, 3, 6

Order the scores from lowest to highest:

3, 4, 4, 5, 5, 6

As there is no middle score, take the numerical midpoint between the 4 and 5 (the two middle scores) to give a median of 4.5. The median is not distorted by any very high or low values, but it is less sensitive than the mean because it does not take account of the value of each score.

The **mode** is the most frequently occurring score in a set of scores. Sometimes there is no mode, and sometimes, as in the data for the male scores above, there are two modes (4 and 5). The mode is very easy to calculate (in fact, there is no calculation), but it is the least sensitive measure of central tendency and is often not very useful.

Measures of dispersion

We have seen how it is important to summarise a set of scores by showing a measure of central tendency to give a representative score for the set as a whole. In addition to showing a measure of central tendency, it is also important to use a descriptive statistic to indicate how much spread there is in a set of scores. The importance of the spread of scores can be illustrated when we look at two sets of scores that have the same mean, but show a very different pattern of performance within each set.

Number of successful basketball shots – Group 1:

5, 6, 8, 9, 10, 10, 11, 12, 14, 15

Number of successful basketball shots – Group 2:

1, 2, 2, 3, 3, 16, 16, 18, 19, 20

In each case above, the mean number of successful basketball shots is 10. However, it is clear by simply looking at the scores that there is something very different about the performance in each group. While the scores for Group 1 are spread fairly evenly around the mean, there is not an even spread for Group 2. In fact, it looks as if there are two distinct types of performance within Group 2; people who are fairly hopeless at basketball and people who are extremely good at it.

To describe the dispersion (or 'spread-outness') of a set of scores, we can use the following statistics:

- the range;

- the standard deviation.

The **range** is the numerical difference between the lowest score and the highest score in a set. It is calculated by subtracting the lowest score from the highest score. Taking the basketball data:

● the range for Group 1 would be $15 - 5 = 10$;

● the range for Group 2 would be $20 - 1 = 19$.

One problem with the range is that it is distorted by any anomalous or extreme scores. More importantly, it can also be rather misleading as it is based just on the lowest and highest values. This means that the range appears to suggest a set of scores that are quite spread out, when in fact most scores are close to the mean. Look at the two sets of scores below. They both have the same range, but it is obvious that there is a different amount of spread in each case:

3, 4, 5, 5, 5, 6, 6, 6, 7, 9   Range = 6

3, 3, 3, 3, 4, 4, 4, 5, 5, 9   Range = 6

The **standard deviation** is a measure of dispersion which takes account of every score in a set. A low standard deviation indicates that there is little spread in a set of scores, and a high standard deviation indicates that the scores are more widely spread. The standard deviation is calculated on the basis of the distance of each individual score from the mean for the set of scores. It is a much more sensitive measure of dispersion than the range.

To calculate the standard deviation, you can use a scientific calculator or apply the formula as follows:

$$s = \sqrt{\frac{\Sigma d^2}{N-1}}$$

where:

s is the standard deviation;

N is the sample size;

Σ is sum of;

d^2 is each difference between the mean and each individual score squared.

Below is a simple, step-by-step procedure for calculating the standard deviation:

1 Calculate the mean for the set of scores.

2 Find the difference between each individual value and the mean.

3 Square each answer to step 2.

4 Add all answers to step 3.

5 Divide the answer to step 4 by the number of scores minus 1.

6 Find the square root of step 5.

(**Note:** the above formula and procedure give the population standard deviation, which may be different to the one used in maths. This is because psychological research involves studying a sample and then generalising the findings to a wider population.)

Raw data Number of successful basketball shots: 5, 6, 8, 9, 10, 10, 11, 12, 14, 15		
Individual scores	**Step 2:** Find the difference between each score and the mean	**Step 3:** Square each difference
5	5	25
6	4	16
8	2	4
9	1	1
10	0	0
10	0	0
11	1	1
12	2	4
14	4	16
15	5	25
Step 1: Find the mean score = 10		**Step 4:** Find the total of the differences = 92
Step 5: Divide the answer to step 4 by the number of scores minus 1: 92 ÷ (10 − 1) = 10.22		
Step 6: Find the square root of step 5: $\sqrt{10.22}$ = 3.19		
Standard deviation = 3.19		

Figure 4.13. Calculating the standard deviation for the basketball data (Group 1 – see page 132), using the step-by-step procedure.

4.2.2 Representing data

Tabular displays – the use of summary tables

Tables must always be fully labelled, with a clear title and column headings. It is important that the title includes reference to the units of measurement – in other words, what the numbers in the table are – and to the two conditions by name. In the table in Figure 4.14, you will see summary statistics for the study investigating the number of errors made by males and females in a driving simulator (see Figure 4.12). Notice that there is a full title which refers explicitly to 'males' and 'females' and to the 'number of errors'.

	Males	**Females**
Mean	4.5	7.0
Standard deviation	1.05	1.41

Figure 4.14. Mean and standard deviation number of errors made in a simulated driving task for males and females.

It is usual to present a verbal summary of the results with a table of descriptive statistics. This is to describe what the table shows and to draw the reader's attention to the main points. Here a verbal summary would say something like: *Notice from the table that males on average make fewer errors than females. The standard deviations indicate that there is a greater variation in ability in the females than in the males.*

Graphical displays

Numerical data can be visually displayed using the following types of graphs:

● bar charts;

● histograms;

● line graphs;

● scattergrams.

A **bar chart** shows columns representing frequencies or amounts of variables. The variables are usually displayed on the x-axis and the frequencies or amounts on the y-axis. For the driving simulation study (Figure 4.12), a bar chart displaying the mean number of errors for males and females could be drawn (see Figure 4.15).

A **histogram** is suitable for displaying continuous data where the variable under investigation has been divided up into intervals of the same size, for example years. The variable intervals are usually displayed on the x-axis and the frequency of occurrence on the y-axis. If there is no score for a particular interval, the interval is left on the x-axis with the nil score showing as an empty space. Histograms are normally shown as columns (see Figure 4.16); however, the midpoints of each column on the histogram can be joined to produce what is known as a frequency polygon – in effect, this would be a line graph.

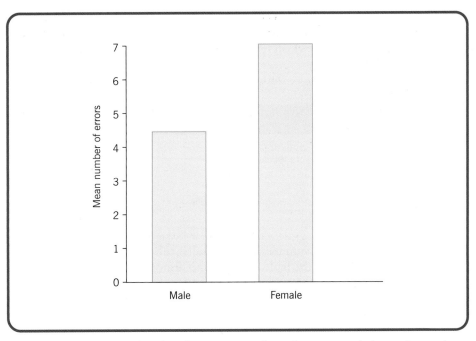

Figure 4.15. Bar chart showing the mean number of errors made by males and females in the driving simulation task.

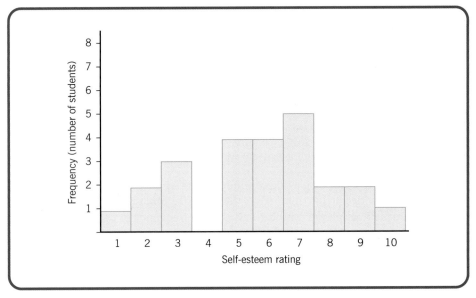

Figure 4.16. Histogram showing the frequency of self-esteem ratings among 18-year-old students.

Line graphs are often used to display a relationship between independent and dependent variables. It is usual to place the IV on the x-axis and the DV on the y-axis. For example, in studies of the effect of the passage of time on recall, it has been found that the more time which elapses between learning and recall, the fewer items are remembered. This effect could be illustrated using a line graph, as in Figure 4.17. Here, using a continuous line is appropriate because there is a connection between the points on the x-axis – the passage of time is a continuous variable. Contrast this with Figure 4.15, the bar graph of means, where it would not make sense to join the means for males and females as they are quite separate sets of scores.

A **scattergram** displays data obtained using a correlation technique where the data are in pairs. One of the paired values is plotted on the x-axis and the other paired value is plotted on the y-axis. Each pair of data is represented on the scattergram as a point, usually shown as a cross. The pattern of points will indicate whether there is a positive, negative or zero correlation. Figure 4.18 shows a scattergram of data from a study into the relationship between self-esteem and attractiveness rating. Notice that the pattern here indicates a positive correlation, meaning that as one variable increases so does the other. Remember that correlation studies do not allow us to infer a cause-and-effect relationship between the two variables. For this reason it does not matter which variable is plotted on which axis on a scattergram.

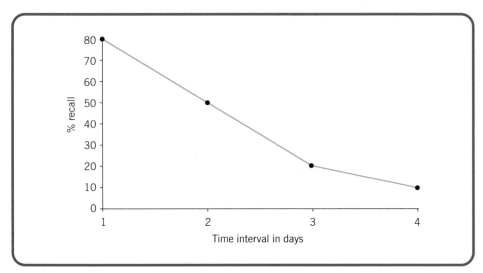

Figure 4.17. Line graph showing the percentage recall at time intervals of one, two, three and four days.

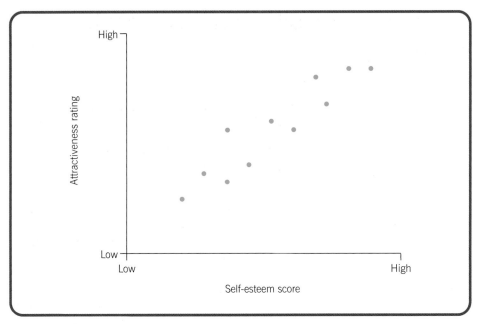

Figure 4.18. Scattergram showing the relationship between self-esteem score and attractiveness rating.

4.3 Ethics

4.3.1 The code of ethics as specified by the BPS

The ethical guidelines covering the activities of psychologists in the UK is the Code of Ethics and Conduct (2006), produced by The British Psychological Society. This code governs the activities of all practising and research psychologists, and psychology students. It is organised under four key headings: Respect, Competence, Responsibility and Integrity, and it serves several purposes:

● It protects participants, patients and clients.

● It helps maintain and promote professional standards.

● It provides a framework within which psychologists work.

● It guides decisions about appropriate and acceptable conduct.

Much of the Code's content is applicable to those working as professional psychologists in a professional context, such as clinical or educational psychology. However, there are also guidelines for those working as researchers. These guidelines apply to everyone carrying out psychological research, including investigations carried out by students at all levels. You should be able to understand ethical issues as they relate to psychological research and adhere to the principles in any practical activities.

4.3.2 Applying the code of ethics in research
Respect

The principle of Respect states that:

- Psychologists should **respect** people as individuals, taking account of factors such as gender, race, culture and religion. Unfair or prejudiced practices should be avoided.

- Psychologists should keep information about people **confidential**, including data collected in research. This is especially important with case studies, where in-depth, personal information about a person has been gathered.

- Psychologists should seek **informed consent** from those taking part in research. Informed consent means that the people consenting know what they are consenting to. This means that prospective participants should be told about the purpose of the research before they are asked to agree to take part. Particular care should be taken with children and vulnerable adults. If they are incapable of understanding what is involved, consent should be sought from someone who is able to make decisions for them, such as a family member. It is normal practice to gain parental consent, or consent from those acting in place of parents (*in loco parentis*), if carrying out research with participants under 16 years. For observational research, where consent cannot be gained, psychologists are advised to respect people's **privacy** and restrict their observations to places where people might normally expect to be observed.

- Psychologists should avoid **deception** unless it is absolutely necessary for the research. Participants are deceived if they are misled about some aspect of the research. Where deception has occurred, participants should be informed at the earliest opportunity.

- Psychologists should make it clear to participants that they have a **right to withdraw** from research at any time. In addition, participants have the right to withdraw their data and have records of their participation destroyed if they wish.

Competence

The principle of Competence states that:

- Psychologists should only **give advice** if they are qualified to do so.

Responsibility

The principle of Responsibility states that:

- Psychologists should **protect their participants from harm**. There should be no risk to their psychological wellbeing, physical health, personal values or dignity.

● Psychologists should **debrief** research participants after the investigation, informing them of the aims and nature of the research.

Integrity

The principle of Integrity states that:

● Psychologists should be **honest** and accurate, maintain professional boundaries and avoid exploitation.

In carrying out any research, psychologists should always consider whether the costs to participants outweigh the benefits to be gained from the research.

How Psychology Works

Planning an observation – devising category systems

Working with a partner, you are going to devise three category systems for use in observational research.

1 Observation of aggression in primary school children.
2 Observation of social behaviour in teenagers on the beach in summer.
3 Observation of mother–infant behaviour in chimpanzees.

● Devise a category system for each of the three observations. Remember that a good category system should include all the target behaviours you are likely to see. For example, if your target behaviour is 'aggression', your category system should accommodate all possible aggressive behaviours that might occur. It should also be unambiguous; you should be able to assign each behaviour to just one category. Remember that the behavioural categories should be objective; they must be behaviours that you can actually see.
● Draw up a record sheet for use in each of the three observations to be used to record the frequencies of behaviour in each category.
● Now you need to operationalise the behaviours in your category systems. This means you need to decide with your partner exactly what is meant by each behaviour. For example, if you have included 'kicking' as one of the behaviours in the observation of aggression, you will need to decide exactly what you mean by 'kicking'. Write down your definitions of each behaviour.
● Write a paragraph explaining why it is important for two observers to work together when making recordings of observations.
● With your partner, discuss the ethical considerations that would be involved in carrying out these observations.

How Psychology Works

Exploring sampling techniques

You are going to carry out an exercise in sampling techniques with students from your school or college. Sampling techniques involve the selection of a group of people to take part in an investigation. Ideally, the characteristics of the sample should reflect the characteristics of the target population, so that psychologists can generalise the findings from the sample to the target population. In psychology, you need to know about opportunity, random, stratified and systematic sampling.

- Decide on the target population for this exercise. If you have a large class, perhaps your class will be sufficient. If it is a smaller class, you should aim to use two or three classes as the target population.
- Decide on the number that should be in the sample. If you have a population of 20 students, a reasonable sample would be 8 students.
- Now select an **opportunity sample**. These will be the people you have easiest access to. Which people will they be? Make a record of their names.
- Now you need to select a **random sample**. To do this you will need everyone's name or should assign everyone a number. These names or numbers can then go in a hat. Draw out the first eight names and these will be your sample. Alternatively, use a computer or calculator to generate eight random numbers between 1 and 20. When you have selected your random sample, make a record of their names, as before.
- Now you need to select a **stratified sample**. Consider your population and identify any subgroups in the population. For example, you may have a subgroup of males and a subgroup of females. Other subgroups might be identifiable, for example people who come from different feeder schools or live in different parts of town. Once you have identified the subgroups, work out how many people are in each one. You then need to calculate how many should be sampled from each subgroup for the sample to reflect the make-up of the population. For example, if 25 per cent of the population is male and 75 per cent is female, then these proportions should be reflected in the sample. When you know how many of each subgroup you need for the sample, these should be selected using random selection, as above. When you have selected your stratified sample, make a record of their names, as before.
- Now you need to select a **systematic sample**. Decide on a system to select every nth person in the class. If you have access to the register you could use that. When you have selected your systematic sample, make a record of their names, as before.
- Now compare the four different samples. Look at who appears in each sample and consider how well each sample reflects the target population. Which of the four techniques produces the most representative sample?
- Write a few sentences to evaluate the sample obtained using each of the different methods.

How Psychology Works

A discussion of ethics in psychology

For the following, write a paragraph summarising key ethical considerations:

1 A study into frustration as a cause of aggression where student volunteers are given an impossible jigsaw to do and then criticised by the researchers for not being able to complete the jigsaw. All the volunteers have been paid £5 each for taking part. The aim of the study is to see whether the participants become aggressive as a result of frustration.

2 A study where passers-by are observed entering a telephone booth where a £5 note has been left behind by the researcher. The aim of the study is to see whether people over the age of 40 years are more or less likely to take the money than people under the age of 20 years. Observers watch from an upper-floor window of a nearby building.

3 A study where children are given an IQ test. Their teacher is then told that some of the children are very clever and others are not. In fact, there is no difference in the IQ of the two groups. Some time later the children are tested again, and the researchers find that those earlier labelled as 'clever' now get higher IQ scores on average than the other children.

4 A study into sociability in nursery school children. Parents are interviewed about how often they read to their children at bedtime, and the researchers then rate each child on a sociability scale. The researchers discuss the outcome of their research with parents.

5 Researchers decide to investigate the hypothesis that good-looking people are judged more positively than people who are not good-looking. They take photographs of their friends and then get other sixth-formers to rate each photograph for attractiveness on a scale of 1–10. Those photographs rated as most attractive and least attractive are then used in an experiment where participants have to look at the photographs and rate each photograph for intelligence and friendliness.

How Psychology Works

Designing a banana experiment

Imagine that you have to find out whether eating bananas has any effect on people's ability to complete anagrams. In pairs or small groups, decide on the following:

- What **experimental design** should you use? Remember you can use repeated measures, independent groups or matched pairs. There is never a perfect way to use your participants in a study, so whichever design you choose there will be advantages and limitations.
- How will you operationalise the **independent variable** (banana eating) in your study? Are you going to use existing banana eaters and non-eaters, or ask people to eat or not eat a specified number of bananas per week?

- How will you operationalise the **dependent variable** (anagram ability)? Will you see how long it takes people to complete a set of anagrams, or will you see how many they complete in a specified time?
- Decide what **materials** you will need. How many anagrams should you use? How many letters should there be in each anagram? Will you need any other special materials? Prepare a set of anagrams that would be suitable.
- Is there anything special you need to consider when you select your **sample**? Is there anyone you would need to exclude?
- How long do you expect the study to last? Will you check on the performance at intervals, or do it all on one day? How many times should you test each person?
- Once you have decided how the study should be conducted, you will need to formulate an **alternative hypothesis** and a corresponding **null hypothesis**. Write these down, making sure that they are clear and testable.
- Write a brief paragraph summarising any relevant **ethical considerations**.

How Psychology Works
Descriptive statistics exercise

Below are arithmetic test results from two junior classes. For both sets of data:
- Calculate the mean, median, mode, range and standard deviation.
- Display your results in a table – your table should be labelled and have a title.
- Write a few sentences below your table, commenting on what the statistics show – refer to measures of central tendency and dispersion.
- Draw a bar graph of the means for each condition – make sure that you give your bar graph a title and that the axes are clearly labelled.

Mrs Popple's class	Mrs Tipple's class
2	1
3	2
4	4
4	5
4	6
4	6
5	6
5	6
5	7
5	8
6	9
10	10

Further reading

Introductory texts

Coolican, H. (2006) *Introduction to Research Methods in Psychology*, London: Hodder Education.

Gross, R. (2005) *Psychology: The Science of Mind and Behaviour*, 5th edn, London: Hodder Education.

Roberts, C. and Russell, J. (2001) *Angles on Psychological Research*, Cheltenham: Nelson Thornes.

Searle, A. (1999) *Introducing Research and Data in Psychology: A Guide to Methods and Analysis*, Routledge Modular Series, London: Routledge.

Specialist sources

Breakwell, G.M., Hammond, S. and Fife-Shaw, C. (2000) *Research Methods in Psychology*, 2nd edn, London: Sage Publications.

British Psychological Society (2006) *Code of Ethics and Conduct*, Leicester: BPS Publications.

Foster, J.J. and Parker, I. (1995) *Carrying Out Investigations in Psychology: Methods and Statistics*, Leicester: BPS Books.

Social influence

5 Chapter

5.1 Introduction

Social influence is about how people influence and change other people's attitudes and behaviours. A useful definition is as follows: 'Efforts by one or more individuals to change the attitudes, beliefs, perceptions or behaviours of one or more others' (Baron et al. 2006). This definition is useful because it implies that at times you may be the target of social influence, while at other times individuals may attempt to change your attitudes or behaviour. It also highlights the fact that social influence may affect both your cognitions (attitudes, beliefs, perceptions) and your actual behaviour. Social influence may occur from real or imagined pressure to change from other people. Therefore, sometimes you may be very aware that another person or group of people is trying to change your attitude or how you behave; at other times, you may not be aware of attempts at social influence (for example, when you are with a group of friends and you go along with their views so as not to cause any tension in your relationships).

In this chapter we will look at a number of different types of social influence. This includes social facilitation, conformity and obedience. We will also consider factors that may lead a person to defy authority. Finally, we will discuss ethical and methodological issues that face social psychologists wishing to conduct research into social influence.

5.2 Social facilitation

Think about a sport that you play, such as hockey, rugby or football, or a game, such as pool or darts. With team sports such as hockey or football, it is common for other people to be watching while you are playing. Think about the games you play frequently, and occasions when people have been watching you play and when there has not been an audience. Can you recall whether or not your performance at the game was affected by having an audience present? **Social facilitation** is where your performance at a task or a sport is affected by the mere presence of other people. Depending on certain factors (which we shall explore below), performance may be either enhanced or made worse by the presence of others. Social facilitation effects can be found for many types of behaviour. For example, dancers may perform better in front of an audience; a skilled typist may type faster and more accurately when working alongside other skilled typists.

Over a hundred years ago, Triplett (1898) published one of the first experiments in social psychology. This study was based on the observation that competing cyclists produced faster times when racing with another cyclist, rather than simply competing on their own against the clock. In the first part of the study, Triplett used archive data from the Racing Board of the League of Wheelmen. He compared times taken by cyclists to cover certain distances in three different conditions: alone (unpaced), with another cyclist as a pacemaker, and in a racing group. Figure 5.1 shows Triplett's findings, and shows that cyclists were slowest when racing alone and fastest when racing with a pacemaker or in a racing group.

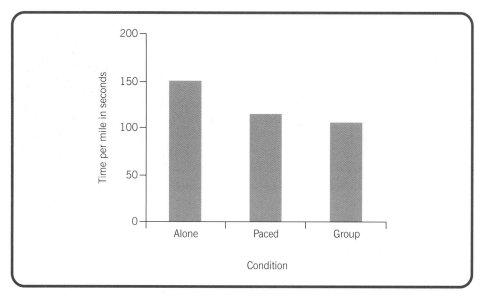

Figure 5.1. Average time, in seconds per mile, for cyclists racing alone, paced and in a group. Notice that the times for paced and group are similar, but both are faster than when the cyclist races alone. (Adapted from Triplett 1898)

Study

Aim Triplett (1898) devised a laboratory task to investigate whether or not performance would be enhanced in the presence of other people performing the same task.

Method Participants were instructed to wind in a line on a fishing reel as quickly as they could. Following a practice period, participants performed the task both alone and in pairs, alternating between the two conditions. In each trial, participants were timed to determine how long it took to make about 150 winds of the reel.

Results Performance was faster in the presence of another person than when the task was performed alone. Participants were about 1 per cent faster when working in pairs than when working alone.

Conclusion Participants' performance at the task was enhanced or **facilitated** by the presence of another person performing the same task. In other words, the mere presence of another person performing the same task results in **social facilitation.**

Early findings with respect to performance in the presence of others seem to be contradictory; sometimes performance is enhanced, but at other times it is worse. For example, Allport (1924) conducted a series of experiments where participants worked alone in cubicles or sitting together round a table. Allport found that with simple tasks, such as crossing out certain letters in words, performance was better in front of other people. However, with more complicated tasks, such as solving complex problems, performance was better when participants worked alone. Dashiell (1930) found that the number of arithmetic problems performed by participants increased in the presence of others, but so did the number of errors made. Schmitt et al. (1986) found that participants typed their name faster in front of an audience, but when asked to type their name backwards, performance was better when they worked alone. Studies with animals have shown that simple mazes are learned faster in the presence of other like animals, while complex mazes are learned faster when the animal is on its own (Zajonc et al. 1969).

Figure 5.2. If you have not danced much before, the audience may make you dance badly.

5.2.1 Dominant responses

Zajonc (1965) put forward a theory to explain these apparently contradictory findings. The rule that Zajonc observed was that performance of a well-learned or well-practised task is enhanced by the presence of other people. In contrast, performance of new or complex tasks is inhibited by the presence of other people. In other words, 'performance is facilitated and learning is impaired by the presence of spectators' (Zajonc 1965).

Zajonc used the term **dominant response** to refer to behaviour we are most likely to perform in a given situation. Zajonc claimed that dominant responses are facilitated by the presence of other people. When a person has learned a behaviour or is highly skilled at a particular task, then this is their dominant response. For example, a world-class basketball player who is skilled at throwing the ball through the hoop can be regarded as having this as a dominant response. The basketball player would have practised this behaviour again and again. In a match, therefore, the presence of both other players and the audience enhances or facilitates this dominant response: the player will pass more balls through the hoop in front of an audience than when training alone. By contrast, imagine someone learning to touch-type using all their fingers: this person would not be skilled at touch-typing, so it would not be a dominant response. In front of other people, the person learning to touch-type would make many more errors than if they were learning on their own.

Study

Aim Michaels et al. (1982) conducted a study to test the prediction that the presence of an audience would facilitate well-learned behaviours and inhibit poorly learned behaviours.

Method In the first part of the study, student pool players were observed in a Students' Union building. Following observation, twelve players were selected: six were identified as above average, and six as below average at playing pool. In the second part of the study, four observers stood round a pool table and observed the players over a number of games.

Results The above-average players potted 80 per cent of their shots when observed, compared to 71 per cent when not observed. In contrast, below-average players only potted 25 per cent of their shots when observed, compared to 36 per cent accuracy when not observed.

Conclusions The presence of an audience resulted in performance being affected as predicted by Zajonc's theory of dominant responses. The dominant response of skilled pool players is to pot balls, and the dominant response of unskilled players is to miss shots and not pot balls. An audience facilitates, enhances or exaggerates each of these dominant responses.

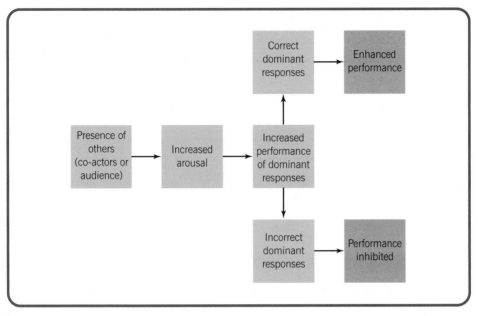

Figure 5.3. The arousal or drive theory explanation of social facilitation.

5.2.2 Social facilitation and arousal

Zajonc (1965) put forward the drive theory of social facilitation. This states that the presence of other people increases a person's general level of arousal (we become more energised and alert); this, in turn, increases the tendency to perform dominant responses. Generally, when arousal is low, such as when we are sleepy, performance at tasks tends to be poor. Similarly, when we are very highly aroused, we show signs of panic and disorganisation, which also results in poor performance. Performance tends to be optimum when arousal is moderate. Zajonc's drive theory of social facilitation suggests that the presence of others when performing dominant responses increases arousal to an optimum level for performance. The presence of others increases arousal level to cause better performance of a dominant response.

Figure 5.3 provides a diagrammatic representation of the arousal explanation of social facilitation. Note that the response has to be correct or appropriate for the situation.

Evaluation apprehension

Why should the mere presence of others cause arousal? One explanation, put forward by Cottrell (1972), revolves around the idea that, when in the presence of others, we are concerned that they are evaluating our performance. When performing a task in the presence of others, Cottrell claimed that people experience **evaluation apprehension**. The effect of evaluation apprehension on a simple or well-learned task produces arousal, which results in the performance being enhanced. For a new or complex task, evaluation apprehension increases arousal to a very high level, with the consequence that performance is worse than when alone.

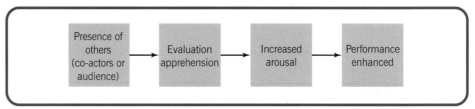

Figure 5.4. The evaluation apprehension explanation of social facilitation.

Study

Aim Bartis et al. (1988) conducted a study to investigate whether or not evaluation apprehension would lead to improvement in performance on a simple task, and inhibition of performance on a complex task.

Method Participants were all presented with the same basic task, which involved thinking of many different uses of a knife. One group was asked simply to list all the different uses of a knife that they could think of. Another group was asked to think only of creative uses of a knife. Some participants in each condition were told that their performance would be identified (the evaluation apprehension condition). Other participants in each condition were told that their ideas would be collected together as a group, but that no individual would be identified.

Results When performing the simple task, participants in the evaluation apprehension condition produced more uses for a knife than participants in the other condition. By contrast, when performing the complex task, those in the evaluation apprehension condition produced fewer creative uses for a knife.

Conclusion Evaluation apprehension increases performance on simple tasks, but decreases performance on complex tasks.

Distraction

Saunders (1983) proposed an explanation of social facilitation based on the idea that the presence of other people creates a distraction to the person attempting to perform the task. This, in turn, interferes with the amount of attention the person can give to the task. The person then experiences a conflict between whether to attend to the task or to the audience. This conflict over what to attend to produces an increase in arousal, thus facilitating performance on simple or dominant tasks, and inhibiting perform-ance on complex or non-dominant tasks.

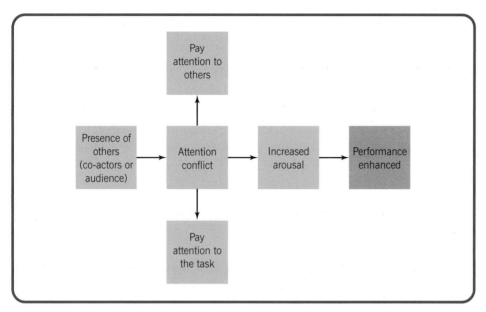

Figure 5.5. The distraction of social facilitation.

Study

Aim Saunders et al. (1978) conducted a study to test the effect of distraction conflict on performance of a task.

Method Participants were presented with either a simple or a difficult task to perform in the presence of others, performing either the same or a different task. It was hypothesised that a co-actor performing the same task as the participant would produce more distraction, since they would be a source of comparison for the participant's performance.

Results Participants in the high-distraction condition (same task as co-actors) performed at a higher level on the simple task, but produced more errors on the complex task.

Conclusion The results of this study produced evidence in support of the distraction-conflict theory of social facilitation.

The distraction-conflict theory of social facilitation may also help to explain the results from studies using non-human animals. Social facilitation has been shown to occur in ants and cockroaches (Zajonc et al. 1969). This is hardly likely to be due to evaluation apprehension! The presence of other animals of the same species may be distracting and hence may draw attention away from the task the animal is trying to perform.

5.3 Effects of arousal on task performance

We have seen how the optimal level of arousal is different for new and well-learned tasks. This can be applied to many different types of sport. For example, using a golf club to hit a golf ball a long distance down the fairway is a highly skilled task. If you have never or rarely played golf, you will almost certainly perform better alone than with other people watching you, even if those other people are poor at golf as well. Using a golf club requires concentration on many things (the ball, the fairway and swing), and therefore results in quite a high level of arousal in the first place. The effect of people watching may push the arousal level too high. The result is that performance will be poorer than if you played a golf shot on your own. This is equally likely to apply to other sports, such as tennis and ice skating, and to field events such as the javelin and the high jump.

In the entertainment world, actors who perform on the stage in front of an audience, and who know their lines well, are likely to act much better than actors who are not confident of their lines.

In the workplace there is also evidence for the effects of arousal on task performance. For example, Aiello and Kolb (1995) showed that highly skilled workers performed better when they were being monitored. By contrast, unskilled workers performed worse when monitored. Henchy and Glass (1968) found that typing performance was worse in the presence of an expert typist, but not in the presence of someone who did not type. People commuting to work on crowded buses or trains may also show arousal, since being close to many other people may cause distraction and fear of evaluation. Thus it may be best only to try to do simple tasks in a crowded situation, as these will benefit from social facilitation.

Figure 5.6. Actors who know their lines well will act better in front of an audience.

MacCracken and Stadulis (1985) found that the presence of an audience had little effect on young children (under eight years of age). This suggests that evaluation apprehension may be something that develops as we get older.

Evaluation

- More recent research has challenged the view that it is arousal alone which explains social facilitation. It is now thought that both arousal and cognitive processes, such as attention, are involved.

- It may be that arousal results from the cognitive demands of having to pay attention to both the task and the audience. This may cause reduced or narrowed attention to the task.
- Another explanation offered is concerned with self-awareness (Wicklund 1975). Here it is proposed that, when in front of other people, the immediate response is to focus on oneself. This then causes the person to compare how he or she would like to perform ideally with how they actually perform. If there is a significant difference between the ideal and the reality, the person tries to perform to their ideal. This will work on easy tasks, but not on complex and difficult tasks that have not been learned.
- Social psychologists have offered a number of different explanations for social facilitation, but after more than a hundred years of research, no one explanation is agreed on by all psychologists.
- There are a number of criticisms of the research. First, audiences in experiments tend to be passive and simply observe someone performing a task. Real audiences are often noisy and judge behaviour, for example in the theatre or at a sports stadium. Second, research has largely ignored personality differences between individuals: for example, Triplett (1898) found that 25 per cent of participants showed worse, not better, performance in front of an audience. Third, many of the tasks given to people to perform are artificial and hence lack ecological validity (see section 5.5.6, below).

5.4 Conformity

Imagine that you and a small group of your friends are standing in a public place, such as a park or a shopping area. You have all agreed in advance to look up at the sky for at least five minutes and to show interest in what you are looking at. In fact, there is nothing to see, but you are interested in how many passing strangers will stop and look up also. How many people do you think would stop and look? What explanations can you offer for those that do? What is described here is an old trick that you may have played on others yourself – it is a good example of conformity to what others are doing.

Conformity may be defined as follows: 'A type of social influence in which individuals change their attitudes, beliefs or behaviour in order to adhere to existing social norms' (Baron et al. 2006). This definition emphasises the importance of social norms as a key social cause of people conforming. Social norms are just one example (albeit an important one) of a majority view. As such, conformity can be said to occur in any situation where a person or small group of people is exposed to a majority and conform. Conformity, then, can be seen as majority influence.

5.4.1 Classic studies of conformity

The first study of conformity appears to be an informal experiment conducted by Jenness (1932). Jenness asked students, first, to estimate individually the number of beans in a bottle. Subsequently, he put students in small groups and asked each student to estimate the number of beans again. Finally, he asked the same students, on an individual basis, to estimate the number of beans in the bottle. He found that in the group condition students moved to a group position which then persisted when students were asked individually again. In what follows, two classic studies of conformity are described.

The autokinetic effect

Study

Aim Sherif (1936) conducted an experiment with the aim of demonstrating that people conform to group or social norms when they are put in an ambiguous or novel situation.

Method Sherif made use of what is called the autokinetic effect. If you are put in a completely dark room and then a small spot of light is projected onto a screen, the spot of light will appear to move, even though it is really stationary. It has been found that individuals in the room on their own make different judgements about how much the light moves – estimates from 20 to 30 centimetres and 60 to 80 centimetres are common. The influence of group norms or majority influence was investigated by Sherif by putting three people in the room together. Sherif manipulated the composition of the group by putting together two people whose estimate of the light movement when alone was very similar, and one person whose estimate was very different. Each of the three people in the darkened room had to say aloud how much they thought the light moved. They did this a number of times.

Results Sherif found that, over numerous estimates of the movement of the light, the group converged. In effect, as Figure 5.7 shows, the person whose estimate of movement was greatly different to the other two in the group conformed to the view of the other two.

Conclusion The results showed that the 'deviant' in the group conformed to the majority view. This took place over a small number of trials of the autokinetic task.

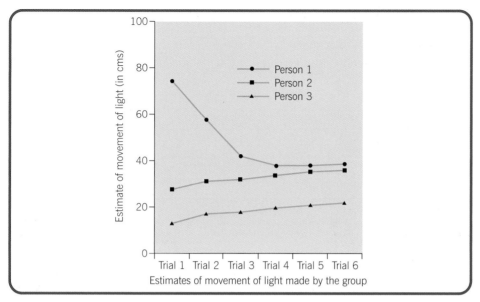

Figure 5.7. Graph showing the coming together of estimates of the movement of light in a three-person group.

Sherif (1936) conducted numerous other experiments using the autokinetic effect. Where participants had no previous experience of the autokinetic effect, he found that conformity to a majority view happened very quickly. In general, Sherif found that in ambiguous situations, such as those presented by the autokinetic effect, the less previous experience a person has of the situation, the more powerful conformity to the majority view will be.

Evaluation

The autokinetic effect is not something we come across in everyday life. However, majority influence resulting in conformity occurs in ambiguous social situations where we do not know the correct or accepted way to behave. For example, if you go to an expensive restaurant for a seven-course meal, you will find a large number of knives, forks and spoons laid out at each place setting. You sit down, look at all this cutlery and do not know which knife, fork or spoon to use with which course. What do you do? You could ask, but this may make you feel that you are showing your ignorance. Most likely you will wait until other people start to eat and then copy them. You follow the behaviour of the majority. The difference between the autokinetic effect and ambiguous social situations, such as the restaurant scenario, is that in most social situations there are social norms or rules about how to behave. With the autokinetic effect, there is no right or wrong answer, since the movement of the light is an illusion anyway.

Asch's study of conformity

Asch (1955) said that while the studies of Sherif (1936) showed some aspects of conformity, they did not demonstrate how social or group pressure would affect the judgements people make when there is clearly a right or wrong answer. Asch wanted to know whether or not people would conform to a majority view when the majority view was obviously wrong. He investigated conformity using a simple perceptual task in which participants were asked to state which of three comparison lines was the same length as the target line. An example of the task is given in Figure 5.8.

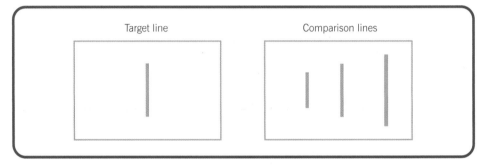

Figure 5.8. An example of the target line and comparison lines used by Asch in his conformity experiments.

Asch (1951) conducted a pilot study to ensure that the line judgement task was easy. In the pilot study, Asch asked 36 people, on an individual basis, to match the target line with one of the comparison lines. Each person did this 20 times, with slightly different versions of the task shown in Figure 5.8. In all, 720 judgements were made, with 717 correct responses given, thus showing the task to be clear and easy.

Study

Aim Asch (1951) conducted an experiment aimed at investigating the influence of an incorrect majority view on an individual exposed to this view.

Method Using the line judgement task shown in Figure 5.8, Asch put a participant in the same room as seven other people. These seven people had agreed in advance the responses they were going to give when presented with the line task. The real (naive) participant did not know this and was led to believe the other seven people were participants too. Each person in the room had to state aloud to the others which comparison line was most like the target line in length. The naive participant sat at the end of the row and gave his or her view last. In some trials, the seven confederates of the experimenter all gave the same, wrong comparison line as the answer (for example, the third line in Figure 5.8). Asch was interested in whether or not the naive participant would conform to the unanimous, but wrong, majority view.

Results Asch measured the number of times each participant gave a correct answer or conformed to the incorrect majority view. Just over 22 per cent of participants gave the correct answer on all 12 occasions. This means that 78 per cent of participants gave at least one incorrect response in line with the majority view. About 5 per cent of participants gave the same answer as the incorrect majority on all occasions.

Conclusions Asch demonstrated that people will conform to a majority view even when it is obvious that the majority is incorrect. Think back to Asch's pilot study, where only three incorrect judgements were made out of 720 answers. Asch concluded that groups exert pressure on an individual in some way to conform to a majority view.

Asch interviewed each participant after they had taken part in his study. The participants who had agreed with the majority gave various reasons for their behaviour: for example, that they did not want to spoil the experimenter's results; that they did not want to be different to the others; that they had actually made the correct judgements; and that they might have been suffering from eye strain. We will consider different explanations for conformity later.

Evaluation

- Asch used students in his experiment who did not know each other. The social pressure to conform is likely to be much greater among a group of friends, or where the other participants are teachers of the student.
- There are many ethical and methodological issues with the Asch experiment which we will consider generally at the end of this chapter.

5.4.2 Types of conformity

There are two main types of conformity: internalisation and compliance.

Internalisation is where the individual accepts the majority group view *and* believes that view to be correct. We may call this 'private acceptance', where a person conforms to other people's behaviour in the genuine belief that they are right. The Sherif experiment, described earlier, is a good example of internalisation or private acceptance. Sherif demonstrated this in a follow-up study, where the same participants were asked to judge the movement of the light after the original group study. Sherif found that the participants gave very similar estimates of the movement of the light as they had the first time. These findings suggest that, in ambiguous situations, people rely on each other to decide what is right and then they stay with this view.

Compliance is where a person conforms to other people's behaviours or attitudes, but does not believe them to be correct. This is when you go along with other people's views, or do what they do, to 'keep the peace', or not cause any conflict or disagreement with others. Strictly speaking, it would be best to call this 'public compliance' because you are agreeing with others publicly, even if you think they are wrong. The Asch experiment is a good example of compliance, since (as we have seen above) participants gave various reasons for agreeing with the majority that were to do with not upsetting other people. Very few of the participants in Asch's experiment actually believed the incorrect majority view.

5.4.3 Explanations for conformity

One obvious explanation of conformity is that people follow social norms. Social norms are rules, which may be written or unwritten, guiding how people are expected to behave in many social situations. For example, if you go to a classical music concert, speaking while the orchestra is playing would break the social norm of silence. Many social norms are a product of our upbringing and socialisation. However, other explanations are needed to account for the conformity to majority influence found in the Asch study. Deutsch and Gerard (1955) put forward a distinction between normative social influence and informational social influence to account for conformity.

Normative social influence

This is where people conform to maintain the harmony of the group, to avoid rejection by the group or to gain approval from others. The result of normative social influence is that people publicly comply with the majority view or the social norms of the group. However, privately they disagree or hold different views to the majority. Think back to what the participants said when interviewed by Asch after taking part in the study. Some said they wanted to please the experimenter

Figure 5.9. Glamorous models may influence the ideal body image that young women have.

or maintain group harmony, but did not see the target line and comparison line as the same length. This is normative social influence.

Normative social influence can be seen in many aspects of our daily lives. For example, clothing fashions change every year. Also, the group you identify yourself as belonging to will have norms for dressing (for example, 'goths' in black and 'chavs' with hoods). Men in executive jobs wear a suit and tie. Women's perceptions of their ideal body size is a major issue in western society, where slim or thin models have a normative influence.

Study

Aim Anderson et al. (1992) attempted to show that women's ideal body size is related to reliability of food supply in a culture. It was hypothesised that in cultures where women had a reliable food supply the ideal body size would be 'slender'.

Method Women from 54 different cultures were asked about their ideal body size in relation to the categories of slender, moderate and heavy body size. Each culture was categorised as having a reliable, moderately reliable and unreliable food supply.

Results It was found that women in cultures where the food supply was unreliable regarded a heavy body size as ideal, while in cultures where the food supply was reliable, women said their ideal body size was slender or thin.

Conclusions Cultural norms concerning women's ideal body size are influenced by factors such as the reliability of the availability of food. Where food supplies are very reliable, there is evidence of normative social influence.

Informational social influence

This is conformity to the majority as a result of information (things you did not know, persuasive arguments, and so on) presented to you by others in the group. This form of influence results in private acceptance of the majority view. That is, the group is believed to be correct in what it is saying. Private acceptance or internalisation of views (Kelman 1958) results in a person repeating that view to others. This does not happen with public compliance in normative influence. Informational social influence is more likely to cause conformity in more ambiguous situations, such as the autokinetic effect. In situations where there is less or little uncertainty, normative social influence is more likely to produce conformity. The reason that informational social influence occurs where uncertainty is high is that people have a need to be sure, or a desire to be right, as often as possible. This motive was suggested by Deutsch and Gerard (1955).

Study

Aim Baron et al. (1996) hypothesised that conformity would be greater where people have less confidence in their judgement.

Method In a novel variation of the Asch line judgement study, participants were shown a drawing of a person and then asked to match this drawing with one of three other drawings. In one condition the drawing was shown for just half a second; in the other condition participants were shown the drawing for five seconds. Before being asked to match the drawing, participants heard the wrong judgements of two assistants of the experimenters.

Results Conformity to the wrong matching of the drawing by the assistants was much higher when the drawing was shown to participants for just half a second, rather than for five seconds.

Conclusions The information gained from seeing the drawing for just half a second is much less than from seeing the drawing for five seconds. Hence, when there is not sufficient information to be sure of a judgement, informational social influence will cause people to conform more.

5.4.4 Factors affecting conformity

We have seen in the above study by Baron et al. (1996) that one factor affecting conformity is the degree to which a person has full information available to them: when information is scarce or poor, conformity to a majority view is likely to be high. Conversely, when a person has full or good information, conformity to a wrong majority view will be low. Psychologists have researched factors that are likely to make us conform more and conform less to a majority view.

Decreasing conformity

Asch (1955) conducted a series of experiments using the same line judgement task and seven confederates.

- In one study, one of the confederates always gave the right answer. Asch found that the conformity level of the naive participant dropped to around 10 per cent.

- In another study, which Asch called the 'extreme dissenter', six of the confederates gave the same wrong answer, while the seventh confederate gave a different wrong answer. Conformity levels dropped among participants to around 10 per cent.

- Asch also looked at the effect of group size on conformity. Generally, he found that, as group size increases, a larger incorrect majority results in higher levels of conformity. With small groups of two or three, where there are only one or two confederates giving the wrong answer, conformity drops to below 10 per cent among naive participants.

It must be remembered that, in the original Asch study, almost 25 per cent of participants did not conform with the wrong majority view. These participants did not give in to group pressure.

Asch (1955) also made a variation of his original study by asking participants to write their answer on a piece of paper, after hearing the wrong views of others in the group. Here Asch found that conformity levels were very low. Not having to say the answer out loud allowed the participants to express their private view without having to be concerned about what other members of the group might think.

Crutchfield (1955) investigated conformity by putting each participant alone in a cubicle, but making the participants believe that they were communicating with other people in a small group.

Study

Aim Crutchfield (1955) conducted a study to investigate conformity, but where participants sat alone in separate booths. The aim of the study was to determine levels of conformity when other people are not present.

Method Participants sat in separate booths, side by side. In each booth was a set of switches and lights. Each participant was told that they would be given a simple task (some of which were Asch's line judgement tasks) to make a decision about. They were also told that five other people would be doing the same task and that the participant would see their answers (shown as lights) before being asked their own view or decision. Participants had to indicate their view by flipping one of the switches representing their choice.

Results Conformity with incorrect majority views by participants dropped to below 50 per cent (in the Asch study, 77 per cent conformed at least once to the majority view). With statements of opinion, conformity was below 35 per cent.

Conclusions When people are placed in situations where they are exposed to an incorrect majority view, but not to the other people, conformity levels are low. Hence, the actual presence of people increases the likelihood of a person conforming to a majority view. This indicates that social pressure has a strong effect on behaviour.

Generally, decreases in conformity are found when information is good or of high quality, and when exposure of an individual's view to a group is reduced or kept private to the individual.

Increasing conformity

Stang (1973) found that the attractiveness of belonging to the group for the individual affects conformity. Generally, the more attractive a group is to the participant, the greater will be conformity to the majority view. The cohesiveness of a group has also been found to affect conformity. Cohesiveness concerns the extent to which the individuals in a group like each other and prize being a member of the group. Highly cohesive groups, where each member likes the other and values being part of the group, show higher levels of conformity, while low cohesive groups show low levels of conformity (Latane and L'Herrou 1996).

Smith and Harris Bond (1993) carried out a review of conformity studies conducted in different cultures around the world between 1957 and 1985. Smith and Harris Bond make a distinction between individualistic and collectivistic cultures. Individualistic cultures are ones such as the USA and the UK, where personal choice and individual achievement are valued. Collectivist cultures, such as China and Asian countries, value the good of the group over individual achievement. Studies conducted in different cultures showed that conformity is higher in collectivist than in individualistic cultures. The main explanation for this is that collectivist cultures strive to achieve group harmony more than individualistic cultures do.

Personality and conformity

We have seen above that different situations may serve either to increase or decrease conformity. In view of this, some psychologists have looked at personality and conformity. Crutchfield (1955) suggested that personality characteristics associated with high levels of conformity include low self-esteem, low intelligence, high levels of anxiety and high need for social approval. The 'authoritarian personality' (Adorno et al. 1950) is also associated with high levels of conformity. According to Adorno, the authoritarian personality is one in which a person values convention, rules and obeying those in authority. The authoritarian personality is associated both with obedience to authority and with prejudice.

5.5 Obedience to authority

Obedience to authority has a positive and a negative side. On the positive side, people obey laws of society, authority figures (such as the police and people in high positions in society), and orders or instructions which seem sensible and reasonable. Obedience in this context is essential to the smooth running of society, and if people did not obey, chaos and disorder would quickly develop. On the negative side, obedience can be destructive and result in terrible crimes. There are plenty of examples from history where one group of people has killed another group, for example, the Nazis ordering German soldiers to torture and kill millions of Jews during the Second World War. The Bosnians and Serbs in Eastern Europe, and the Tutsis and Hutus in Rwanda are also examples of mass slaughter resulting from obedience to orders given by high-ranking army officers or government officials.

Figure 5.10. Racial hatred can result in many people obeying the orders of a few, sometimes with destructive consequences.

5.5.1 Milgram's classic study of obedience

Milgram conducted a series of highly controversial studies in the 1960s (Milgram 1963, 1965, 1974), investigating obedience to authority. The studies explored the effect of a range of factors on levels of obedience. Milgram recruited participants by placing advertisements in local newspapers, asking for volunteers to take part in an experiment on learning. Volunteers were told that the experiment required one person to act as a 'teacher' and another person to act as a 'learner'. Participants each drew a piece of paper from a hat to assign the role of teacher and learner. In reality, this was fixed so that the true volunteer, or participant, was always assigned to the role of teacher, and the other person, who was a confederate of Milgram's, to the role of learner.

Milgram then explained to the teacher that they had to read a series of word pairs (such as 'blue–girl', 'fat–neck') to the learner. Subsequently, the teacher had to read the first word of the pair, and the learner had to choose the correct second word of the pair from a list of a few words. The teacher was told that, if the learner responded with the wrong word, the teacher had to give the learner an electric shock. This continued over many sets of word pairs, and each time the learner gave a wrong answer, the teacher was told they had to give an electric shock of increasing intensity.

A sophisticated piece of equipment, with a long line of switches and lights, was placed in front of the teacher, allowing them to see what the next level of electric shock should be (see Figure 5.11). On the front panel of the equipment was a voltage scale running from 15 to 450 volts, with an indication of the severity of shock, as shown below:

- 15–60 volts: slight shock;

- 75–120 volts: moderate shock;

- 135–180 volts: strong shock;

- 195–240 volts: very strong shock;

- 255–300 volts: intense shock;

- 315–360 volts: extremely intense shock;

- 375–420 volts: danger, severe shock;

- 425–450 volts: XXX.

Figure 5.11. Stanley Milgram's complex-looking electric shock equipment (left), and the 'learner' having electrodes attached to his wrist (right). (From Milgram 1974)

Prior to beginning the experiment, the teacher was given a sample shock of 45 volts (which is quite painful). The learner (a confederate of Milgram's) did not actually receive any shocks during the experiment, but the teacher did not know this. The teacher would see the learner 'wired up' and would be told that he had complained of a weak heart. As the learner kept getting the second word in the word pair wrong, Milgram would order the teacher to carry on giving electric shocks. This would consist of saying, 'Please go on', or 'The experiment requires that you continue', or 'You have no other choice, you must go on'.

Before conducting his series of experiments, Milgram asked psychiatrists, students and middle-class adults the shock level at which they thought teachers would refuse to go on. All said they would refuse beyond the 'very strong shock' level (195–240 volts), and over 80 per cent said they would refuse to go on beyond the 'strong shock' level (135–180 volts).

The first experiment was conducted in the psychology department at Yale University (a highly prestigious US university). The teacher and learner were put in different rooms so that the teacher could hear the learner but not actually see him. Figure 5.12 shows the results that Milgram obtained.

As can be seen, 63 per cent continued to deliver electric shocks up to the very maximum. In dramatic contrast to the predictions made by psychiatrists, students and middle-class adults, all continued to 240 volts, whereas between 90 and 100 per cent were predicted to discontinue at this level.

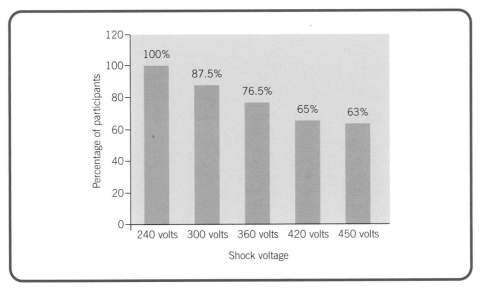

Figure 5.12. Percentage of participant 'teachers' who continued to give shocks to learners. (Adapted from Milgram 1974)

There are many ethical and methodological issues raised by Milgram's experiments which we shall consider towards the end of this chapter. What Milgram demonstrated was that the situation a person is placed in may cause that person to blindly obey authority without apparent concern for other people. In another experiment, Milgram used only female participants and learners (in the classic experiment all were male), but he found only very slightly lower levels of obedience with females. Sixty-five per cent of females continued to the highest shock level.

Evaluation

- Milgram's experiments have been enormously important in the study of social influence, and the findings have disturbed generations of psychologists. Milgram made people confront a potentially disturbing aspect of their own behaviour: that anybody, given appropriate situational factors, may behave with destructive obedience to authority.
- Much criticism has been levelled at Milgram for conducting experiments which many now regard as both unethical and methodologically flawed. For example, the experiments all involve deception of the participant and caused high levels of stress to them at times.
- Milgram did debrief every single participant in his studies and informed them of the real purpose of the experiment. Participants were informed that they had behaved in ways similar to other participants. Milgram reported that, following a full debrief, over 80 per cent of participants said that they were happy to have participated in the experiment.

5.5.2 Explanations of obedience

Kelman and Hamilton (1989) suggest three main factors to explain obedience, and destructive obedience in particular. These are:

- legitimacy of the system;

- legitimacy of authority within the system;

- legitimacy of demands or orders given.

The **legitimacy of the system** concerns the extent to which a government, army, religious group or even family is a legitimate source of authority. Where one or more of these is seen by the individual to be a legitimate source of authority, obedience to the system will be high. When the system is not seen as legitimate, obedience will be low. For example, if a car driver does not believe the law penalising drivers for using a mobile phone while driving is right or legitimate, that driver may risk the penalty and use the mobile phone while driving. In Milgram's experiment described above, the experiment took place at the highly prestigious psychology department at Yale University. It is most likely that participants would have seen the setting as legitimate and believed that, in the university, harm to another would not take place.

The **legitimacy of authority** is the power individuals hold to give orders because of their position in the system. For example, the prime minister in government or a general in the army would have a high degree of legitimacy. Where someone attempts to give orders but is not seen to be in a position to do so, obedience to the orders will be low. In the Milgram study described above, the experimenters wore white coats to make them look like scientists. This gave the experimenters legitimacy of authority in the eyes of the participants. This can also be seen as the experimenter having both expert and legitimate power over the participant (French and Raven 1959).

The **legitimacy of demands or orders** refers to the extent to which the order is perceived to be a legitimate area for the authority figure. For example, if the prime minister tried to order people not to eat meat because he was a vegetarian, you would be unlikely to regard the order as legitimate. In Milgram's study, the participant in the role of the teacher was repeatedly asked and told to continue in the name of science, and that the experiment demanded that they continue. Hence, the order to continue, even when the participant wanted to stop, can be seen as legitimate because of the setting and the belief we have in the legitimacy of science.

Finally, the classic Milgram study physically separated the participant (teacher) from the learner. While participants heard the learner express sounds of distress, this was not actually seen by the participant. As we shall see below, when the participant is in close proximity to the learner, obedience levels drop dramatically.

5.5.3 Situational factors affecting obedience

Milgram (1974) investigated various situational factors affecting obedience in the teacher–learner experiment described above. These include legitimacy of authority, proximity of the learner, proximity of the experimenter, conflicting orders and gender differences. In all, Milgram conducted 18 experiments using the basic learner–teacher set-up.

The legitimacy of system and authority was varied by conducting the experiment in a run-down office in a less respectable part of town. This 'low legitimacy' experiment resulted in lower levels of obedience – just 48 per cent of participants delivered the maximum shock. The legitimacy of the authority figure, the experimenter, was varied by allowing another casually dressed participant to give orders to the teacher to carry on, rather than the experimenter dressed in a white laboratory coat. Here, obedience dropped to just 20 per cent giving the maximum shock.

The proximity of the learner was varied by placing the teacher and the learner in the same room. Here, obedience dropped to 40 per cent. When the teacher had to put the hand of the learner on a metal plate to deliver the electric shock, obedience dropped to 30 per cent. In another experiment, the experimenter left the room after giving the teacher instructions on what to do. Here, obedience dropped to 20 per cent. Where two experimenters were present with the teacher and one instructed the participant to continue and the other to stop, obedience dropped dramatically, with no one giving the maximum shock.

The proximity of the authority figure or experimenter also affected levels of obedience. When the experimenter was not in the same room as the participant, but gave orders over the telephone, obedience was reduced to about 20 per cent. When the experimenter did not order the participant to continue and made it clear that the participant could leave at any time, only 2.5 per cent continued to give the highest level of shock.

Numerous replications of the basic Milgram set-up were conducted in different countries in the 1970s and 1980s. Figure 5.13 summarises some of the findings. However, some caution is needed in the interpretation of these, since slightly different methods to Milgram's were used in different studies. Nevertheless, all show a worryingly high level of obedience to authority!

Study	Country	Participants	Percentage
Milgram (1963)	USA	Male general public	63%
Mantell (1971)	Germany	Male general public	85%
Burley & McGuiness (1977)	UK	Male students	50%
Shanab & Yahga (1978)	Jordan	Students	62%
Miranda et al. (1981)	Spain	Students	90%
Scharz (1985)	Australia	General public	80%

Figure 5.13. Levels of obedience in different countries using the classic Milgram procedure. (Adapted from Smith and Harris Bond 1999)

5.5.4 Dispositional factors affecting obedience

In considering dispositional factors that may explain why people obey authority, we are concerned with the question of whether or not particular personality types are associated with high and low levels of obedience. The **authoritarian personality** is most commonly associated with obedience to authority. It was Adorno and his colleagues (1950) who put forward the idea of an authoritarian personality, which they described as a person who submits to the authority of those in a higher position (this may be due to status or power) and is authoritarian with those of lower status or power. Someone with an authoritarian personality is characterised by excessive and blind obedience to authority.

Adorno was originally concerned with constructing a questionnaire to measure anti-Semitism, and developed an attitude questionnaire which became known as the F-scale (the 'F' standing for fascist). This measures different aspects of personality – such as conventionalism, preoccupation with power, puritanical sexual attitudes and superstition – which were all thought to be different components of the authoritarian personality.

The authoritarian personality offers an obvious explanation of obedience to authority, since you would expect people with an authoritarian personality both to obey the orders they are given, and to expect others to obey orders.

Evaluation

- Hyman and Sheatsley (1954) found that the authoritarian personality is more likely to exist among people who are less well educated and are of low economic social status. Thus personality is not needed to explain obedience to authority.

- Another problem with the authoritarian personality is that it was assumed to be associated with only the extreme political right wing. Rokeach (1960) showed that authoritarianism is equally likely to be seen on the extreme political left. Rokeach called this a 'closed mind', which involved very rigid thinking and intolerance of different views.
- Generally, the explanation of obedience to authority using the authoritarian personality has not fared well. Psychologists regard powerful situational, social and cultural factors to offer better explanations.

A more recent attempt to link personality and obedience to authority is the idea of social dominance put forward by Sidanius and Pratto (1999). A person is said to have high social dominance when he or she wants their own group to be better and more dominant than another group or groups. People with high social dominance will therefore tend to reject the views of others and want their own view to prevail. With respect to the classic Milgram experiment, seeing yourself as a member of a scientific group or a member of a sub-cultural group would mean that you are more likely to obey orders from people you see as belonging to that group.

5.5.5 Defiance of authority

We have looked at some of the factors which encourage obedience to authority; now we will consider what factors reduce our likelihood of obeying authority. We have already seen that some variations to Milgram's classic experiment resulted in low levels of obedience, for example, shabby building, experimenter not in the room, learner physically in same room as the participant (teacher). When individuals are reminded that they are responsible for the consequences of what they do and of the harm that may be caused, research has shown significant reductions in obedience (Hamilton 1978). Research has also shown that if participants in a study of obedience watch another person acting disobediently, then levels of obedience will be low (Rochat and Modigliani 1995).

Study

Aim Feldman and Scheibe (1972) conducted a study to discover what factors cause people to rebel against an authority figure.

Method College students were asked to complete a very personal and embarrassing questionnaire in the presence of other students. The other students were confederates of the experimenter. In one condition, the confederates appeared to complete the questionnaire willingly. In another condition, the confederates refused to complete the questionnaire and asked to leave the experiment.

Results The real participants in the first condition were much more likely to complete the questionnaire than those in the condition where the confederates refused.

Conclusion People are likely to refuse authority requests which are unpleasant or harmful when social support is available from others. In this experiment, social support came from others refusing to fill in the questionnaire.

We may use the idea of informational social influence (discussed earlier with respect to conformity) to explain conditions under which people might defy authority or resist destructive obedience. You will recall that when a person is not sure of what to do in a social situation, the influence of another person may be great. In the Milgram study, the participant is in the role of the teacher. This is a highly unusual situation for most people and therefore one in which they would tend not to be confident about how to behave in an appropriate way. Hence the experimenter, as an authority figure giving orders, provides strong social information about what to do. Where the credibility of the authority figure is in doubt, informational social influence is less and the participant relies more on his or her own moral judgement about whether or not it is right to continue. In circumstances where informational social influence is low, obedience to authority is also likely to be low.

Similar reasoning may also be applied to normative social influence. Where the experimenter and the setting for the experiment are seen to be legitimate (experimenter wears a white coat and the setting is in a university), normative pressures to obey authority will be high. Normative pressures are low where legitimacy is questioned (casually dressed experimenter and shabby building), resulting in low levels of obedience to authority.

5.5.6 Issues in studying social influence

Research on social influence is a difficult area for social psychologists. This is because both methodological and ethical issues need to be addressed and taken into account. We will consider ethical issues first, and then methodological ones.

Ethical issues

There are four main ethical issues that arise with social influence research, especially with experiments which take place in psychology laboratories. These are:

- deception;
- informed consent;
- potential harm to participants;
- withdrawal from the experiment.

> **Deception** With both the Asch and Milgram experiments, participants were deceived about the reasons for conducting the experiment. In the Milgram studies, participants were told that the experiment was concerned with how people learn. In the Asch studies, participants were told that the experiment was about perception (a visual discrimination task). Participants were only told about the true purpose of each study after taking part.

The British Psychological Society's Code of Ethics and Conduct (March 2006) states that deception should only be used in exceptional circumstances, 'to preserve the integrity of the research' (Section 1.3 xii). Asch and Milgram would probably have argued that the research was of such importance to understanding conformity and obedience to authority that it qualified as exceptional. Kelman (1967) offered two reasons for deception in psychological research:

- to get people to take part in an experiment that would be unpleasant in some respect;
- where revealing the true purpose of the experiment from the outset would not result in finding out how people would really behave.

The first is clearly not an acceptable reason, but the second may be. It is likely that, with the code of ethics that we have these days for psychological research, it would not be possible to conduct Milgram's study. If both Asch and Milgram had informed participants from the outset of the true purpose of their experiments, the participants' behaviour might not tell us much about social influence in everyday life.

> **Informed consent** We can see from the above discussion that participants in the Asch and Milgram studies did not give informed consent. Informed consent means that the participant has had the procedure and purpose of the experiment fully explained to them before taking part, and that having been told about the experiment they have consented to take part. If you consider the different studies described and referred to in this chapter, you will see that virtually none obtained informed consent from their participants.

The British Psychological Society's Code of Ethics and Conduct states that unless informed consent has been obtained, research should be restricted to observations of people in public places. Again, we see that some social influence research may not be possible with today's standards.

Harm to participants It is clear from photographs and a film of the Milgram experiment that participants showed clear signs of distress at times. Baumrind (1964) drew attention to the fact that participants might have suffered long-lasting after-effects from taking part in the experiment. With the Asch experiment, participants of low self-esteem might also have experienced significant after-effects, which could result in them being unsure of their own judgements. Both Milgram and Asch gave an extensive debriefing to each participant.

However, Baumrind (1964) wondered what effect being told that they had been deceived would have on the participants. Would these people trust others less in the future and have lower self-esteem as a result? No longer-term follow-up of participants in either the Asch or the Milgram studies has been carried out. It is difficult to know whether these people suffered long-lasting after-effects arising from having been placed in stressful and upsetting conditions.

Withdrawal from the study Another principle of modern ethical standards for psychological research is that participants must be told that they are free to withdraw from the study at any time they wish. With the Milgram experiments, the participant was very strongly urged and ordered to continue by the experimenter. If Milgram had said before the experiment that they could withdraw at any time, one wonders at what point most would have withdrawn. We can only speculate, but we might expect participants to refuse to continue very early on in the experiment.

Studying social influence presents many ethical dilemmas to social psychologists and, these days, all experiments must conform to modern codes of ethics and conduct for research. This may have the consequence that it is simply not possible to conduct certain kinds of studies now.

Methodological issues

The main methodological issues arising from experimental research in social influence that is conducted in a laboratory setting are:

● ecological validity;

- demand characteristics;

- participants.

Ecological validity This is to do with the extent to which the laboratory experiment can be said to be a clear reflection of everyday life or 'mundane realism'. Critics have argued that judging the length of a line and giving electric shocks are not a reflection of our activities in everyday life. Also, such artificial tasks do not relate to how we conform and obey on a daily basis. The Asch and Milgram experiments are said to lack ecological validity, and this makes it difficult to generalise the findings to conformity and obedience in the real world. In an attempt to overcome this criticism, psychologists have conducted field experiments. For example, Bickman (1974) conducted a field experiment on the streets of New York, where people walking along the street were asked to pick up some litter. In one condition, the person making the request was dressed in military uniform, and in another condition the person was dressed casually. Obedience was highest (around 80 per cent) when passers-by had the request made by the experimenter dressed in a uniform.

Most laboratory experiments in social influence suffer from lack of ecological validity. Field experiments and naturalistic observation may help overcome this criticism if findings using these methods support the laboratory findings. Milgram argued that obedience to authority is the same, regardless of the setting or the task.

Demand characteristics These are where participants in an experiment try to guess what the experiment is about: as a result, they may behave in ways to try to please the experimenter. People are not passive in an experiment. In the Asch and Milgram studies, the participants were not told the true purpose of the experiment in either case, and may not have believed the 'cover story' they were given. As a consequence, the participants may have thought that the experimenter wanted them to agree with others (Asch) or give shocks up to the highest level (Milgram). Participants in the Milgram studies may well have thought that no real harm could come to the learner and continued to obey on the basis of that belief.

Participants Milgram obtained his participants through placing an advertisement in a local newspaper. The participants were volunteers who thought they were taking part in a study on learning. If Milgram had advertised for volunteers to take part in a study on obedience he may have recruited a very different type of person. It is difficult to tell, but volunteers recruited by public advertisement are not representative of the population as a whole: they are self-selecting. The problem then is that it may not be possible to generalise findings from research conducted using volunteers to the population as a whole.

Studying social influence, as we have seen, requires psychologists to take into account and address a range of ethical and methodological issues. There is no right answer, but all research conducted today must conform to an ethical code of conduct.

How Psychology Works

An ethical study of conformity

Studies of conformity using real stooges are no longer thought to be ethical. However, using bogus stooge scores is possible as long as the participants are thoroughly debriefed afterwards.

Some kind of object or stimulus will be shown to people and they will then be asked a question about the object or stimulus. For example:

- People look at a photograph of a person and then estimate their age.
- People view a fashion item, like a handbag, and then estimate its cost.
- People read a job description and then estimate the likely salary.
- People see a photo from a holiday brochure and then estimate the midday August temperature.

- There will be two conditions. In one condition, people are simply shown the stimulus and asked to write their estimate down in a space provided. In the other condition, people are shown the stimulus and asked to write their answer down in a space, apparently below answers that other people have already given. These will be a set of 6/7 bogus estimates, written in different handwriting and different ink.
- Each response sheet in the bogus condition must have the same set of estimates. You will need to decide what they should be. Ideally they should all be close to each other and either quite high or quite low.
- Prepare a suitable debrief, then try your materials out with a few people.
- Calculate the mean and median estimates and the standard deviation for each condition.
- Show these statistics in a table with title and labels.
- Write a verbal summary of your findings, referring to the averages and the standard deviations. Say whether the independent variable has affected the dependent variable, and how.

How Psychology Works

A study of social facilitation

Studies of social facilitation show how performance at a very simple task can be enhanced by the presence of other people, or if other people are carrying out the same activity nearby. Various tasks are suitable:

> In the classroom: You could use a simple manual task that is quick to perform and would yield some easily quantifiable data. Good examples would be a pencil maze or a dot-to-dot. Using this type of task, you could record the time taken to complete the task as quickly as possible, without making any errors.
>
> At the gym or sports field: If you have access to sports or gym facilities, you might like to compare distances rowed on a rowing machine in solitary and co-acting/audience conditions, within a specified time.

- Identify a suitable task.
- Prepare a set of materials, including a record sheet on which to record data for each participant.
- Prepare a set of standardised instructions and a debrief. Remember that the debrief should explain the purpose of the study, but should not include technical language that ordinary people would not be able to understand.
- Decide whether this study should be a repeated measures (same people in each condition) or an independent groups design (different people in each condition).
- Write a justification for the type of design you have chosen. The justification should refer specifically to this study of social facilitation.
- Identify two extraneous variables that might affect the outcome of this study.
- Explain whether your chosen task and design have high ecological validity.

Further reading

Introductory texts
Baron, R.A., Byrne, D. and Branscombe, N.R. (2006) *Social Psychology*, 11th edn, London: Allyn & Bacon.
Smith, E.R. and Mackie, D.M. (2007), *Social Psychology*, 3rd edn, Hove: Psychology Press.
Vaughan, G.M. and Hogg, M.A. (2004) *Social Psychology*, London: Prentice Hall.
Specialist sources
Guerin, B. (1993) *Social Facilitation*, Cambridge: Cambridge University Press.
Milgram, S. (1974) *Obedience to Authority*, New York: Harper and Row.
Pennington, D.C. (2002) *The Social Psychology of Behaviour in Small Groups*, London: Psychology Press.
Smith, P. B. and Harriss Bond, M. (1998) *Social Psychology Across Cultures*, 2nd edn, London: Prentice Hall.

Social cognition

6.1 Impression formation

We constantly form impressions of people we meet for the first time, and we revise those first impressions on further acquaintance with a person. Of course, other people are doing the same to us: forming first impressions and changing them as a result of getting to know us better. It is often said that first impressions are very important and may be long-lasting, but despite the fact that they may have important consequences, they are often based on very little information about a

Figure 6.1. First impressions matter!

person. For example, a person may be interviewed for a job and the interview lasts for just 30 minutes. Sometimes on the basis of this very brief interaction the person may be offered a job. While this may work well when a good decision has been made, at other times it may turn out that the person is really not suited to the job and may have to leave or have their employment terminated.

Imagine yourself in an interview situation and think about what you would be trying to do. Like most people, you would probably be trying to manage the impression that you are giving to the interviewer. This is called **impression management** (Sharp and Getz 1996). Psychologists have shown that people who actively manage the impression they make on others do gain advantages (Wayne and Liden 1995). Research has shown that two general tactics are used in impression management: self-enhancement and other-enhancement. Self-enhancement is where people try to make themselves look good to others by dressing well, describing themselves in a very positive way and generally enhancing their appeal to others. Other-enhancement is where people try to make themselves be liked by making others feel good. Tactics such as flattery, showing a high degree of interest in the other person and asking for their advice (Byrne 1992) have all been shown to be effective. Caution is needed in terms of how far to take other-enhancement. Vonk (1998) found that if other-enhancement is taken too far it can have the opposite effect to that desired. Vonk called this the **slime effect**, claiming that this results in a negative impression: the opposite of what the individual is trying to achieve by impression management.

The impressions we form of other people start with cues that come before any social interaction takes place. These initial cues may come from what we see, hear and smell. For example, physical appearance, both in terms of how we look physically and how we dress, is very important. People try to manage the impression they make by their dress and their looks, and may go to extremes to create a good impression. This may be done, for example, by 'nip-and-tuck' cosmetic surgery, breast enhancement for women and muscle building for men. Also of importance is what other people may tell you about the person before you have had a chance to meet them. If your friend informs you that the person you are about to meet is difficult and irritable, this very short description may well influence and bias the impression you form of the person: the impression may be a negative one because of this information. Figure 6.2 summarises the main factors that influence impression formation before social interaction takes place.

Factor	Positive impression	Negative impression
Eye contact	Looks at person while being spoken to	Avoids eye contact while speaking and listening
Body orientation	Orients body towards person	Orients body away from person
Facial expression	Smiles and laughs at appropriate times	Does not smile or laugh at appropriate times
Physical appearance	Attractive to the other person	Not attractive to the other person
Familiarity	People we encounter every day	People we encounter rarely or infrequently
Behaviour	Donates to a charity or gives time to a voluntary cause	Only does things for themselves

Figure 6.2. Some important factors in impression formation and when positive and negative impressions are formed.

When social interaction takes place, what a person says and their non-verbal communication play important roles in impression formation. Whether or not a person looks you in the eye or avoids eye contact when you are speaking, along with their general facial expression, will affect the impression you form of that person. Another non-verbal cue is body orientation: does the person orient their body towards you or away from you, for example? If it is the latter, you may form a negative impression of the other person. The behaviours of the person are important here. For example, you are likely to form a positive impression if you know that a person does voluntary work for a good cause. Gilbert (1998) states that, after the initial cues, such as those identified in Figure 6.2, the actual behaviours of a person are the most influential in impression formation.

From this general consideration of how we form impressions of other people, and how we try to manage the impressions others form of us, we will now consider key factors affecting impression formation. These are social schemas, primacy and recency effects, central traits and stereotyping.

6.1.1 Social schemas

A social schema is a mental framework for representing information about oneself, other people, and specific and common social situations and events (Fiske and Taylor 1991). For example, a common social schema is associated with eating out at a restaurant. This schema includes:

- arriving at the restaurant and being shown to your table (assuming you have booked in advance);

- being presented with the menu and wine list, then ordering;

- eating your meal with friends and chatting;

- asking for the bill, paying and leaving the restaurant.

Social schemas are organised collections of information based on past experience and stored in memory. Many social schemas are formed in childhood and developed to become more complex as a result of experience and growing up. Social schemas help with encoding new information and guide us towards what requires attention. Often information consistent with a social schema is remembered, and inconsistent information is ignored or paid little attention.

Social psychologists have identified four main types of social schemas that are involved in impression formation (Pennington et al. 1999). These are as follows:

- Self schemas are generalisations about the self based on past experience.

- Person schemas are mental representations about the personality, traits and motives of other people.

- Role schemas are knowledge that people have about social norms and expected behaviours of individuals who hold specific positions in society.

- Event schemas are mental frameworks that relate to specific social situations. (The restaurant example given above is an event schema.)

The **self schema** organises and guides how information about the self is processed. Self schemas include a person's self-concept, self-image and level of self-esteem. This schema also represents those traits and aspects of personality which we regard as best describing what kind of person we are. Self schemas can play an important role in impression management (which we considered earlier in this section). Another aspect of the self schema is the idea of **possible selves** (Markus and Nurius 1986). This recognises the fact that we have ambitions for the future, for example, in terms of career, happiness and relationships.

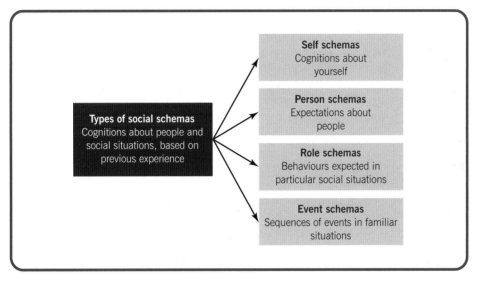

Figure 6.3. Four types of social schemas.

The **person schema** consists of the knowledge we have of other people. For example, the person schema for your best friend will be built from the interactions and experiences that you have shared. You are most likely to have a very positive person schema for your best friend. Now think of a person you do not like. This may be based on previous negative experiences that you have had with this person. Your person schema here is likely to be negative. If you were asked by a friend who had not met this person before what they were like, you are going to say negative things. Hence, person schemas used in this way may have a strong influence on others' impression formation.

The **role schema** is a set of behaviours that we expect of a person in a specific social situation (Fiske and Taylor 1991). We each have a large number of role schemas. For example, the roles of husband/wife, son/daughter, teacher, policeman, best friend and shop assistant. For each of these roles we have expectations about how people will behave towards us. Role schemas may guide how people behave in a given role. They also influence impression formation. This is because knowing the role (or roles) that a person has will lead us to expect the person to behave in certain ways. We also attach values to roles, for example we expect our teacher to uphold the laws and rules of society and to behave in sensible ways. Generally, knowing that a person is a teacher will bring into play the associated role schema and will usually result in a favourable impression being formed.

Event schemas are mental representations of common social events that we have experienced, seen in films, read about, and so on. Most people will have event schemas for restaurants, interviews, behaviour at college, parties, going to a nightclub, playing a game with friends, a mobile phone conversation, and many more. Event schemas provide people with expectations of the sequence of events most likely to occur in a specific social situation. Event schemas also guide our behaviour, for example what to wear at a wedding.

Social schemas play a key role in impression formation. Such schemas, as we have described above, may cause us to form an impression of a person before we have even seen or met them. Social schemas may also guide us to expect a person to behave in a certain way, hold certain attitudes and beliefs, and have certain personality characteristics. Social schemas may also help to explain why first impressions can be both lasting and hard to change. This is because our actual experience of a person is strongly influenced by the social schemas that we think apply to that person.

6.1.2 Primacy and recency effects

Impressions are often made on the basis of little information. The order in which information is presented may have an influence on the impression formed. The **primacy effect** is where information presented first has the strongest influence on the impression formed. The **recency effect** is where information presented last has the greatest influence on the impression formed. Both have been shown to operate in the process of impression formation.

Study

Aim Asch (1946) conducted a study to discover whether the order of information given about a person influenced the impression formed of the person.

Method Asch gave participants one of two lists of adjectives describing a person. Each list contained the same adjectives, but in a different order:
- List 1: intelligent, industrious, impulsive, critical, stubborn, envious.
- List 2: envious, stubborn, critical, impulsive, industrious, intelligent.

Participants were then asked to rate the person on another list of adjectives, including honest, sociable, humorous, reliable and happy.

Results Asch found that participants who had been given List 1 rated the person more positively than participants given List 2. That is, those given List 1 rated the person as more honest, sociable, humorous, reliable and happy than those given List 2.

Conclusion The order in which adjectives describing a person appear is important in influencing impression formation. People given a description where positive characteristics are listed first form a more positive impression than when negative characteristics are listed first. This demonstrates the **primacy effect**.

Evaluation

The Asch study described above has been criticised for lacking ecological validity. This means that the experiment does not represent how people actually receive information about another person and then go on to form an impression of that person. It is artificial in the sense that this is all the information participants were given about the person's characteristics. In real life, you are likely to know much more about a person when forming an impression. However, the Asch experiment does demonstrate how first impressions may be formed, and the importance of the very first impression that is made. For example, when you first walk into an interview and sit down, ready to be asked questions, the interviewer will already have formed a first impression of you from your dress and facial expression when saying hello. The primacy effect may result in a long-lasting impression, because people may look for information to confirm the first impression, and ignore subsequent information inconsistent with that impression.

Recency effects occur when information presented last has the greatest influence on the impression formed. Recency effects are less common than primacy effects (Jones and Goethals 1972). Recency effects are more likely to occur when there is a time delay between two sets of information about a person. This was demonstrated in an experiment by Luchins (1957).

Study

Aim Luchins (1957) conducted a study to show that recency effects occur when there is a time delay between two pieces of information about a person being read.

Method Participants were given two paragraphs describing a person called Jim. One paragraph described Jim as extrovert, outgoing and someone who enjoyed talking to people. The other paragraph described Jim as introvert, preferring to be alone and not wanting to talk to people.

Participants in one condition read the extrovert paragraph first, followed by the introvert paragraph after a delay of 15 minutes, during which they read a magazine. Participants in another condition read the introvert paragraph first, with the same time delay and magazine to read before reading the extrovert paragraph.

Results Luchins found that participants were more influenced by the second paragraph when stating whether they would like to talk to Jim and if they thought they would like him. For example, participants who read the introvert paragraph last said they would not want to talk to Jim and that they would not like him.

Conclusion Recency effects are more likely to occur when two sets of information are read with a time interval between them, and the time interval is used on a different or 'distracter' task, such as reading a magazine.

Luchins (1957) also included a condition in this experiment where there was no time gap or distracter task between participants reading the two paragraphs. In this condition he found a primacy effect. Other conditions likely to lead to a primacy effect in impression formation include when a person is tired, where there is little interest in the other person and when a large amount of information about a person is provided. Generally, primacy effects are more common, and are therefore more important in forming first impressions of a person.

6.1.3 Central traits

If you look back to the Asch (1946) study described above, the importance of the order of the adjectives Asch used may also be to do with the representation of central traits described by these adjectives. **Central traits** are descriptions of personality which have a strong and disproportionate influence in impression formation. **Peripheral traits** are those descriptions of personality which have little or no influence on the formation of impressions.

Study

Aim Asch (1946) devised an experiment to show that some traits are more central and important in impression formation than other traits.

Method Participants were given one of two lists of adjectives describing a person, and then asked to rate the person on characteristics such as generous, happy, good-natured and humane.
- List 1: intelligent, skilful, industrious, warm, determined, practical, cautious.

- List 2: intelligent, skilful, industrious, cold, determined, practical, cautious.

The only difference between List 1 and List 2 is the words *warm* and *cold*.

Results Asch found that the person was rated more positively (happy, generous, good-natured, and so on) by participants given List 1 than by those given List 2.

Conclusion The traits of warm and cold are central traits and have a strong influence on impression formation.

Asch (1946) included another condition in this experiment in which the words *polite* and *blunt* were used instead of *cold* and *warm*. Here Asch found no difference in the way in which participants formed impressions of the person. Hence Asch said that adjectives such as *polite* and *blunt* are peripheral traits and have little influence on impression formation.

Evaluation

- Other traits that have been shown to be central are those of extroversion and introversion. This may explain why, in the Luchins (1957) experiment described above, the extrovert and introvert paragraphs influenced the impression which participants formed of Jim. It may also explain the fact that both primacy and recency effects occur, depending on conditions, with these two traits.
- Central traits may also have such a strong effect on impression formation because they are central to the person schema that we considered earlier.
- Asch's experiments on central traits have been replicated in more natural settings. For example, Kelley (1950) introduced students to a guest speaker by describing him with either List 1 (warm) or List 2 (cold) adjectives. After the lecture, students were asked to rate the speaker, and similar results were found to those of the classic Asch study.

6.1.4 Stereotypes

Stereotypes may be defined as 'beliefs that all members of specific social groups share certain traits or characteristics' (Baron et al. 2006). Stereotypes are mental representations that influence the impression we form of a person when we know that the person belongs to a specific social group. Stereotypes extend beyond social groups to include groups based on gender (male and female) and disabled people. Stereotypes help an individual to deal with a potentially vast amount of social information about a person or group of persons. To this extent, stereotypes help to simplify our social world and make it more manageable, controllable and predictable. However, this comes at a price in that stereotypes often oversimplify and misrepresent a person. Stereotypes are seen as a prime factor of many of the disagreeable and unfair aspects of the social world in which we live. For example, stereotypes may result in racist, sexist or homophobic attitudes, which may lead to prejudice and discrimination.

Figure 6.4. What stereotype does this picture produce for you?

Hogg and Vaughan (2002) summarise the main findings from over fifty years of research by social psychologists as follows:

● Stereotypes are quick to form and difficult to change.

● People show a general tendency to rapidly stereotype others on the basis of a small number of traits or characteristics.

● Many stereotypes are formed in childhood and early adolescence, when the young person has very little experience of people or other social groups.

● Stereotypes become more strongly held and more openly expressed when conflict and tension exist or develop between two or more social groups.

● Stereotypes are often associated with political, social or economic changes.

● Stereotypes oversimplify people and groups of people, but have a degree of truth in them.

● Stereotypes overestimate differences between groups and underestimate differences of individuals within a specific social group.

Psychological research has found that people hold clear stereotypes about males and females, as the classic study on sex stereotypes outlined below demonstrates.

Study

Aim Broverman et al. (1972) conducted a study to demonstrate that males and females hold clear stereotypes about their own and the opposite sex.

Method Female and male students were asked to list the ways in which they thought men and women differed. From this, the researchers constructed a list of the most commonly used adjectives to describe men and women. This list was then given to adults between the ages of 17 and 60 years, who were asked to rate how typical and desirable each trait was for men and for women. Some of the adjectives used were: independent, aggressive, ambitious, passive, emotional, talkative, submissive, adventurous, easily influenced.

Results Adult males and females agreed on gender stereotypes. Men were stereotyped as more independent, aggressive and ambitious; women as more passive, emotional and talkative.

Conclusions Gender stereotypes are clear and consistent for men and women. It was also found that the stereotypes associated with males were rated as more socially desirable than those associated with females.

Broverman et al. (1972) generally found that men were seen as more confident and stronger than women, and women as more expressive and weaker than men. More recent research has demonstrated that these stereotypes have persisted over time (Berger and Williams 1991).

Stereotypes are an important influence on impression formation. This is because when we first meet a person, we may well assign them to a social group with which a number of stereotypes are associated. Hence, even before we have spent time finding out what a person is like by talking to them and finding out more about them, we have formed a first impression from our pre-existing stereotype.

Evaluation

- Stereotypes commonly exist for all people. They have both positive and negative aspects. On the negative side, a stereotype may strongly determine impression formation even before we have met a person. On the positive side, they do help us to make sense of the complicated social world in which we live.
- Stereotypes may be seen as being made up of the four social schemas that we considered earlier in this chapter. The self, person, role and event schemas can all be seen to be involved in stereotypes.

6.2 Attribution

The main concern of the attribution approach in social psychology relates to how we attribute or perceive causes of our own and other people's behaviour. We want to know not only *what* people do (how they actually behave), but also *why* they behave in such a way. Consider, for example, that you have just taken a mock psychology examination and have been told that you did not do very well. How might you explain the cause or causes of your poor performance? You have been revising hard for the examination for the past two weeks. One attribution that you might make is that the examination questions were very hard; another might be that they were unfair. Additionally, you might attribute poor performance to your lack of interest in the subject of psychology. Even though you spent a lot of time revising, you might admit that not much 'went in', and therefore that you were not able to answer the questions in the examination very well. We will return to this example shortly.

Heider (1958) was the first social psychologist to be interested in how people attribute causes to their own and other people's behaviour. He said that the main reason people attribute causes to behaviour is to help them predict and control their social world. Baron et al. (2006) define attribution as follows: 'The process through which we seek to identify the causes of others' behaviour and so gain knowledge of their stable traits and dispositions.' Notice that, with this definition, Heider's idea of attribution helping people to predict and control their social world is seen as being related to knowing the traits and dispositions of people. In short, what is being claimed is that knowing the personality traits of a person will help us to predict how they will behave in a social situation. Three principles underpin the concept of attribution in social psychology:

1 People have a desire and need to attribute causes to behaviour.

2 People search for information about the person and the social situation in order to attribute causes to behaviour.

3 People act like **naive scientists** (adopting a scientific-like approach) when trying to attribute causes to behaviour.

The attribution approach in social cognition, as we shall see, has investigated biases and errors that people commonly make when attributing causes to both their own and other people's behaviour.

Evaluation

We have said that people want to attribute causes to all behaviour. While this may generally be true, we do not spend all our time thinking about the causes of behaviour. Weiner (1985) identified two main types of behaviour that trigger the need to attribute causes. These are when something surprising or unexpected happens, and when a person fails to achieve a desired outcome. An illustration of the latter is our example of doing poorly in an examination.

6.2.1 Dispositional and situational attributions

Think back to our example of taking a psychology examination and getting a poor mark. One causal attribution we considered was that, while you had revised, you had not assimilated much of the information because you are not interested in psychology. This is a causal attribution about yourself and certain aspects of your personality. This type of attribution is called a **dispositional attribution** because it is to do with the individual's disposition, likes and dislikes, and personality traits. Consider this in another way: suppose that it was a classmate who had done poorly in the examination and you attributed this to that person being lazy. Again, this is a dispositional attribution because you are attributing the cause to a personality trait – in this case, laziness.

We also considered attributing the cause of your performance to either an unfair examination or to the questions being very hard. This type of causal attribution is not to do with the person, but is due to something in the outside world. Such an attribution is called a **situational attribution**. To understand this better, let's take another example. Imagine you meet someone who is unemployed. You learn that the person worked in the car industry in the Midlands and that thousands of people were made redundant when the car production plants were shut down. Are you likely to make a dispositional or situational attribution here? It is most likely that you would attribute the cause of unemployment to no jobs being available, and hence you would be making a situational attribution.

Another way in which dispositional and situational attributions are described is by calling them **internal** (dispositional) or **external** (situational) attributions. Internal refers to the individual's personality, and external refers to something outside the person (the social situation).

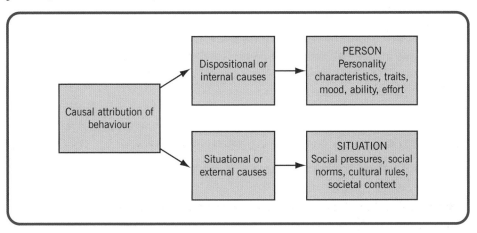

Figure 6.5. Internal and external causes in the attribution of behaviour.

6.2.2 Attributional biases

In classifying people as naive scientists, theory and research in attribution characterised people making causal attributions as operating in a rational and logical way.

Such a characterisation would mean that people would not be subject to any errors or biases when making attributions. Social psychological research has found that people are indeed subject to attributional biases. The three most important and well-evidenced by empirical research are:

● the fundamental attribution error;

● the actor–observer effect;

● the self-serving bias.

The fundamental attribution error

The fundamental attribution error is the tendency people show to overestimate the importance of dispositions, and to underestimate the importance of situational factors when attributing causes to another person's behaviour. Put another way, people too readily make internal attributions and ignore the powerful influence of external (social situation) factors. This was demonstrated in a classic experiment by Ross et al. (1977).

Study

Aim Ross et al. (1977) conducted a study to show that people make dispositional or internal attributions when it is not appropriate to do so.

Method Participants were assigned to the role of either questioner or answerer in an experiment based on a general knowledge quiz game. Participants assigned to the role of questioner were asked to make up their own general knowledge questions. These questions were then put to the participant assigned to the role of answerer. The answerer is at a strong disadvantage here. Another group of participants observed the quiz game. When the quiz was over, the observer participants were asked to rate the general knowledge of both the questioners and the answerers. The questioners and answerers were also asked to rate each other's general knowledge.

Results It was found that both the answerers and the observers rated the questioners as having superior general knowledge to the answerers. The observers rated the general knowledge ability of the questioners higher than the ratings assigned by the answerers.

Conclusion These findings provide evidence for the fundamental attribution error. This is because both the observers and the answerers ignored the situational factor – this being the obvious advantage that the questioners had by being allowed to make up questions from their own general knowledge, which is highly likely to be different to that of the answerers.

The fundamental attribution error is shown in many different aspects of our lives. For example, Barjonet (1980) found evidence that people attribute car accidents to driver error and ignore situational factors such as the condition of the road or general driving conditions. Gilbert and Malone (1995) offer three main reasons why people make the fundamental attribution error:

- People do not pay sufficient attention to the situation and focus too much on the person.

- People assume that what a person says and does is always consistent with their attitudes and personality traits.

- People make snap or spontaneous causal attributions much of the time, and do not adjust such attributions on getting further information.

The actor–observer effect

The fundamental attribution error only applies when one person is making attributions about the behaviour of another person. Social psychologists have found that when a person is making attributions about their own behaviour, there is a strong tendency to focus on and overemphasise situational or external factors. In contrast, when making attributions about another person, dispositional or internal causes are overemphasised. This difference in causal attribution has been called the actor–observer effect. Actors – or the self – tend to make situational attributions about their own behaviour. Observers tend to make dispositional or internal attributions about the behaviour of other people. Baron et al. (2006) define the actor–observer effect as follows: 'The tendency to attribute our own behaviour to mainly external (situational) causes but the behaviour of others to mainly internal (dispositional) causes.'

Study

Aim Nisbett et al. (1972) conducted a series of experiments to demonstrate the actor–observer effect and to show that it occurred in a wide range of situations.

Method In one experiment, students studying psychology at university were asked why they had chosen to study the subject, and why they thought their colleagues had chosen to study it.

Results Students attributed causes to themselves for studying psychology as to do with the topics covered in the course, the quality of the university and the sports facilities available – all situational or external causes. By contrast, attributions to their classmates were to do with being interested in people and career prospects as a psychologist – all dispositional or internal causes.

Conclusion The actor–observer effect is commonplace and occurs in a wide range of circumstances.

Figure 6.6. Did do he do it intentionally or did the situation cause the criminal behaviour?

Nisbett et al. (1972) offered two main explanations why causal attributions were different for the actor (self-attributions) and the observer (other-attributions):

- The perceptual focus of the actor (self) is much more on situational factors than his or her dispositions. In contrast, the perceptual focus of the observer is clearly more on the person than the situation in which the person is behaving.

- There are important informational differences. The actor (self) has extensive information about how they have behaved in the past and the kind of person they are. In contrast, the observer has limited knowledge of the person being observed and knows little about how the person has behaved in similar situations. This results in a focus on the dispositions of the person.

Study

Aim Storms (1973) conducted a study to demonstrate that the actor–observer effect could be reversed by changing the focus of attention of the person making causal attributions.

Method Participants were arranged in 'conversing' pairs and asked to engage in conversation. Another group of participants were put in 'observing' pairs and were assigned to the conversing pairs. Each observing participant was assigned to watch one of the conversing pair in conversation. Following this, half of the conversing participants were shown a videotape of themselves. The observer who had watched this conversing participant was also shown the same videotape. This was called the **same orientation condition**. In the **opposite orientation condition**, the observers were shown a videotape of the non-assigned conversing participant from their conversing pair.

Results Participants were asked to rate the extent to which friendliness, nervousness and dominance were due to the person or the situation. They found that participants in the same orientation condition showed the traditional actor–observer effect. By contrast, participants in the opposite orientation condition gave more dispositional attributions to the actor and more situational attributions to the observer – a reversal.

Conclusion The actor–observer effect can be reversed if the actor (self) is forced to focus on dispositional factors and the observer is forced to focus on situational factors that another person is in.

Evaluation

Overall, considerable evidence from experiments shows the actor–observer effect to be present and consistent in many different circumstances and conditions. Reversing the orientation of the person making causal attributions can reverse the effect. It has also been found that people tend to make more dispositional attributions for socially desirable behaviour, regardless of whether the person is making an attribution about self or other (Taylor and Koivumaki 1976).

The self-serving bias

The self-serving bias is where a person attributes causes to their own behaviour which results in self-enhancement of their abilities and/or self-esteem. Fiske and Taylor (1991) characterise the self-serving bias as 'the tendency to take credit for success and deny responsibility for failure'. Generally, research has shown stronger support for people taking credit for success than for people not accepting responsibility for failure.

Two main explanations have been offered for the self-serving bias. The first is a motivational explanation, based on the idea that people need to protect themselves from harm and present themselves to others in a positive way. Taking credit for success and blaming others for failure achieves this. Second is a cognitive explanation, based on expectations that people have. You expect to succeed at tasks you set yourself and believe that you can be successful in many different ways. People like to think that success is under their own control and not a product of luck or what others may do for them.

The self-serving bias has been shown to vary across different cultures. For example, Oettingen (1995) found that cultures which value collective or group outcomes show the bias less than cultures which value individual success.

Evaluation

- We have looked at three attributional errors that people commonly make when attributing causes to their own or other people's behaviour. This needs to be considered in the context that, generally, people make accurate and appropriate causal attributions most of the time. In the main, people do make accurate dispositional and situational attributions.
- The internal–external (dispositional–situational) distinction is essential to understanding biases and error in attribution. However, the distinction

may not always be that clear-cut. Consider, for example, why someone would want to buy a house in a particular location. The person might say they bought the house because it is in a secluded location (external attribution), or they might say they bought the house because they need to have privacy (internal attribution). Often, an external attribution (secluded location of the house) reflects an internal attribution (need for privacy). So internal (dispositional) and external (situational) may be two sides of the same coin.

6.3 Attitudes

An attitude cannot be seen or measured directly. This is in comparison to many phenomena in the sciences of biology and chemistry. As a consequence, social psychologists have developed many different ways of understanding attitudes. The term is used to represent quite complex mental processes. Attitudes are important in social psychology. In virtually all aspects of our social lives, we continually seek to discover other people's attitudes, tell others of our views, and try to change other people's opinions. Attitudes are also regarded as an important influence on our behaviour. Petty and Cacioppo (1986) define attitudes as: 'general evaluations people make about themselves, others, objects or issues', and they go on to say: 'attitudes have a past, present and future; they were developed from past experience, they guide our current behaviour, and can direct our development in the future'.

This definition is helpful because it draws our attention to the generally held view that attitudes have a strong influence on how we behave. Also, using the term 'general evaluations' indicates that attitudes have both a cognitive and an emotional or affective component. The word 'evaluative' further indicates that people hold positive, negative and neutral attitudes to different things.

In what follows we will look at two different approaches to understanding attitudes: the **structural** approach and the **functional** approach. Both approaches are concerned with the link between attitudes and behaviour, and with how attitudes may be changed.

6.3.1 The structure of attitudes

The structural approach (Katz 1960) to understanding attitudes states that attitudes are an evaluation (positive or negative) of an attitude object (person or issue). An attitude object is anything that we hold an attitude about, and can range from attitudes about people to attitudes about laws or government policies. For example, it would be expected that you hold a positive attitude towards your best friend; conversely, you might hold a negative attitude towards laws allowing abortion in the UK. You may also hold neutral attitudes; this may be the case particularly if you do not have much information about an attitude object.

> The structural approach breaks attitudes down into three components:
> - cognitive – which is to do with our thoughts;
> - affective – which is to do with our feelings or emotions;
> - behavioural – which is to do with our behaviour.

The **cognitive** component is to do with what you know about an attitude object. This may include facts, beliefs and other information. These are our thoughts about an attitude object and are best seen 'cold', without any feelings attached. For example, you may believe that smoking causes lung cancer because you have read articles and watched scientific programmes about the topic on television.

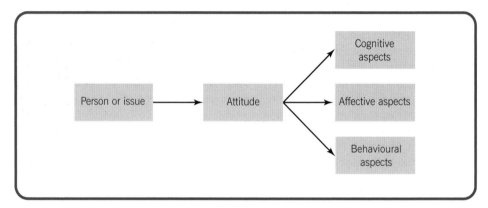

Figure 6.7. The structural approach to attitudes.

The **affective** component is to do with feelings, emotions and gut reactions to something. Seeing somebody you do not like or being in a noisy restaurant when you have gone out for a quiet time will arouse strong negative feelings for you. In the latter case, this may mean that you develop a negative attitude about the restaurant and will not go there again.

The **behavioural** component concerns what you know about how you have behaved in the past towards an attitude object. It also includes how you think you would behave or intend to behave in the future. In a sense, the behavioural component is cognitive in that it is referring to what you can remember about how you have behaved in the past, and the intentions you have for how you will behave in the future.

According to the structural approach, a person's attitude is a combination of these three components. This approach also implies the following:

- There is a high degree of consistency between the three components. For example, suppose that you hold a negative attitude towards racial discrimination. The structural approach would assume that you think that all people are equal, that you are upset when you read about a case of racial discrimination, and that you have behaved towards others from a different ethic group to your own in a fair way.

- Attitudes are relatively enduring and do not change moment to moment. For example, if a friend of yours holds a positive attitude to the prime minister, you would not expect this attitude to change the next day. Attitudes can change, but it is often gradually rather than suddenly.

Edwards (1990) conducted research to show that there may not always be a high degree of consistency between the three components. At times, the affective or emotional component can dominate the other two (Edwards and von Hippel 1995). The heart, so it is said, often dominates the mind. There may be good reason why emotions take pole position. First, when we have a gut reaction to someone we have not met before, this can often result in a negative attitude. This negative attitude is formed in the absence of any knowledge about the person and without having interacted (behaviour) with them. Second, strong emotions can quite literally overwhelm thoughts and stop us retrieving memories about an attitude object. Third, you may actually experience pain or become unwell because of very loud noise, for example. Again, your emotional reaction will dominate your senses.

Figure 6.8. What attitude does a person who smokes have to smoking?

Attitudes may also be **ambivalent**. By this we mean that an attitude towards an object might represent a mixture of both positive and negative aspects, such that we are not really sure what attitude we hold. For example, a person who smokes cigarettes may know (cognitive component) that smoking damages a person's health. At the same time, this person may enjoy (affective component) smoking. In terms of behaviour, the person will know that he or she has smoked for the past ten years. If you ask a person what their attitude to smoking is, they may have difficulty giving a simple positive or negative indication of their attitude because of these inconsistencies between the three components.

Evaluation

- The structural approach to attitudes is often called the **three-component model**. Psychologists have questioned whether three components are needed to understand attitudes. Fishbein and Ajzen (1975) proposed a one-component or one-dimensional model. Here, the evaluation, from positive to negative, is all that is needed (i.e. the affective component).

- A **two-component model** has also been put forward (Petty and Cacioppo 1986). Here, the two components are a predisposition to behave and an evaluation. An attitude is seen as a 'mental readiness' to behave in a positive or negative way to an attitude object.

The structural approach assumes that there is a strong link between the attitude a person holds and how they actually behave. This is the principle of **consistency** between attitudes and behaviour. However, it is easy to think of numerous examples where people behave in inconsistent ways. For example, suppose that the government were to hold a referendum on whether Britain should adopt the euro as common currency. You find out that your friend voted for the euro. From this, you might assume that your friend has a positive attitude to a common European currency and wants greater integration for Britain in Europe. But there are other reasons why your friend might have voted in this way which are not related to their attitude. For example, they might want to vote the same way as their parents, or they might support the government in power no matter what. It is not always easy or obvious to establish a consistent link between an attitude and a person's behaviour.

Study

Aim La Piere (1934) devised a study aimed at investigating differences between what people say they will do and what they actually do in a given situation.

Method La Piere travelled round America with a Chinese couple and recorded how they were treated at hotels and restaurants. On only one occasion were they treated inhospitably. Six months later, La Piere sent a letter to all the places he had visited, asking them if they would accept Chinese clientele.

Results Over 90 per cent of the replies were negative: 92 per cent of restaurants and 90 per cent of hotels said that they would refuse Chinese clientele.

Conclusion The study demonstrated an enormous difference between what people say they would do and what they actually do.

The La Piere study is a classic study in social psychology. The findings question the extent to which the structural approach can provide a full enough understanding of attitudes.

6.3.2 The function of attitudes

The structural approach only considers the different mental structures that help us to understand attitudes. The **functional** approach attempts to understand and explain what functions or purpose attitudes serve for the individual. Katz (1960) proposed that attitudes generally serve the function of promoting the wellbeing of an individual. This is achieved by attitudes serving five different functions, as follows:

- **Adaptive function:** this concerns the extent to which attitudes help a person achieve a desired goal and avoid something that is undesirable. This function is hedonistic in that it serves to increase pleasure or satisfaction and avoid unpleasant situations or punishment.

- **Self-expressive function:** this is concerned with letting other people know our opinions, attitudes and views. It represents the fact that we are humans who are essentially social creatures, who need to communicate with each other.

- **Ego-defensive function:** this protects the individual from themselves or from other people. Effectively, it serves to maintain and protect a person's self-esteem and promote a positive self-image to others. As its name implies, this function is rooted in Freudian psychoanalytic theory.

- **Knowledge function:** this helps us to structure and organise our social world and to think that the world (especially in terms of other people) is a predictable place in which to live.

- **Social adjustment function:** this helps a person to manage social situations by holding or communicating attitudes that impress other people and maintain harmony in a social group.

The basic idea behind the functional approach is that attitudes help us to mediate between our own inner needs (self-expression, need for high self-esteem) and the external social world (social information).

The adaptive function of attitudes helps an individual to achieve the greatest rewards and to minimise punishment or failure to realise desired outcomes. Clary et al. (1994) showed that people who hold a positive attitude to voluntary work and wish to help those in society who are less well-off may hold the positive attitude because other people will value it. In this situation the person genuinely holds a positive attitude to voluntary work, and the function of the attitude is primarily an adaptive one. In a sense, the attitude is held because other people, and society in general, value and reward such an attitude. Another way to look at this is that the adaptive function will help people to manage and determine the impression other people have of them. The adaptive function helps a person to master and gain control over their social environment.

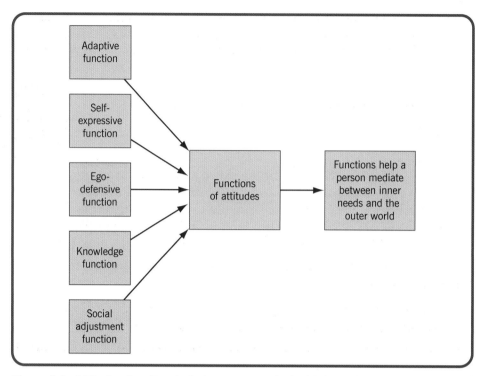

Figure 6.9. Attitudes function to help a person deal with inner needs and the outside world.

The self-expressive function is most important for expressing to other people deeply held beliefs and attitudes which, in a sense, define who we are. Self-expression is bound up with self-identity. Erikson's (1968) theory of identity states that a clear sense of identity and understanding of what we are about is important for our general well-being. Attitudes that we regard as most important and central to us are most resistant to change and may, in the extreme, lead to psychological ill health if attempts are made to change them. A person who is not able to express deeply held beliefs and attitudes, because he or she does not hold any, may suffer from a lack of self-identity. Shavitt and Nelson (2000) showed that the impression people have of an individual is clearly influenced by the attitudes which that individual expresses. The expression of your 'real self' through telling others about your attitudes also identifies which social groups a person does and does not belong to.

The ego-defensive function indicates that attitudes can serve to protect how a person thinks and feels about him or herself by maintaining high self-esteem and positive self-image. Ego-defensive function of attitudes can work in two ways. First, when feeling psychologically threatened, we may exaggerate the strength with which we hold an attitude in order to deny the credibility of another person holding the opposite attitude. As a result, this justifies dismissing an attitude different from our own. This gives us self-protection. Second, take the example of waking up in the morning with a terrible hangover from drinking too much the night before. To think about what we did the night before when drunk may threaten our self-image as a sensible, rational person. This positive self-attitude will allow us to not think about the night before, since it is not generally how we behave. Again, this use of the ego-defensive function offers self-protection.

Study

Aim A study was conducted by Herek (1987) to investigate the ego-defensive function of attitudes towards lesbians and homosexuals.

Method Students were asked to write an essay about why they had a negative attitude towards lesbians and homosexuals. Herek scored each essay on the frequency of ego-defensive functions being demonstrated.

Results The researchers found that over 20 per cent of essays contained ego-defensive attitudes.

Conclusion The attitudes portrayed in the essays tended to overemphasise the individuals' identity with their own heterosexual status.

The knowledge function concerns how people organise, structure and process information about their social world. It also allows us to simplify the world in which we live, and not to see it as an unpredictable, chaotic and threatening place. This simplification has both positive and negative aspects. The positive aspects are that we can bring order and a degree of predictability to our own thoughts, beliefs and behaviour; and also that other people are thought to be predictable in what they will say and how they will behave. The negative aspects are that the simplification can be an oversimplification, leading us to hold stereotypes about people and different groupings of people. Stereotypes are one of the foundations on which prejudice and discrimination are based (see section 6.4). The knowledge function also helps a person to decide what it is important to pay attention to and what can be ignored (Fazio et al. 1994).

The social adjustment function recognises that expressing socially desirable or acceptable attitudes helps to uphold positive interpersonal relations and to ensure that conflict is not brought into a social setting. Snyder and DeBono (1989) have shown that use of the social adjustment function may vary according to a certain type of personality. People who pay close attention to social situations and the impression they are making are called **high self-monitors**. People who are less concerned about the social situation and the impression they are conveying are called **low self-monitors**. Snyder and DeBono (1989) produced evidence that high self-monitors make greater use of the social adjustment function of attitudes than do low self-monitors. Low self-monitors are more likely to use the self-expressive function of attitudes than high self-monitors.

199

Evaluation

- The knowledge function and self-expressive function of attitudes are used most when people want to be seen to be right. By contrast, the ego-defensive and adaptive functions are used most to make a person likeable to others and to themselves.
- Cultural differences have been demonstrated with respect to the most frequently used functions (Aaker and Smitt 2001). Here it was shown that western cultures that are more individualistic make greater use of the self-expressive and knowledge functions. By contrast, cultures which value social groups (known as collectivism), typically eastern cultures, make greater use of the social adjustment function.
- More recent approaches to understanding the function of attitudes have placed emphasis on one overriding function – that of information processing (Olson and Zanna 1993).
- The functional approach has implications for understanding what may be most effective when attempting to change a person's attitude. For example, an attitude serving a knowledge function is best changed through the use of evidence and information. An attitude serving an ego-defensive function may be changed by an appeal to a person's self-image and by raising self-esteem.

6.4 Explanations of prejudice

6.4.1 Prejudice and discrimination

The terms prejudice and discrimination are often used interchangeably in everyday life; however, social psychologists make a clear distinction between the two:

- **Prejudice** is an unjustified or incorrect negative (or positive) attitude towards an individual, based solely on the individual's membership of a group.

- **Discrimination** is the behaviour or actions, negative or positive, towards an individual or a group of people.

Note that it may not always be the case that attitudes towards an individual are negative, since one can also be prejudiced in favour of an individual or group. Nevertheless, most theory and research have looked at negative attitudes and behaviours because these are often a source of conflict in society. By distinguishing between prejudice (attitudes) and discrimination (behaviour), it is assumed that a direct link exists between the two. In the previous section of this chapter we have questioned this assumption.

Categories of prejudice

We have seen that prejudice refers to negative (although it could be positive) evaluations of individuals seen to be members of a specific group. This is based on the perception that the group has certain characteristics which are believed to be possessed by every individual in the group. In effect, a **stereotype** of the group is applied to the individual. Stereotypes are highly simplified descriptions of a set of characteristics believed to be typical of members of a group. Stereotypes are unfair and misleading because they fail to take account of the uniqueness of each person.

Prejudice, discrimination and stereotypes are usually aimed at minority groups, or shown by dominant groups over subordinate groups. A minority group should not

Figure 6.10. An extreme example of prejudice and discrimination.

always be seen as a group in the numerical minority. For example, in the southern states of the USA (Mississippi, Missouri), black African Americans outnumber white Americans. However, it is the black Americans who experience prejudice and discrimination. Categories of groups that experience prejudice and discrimination range from those which are in a numerical minority (such as homosexuals, Jews or Muslims in the UK) to groups which may be in the majority in an area or country (for example, sexism towards female, black African Americans in southern US states). Figure 6.11 shows a number of categories of prejudice, together with a brief explanation and an example of each.

Perhaps the most prevalent and historically common form of prejudice is racism. In the nineteenth and early twentieth centuries, native Africans and Aborigines in Australia were blatantly discriminated against – used as slaves or massacred. In the 1990s and early 2000s, psychologists have talked about 'modern racism' (Surin et al. 1995). This type of prejudice is covert and subtle, and is revealed in three ways:

- denial by members of the dominant group that a minority group is discriminated against;

- impatience and irritation at the continued demands made by the minority group;

- resentment that minority groups may be treated favourably or with positive action.

Most, if not all, people hold prejudiced attitudes and act, at times, in discriminating ways towards other people. Britain has laws to try to stop this, for example, the Race Relations Act and the Sex Discrimination Act. Pettigrew and Meertens (1995) introduced the ideas of subtle and blatant racism, since many people deny that they are directly or openly prejudiced (blatant), but do exhibit covert or subtle prejudice.

Category of prejudice	Explanation	Examples
Racism	Negative treatment and stereotyping of races other than the dominant one in the society in question	Jews in Nazi Germany in the 1930s/40s; bullying of an Asian by white students
Sexism	Negative treatment of females by males in a particular society; negative stereotype of men as aggressive, 'spraying testosterone everywhere'	Male view that a woman's place is in the home; 'glass ceiling' for women trying to reach to top positions in business;
Ageism	View that older people are less able, less competent and suffer memory loss	Not employing people in their 50s and early 60s for jobs they could do
Tokenism	Is where positive action is taken towards a person belonging to a group discriminated against	The token 'female' on an all male panel; the token 'ethnic minority person' in a group
Homophobism	Prejudice shown towards homosexuals by heterosexual people	Refusing to serve a homosexual (or lesbian couple) in a public house

Figure 6.11. Categories of prejudice.

Prejudice may be specific to a situation. This means that an individual may show prejudice in one situation, but not in another. The classic study demonstrating this was Minard's (1952) research into the behaviour of miners in a mining community in the USA. Segregation of and discrimination against blacks by whites existed in the town. However, below ground, in the mine, this disappeared, with black and white workers showing mutual support, interdependence and collaboration.

In what follows we will look at three different explanations for prejudice: competition for resources, social identity theory and the authoritarian personality.

6.4.2 Competition for resources

Where two or more groups are in competition for resources, prejudice between the groups may arise. This is most likely to happen if resources are scarce or in limited supply. Economic, political and celebrity status can all be seen to be limited resources in the sense that not everybody can be rich, or be a Member of Parliament or an international pop star. Limited resources between groups can lead to prejudice and conflict between the groups. This explanation of prejudice is called **realistic group conflict**. The word 'realistic' is used to indicate that two or more groups are competing for the same limited resource. For example, Arabs and Israelis compete over the limited resource of land that they both wish to possess. Conflict in the Middle East has been going on for over 50 years. Within society, competition may exist over housing, jobs, access to good schools and other desired objectives.

As competition for a resource continues, members of each group come to hold increasingly negative and prejudiced attitudes towards one another. At the extreme, this may result in each regarding the other as the enemy, and each group thinking they are superior to the other group. This progress from simple competition through to hatred is shown in Figure 6.12.

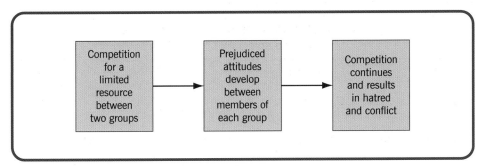

Figure 6.12. Continued competition for limited resources often results in extreme attitudes and physical conflict.

A classic study by Sherif (1936) investigated how conflict develops, using boys aged between 11 and 12 years who were attending a summer school camp in America. This was a field experiment which lasted for three weeks. The boys were normal and well-adjusted. They were randomly assigned to one of two groups, called the Rattlers and the Eagles. Each group lived in a cabin and the cabins were a good distance apart. Sherif set up a series of competitive activities between the two groups. They played games such as football and tug-of-war, and the winning team won prizes. Activities were set up where the two groups competed for resources, for example, the researchers allowed one group to get the best food at a party.

Sherif found that conflict rapidly developed between the Rattlers and the Eagles, for example name calling, refusing to eat with the other group, raids on each other's cabins, and fighting. Sherif said that, at this point, an outside observer would have thought the boys to be a 'wicked, disturbed and vicious bunch of youngsters'.

Sherif then attempted to reduce the prejudice and conflict between the two groups by stopping the competitive games and getting the two groups to work together. Eventually Sherif did reduce the animosity between the Rattlers and the Eagles.

More recent research has shown that prejudice develops from competition for limited resources when groups in a position of power have an interest in maintaining inequality. Murrel et al. (1994) showed that in the USA white people support the idea of equality of employment, but do not support taking positive action to help black people get better jobs. The limited resource of good jobs, the researchers showed, resulted in white job seekers thinking that they would be disadvantaged by the taking of such positive action. Bobo (1988) argued that when members of a majority or dominant group think that their own interests are threatened, they will produce reasons to justify their prejudicial attitudes.

Evaluation

- Prejudice cannot be explained solely by competition for resources. We shall see in the next section that simply being a member of a group, without consideration of resources, is a sufficient condition for prejudice to arise.
- Concerns have been expressed over the ethics of the field experiment conducted by Sherif. The study deliberately set out to create conflict and tension between the Rattlers and the Eagles. This was distressing to some of the boys attending the summer camp.
- Competition for limited resources has also been investigated, where self-interest is set against the common good. For example, this may occur when an individual fells rainforest trees for profit and ignores the destruction of the rainforest, to the detriment of others. Research finds that the normal outcome is for self-interest to prevail and the resource to be destroyed (Kerr and Park 2001).
- Explaining prejudice through realistic group conflict is valuable when applied to real issues where there is competition for a resource.

6.4.3 Social identity theory

Social identity theory emphasises the role of both cognitive and motivational factors in the development and maintenance of prejudice (Tajfel and Turner 1986). The theory assumes that we divide the world into two basic categories: 'us' and 'them'.

These are called the 'ingroup' and the 'outgroup'. This occurs through a process called **social categorisation**. Social identity theory states that an ingroup will be prejudiced and, as a result, will discriminate against an outgroup. The advantages for the ingroup in doing this are that the members of the ingroup enhance their self-esteem and provide rewards for themselves. The central assumption of social identity theory is that group members will seek to promote positive aspects for the ingroup. Conversely, members of an ingroup will seek to find and believe in negative aspects of an outgroup. Comparisons of an ingroup with an outgroup result in the following:

- over-evaluation of the ingroup and devaluation of the outgroup;

- comparisons made between an ingroup and an outgroup in relation to status and perceived worth of each group, resulting in social competition;

- people desire to be members of high-status, high-value and worthwhile groups;

- stereotypes are used to enhance the ingroup and devalue the outgroup.

Social identity theory is concerned with social competition, which is different from realistic competition (competition for resources). With social competition, people are not competing for physical resources. Instead, they compete for the social values of positive identity, high self-esteem and a positive self-image. Considering yourself to be a member of a highly valued group (your ingroup) is said to provide the individual with these positive social aspects.

Study

Aim Tajfel (1970) conducted an experiment to show that random assignment to a group would be sufficient to result in prejudice between an ingroup and an outgroup.

Method Schoolchildren aged between 11 and 14 years were randomly assigned to one of two groups. However, they were told that they had been assigned to a group on the basis of their preference for one of two famous artists. No interaction took place between the members of a group. Each person was asked to make models. Each schoolchild was asked to allocate monetary rewards to each of the two groups.

Results Generally, it was found that the allocation of monetary rewards maximised the difference in favour of the ingroup.

Conclusion The results clearly showed that people show prejudice to an outgroup and act in favour of the ingroup when membership of the group is anonymous and no interaction takes place among group members.

The experiment described above has become known as the **minimal group paradigm**. This is because the group does not know who the other members are and the members do not engage in any form of interaction. A great many experiments investigating social identity theory have used this type of minimal group.

Factors that make a person aware of a group he or she belongs to (the person's ingroup) may increase prejudice to an outgroup and enhance favouring your ingroup. When social identity is made more important than personal identity, members of an ingroup will see outgroups as increasingly different to their own group; they will become ethnocentric and show favouritism to their own group.

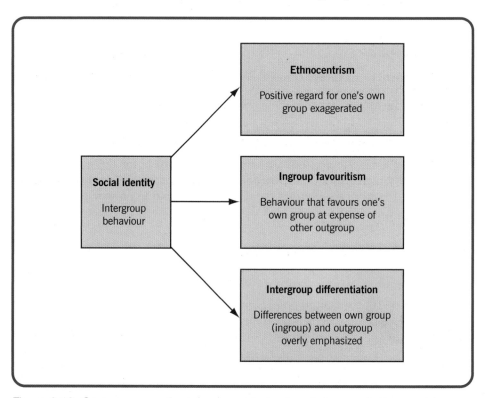

Figure 6.13. Consequences for inter-group behaviour in terms of ethnocentrism, ingroup favouritism and inter-group differentiation resulting from social identity.

A number of cognitive and social factors have been shown to enhance a person's awareness of the ingroup. These are as follows:

● direct reminders that a person is a member of a group;

● the presence of members of an outgroup;

● the ingroup is a minority group;

● conflict between the ingroup and the outgroup.

Mullen (1991) demonstrated that the presence of members of an outgroup affected members of an ingroup. He placed a small number of people representing an ingroup in the same place as a large number of people from an outgroup. He found that this made the members of the minority ingroup much more aware of their membership of that group.

Evaluation

- Experiments using the minimal group paradigm have been criticised for being too artificial to generalise the results to real prejudice.
- Most people are members of many different groups, and social identity theory does not help us to understand which are the most important for the individual.
- Most research on social identity theory has only looked at membership of one group, when, in real life, we are all members of many groups at once. Research has oversimplified real life.
- Social identity theory and realistic group conflict (competition for resources) are complementary, not contradictory. Each explains how prejudice can arise as a consequence of competition and membership of a social group.

6.4.4 The authoritarian personality

The previous explanations of prejudice have not taken the personality of the individual into account. Is there a certain type of personality that is associated with prejudice? Adorno and his colleagues (1950) suggested that a personality type they called the **authoritarian personality** exhibited prejudice, discrimination and negative views of different groups. The origins of this come from Freudian theory, where this personality type is said to develop in childhood. Here Adorno claimed that parents are overly harsh and disciplined, and disapprove of unconventional behaviour. Such a parenting style is said to result in a person with a weak ego. A person with an authoritarian personality willingly obeys authority and is authoritarian with those in lower positions. The authoritarian personality is said to have the following characteristics:

- excessive and blind obedience to authority;

- conventional and conservative;

- stereotypes others readily;

- submissive to superiors or those in higher positions of power;

- aggressive to inferiors or those in weaker positions of power.

Adorno et al. (1950) investigated the extent to which a person with an authoritarian personality was likely to be anti-Semitic and ethnocentric. Both this original research and subsequent research (Christie and Cook 1958) have shown strong, positive correlations between:

- authoritarianism and ethnocentrism;

- authoritarianism and political and economic conservatism;

- authoritarianism and fascist tendencies.

Adorno developed a questionnaire designed to measure the authoritarian personality. This is called the F-scale ('F' standing for fascist). The major problem with this was that the wording of each question was such that agreement scored as authoritarianism. More recent research by Altemeyer (1996) has produced a new authoritarian personality questionnaire, which is both reliable and valid. This scale consists of three main aspects: authoritarian submission, authoritarian aggression and conventionalism. Altemeyer has used this new questionnaire to show that people who score highly as an authoritarian personality are prejudiced towards groups such as homosexuals and people with AIDS. Research has also shown that such a personality type is conventional, in that individuals of this type give support to fundamental religious beliefs and are against abortion. People with an authoritarian personality have also been shown to hold highly punitive views on the treatment of criminals.

The original research of Adorno et al. was motivated by the anti-Semitism viciously expressed by Nazi Germany during the Second World War. Adorno initially thought that there was a 'German personality' which was authoritarian in nature. He quickly found from his research that authoritarianism or, more generally, ethnocentrism, was just as common in the USA as in Germany. Recent research using Altemeyer's questionnaire has shown authoritarianism to be present in many different cultures and societies.

Evaluation

- Rokeach (1960) criticised Adorno's concept of the authoritarian personality because prejudice is shown by people on both the extreme right and the extreme left of the political spectrum. Rokeach developed the idea of the 'closed mind'. People with closed minds, according to Rokeach, have rigid styles of thought and are intolerant to views different to their own. Rokeach separates authoritarianism from extreme political views, something which Adorno failed to do.
- The F-scale developed by Adorno suffers from an acquiescent response set. A high score may indicate a person's tendency to agree with a question rather than an authoritarian personality. This means that it is unclear exactly what a high score means.
- On the positive side, the idea of an authoritarian personality as a prejudiced person generated a huge amount of research using the F-scale. This is still an active area of research, but using Altemeyer's revised authoritarian scale.

- Evidence (Brown 1995) does suggest that there is a relationship between authoritarian personality and prejudice. What is not clear is just how strong or important this relationship is, and whether social factors, such as those we have looked at earlier in this section, are more influential.

How Psychology Works

Self-serving bias in attribution

The area of self-serving bias lends itself easily to practical work. You will need to identify a topic for success/failure (e.g. driving test, sports results, school tests), and will need access to two groups of people: those who have succeeded and those who have not. To avoid the problem of having to categorise open-ended responses, give people a tick list of options to explain the outcome – some should be external and some should be internal attributions. Ask people to tick the one that is the single most important factor. Alternatively, they could be asked to give each factor an importance rating.

> In your view, what do you think was the single most important factor in your passing/failing your driving test?
>
> - I tried really hard.
> - I didn't pay attention.
> - I was too nervous.
> - My instructor was good.
> - The examiner was harsh.
> - It was quiet on the roads at the time.
> - I have a good natural ability.
> - The car was unfamiliar.

- Produce your own set of materials, based on the model above.
- Write a brief and debrief to use in this study.
- This will be an independent groups design, with different people in each condition. Can you explain why it has to be this design?
- What is the independent variable in this study?
- What is the dependent variable in this study?
- You have probably used an opportunity sample of any people who were available to carry out your investigation. Explain how you would find a random sample of people in a badminton club to take part in a similar study.
- Display your results in a frequency table. These can then be converted into percentages and displayed as pie charts. Don't forget to label and title your tables and graphs in full.

How Psychology Works

The authoritarian personality – a study in questionnaire design

First you will need to find out about the F-scale questionnaire used by Adorno et al. in the 1950s. Have a look at some of the items on the scale and think about what the questionnaire was meant to assess.

Notice how the items on the questionnaire are not really questions at all, but statements. People read each statement and then decide whether they agree with it or not. This is a form of Likert scale, or attitude scale.

- Your task is to devise a set of statements that could be used in the present day to assess the same kinds of issues that Adorno et al. were investigating.
- Aim to have at least ten statements: five positive and five negative. Make sure you have an equal number of each.
- Try to make each statement very clear and unambiguous. You might have to reword them a few times.
- Decide on a suitable scale. Are you going to ask people to simply agree or disagree, or are you going to give them a scale on which they can mark their extent of agreement or disagreement?
- If you are going to use a scale, will it have three points, five points or ten points? Think about how this might affect people's responses.
- Arrange the statements in random order and type them up with the response options next to them.
- You will need to have a set of instructions at the top of the page so that people know what they are being asked to do.
- Carry out a pilot study to see whether people find your questionnaire easy to use. This will demonstrate whether the instructions are clear, whether the items are easy to understand and whether the scale works in the way you hoped.
- Consider the outcome of the pilot study and identify any adjustments you would need to make if you were going to carry out this study on a larger scale.

How Psychology Works

A study of central traits

Asch demonstrated how the traits 'warm' and 'cold' can have a significant effect on how we view another person. You are going to devise your own materials to study the effects of the adjectives 'warm' and 'cold', and then use the materials to see whether you get the same effect as Asch.

Here are some options:

- Job application letters where the applicant describes him or herself as a 'warm' or 'cold' person.
- Reference letters which describe the character as either 'warm' or 'cold'.
- MySpace website descriptions that describe someone as either 'warm' or 'cold'.
- Short-story accounts of someone in court for a minor offence whom the judge describes as either 'warm' or 'cold'.
- Newspaper reports about a person who has cycled the whole length of the UK, and in which the person is described as either 'warm' or 'cold'.

- Prepare two versions of your stimulus material, based on the ideas above or an idea of your own. Make sure the two versions are identical apart from the words 'warm' and 'cold'. (Why is it important that the content is exactly the same apart from changing these two words?)
- Decide how you are going to measure the effect this change has on behaviour. For example, people could be asked to rate the character on a scale of 1–10, according to how 'sociable' they think he or she might be.
- Write a suitable hypothesis for your study.
- Write a set of standardised instructions and try your materials out on a few people. See whether your results follow the pattern observed by Asch.

Further reading

Introductory texts

Aronson, E., Wilson, T.D. and Akert, R.M. (2005) *Social Psychology*, 5th edn, New Jersey: Prentice Hall.

Baron, R.A., Byrne, D. and Branscombe, N.R. (2006) *Social Psychology*, 11th edn, London: Allyn & Bacon.

Pennington, D.C. (2000) *Social Cognition*, London: Routledge.

Vaughan, G.M. and Hogg, M.A. (2004) *Social Psychology*, London: Prentice Hall.

Specialist sources

Augoustinos, M. and Reynolds, K.J. (2001) *Understanding the Psychology of Prejudice and Racism*, London: Sage.

Bohner, G. and Wanke, M. (2002) *Attitudes and Attitude Change*, Hove: Psychology Press.

Fiske, S.T. and Taylor, S.E. (1991) *Social Cognition*, 2nd edn, New York: McGraw-Hill.

Forsterling, F. (2001) *Attribution: An Introduction to Theories, Research and Applications*, Hove: Psychology Press.

Remembering and forgetting

7.1 What is memory?

Memory is the retention of what we learn and what we experience. Three memory processes identified by psychologists are encoding, storage and retrieval.

- **Encoding** refers to the process of translating information into a form in which it can be used, and then putting that coded information into our memory. For example, memory for historical events would probably be encoded verbally, whereas a memory of a beautiful beach would most likely be encoded visually.

- **Storage** refers to the process of retaining the information we have encoded.

- **Retrieval** occurs when we access stored information. Retrieval can take different forms: **free recall** is when we simply remember information; **cued recall** is when something acts as a cue or trigger for stored information; and **recognition** is where we identify information previously learned. Examinations can involve various forms of retrieval: essay writing from memory would be an example of free recall, while multiple-choice questions involve recognition.

7.2 Models of memory

7.2.1 The multi-store model (Atkinson and Shiffrin 1968)

The multi-store model was proposed by Atkinson and Shiffrin in 1968 and quickly became the basis for decades of research into the structure of memory. Atkinson and Shiffrin proposed three separate memory stores or components that vary in terms of coding, duration and capacity. The model is a good example of an information-processing theory, seeing cognitive processes as a sequence of stages and comparing them with the operations of a computer (Eysenck 1993).

According to the multi-store model, all our sensory experiences are recorded in the sense organs as a very brief sensory memory, most of which is lost when the brief memory trace fades. Different types of sensory memory have been identified: **iconic**

213

memory refers to the visual sensory memory, and **echoic memory** to the auditory sensory memory.

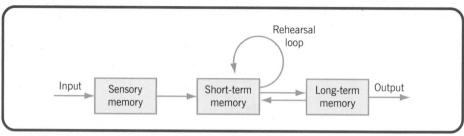

Figure 7.1. The multi-store model of memory. (Based on Atkinson and Shiffrin 1968)

Moving from sensory memory, the information we attend to is not lost, and is transferred to our short-term memory, where it is retained for a period of 18–30 seconds. However, it is possible to maintain information in the short-term store for longer than 30 seconds by verbally rehearing information in the **rehearsal loop**. For example, you might verbally rehearse a set of directions in your head as you follow a route in a car. Such an example illustrates the limited capacity of short-term memory: it is extremely difficult to retain a long set of directions; most people would manage to retain around seven pieces of information in this situation. A process know as **chunking** (Miller 1956) does allow us to cope with more than seven items at a time in short-term memory: chunking involves grouping separate items into lots or chunks, with each chunk then constituting a single item. Amazingly, Ericcson et al. (1980) found that a volunteer participant was able to increase his memory capacity for individual digits (digit-span) to nearly 80 items after 230 hours of training. His technique involved storing the digits as running times, imposing his own pattern on the information to make it more memorable.

Single items: 1 7 7 3 5 2 8 8 7 (nine separate items)
Chunks: 177   352   887 (three items)

According to Atkinson and Shiffrin, verbal rehearsal is also the means by which selected information passes from the short-term store to the more permanent long-term store. Information to be transferred to the long-term store is usually selected on the basis of its current importance to us, or its relevance in relation to what we already know about the world. For example, a teacher might rehearse the names of students in a new class in order to transfer their names to her long-term memory, but she would be particularly motivated to retain the names of certain students, for example very clever or challenging students, so that she could manage future lessons more effectively.

Several studies support the multi-store model, either by demonstrating the existence of separate stores, or by illustrating the features set out in Figure 7.2.

	Sensory memory	Short-term memory	Long-term memory
Capacity *How much does it hold?*	All sensory experience	7$^{+/-2}$ items (can be increased by chunking)	Unlimited
Duration *How long does it last?*	¼ second – visual 4 seconds – auditory	18–30 seconds	Unlimited
Coding *In what form is it stored?*	In the form in which it is received (i.e. sense-specific)	Mainly phonological (i.e. auditory or sound-based)	Mainly semantic (i.e. based on meaning)

Figure 7.2. Characteristics of the different aspects of the multi-store model of memory.

Here we shall consider the following evidence:

- Sperling's research into sensory memory;
- digit-span tasks;
- the primacy–recency effect;
- coding studies;
- clinical evidence.

A study by Sperling (1960) illustrated the capacity and duration of the visual sensory memory.

Study

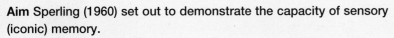

Aim Sperling (1960) set out to demonstrate the capacity of sensory (iconic) memory.

Method Using a tachistoscope, a visual array of 12 letters was displayed to participants for 50 milliseconds.

L V F D
S R K J
T P B Z

Fifty milliseconds is too short a time to consciously focus on the letters and read them. A previous study had shown that if participants were asked to recall the letters they had seen immediately after presentation, they could typically recall only around 4 of the 12 letters. Sperling suspected that

215

sensory memory could hold far more than four items, but that the reason participants only managed to report four was because the information faded so rapidly that most items were lost before they could be reported out loud. To test this, he arranged for participants to hear a tone of either a high, medium or low pitch immediately after presentation of the letter array had ceased. The participants' task was to report the letters they had seen from either the top, middle or bottom row, depending on which tone they had heard.

Results Sperling found that most participants could report the four letters from the selected row, whichever row was cued. It seems that the image of all the letters was available to be 'read off' for a very short time after display.

Conclusion Sperling concluded that a large amount of sensory information could be stored in sensory memory, but that it faded very rapidly, probably within ¼ of a second, after presentation ceased.

The capacity of short-term memory is usually investigated in what is known as a **digit-span** task. Participants hear a series of numbers or letter sequences which they have to recall one at a time. The length of the sequence is increased by one item every time. The participant must recall each sequence in the order in which it is presented.

Read each sequence, then cover it and repeat the sequence out loud.

C M F G
R P L J B
S F H P R K
V T D P B G L
G J L D C M R F
D K S L H C F T Q

It is usually found that most people can recall sequences of a maximum of seven items in the correct order. Since rehearsing information in our head like this involves the use of short-term memory, these findings support the view that short-term memory has a capacity of seven, plus or minus two items. Research shows that children who are experiencing problems learning to read and write often have a very limited short-term memory capacity when tested using a digit-span task.

Research into the **primacy–recency effect** has been used to support the existence of separate short-term and long-term stores. If you are given a series of 15–20 letters and asked to recall them in any order, you will usually find that you remember several items from the start of the list and some from the end, but you are less likely to recall the items from the middle of the list. Items recalled from the start of the list (the earliest items) are due to the primacy effect, and items recalled from the end of the list (the most recent items) are due to the recency effect. The effect is also known as the **serial**

position effect, because the likelihood of an item being remembered depends on its position in the series.

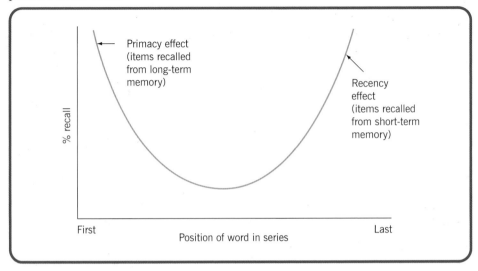

Figure 7.3. The primacy–recency effect occurs when we try to recall a list of words in any order.

How does the primacy–recency effect support the multi-store model?

When we hear the first words from the list we start to mentally rehearse them so we will be able to remember them later; this rehearsal transfers the words to our long-term memory. The rehearsal means that we tend to miss the words from the middle of the list altogether, unless they are especially unusual or relevant. The last few words in the list are retained in our short-term memory for long enough when the reader has finished speaking to enable us to recall them straightaway from our short-term memory. Thus the primacy effect is a long-term memory effect and the recency effect is a short-term memory effect. Glanzer and Cunitz (1966) varied the original primacy–recency task and provided further evidence for the existence of separate stores with different features.

Study

Aim Glanzer and Cunitz (1966) decided to explore the role of rehearsal in relation to the capacity and duration of short-term memory.

Method One group of participants recalled a list of words immediately after presentation. The other group of participants had the same list of words to recall, but, immediately following the list, participants were given a distracter task of counting backwards in threes for 30 seconds.

Results When asked to recall the words in any order, it was found that the control group showed both the primacy and the recency effect. However, participants given the distracter task showed only a primacy effect, recalling the items from the start of the list.

Conclusions Glanzer and Cunitz concluded that the distracter task took up the limited capacity of the short-term memory so that the final few words from the list were no longer available to be recalled. However, the first few words from the list were still safely stored in long-term memory, so that the primacy effect was unaffected by the distracter task.

Coding studies (Baddeley 1966a, b) illustrate how information in the different memory stores is coded or represented differently. In short-term tasks requiring information to be stored for less than 30 seconds, it is usually found that there is confusion with material that is sound-based (e.g. mat, mad, man, map). This confusion over same-sounding words suggests that short-term memory must involve coding of information according to how it sounds. Conversely, in a long-term task with a duration of more than 30 seconds, it is typically found that participants get confused over information with the same or similar meanings (e.g. huge, wide, great, big), suggesting that long-term memory involves the use of a semantic or meaning-based code.

Clinical studies offer convincing evidence for the existence of separate short-term and long-term stores. Clinical cases involve people who are experiencing memory impairments, perhaps because of some brain damage or disease. Such cases demonstrate how some memory functions are relatively normal, while others can be severely impaired.

The case of HM (Milner et al. 1968)

HM had brain surgery in 1953, when he was 27 years old, to reduce the symptoms of epilepsy. As a side effect, he suffered serious memory loss. His short-term memory was normal, but he was completely unable to transfer new information into his long-term memory. He showed almost no knowledge of current affairs, because he forgot news items as soon as he had read them; he knew nothing of recent family events, including moving house and the death of his father. He could remember people from long ago, but could not store information about new people he met. Generally, HM seemed cognitively 'normal', as he was able to use language, and perceptual and motor skills. Pinel (1993) suggests that the case of HM has contributed more than any other to our understanding of memory.

Evaluation of the multi-store model

- Many different studies seem to support various aspects of the model, although a lot of the research might be criticised because it involves testing memory in an artificial way. For example, we never normally need to recall lists of unrelated words or a sequence of digits.
- Perhaps the model is oversimplified, as it suggests that we have a single store of long-term memories. Other researchers, notably Tulving (1972), have suggested that there is more than one type of long-term store (see episodic, semantic and procedural memory in section 7.2.4).
- The view of short-term memory as a single store, holding up to seven pieces of information for 18–30 seconds, is also an oversimplification. The problem can be illustrated with the case of KF, who suffered brain damage following a motorcycle accident. His short-term memory for verbal materials was very poor, but was more or less normal for visual material (Shallice and Warrington 1970). Findings such as this suggest that short-term memory is not a single store. A more sophisticated understanding of short-term memory was proposed by Baddeley and Hitch (1974), in the form of the working memory model.
- One problem for the multi-store model is the view of rehearsal as simple rote rehearsal or verbal repetition. Studies have shown that rehearsal involving elaboration of materials, into a story for example, is more effective than simple rote rehearsal. Also, we know from experience that some material is remembered whether we rehearse it or not. **Flashbulb memories** of highly significant or emotional events and images, such as the devastation of the World Trade Center in 2001, seem to be readily remembered without any need to rehearse. Indeed, in everyday life we rarely rehearse information, yet as Eysenck and Keane (2000) note, we have little problem in storing huge amounts of it.

Figure 7.4. Some memories are so significant that they are remembered easily, without the need for rehearsal.

- Recently, many researchers have questioned the idea of separate short-term and long-term memories. Nairne (1996) sees short-term memory as a tiny, highly active part of long-term memory.
- Despite these criticisms, the multi-store model provided the basis for much research into memory and remains an important milestone in our understanding of the structures and processes involved in memory (Matlin 2002).

7.2.2 The working memory model

In 1974 Baddeley and Hitch extended Atkinson and Shiffrin's work on the multi-store model and developed a much more sophisticated understanding of short-term memory, the working memory model. According to Baddeley and Hitch, working memory consists of three main components:

- **The central executive** (THE CONTROLLER) controls and coordinates the operation of the other components. It has a limited capacity.
- **The phonological store** (THE SOUND SYSTEM) is responsible for processing sound-based information. Later investigations led to the proposal of two sub-components of the phonological store:
  - **The articulatory loop** (INNER VOICE) is a limited-capacity verbal rehearsal component, which is used to prepare speech and to think in words, as when doing mental arithmetic or memorising a phone number. The capacity of the articulatory loop is determined by how long it takes to say something and not simply by the number of items.
  - **The primary acoustic store** (INNER EAR) is a limited-capacity auditory rehearsal system which receives sound information from the environment. The primary acoustic store also receives auditory information from our own internal speech via the articulatory loop, for example, when we 'hear' in our head what we are thinking.

If the articulatory loop has a limited capacity determined by the length of time it takes to verbally rehearse information, then we should be able to remember more single-syllable names than triple-syllable names, given the same amount of time. See whether this happens, using the following lists of names.

Luke	Marianne
Sam	Josephine
Jack	Susannah
Jed	Carolyn
Mark	Rhiannon
Tom	Angelina
Dave	Patricia
Ben	Jacqueline
Rick	Alison
Steve	Barbara

- **The visuospatial scratch pad** (INNER EYE) is a visuospatial rehearsal system where we can image and manipulate visual and spatial information. The best way to understand the visuospatial scratch pad is to shut your eyes and imagine the layout of the room around you. Imagine standing and making your way to the door. According to Baddeley (1997), the visuospatial scratch pad helps us to monitor where we are in relation to other objects as we move around our environment. The scratch pad can also be used to store visual information that has been encoded from verbal stimuli, such as words. For example, if someone says the word 'beach', you might conjure up an image of a sandy white beach with palm trees. Due to the limited capacity of the visuospatial scratch pad, it is difficult to perform several visuospatial tasks at the same time, as any learner driver will testify.

Evidence for two separate subsystems in the phonological loop comes from experiments which involve measuring the blood flow in participants' brains when they are carrying out different types of memory task.

Figure 7.5. Learning to drive makes us aware of the limited capacity of the visuospatial scratch pad.

Study

Aim Paulesu et al. (1993) set out to investigate the phonological loop in working memory.

Method Participants were asked either to memorise a series of letters or to rehearse the sounds of the letters in their heads. At the same time, the blood flow in their brains was monitored using a PET scanner (positron emission tomography).

Result Each type of task produced a very different pattern of blood flow in the brain. The sound rehearsal produced increased blood flow in Broca's area of the brain, while the letter-memory task was associated with another part of the brain.

Conclusion It appears that the phonological loop has two components, one which stores sounds (the primary acoustic store), and one which involves mental rehearsal (the articulatory loop) (Logie 1999).

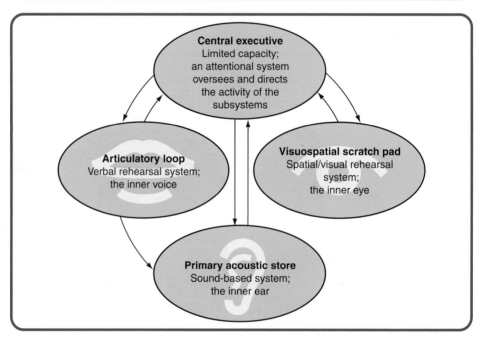

Figure 7.6. A simplified version of working memory. (After Baddeley and Hitch 1974; Baddeley 1997)

Study

Aim Logie et al. (1989) examined the role of working memory in performance on a complex computer game.

Method Performance at the computer game involved manual responses, using a joystick, and the processing of verbal elements. Participants were required to play the game and at the same time carry out either a visuospatial distracter task or a verbal memory distracter task.

Results The visuospatial distracter task impaired performance on perceptual-motor aspects of game performance, while the verbal memory distracter task disrupted performance on the verbal elements of the game.

Conclusion The study demonstrates the existence of separate visuospatial and sound-based components of working memory. It also shows how these components have a limited capacity and can only cope with a certain amount of processing at any one time.

The **central executive** is the key component of the working memory system (Eysenck and Keane 2000), acting more like a system which controls attention processes than as a memory store. The central executive enables us to selectively attend to some stimuli and ignore others. It also plays a role in retrieving information from long-term memory. In our everyday activities, the central executive helps us to decide when and how to act (Matlin 2002). Baddeley (1986, 1999) has compared the central executive to a company boss making decisions, selecting strategies for dealing with problems. It also integrates information from assistants (the other components), and calls on information held in a large database (long-term memory) (Matlin 2002). If the central executive is heavily involved in controlling one task, it is very difficult for it to do another job at the same time. This is shown in a study by Robbins et al. (1996).

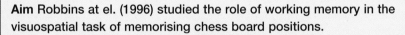

Study

Aim Robbins at el. (1996) studied the role of working memory in the visuospatial task of memorising chess board positions.

Method Twenty male chess players from two university chess clubs were asked to memorise the board positions of 16 chess pieces from actual chess games. They were shown the board positions for 10 seconds, then asked to recreate the positions from memory on another board. In three of the conditions, participants had to recreate the positions while doing another task at the same time.

1 In the articulatory suppression condition, participants were asked to repeat the word 'the' over and over in their head.
2 In the visuospatial blocking condition, participants had to press numbers on a calculator keypad with their non-preferred hand.
3 In the central executive blocking condition, participants had to say out loud random letters in time with a beat.

There was also a control condition with no accompanying task. Participants were scored according to how many chess pieces they placed on the board correctly.

223

Results It was found that the articulatory suppression task had no effect on performance, producing very similar results to the control condition. However, both the visuospatial and central executive blocking tasks seriously affected performance.

Conclusions The articulatory and visuospatial components of working memory are quite separate, and the visuospatial component has a limited capacity. The central executive is of crucial importance and has a limited capacity.

Evaluation of the working memory model

- As the role of the central executive is very broad, the model helps us to understand the link between the different cognitive processes, such as memory, perception and attention.
- Working memory is a much more flexible alternative to the fixed-capacity, short-term store of the multi-store model, and it sees memory as active rather than passive (Eysenck and Keane 2000). It considers how we use our short-term memory for everyday activities.
- The theory has important implications for the assessment and treatment of people with processing difficulties.
  - Problems with the phonological loop system may be responsible for difficulties in learning to read (Baddeley et al. 1998). Children who have difficulty reading often perform badly on tasks which use the phonological loop, such as deciding whether or not two words rhyme.
  - Problems experienced by patients with brain damage can be explained using the working memory model. For example, if only the visuospatial scratch pad is damaged, then performance on tasks which rely on the phonological loop will remain unimpaired.
- The working memory model explains only the short-term memory and makes no attempt to explain long-term memorising. As such, it does not provide an overall theory of memory.
- We know relatively little about the central executive, even though it is the most important component of the model (Baddeley 1997).

Baddeley continues to develop and refine the working memory model. He has recently proposed the existence of another sub-component, the episodic buffer, that enables communication between working memory, long-term memory and present experience or consciousness.

7.2.3 Levels of processing

Craik and Lockhart (1972) proposed an alternative to structural models of memory, focusing instead on memory processes. They suggested that information can be processed at different levels, and that the way in which information is processed can affect the likelihood of it being retrieved in the future. Depending on what we do with information at the time of encoding, processing can be shallow and superficial, or deeper and more meaningful. Craik and Lockhart argued that deeper levels of processing result in more long-lasting and more retrievable memories, whereas shallow levels of processing result in memories that are less long-lasting and less likely to be retrieved.

Tasks that require different levels of processing

- Structural

  An example of shallow, superficial processing would be looking at words and deciding whether the letters are upper or lower case, or whether the print is in one colour or another.

  Upper or lower case?   'BOY'

- Phonological

  An intermediate level of processing would be making judgements about the sound of words, deciding whether or not one word rhymes with another.

  Rhymes with lark?   'PARK'

- Semantic

  An example of deep processing would be looking at a word and judging whether or not it fits into a sentence, or sorting sets of words into different categories (e.g. vehicles, foods).

  Fits into this sentence?

  'The _____ ran on ahead of the group.'   'TABLE'

In order to complete the first type of task, it is necessary simply to process the word structurally, scanning the word visually. In order to complete the second type of task, it is necessary to carry out phonological or sound-based processing, mentally sounding out the words. In order to complete the third type of task, it is necessary to process the information semantically, thinking about the meaning of the word and relating it to the rest of the sentence, or putting it into a meaningful category. Craik and Lockhart's theory would predict that words which are processed for meaning (deep processing) will be remembered better than words processed for sound (intermediate processing) which in turn will be recalled better than words which are processed for superficial characteristics such as shape, size or colour (shallow processing).

Study

Aim Craik and Tulving (1975) investigated the effects of different types of processing on the recall of words.

Method Participants were shown 60 words, one at a time, and for each word they had to answer one of three questions. The questions required participants to make decisions about the case of the word (visual or structural processing), the sound of the word (auditory processing), or the meaning of the word (semantic processing). Participants heard each question and then were shown the corresponding word for a brief period. Participants then answered the question. When the 60 questions had been completed, participants were given a recognition test. They were shown a list of 180 words and had to pick out the original 60 words.

Result Approximately 17 per cent of words in the visual question condition were correctly recognised, 37 per cent in the auditory question condition, and 65 per cent in the semantic question condition.

Conclusion The findings confirmed Craik and Lockhart's (1972) theory about depth of processing: that the type of processing which takes place when information is encoded affects later recall.

This type of research technique is sometimes referred to as an incidental-learning task because the participants did not know that they would be required to recall the original words at the end of the procedure.

Here are some examples of the types of question used by Craik and Tulving:

Does it come from a cow?	Milk
Does it rhyme with 'boat'?	Sun
Is it in capital letters or small letters?	HEART

Although they emphasise process rather than structure, Craik and Lockhart do assume the existence of separate short-term and long-term memory systems. However, they see the function of short-term memory in terms of the processes it carries out (Baddeley 1997).

Evaluation of levels of processing theory

- Craik and Lockhart's (1972) theory provided a realistic and credible alternative to the structural approach to memory.
- They emphasised how processes which occur during learning affect the extent to which material can be retrieved from long-term memory (Medin et al. 2001).
- The theory would explain why some things, for example deeply significant and meaningful events, can be readily remembered without rehearsal.
- The theory also explains why elaborative rehearsal is more effective than maintenance or rote rehearsal (Craik and Watkins 1973). Elaborative rehearsal involves elaboration of the material to be recalled, perhaps by weaving a list of words into a story. Maintenance or rote rehearsal is simply repeating the information over and over. Since elaborative rehearsal involves thinking about the meaning of the material, it is a deeper level of processing and therefore leads to better recall. Elaborative rehearsal can add all kinds of extra images, associations and memories to enrich the material which has to be learned, resulting in better recall (Matlin 2002). Contrast this with the Atkinson and Shiffrin (1968) view of rehearsal as simple verbal repetition.
- A key problem for the theory concerned the way in which depth of processing was measured. There was no independent way of assessing whether processing was deep or shallow. Determining this relied on a circular definition which argued that if recall was good, then deep processing must have taken place, and if recall was poor, then the processing must have been shallow. However, just because participants were asked to say whether or not a word was in capital letters, it should not be assumed that they did not engage in further deeper processing.
- Lockhart and Craik (1990) have updated their model in response to criticisms and recent research findings. The basic ideas remain the same, but they accept that their original model was rather oversimplified, and agree that they had not considered retrieval processes in sufficient detail. In addition, Lockhart and Craik (1990) accepted that in some cases shallow processing does not lead to rapid forgetting.

7.2.4 Types of long-term memory

One criticism of the multi-store model of memory was that it presented an oversimplified view of long-term memory. In an elaboration of long-term memory, Tulving (1972) proposed a distinction between different types of long-term memory.

Episodic memory is the long-term memory for events or episodes which we have experienced ourselves, or which we have heard about from another source. Examples of episodic memory would be remembering the events of our first day at college, or from a day out at the seaside with friends. Such memories are usually linked in our memory to a particular time and place. (See Autobiographical memory, on page 231.)

Semantic memory is the long-term memory for information about the world or world knowledge. This includes knowledge about the meanings of words and general knowledge. Examples of semantic memory would be the knowledge that grass is green, recalling the date of your mother's birthday, or knowing that a giraffe is an animal with a long neck. Such semantic memories can be used without reference to when and where the information was learned. Indeed, very rarely do we know exactly when we first learned such information.

Both episodic and semantic memory can be inspected consciously and are described by Cohen and Squire (1980) as **declarative**, meaning that they can be put into words quite easily. For example, you can tell someone what happened on your first day at college and you can tell someone what a giraffe is like. These two types of memory are very closely linked: for example, the memory for events on your first day at college can become integrated into your semantic memory or general knowledge about college. Episodic memory and semantic memory are sometimes referred to as 'knowing that' memories.

A further type of long-term memory was proposed by Cohen and Squire in 1980. **Procedural memory** is a motor- or action-based memory. Examples of procedural memory would include the memory of how to ride a bike or how to swim. Unlike episodic and semantic memory, procedural memory cannot be consciously inspected and is non-declarative, meaning that it is very difficult to put into words. You will soon understand this if you try to explain to someone in words how to do the breast-stroke. In your explanation you are not allowed to move your arms or legs, and you cannot refer to frogs. Procedural memory is sometimes referred to as 'knowing how' memory.

Episodic and semantic are **declarative** and involve 'knowing **that** ...'
Procedural is **non-declarative** and involves 'knowing **how** ...'

Some evidence to support the existence of separate and distinct long-term memory stores has come from studies monitoring blood flow in the brains of participants while they complete different types of memory task.

Study

Aim Tulving (1989) investigated episodic and semantic memory to see whether they were separate memory systems located in different areas of the brain.

Method Tulving himself was the participant. Quantities of radioactive gold were injected into his bloodstream. He then thought about semantic memories (e.g. historical facts, such as the work of famous astronomers), or about episodic memories (e.g. events from the summer holidays when he was a child). Scanners were used to monitor the blood flow in his brain.

Result The two different memory tasks showed distinct patterns of blood flow in the brain. Episodic memories involved increased blood flow in the front of the brain, whereas semantic memories involved increased blood flow in areas towards the back of the brain.

Conclusion The results supported the view that episodic memory and semantic memory are located in different areas of the brain. However, as this was a preliminary study involving a single participant, the findings should be interpreted with caution.

Patients with amnesia provide evidence for the distinction between declarative and procedural memory. Such patients often have problems remembering episodic and semantic information they encounter after the onset of their amnesia, although their memory for events and knowledge acquired before the onset of amnesia tends to remain intact. In other words, it appears that their ability to retain any new declarative information is impaired. However, these amnesic patients seem to be able to learn and remember new motor skills, suggesting that their ability to acquire procedural knowledge remains intact (Cohen 1984).

Study

Aim Corkin (1968) investigated the ability to acquire new motor or procedural skills in a person with amnesia.

Method A case study of an amnesic patient (HM) was carried out. HM's memory problems were so serious that he appeared to be unable to remember new information. Over several days, HM was trained to carry out a task which involved tracking or following a curvy line on a rotating disc.

Result At first, his performance at the tracking task was poor, but he improved with practice. Several days later, when he carried out the task again, he had no conscious memory of the first session. Despite this, his performance was as good as it had been at the end of the first session. Evidently he had retained his procedural memory for the task, but had no episodic memory of the training episode.

Conclusions HM was unable to acquire any new declarative knowledge, but was able to learn and retain new motor skills. This supports the view that procedural knowledge and episodic, declarative knowledge involve separate memory systems.

Evidence for the opposite effects has been reported in patients with the brain disease known as Huntington's disease. Huntington's patients have problems learning new motor skills, so probably have some damage to their procedural memory system. However, they can acquire new declarative knowledge (Heindel et al. 1988). Together with the findings of Corkin (1968), this pattern suggests that there are different systems underlying procedural and declarative memory.

The distinction between different types of long-term memory

- It seems sensible to make a clear distinction between episodic, semantic and procedural memories in terms of their content, as each type of memory holds a different type of information.

- Exactly how much episodic memory and semantic memory involve different brain structures and processes is unclear, supported by limited evidence, such as the study by Tulving (1989).

- Some researchers (e.g. Medin et al. 2001) suggest that episodic memory and semantic memory are part of the same system.

- Evidence from clinical studies indicates that declarative memory and procedural memory rely on different encoding systems and brain structures.

- Wheeler et al. (1997) expanded on the distinction between episodic memory and semantic memory by focusing on different thoughts and feelings that are experienced when the two types of memory are recalled. They suggest that episodic memories are associated with a conscious awareness of the self actually experiencing the event. In contrast, the recall of semantic memories involves thinking objectively about something that we know, rather than a conscious recollection.

Autobiographical memory – a special kind of episodic memory

An autobiography is a person's own life story, as written by him or herself. Thus, autobiographical memory is the episodic memory we have specifically for events we have experienced in our own lives. It is very difficult to check the accuracy of autobiographical memory, since most people do not keep an accurate record of the daily events in their lives. One way of checking autobiographical memory is to use a diary.

Study

Aim Linton (1975) set out to investigate the accuracy of her autobiographical memory.

Method She used a diary method, noting down two or three events in her own life every day for six years. At the end of each month, she randomly chose two of the events and tried to recall as much detail about them as possible.

Result Linton found that events which had been retrieved on more than one occasion were recalled in more detail on later occasions. She also found that there was a strong tendency for better recall of pleasant events in her life.

Conclusion Findings are consistent with laboratory studies, which show that frequent retrieval of information keeps the memory trace accessible and therefore makes it easier to remember. Estgate and Groome (2005) suggest several explanations for enhanced recall of pleasant memories: perhaps the upset involved in unpleasant memories makes them harder to recall; perhaps we repress unpleasant memories; perhaps we think about pleasant events more often and the enhanced recall is therefore due to this rehearsal.

Other researchers have used photographs as a cue for recall of autobiographical memories.

In a series of experiments, Bahrick et al. (1975) used old school photographs to test the ability of American adults to recall their former classmates. Participants were required to either recall the names of the people in the photos, or to match the photos to a list of names they were given. Despite an average time lapse of 47 years, participants managed to match correctly more than 70 per cent of the names they were given to the photos. Participants were

Figure 7.7. Photos are often used in the study of autobiographical memory.

less able to recall the names from memory, but even on this task performance was still quite impressive and showed little decline over the years.

Studies have found that older people tend to show a better autobiographical memory for information from their adolescence and early adulthood (between the ages of 11 and 30 years) than for other periods in their lives. Rubin et al. (1986) referred to this increased ability to recall information from a particular point in one's life as the 'reminiscence bump'. This is illustrated in Figure 7.8.

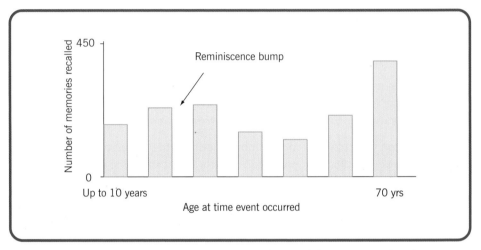

Figure 7.8. We are better able to recall events from adolescence and early adulthood than from our later adult years.

According to Estgate and Groome (2005) there are several explanations for this effect. Perhaps we are more likely to recall events from this period because they were new experiences at the time, and were memorable because they were distinctive. For example, who can forget their first date or the first time they moved away from home? Possibly the reminiscence bump occurs because we enjoy thinking about our younger days, and therefore these memories have been rehearsed more often. The same effect seems to occur for other types of personal memory; for example, older people show a better memory for songs that were popular in their younger years than they do for more recent music (Schulkind et al. 1999).

For most people, their earliest autobiographical memory is of something that happened to them around the age of three years. The inability to recall information from any earlier than that is usually referred to as 'infantile amnesia' and may occur for several reasons. Freudian theory would suggest that these memories have been repressed because the early years are a time of anxiety and emotional conflict. Biological evidence would suggest that the prefrontal area of the brain is not fully developed in young infants and this is why they cannot store any permanent conscious memories (Newcombe et al. 2000).

We forget things all the time. We forget to do our homework, miss dentist appointments, have trouble remembering names, lose our keys and cannot remember the detail of things that happened to us just last week. Several explanations for forgetting have been proposed. The following explanations will be covered in this chapter:

- decay;

- interference;

- retrieval failure (absence of context or cues);

- lack of consolidation;

- displacement;

- motivated forgetting, including repression.

7.3.1 Decay

Decay theory offers an explanation for forgetting in both short-term memory and long-term memory. Memories have been shown to involve structural changes in the brain and the establishing of fixed connections between neurons (Rose 1992). The decay explanation for forgetting is really a biological explanation which suggests that, unless information is rehearsed, the trace connections between neurons which make a memory permanent are not sufficiently fixed and simply fade away (Hebb 1949). This would explain forgetting in short-term memory. In long-term memory, it is proposed that memories that have been rehearsed and have become fixed as a structural change in the brain can nevertheless fade away over time if they are not used regularly.

Studies by Brown (1958) and Peterson and Peterson (1959) offered support for the decay theory of forgetting from short-term memory. The experimental technique they used has become known as the Brown–Peterson task. The task involved displaying sequences of three consonants (three consonant trigrams), such as 'B T F', to participants for a few seconds. Immediately after the display, participants heard a number and were then required to count backwards from this number in threes. The task of counting backwards was designed to prevent rehearsal of the trigram. It was usually found that when people are prevented from rehearsing information, it is very quickly lost from short-term memory. Performance drops by more than 50 per cent in less than six seconds (Figure 7.9). The findings of studies using the Brown–Peterson technique support the view that information is lost from short-term memory through a process of decay.

Other research has shown that the passage of time does not affect recall from short-term memory.

AO2

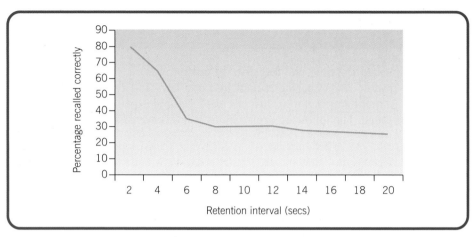

Figure 7.9. *Typical findings from a Brown–Peterson task. Recall of the trigram is very difficult if rehearsal is prevented.*

Study

Aim Waugh and Norman (1965) set out to investigate forgetting in a short-term memory task.

Method Participants heard a list of 16 digits. In one condition, the list was presented at the rate of one per second. In the other condition, the list was presented at a rate of four per second. Thus, in the first condition, the list took 16 seconds to read out, whereas, in the second condition, it took only 4 seconds to read out the list. After presentation of the list, participants were given a cue to indicate which of the sequence of 16 digits they had to recall. Waugh and Norman thought that if decay alone is responsible for forgetting, then the more time that had passed, the more information would be forgotten. They therefore expected that there should be more forgetting from the first condition where the list has taken 16 seconds to read out than from second condition where the list took only 4 seconds to read out.

Result No significant difference in recall was found between the two conditions.

Conclusion The findings do not support decay theory, as they suggest that the passage of time alone cannot explain forgetting in this short-term memory task.

Long-term decay

Ebbinghaus (1885) argued that even established memory traces decay over time. In other words, if memories are not used they gradually fade away as time passes. This is sometimes referred to as the Law of Disuse. Ebbinghaus investigated this himself by learning 169 different lists of 13 nonsense syllables, made up of consonant-vowel-consonant sequences (e.g. BEJ, ZUX), and then testing himself after different intervals of time. He used nonsense syllables rather than real words so it would be a true test of memory, and not a test of existing memories for words he already knew and could link to other things. He found that forgetting followed a particular pattern (see Figure 7.10), known as the 'forgetting curve', with rapid forgetting at first and a gradual levelling off.

Try Ebbinghaus's experiment yourself. Make a list of 13 nonsense syllables and learn them. After a few hours, test yourself to see how many you can remember, then test yourself again a few hours later, and again the next day.

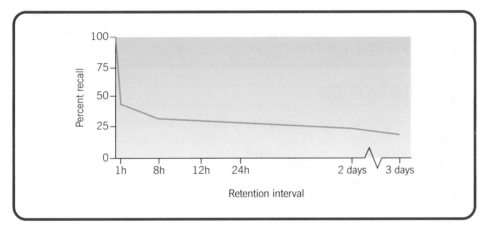

Figure 7.10. A typical forgetting curve, with most forgetting occurring soon after learning.

Bjork and Bjork (1992) have recently suggested a new theory of 'disuse'. They argue that memory traces compete with each other for access to a retrieval path. Frequent retrieval of one particular memory trace strengthens its access to the retrieval route, making it easier to access in the future. At the same time, this has the effect of blocking off the retrieval route to other rival memory traces. This theory explains why information that is not retrieved regularly becomes less easy to access, supporting the decay theory.

> ## Evaluation of decay theory
>
> - Most studies of decay involve unrealistic tasks and so have very low ecological validity.
> - Decay theory is difficult to investigate in a real-life way because the time between learning something and recalling it will be filled with all kinds of different events. In studies which involve a distracter task, such as Brown–Peterson, it might be the distracter task which causes forgetting, and not simply the passage of time. This would support the interference theory of forgetting rather than decay theory.
> - Decay theory cannot explain why people often remember clearly events that happened several years ago, even though they have not thought about them for a long time.
> - Solso (1995) points out that there is no evidence that neurological decay is responsible for normal forgetting, although it is obviously responsible for forgetting in conditions such as Alzheimer's disease.
> - Sperling's research (1960) (see Study on p. 215) does support the idea that information decays and is lost from sensory memory.

7.3.2 Interference

According to the decay theory of forgetting, events that take place between learning and recall have no effect on our ability to remember. All that matters is the length of time the information has to be retained. However, studies have shown that what happens in between learning and recall can cause us to forget (Baddeley 1999). In other words, forgetting is caused by interference from other information.

There are two types of interference:

Proactive interference occurs when what we have previously learned interferes with what we have learned more recently. Here the interference works forward in time (and hence is proactive), with earlier information causing us to forget information learned later. An example of proactive interference is calling your new boy/girlfriend by your previous boy/girlfriend's name – not recommended!

Retroactive interference occurs when what we have learned more recently interferes with information we had previously learned. Here the interference works backwards in time (and hence is retroactive), with later learning interfering with earlier learning. An example of retroactive interference is forgetting how to use your old mobile phone when you have become used to using a newer model.

Studies have reliably demonstrated proactive and retroactive interference (e.g. Warr 1964; Underwood and Ekstrand 1967). The basic method for testing proactive and retroactive interference involves learning pairs of words. Participants learn the first set

Figure 7.11. Proactive interference in this situation could get you into trouble.

Set A	Set B
Dog – Balloon	Dog – Paper
Carrot – Fence	Carrot – Milk
Moon – Chair	Moon – Ankle
Baby – Market	Baby – Petal
Parcel – Lamp	Parcel – Tent

of word pairs (Set A) and are then given another set of word pairs (Set B) to learn. The first word of each pair is the same for both sets. After learning both sets, participants are given the first word of the pair (e.g. 'Dog') and asked to say which word goes with it.

If retroactive interference occurs, participants would tend to recall the second set of pairs rather than the first set. If proactive interference occurs, participants would tend to recall the first set of pairs rather than the second set. Interference has been found to be far greater where the two sets of information are very similar, for example when trying to learn two different foreign languages or when a teacher has to learn the names of two new groups of students at the start of a new school year.

French lesson followed by chemistry lesson = little interference

French lesson followed by Spanish lesson = lots of interference

Most laboratory studies of interference use unrealistic tasks, like the paired-word task described above. However, researchers have used other, more realistic ways of studying the effect of interference. One such study is a well-known experiment carried out by Jenkins and Dallenbach (1924).

Study

Aim Jenkins and Dallenbach (1924) set out to investigate reasons for forgetting.

Method Participants learned a list of ten nonsense syllables. Their recall was tested at one, two, four and eight hours after learning. During the period between learning the list and recalling it, participants were either:

- awake, carrying out normal daily activities ('awake' condition); or
- asleep, doing nothing – except sleeping ('asleep' condition).

Results The mean number of syllables recalled correctly was far greater when the participants were asleep between learning and recall than when they were awake. In other words, they forgot much less when they were doing nothing between learning and recall.

Conclusions The findings support interference theory, since the daily activities performed between learning and recall in the 'awake' condition appear to have interfered with recall of the nonsense syllables learned earlier. This would be an example of retroactive interference. Furthermore, the findings appear to contradict the decay theory of forgetting. If decay were responsible for forgetting, and forgetting were due simply to the passage of time, then there should have been no difference in recall between the two conditions at the various time intervals.

Unfortunately, Jenkins and Dallenbach did not control for the time at which learning took place. In the 'asleep' condition, participants learned the list in the evening, but in the 'awake' condition they learned it in the morning. This uncontrolled variable means we cannot be sure whether forgetting is due to interfering events or to time of day.

Study

Aim Baddeley and Hitch (1977) wanted to compare interference and decay explanations for forgetting.

Method Rugby players were asked to recall the names of the teams they had played earlier in the season. Through the season, different players had played different numbers of games because some had missed games through injury or for another reason. Baddeley and Hitch looked at how recall was affected by both the number of intervening games (interference) and the amount of time that had passed since each game was played (decay).

Results The results clearly showed that forgetting was affected by the number of intervening games a player had played, rather than by the time that had passed since the game.

Conclusion These findings appear to support the interference theory of forgetting rather than decay theory.

Study

Aim Schmidt et al. (2000) investigated retroactive interference in a naturally occurring situation.

Method Participants were asked to complete a questionnaire which contained a map of their childhood neighbourhood. They had all grown up in the same area. Their task was to name the streets on the map. Other questions included how long they had lived in the area and how often they had moved house to live in other areas. One key variable was the number of times participants had moved to other areas. The other key variable was the number of childhood neighbourhood street names recalled correctly. Schmidt et al. reckoned that moving house would create retroactive interference, because when we move house we have to learn a whole new set of street names for our new locality. Since the two sets of information are very similar, this would be especially likely to cause interference.

Results Schmidt et al. found that participants who had moved house more frequently recalled fewer street names from their childhood neighbourhood than participants who had moved house less often. For example, people who had never moved house recalled on average approximately 23 street names, while those who had moved house more than eight times recalled on average approximately 10 street names.

Conclusion Participants' recall of neighbourhood information is influenced by retroactive interference.

Evaluation of interference theory

- Although the effects of interference have been demonstrated in experiments, there is no real explanation of why these effects occur or of the cognitive processes involved.
- Most research into the effects of interference on forgetting involves artificial stimuli – usually lists of unrelated words – and the studies usually take place in a laboratory. The kinds of circumstances that might lead to interference in real life are much more varied and complex (Eysenck and Keane 2000).
- Some researchers have investigated 'real-life' events and have provided support for interference theory.
- It is clear that interference does have some role in forgetting, but the extent of the effect is uncertain (Anderson 2000).

7.3.3 Retrieval failure (absence of context and cues)

According to the theory of retrieval failure, we forget because we cannot retrieve information from long-term memory without the appropriate retrieval cues. In this case, the information is available, because it is still stored in memory, but not accessible, because we cannot recall it when needed. You only have to think about what happens in exams, when you cannot recall information in the exam hall, but remember it easily when someone cues you by saying something about it outside the examination hall. Brown and McNeill (1966) referred to this type of experience as a tip-of-the-tongue phenomenon (TOT).

Context

One especially useful cue to recall is context. Investigators who study eyewitness testimony are aware that it is possible to aid recall in a witness by reinstating the context, helping the witness to re-experience the event by imagining where the event took place and all that was going on at the time. The effect of context on recall was demonstrated experimentally by Godden and Baddeley (1975). They suggested that memory was context-dependent, meaning that recall is dependent on whether the context in which we learn is the same as the context in which we recall.

Study

Aim Godden and Baddeley (1975) investigated the importance of environmental context in memory and forgetting.

Method Participants were divers who heard a list of 40 unrelated words either on the beach, in the dry condition, or under ten feet of water, in the wet condition. After hearing the 40 words, the participants were tested for recall, either in the same environmental context, or in the alternative environmental context.

Results Participants recalled significantly more words if they were tested in the same environment as where they learned the words. If the words were learned underwater, recall performance was approximately 10 per cent better underwater than on dry land. If the words were learned on dry land, recall performance was approximately 15 per cent better on dry land than underwater.

Conclusions The study demonstrates that recall performance is best when the environmental context for learning and recall are the same. The study supports the retrieval failure explanation for forgetting, because it shows how being in a different context at the time of learning and the time of recall causes us to forget some of the information.

Tulving and Thompson (1973) explained this effect in terms of the encoding-specificity principle, meaning that recall is better if the retrieval context is similar to the encoding context. However, the context need not always be environmental. Sometimes our own internal context, such as our mood state, can act as a cue to retrieval. For example, if a person is depressed when they learn something, they are more likely to recall the information when they are depressed than when they are happy. Eysenck and Keane (2000) suggest that this effect is most noticeable when the moods are a consequence of personal events rather than induced by lists of positive or negative words.

Other cues

A fairly common way of investigating the effects of cues on retrieval failure is to use category headings as cues.

Study

Aim Tulving and Pearlstone (1966) investigated retrieval failure using categories as cues.

Method Participants were given a total of 48 words to remember. The words were organised into 12 categories, with four words in each category. At the start of each four-word set was the category heading. For example:

Fruit
Apple
Orange
Pear
Grape

Participants were instructed to try to remember the sets of four words and were told they would not be asked to recall the headings. At the time of recall, a control group of participants were asked to remember as many of the words as they could (free recall). Participants in the experimental condition were given the category names as retrieval cues (cued recall).

Results Without any cues, participants in the control condition recalled approximately 40 per cent of the words. With the category headings as cues, the experimental group participants recalled over 60 per cent of the words.

Conclusion The poor performance of the control group was explained in terms of retrieval failure due to lack of cues.

Bower et al. (1969) carried out a study which showed how organisation can act as a cue to recall.

Study

Aim To test the effect of hierarchical organisation on recall for a list of minerals.

Method Bower et al. (1969) presented participants with a list of minerals. In one condition, the minerals were presented in a meaningful hierarchy (see Figure 7.12). In the other condition, the same words were presented in a non-meaningful, unorganised way. They then carried out the same procedure with three other sets of material.

minerals				
metals			**stones**	
rare	**common**	**alloys**	**precious**	**masonry**
platinum	aluminium	bronze	sapphire	limestone
silver	copper	steel	emerald	granite
gold	lead	brass	diamond	marble
	iron		ruby	

Figure 7.12. Bower et al. (1969) showed how participants who had the hierarchy as a cue to recall did not forget many words.

Results It was found that meaningful hierarchies produced 65 per cent recall, whereas non-meaningful, unorganised stimuli resulted in 19 per cent recall.

Conclusions The findings suggest that organising material in a meaningful way acts as a cue to recall. The study supports the retrieval failure explanation for forgetting, as it shows that the group without the hierarchy as a cue forgot 81 per cent of the words.

Evaluation of retrieval failure as an explanation for forgetting

- According to Baddeley (1997), there is no doubt about the importance of cues in the retrieval process.
- Godden and Baddeley's (1975) findings in the underwater study occur only when participants are asked to perform free recall, and not when the test involves recognition, so retrieval failure may not explain instances of forgetting that occur with other forms of recall.
- The context-dependent nature of memory has been demonstrated many times and it is not even necessary to be in the same environment. Smith (1979) found that just imagining the room where learning took place was as effective for participants as recalling in the same room as learning.
- Some studies involve artificial stimuli and so lack ecological validity. For example, in the Tulving and Pearlstone study (1966) participants were asked to recall a list of 48 words in 12 categories.
- The retrieval failure explanation is consistent with the levels of processing theory of memory. Deep processing involves making links and associations with what we already know. This increases the chance that one or more of these associations will match with a retrieval cue (Groome 1999).

7.3.4 Displacement

The displacement theory of forgetting was based on Atkinson and Shiffrin's (1968) multi-store model of memory, which stated that short-term memory had a limited capacity of seven, plus or minus two items. In the late 1960s and early 1970s, the concept of displacement became popular as an explanation for forgetting (Groeger 1997).

According to displacement theory, the limited capacity of the short-term memory meant that any extra information would push out, or displace, information already in short-term memory. Information that had been in the short-term store for the longest would be the first to be displaced by new information. Imagine a shelf with seven bottles on it and no room for any more. If you push another one on at one end, the first bottle will fall off at the other end.

Figure 7.13. If short-term memory can only hold seven pieces of information, then any extra will mean that other information is pushed out, or displaced.

Studies using free recall of unrelated items tend to show that most people do indeed remember around seven items of information. Perhaps, once the short-term store is full to capacity, any new items will displace the first items on the list. Displacement can also explain the recency effect in serial position effect studies. Remember that the recency effect is where we recall the last few items from the list (see Figure 7.3). These results are consistent with displacement theory in that the last few words on the list have not yet been displaced from short-term memory and so are available for recall. Furthermore, if displacement theory is correct, it should be possible to disrupt the recency effect by giving participants another task, such as simple repetition of a nursery rhyme, after the end of the list of words but before the free recall. The nursery rhyme task would displace the words held in the short-term store and the recency effect would disappear.

Several studies have demonstrated how the recency effect disappears if other information is presented to participants at the end of the list. Postman and Phillips (1965)
asked participants to count back from 100 in threes, for 15 seconds between the list
being read out and free recall. See also the study by Glanzer and Cunitz (1966) on page
217. Both these studies seem to support displacement theory.

Evaluation of displacement theory

- The theory is consistent with Atkinson and Shiffrin's (1968) model of short-
  term memory.
- As Atkinson and Shiffrin's (1968) description of short-term memory gave
  way to the working memory model, displacement theory became less
  popular.
- Displacement is a fairly limited explanation of forgetting as it can only
  explain forgetting from short-term memory.
- In studies involving an interference task, forgetting may be due to decay
  because of the extra time between learning and recall, rather than being
  due to displacement.

7.3.5 Lack of consolidation

This explanation for forgetting has a biological basis. Parkin (1993) describes the
making of memories as 'permanent alteration of the brain substrate in order to represent some aspect of a past experience'. The permanent change that takes place in the
brain cells when memories become fixed is referred to as consolidation.

An early theory about the biological changes involved in memory was proposed by
Hebb (1949), who referred to 'cell assemblies', which were groups of brain cells, or
neurons. When we receive information from the senses, these cell assemblies act to
hold the information long enough for a permanent memory to be formed. Hebb
thought that the consolidation and formation of a permanent memory took around 30
minutes.

Nowadays, modern techniques enable us to see the changes that take place when new
memories are formed. Brain cells, or neurons, are connected to each other at synapses.
At the synapse, chemicals known as neurotransmitters are passed from one neuron to
another. These chemicals can either stimulate or inhibit the activity of neurons. So in
any network of connecting neurons there will be a pattern of stimulation and inhibition. Brain research suggests that the pattern of activity between connecting neurons
forms the basis for making a memory.

The neurotransmitter acetylcholine has been identified as very important for the consolidation process. It follows, therefore, that interfering with the activity of

acetylcholine could disrupt consolidation, and that this lack of consolidation would lead to forgetting.

Study

Aim Drachman and Sahakian (1979) investigated the effect of chemical interference on the process of consolidation. They aimed to show that interfering with the action of acetylcholine would cause forgetting.

Method A drug which prevents the neurotransmitter acetylcholine passing between neurons was given to one group of participants. A control group received no drug treatment. Both groups were then given a list of words to learn. After learning the list there was a delay of 60 seconds. During this time, both groups of participants performed a distracter task to prevent them from rehearsing the information. At the end of the 60-second interval, participants in both groups were required to recall the words from the list.

Results Participants in the control group recalled around twice as many words on average as the group that had been given acetylcholine, blocking drugs.

Conclusions The findings show that consolidation requires the action of specific neurotransmitters, and also that this process can be chemically disrupted. The study supports lack of consolidation as an explanation for forgetting.

Other factors have also been found to affect our ability to consolidate memories. Yarnell and Lynch (1970) carried out a study of lack of consolidation following a blow to the head.

Study

Aim To investigate the effects of head trauma and concussion on memory loss.

Method Yarnell and Lynch (1970) carried out a field study of American footballers who had been concussed during a game. As soon as they came round, they were asked about the details of play at the time of the incident, and then asked again between 3 and 20 minutes later.

Results When asked immediately, the footballers gave accurate information about the play just before the accident. However, when asked between 3 and 20 minutes after regaining consciousness, they could give no information.

Conclusions The blows to the head received by the players led to a disruption of the consolidation process needed to make a memory trace permanent. Failure to recall events from before concussion cannot be due to a failure to take in the information in the first place, as it was available for recall immediately after regaining consciousness. The findings support the lack of consolidation theory of forgetting.

How long does it take for a memory to be consolidated? Parkin (1993) identified different steps in the consolidation process. The first stage happens quickly and results in an 'initial fixation' of the memory. In the second stage, links are established between the new memory trace and our existing memories. The case of HM (see page 218), who suffered severe amnesia following brain surgery, suggests that consolidation occurs over quite an extended period of time. HM's memory for his early life remained mostly intact, but he did have some memory loss for events which occurred in the two years before the surgery. According to Pinel (1993), this appears to go against Hebb's (1949) idea that the process of consolidation takes about 30 minutes. The fact that HM's memory is disrupted for the two-year period leading up to the surgery indicates that the process of consolidation continues for a number of years.

Evaluation of the lack of consolidation explanation

- The explanation is consistent with what we know about the nervous system and how the brain processes information.
- The theory links both biological and psychological approaches to explaining human behaviour.
- There is still no clear evidence about exactly how long is required for consolidation to take place.
- In the case of HM, there could have been other explanations for his forgetting. In any event, his case was so unusual that we should not generalise from it to cases of everyday forgetting.
- Most instances of forgetting in real life do not involve interference with psychoactive drugs, a blow to the head or brain surgery. Maybe lack of consolidation occurs only rarely in real life.

7.3.6 Motivated forgetting – repression

Repression is sometimes referred to as motivated forgetting, meaning that we forget things because we wish to forget them. According to psychodynamic theory (see Chapter 1), we have a set of unconscious defence mechanisms to protect our conscious self from unpleasant thoughts and events. Repression is a defence mechanism whereby unpleasant or upsetting memories are pushed into the unconscious, so that the conscious self is not upset by them. According to psychodynamic theory, these unpleasant memories can stay in the unconscious for many years, perhaps for ever. However, although we may not be consciously aware of them, our conscious behaviour may be affected by their presence. For example, someone who has repressed a childhood memory of a horrific accident may suffer from an unexplained anxiety disorder as an adult.

Study

Aim Levinger and Clark (1961) attempted to test the repression hypothesis experimentally.

Method Participants were given a set of emotionally negative words like 'sadness' and 'unhappiness', and a set of neutral words. They were then asked to provide an associated word for each stimulus word. For example, if given the word 'sadness', the participant might say 'cry'. Later on, participants had to say the word that went with the cue word.

Results Fewer associated words for the emotionally negative set were recalled than for the neutral set; thus, for example, participants could not recall associated words like 'cry' or 'hurt'.

Conclusion The difficulty recalling the negative word associations was taken as an indication of repression.

There are examples of traumatic experiences which have occurred over a prolonged period being held back from consciousness.

Study

Aim Williams (1994) set out to see whether women recalled incidents of childhood abuse.

Method The participants were 129 women, shown by hospital documentation to have been abused between the ages of 10 months and 12 years. When interviewed later, they were aged between 18 and 31.

Results In extended interviews about their sexual histories, 38 per cent of the women failed to report the abusive episode documented by the hospital authorities. They did, however, quite often report their general experience of having been abused.

Conclusion Some participants failed to recall specific incidents of abuse because these had been repressed.

Psychiatrists refer to a condition known as **dissociative amnesia**, which takes several forms, but usually involves a failure to recall specific unpleasant or traumatic events. In very severe cases, sufferers even forget who they are or where they come from, sometimes even taking on a new identity altogether. Barlow and Durand (2002) reported the case of a woman who was in her early fifties. Family interviews revealed high levels of stress in the home, with continual rows and arguments between father, son and daughter. The mother acted as the peacemaker in the midst of all the upset. Approximately every six months, usually after a significant family battle, the mother completely lost her memory and had to be admitted to hospital. After a few days in hospital, her memory gradually returned and she went home, only to be readmitted again following another serious row.

Study

Aim Groome and Soureti (2004) set out to investigate the link between negative experiences and post-traumatic stress disorder (PTSD).

Method Children were interviewed five months after the Athens earthquake of September 1999. The children lived in three areas of Athens, at varying distances from the epicentre of the earthquake. Questionnaires were used to identify symptoms of PTSD.

Results PTSD and anxiety symptoms were found to be significantly related to closeness to the epicentre of the earthquake.

Conclusion Those children who had been subjected to the most frightening experiences were the most likely to suffer from anxiety-related symptoms, perhaps because they had repressed some of their memory for the events.

Evaluation of repression theory

- The general problem with psychodynamic theory is that it cannot be tested easily. Defence mechanisms are unconscious processes, so do not lend themselves to investigation.
- Word-association studies, like that of Levinger and Clark (1961), are not a very realistic test of repression, because memory for real-life unpleasant events is presumably much more emotionally disturbing than memory for lists of unpleasant words.
- In the Williams study (1994) there may have been other explanations for the failure to recall the incidents of abuse. Former victims of abuse give various reasons for choosing not to talk about events they can clearly recall. For example, they might wish to forget the past and get on with the future; they might be embarrassed; they might wish to protect their parents; or they may simply prefer not to disclose such events to the interviewer (Femina et al. 1990).
- Findings in single cases of dissociative amnesia should not be generalised to explain other cases of forgetting.
- Our own experience tells us that many people do recall unpleasant memories very clearly indeed, so the question arises, why would we repress some unpleasant memories and not others?
- There is evidence that people who have suffered upsetting experiences are more likely to be affected by anxiety disorders, although, in itself, this finding does not directly support the theory of repression.

How Psychology Works

Levels of processing

- Carry out your own version of a levels of processing study like the one conducted by Craik and Tulving (1975) (see page 226).
- Produce a set of materials modelled on the example below. You will probably want between 24 and 30 questions/words in total.

There are three kinds of task in this activity:

1 judging physical appearance (capitals or lower-case letters);
2 deciding whether or not a word rhymes with another;
3 deciding about the meaning of a word (does it fit into a sentence?).

Levels of processing theory would predict that when we process a word for meaning, we are more likely to remember it than if we simply process its physical appearance.

Is the word in capital letters?	horse
Does the word rhyme with GREEN?	MEAN
Does the word fit this sentence: The bank clerk picked up his _____?	house
Is the word in lower-case letters?	TOWER
Does the word fit this sentence: The woman slept on the _____?	tomato
Does the word rhyme with MEND?	stool

- Propose a suitable research hypothesis and null hypothesis for this study.
- Identify the IV and DV in this study.
- Identify at least one possible extraneous variable that would need to be controlled.
- Write a set of standardised instructions you could use to carry out this study with real participants. Carry out the study with a few friends.
- Using data from the whole class, calculate measures of central tendency (means, medians and modes) for the three conditions. Calculate the ranges.
- Display these descriptive statistics in a summary table.
- Write a short conclusion based on the data in your table and relate the results to the findings of Craik and Tulving (1975).

How Psychology Works

Autobiographical memory

- Carry out two separate interviews with older members of your family. The best age group to use would be that of your grandparents.
- The aim is to find out about people's memories for events in their lives. Remember that Rubin et al. (1986) found that people tend to recall more about events that take place between the ages of 10 and 30 years than they do for other periods in their lives; and Linton (1975) found that recall of pleasant events was better than recall of unpleasant events. You can investigate these effects.
- The first interview should be structured, so you will need a set of predetermined questions. Devise about 15 questions. Start with a few closed questions, where participants have to choose from a fixed range of answers. Other questions should be open questions, where participants can give any answer they like.

- The second interview should be unstructured. You will need to have a general aim in mind, asking questions that you think are appropriate as the interview develops.
- Due to the personal nature of autobiographical memory research, it is important that you take account of ethical considerations. When deciding on your questions and carrying out your interviews, consider the following factors and think about why they are especially important in this context:
  - consent;
  - confidentiality;
  - debrief;
  - protection from harm;
  - withdrawal.
- Decide how you are going to record your data. You might want to use a tape recorder, or you might prefer to make handwritten notes.
- Before you collect the information from your interviews, you need to decide how it can be analysed. Will you categorise responses into categories and tally the totals? What categories will you use? How will you display your data?
- Consider your findings. Do they agree with the findings of other researchers or not?
- Consider the relative advantages and limitations of structured and unstructured interviews, and think about the effectiveness of open and closed questions.

How Psychology Works

Retrieval failure – use of cues

- Carry out a version of the Tulving and Pearlstone (1966) study (see page 242) to see whether category headings affect ability to recall a list of words.
- Propose a suitable hypothesis for your study and a corresponding null hypothesis.
- Prepare a set of materials. You will need the following:
  - An A4 sheet with a set of 48 words, with 4 examples for each category arranged under 12 category headings e.g.

Animals	Vegetables
Dog	Carrot
Squirrel	Cabbage
Otter	Leek
Sheep	Onion

  - Another A4 sheet with the same words and headings, but jumbled up.
  - A brief, a set of standardised instructions and a debrief.

- Some plain sheets of paper for participants to write on, and a record sheet to record the total number of words correctly recalled for each participant.
- Decide which experimental design you should use for this study: repeated measures, independent groups or matched pairs. How would you justify your choice of design?
- Try out your study on a small opportunity sample.
- Calculate the mean and median number of words recalled in each condition, and the standard deviation for each condition. Display your results in a table, with labels and title. Write a couple of lines to describe what these statistics tell you about performance in the two conditions.
- Write a brief conclusion of your activity, saying whether the data you have collected support the experimental hypothesis or the null hypothesis.
- Write a brief paragraph explaining how your results relate to the findings of Tulving and Pearlstone and the retrieval failure theory of forgetting.
- Identify at least one problem of using the experimental design that you chose for this study.

Further reading

Introductory texts

Eysenck, M.W. (2001) *Principles of Cognitive Psychology*, 2nd edn, Hove: Psychology Press.

Gross, R. (2005) *Psychology: The Science of Mind and Behaviour*, 5th edn, London: Hodder Education.

Scott, P. and Spencer, C. (1998) *Psychology: A Contemporary Introduction*, Oxford: Blackwell.

Sternberg, R.J. (1995) *In Search of the Human Mind*, Fort Worth, TX: Harcourt Brace College Publishers.

Specialist sources

Andrade, J. and May, J. (2004) *Cognitive Psychology*, Abingdon: BIOS.

Baddeley, A.D. (1997) *Human Memory: Theory and Practice*, Hove: Psychology Press.

Baddeley, A.D. (1999) *Essentials of Human Memory*, Hove: Psychology Press.

Estgate, A. and Groome, D. (2005) *An Introduction to Applied Cognitive Psychology*, Hove: Psychology Press.

Eysenck, M.W. and Keane, M.T. (2005) *Cognitive Psychology: A Student's Handbook*, 5th edn, Hove: Psychology Press.

Groeger, J.A. (1997) *Memory and Remembering: Everyday Memory in Context*, New York: Addison Wesley Longman.

Matlin, M.W. (2005) *Cognition*, Hoboken, NJ: John Wiley & Sons.

Perceptual processes 8 Chapter

8.1 Introduction

When we look at something like an apple, how do we process it? How do we experience and understand what we are seeing? If someone gives us an apple, how do we know whether to eat it, wear it, chase it or smile at it? Psychologists interested in perception try to explain our processing and interpretation of sensory information.

Perception has been referred to as the process of 'assembling of sensations into a useable mental representation of the world' (Coon 1983). Gregory (1966), meanwhile, defines perception as a 'dynamic searching for the best interpretation of the available data'. Look at Figure 8.1 and try to 'assemble the sensations' into something sensible you might later be able to think about or 'use'. As you look, can you feel yourself 'searching' for the best interpretation?

Figure 8.1. At first glance, this may seem like a random collection of splodges, but if you look carefully, especially through half-closed eyes, a picture may emerge. (See page 285 for solution.)

8.2 Perceptual set

Perceptual set can be defined as a predisposition to attend to and perceive certain aspects of a stimulus and disregard others, and a tendency to interpret a stimulus in a certain way. In our everyday lives, perceptual set affects what we notice in our environment. As an example, if your friend has told you about a CD she has just bought by a band you have never heard of before, you will probably notice when they appear in magazines or on television, but you might not have noticed them before. Perceptual set is related to the concept of a schema, which is our own personal way of organising past events into units of knowledge that are meaningful to us. Many factors have been found by psychologists to affect perceptual set, including motivation, expectation, emotion and culture.

8.2.1 Motivation and perceptual set

The idea that wanting something increases its attractiveness is a familiar one, illustrated in old sayings like 'The grass is always greener on the other side of the fence.' This phenomenon of increased awareness and/or attractiveness is known as **perceptual accentuation**. This means that our perception of something we need or want becomes accentuated or heightened simply because of our motivation or desire for it. For example, you might have set your heart on a new jacket or pair of shoes that you cannot afford. Perhaps if you did have the money to buy them there and then, it would not have seemed so desirable. Very often we find that when we eventually get whatever it is we want, it turns out to be a bit of a disappointment.

Study

Aim Gilchrist and Nesberg (1952) set out to test the effect of motivation induced by hunger and thirst on perception of pictures.

Method Participants viewed food-related and non-food-related pictures, which they were then asked to rate on a scale for colour and brightness. One group of participants had been deprived of food and liquid for several hours, the other group had not.

Results The 'deprived' participants rated the food-related pictures as brighter and more colourful than the non-food-related pictures.

Conclusion Gilchrist and Nesberg suggested that hunger and thirst were motives which led to perceptual accentuation, producing perceptions which were stronger and brighter than normal. The study is an example of how motivation can induce a perceptual set.

Evaluation

- In this case, the motivating factor was hunger, but does the same accentuation effect occur with other motivational factors? Other researchers have shown that motivation can affect the perception of the size of coins, with children from less affluent backgrounds estimating the size of coins to be greater than children from more affluent backgrounds (Bruner and Goodman 1947).
- One difficulty with the Gilchrist and Nesberg (1952) study is the use of a rating scale. Rating scales are a subjective measure recording the

participant's opinion on a scale where the units are not of a defined size. As such, they are less scientific than a measure on a fixed-unit scale.

- Consider the implications of the Gilchrist and Nesberg (1952) study. How could the findings be applied to the behaviour of people who are on a strict diet and have reduced their food consumption dramatically? How would this affect their perception of food images, for example in magazines, on TV and in real life? Not surprisingly, diet magazines recommend that dieters should go to the supermarket when they have just eaten, so that they do not end up buying a trolley full of things that look good simply because they are hungry at the time.

8.2.2 Expectation and perceptual set

Expectations arise for many reasons and influence perceptual set very powerfully. Most experiments conducted by psychologists involve creating an expectation by manipulating the context in which a stimulus is shown. This is usually achieved by showing a set of pictures, and then exposing the participant to a stimulus that can be perceived in more than one way. Such a stimulus is known as an ambiguous figure. One very well-known example of an ambiguous figure used in perceptual set experiments is the rat-man figure shown in Figure 8.2 (Bugelski and Alampay 1962). The rat-man figure is shown at the end of a sequence of pictures, either of faces or of animals. It is usually found that participants who see the face sequence perceive the figure as that of a man's face, whereas those participants who see the animal picture sequence perceive the ambiguous figure to be that of a rat or a mouse.

Figure 8.2. 'It's a rat!' 'No, it's a man!' The rat-man figure illustrates how we can have two possible hypotheses for the same stimulus.

Study

Aim Bruner and Minturn (1955) set out to demonstrate how the immediate physical context could influence perception of an ambiguous figure.

Method In an independent design, participants were shown either a series of numbers or a series of letters. In each case, the centre stimulus was exactly the same – I3. Participants were asked to look at the letters or numbers and state what they saw.

Results The perceptions of the two groups were quite different. The group who saw the ambiguous figure alongside letters reported seeing the figure as a 'B', while the number-context group reported seeing the figure as a '13'.

Conclusions Bruner and Minturn concluded that perception of sensory information varies according to the context in which a stimulus is presented, and that by altering the immediate context it is possible to predispose participants to interpret visual information differently. The study therefore supports the existence of context-induced perceptual set.

Evaluation

- The stimuli used in studies of perception are artificial because they are specially produced to 'trick' people into making perceptual errors. Thus, studies using ambiguous figures may lack ecological validity because they are not testing perception as it occurs in real life. However, there are many real-life examples of how perception can be affected by context. We often fail to notice spelling mistakes on signs and notices, simply because we see what we expect to see. How many times have you been reading a book and found that there are errors in typing, or 'typos'? These ought to have been identified by the proofreader, whose job involves going through the text carefully to make sure it is correct. However, some errors are missed because the perception of written words is influenced by context in just the same way as the perception of ambiguous pictures. Next time you go to a park, check carefully to see what the notice says:

  KEEP OFF THE
  THE GRASS

- A general problem arises with the method used in all studies of perception using ambiguous figures; they always use an independent groups design, with different participants in each condition. Of course, this is essential, as once the participants have experienced the ambiguous stimulus they are no longer naive to it and cannot be influenced into perceiving it differently a second time. This does mean, however, that the interpretation they make of the ambiguous stimulus might be due to inherent individual differences or participant variables, rather than their exposure to the immediate context. For example, if one group of participants in a study using the rat-man figure just happen to have pet mice at home, they will probably be more inclined to perceive the figure as a mouse rather than a man's face, regardless of what pictures they are shown beforehand.

Studies of expectation and perceptual set often involve the creation of an expectation due to manipulation of the immediate context. However, more enduring factors, such as training and occupation, have also been found to affect expectation.

Study

Aim Toch and Schulte (1961) investigated the effect of occupational background on perception of stereograms. Stereograms are two different stimuli presented simultaneously to each eye so that each eye receives a different image. When viewing stereograms for a very brief period, we tend to resolve the discrepancy by consciously perceiving either one image or the other.

Method Advanced trainee police officers were compared with two control groups: novice police trainees and university students. Participants were presented with stereograms where one of the stimulus pictures had a violent theme while the other did not. (See Figure 8.3.)

Results The advanced trainees were twice as likely to report having perceived the violent picture from the stereogram than the participants in the two control groups.

Conclusion Toch and Schulte (1961) concluded that occupational background and training created an expectation which influenced the advanced trainees to be especially sensitised to the perception of violent stimuli.

Figure 8.3. Advanced trainee police officers are more likely to perceive the violent than the non-violent option (Toch and Schulte 1961).

8.2.3 Emotion and perceptual set

Both positive and negative emotions have been found to affect perception. An example of a positive emotion that could affect how we interpret what we see or hear is excitement, which might lead us to perceive a forthcoming event more positively because of eager anticipation. An example of a negative emotion that might affect perception is fear, which would lead us to perceive something bad as worse than it really is because we would rather avoid it.

Several studies show that it takes us longer to perceive stimuli we find unpleasant. In a way, this is a form of perceptual set, since we are affected by a predisposition, although in this case, we are less rather than more likely to perceive certain aspects of a stimulus. This phenomenon of delayed perception is referred to as **perceptual defence** and has been illustrated in a study by McGinnies (1949).

Study

Aim McGinnies (1949) set out to investigate the effect of emotion on perception by testing whether offensive or 'taboo' words would take longer to perceive and recognise than neutral words.

Method Using a tachistoscope, participants were presented with words which were either unpleasant and offensive or neutral. A tachistoscope is a machine incorporating a shutter mechanism, which is designed to display a visual stimulus for a very short time. The words were projected very rapidly at first, with gradually increasing display times. The task was to say each word out loud as soon as it was recognised.

Results It took participants a lot longer to recognise offensive taboo words like 'crotch' than it did for them to recognise neutral, inoffensive words like 'plate'.

Conclusion Participants took longer to perceive the offensive taboo words because of perceptual defence, the unconscious defence mechanism acting to protect us from consciously experiencing the unpleasant words.

The perceptual defence interpretation of these findings rests on the Freudian concept of defence mechanisms like repression and denial (see Chapter 1). According to Sigmund Freud (1901), these unconscious defence mechanisms act to protect us from consciously experiencing unpleasant events and thoughts.

Evaluation

- There is no way of knowing whether people really took longer to recognise the offensive taboo words because an unconscious perceptual defence mechanism was operating to protect them. Indeed, critics would argue that the general explanation for perceptual defence in terms of Freudian defence mechanisms is not supported scientifically. Perhaps there was another reason for the delayed recognition of the taboo words: people might have been too embarrassed to say the rude words aloud in front of the experimenter. Even if they were not embarrassed, presumably they wanted to be quite sure that the word was really what they thought it was, probably thinking that it was unlikely to be such a rude word in an experiment. For this reason, perhaps they would have waited fractionally longer before saying the word out loud.
- The study could also be criticised from an ethical point of view, since participants were likely to have been at least a little uncomfortable, if not completely embarrassed and affronted. In this experiment, participants were not been protected from harm as they should have been.

The McGinnies (1949) study seemed to show that we operate an unconscious filter system which makes it more difficult for us to perceive unpleasant information. A further piece of research supports this to an extent, because it demonstrates that perception can operate at an unconscious level.

Study

Aim The question of whether or not unconscious perception can occur was explored in a famous study by Lazarus and McCleary (1951).

Method They presented participants with ten nonsense syllables on a screen; for five of these syllables, presentation was accompanied by a mild electric shock. After the initial training period, they were shown the syllables again without the shocks, but at a presentation rate that was too fast for them to consciously perceive the words. Participants were wired to a galvanic skin response (GSR) meter, recording minute changes in the surface moisture of the skin which occur when a person becomes aroused, as would happen when a person is afraid or shocked in some way.

Results Even though the participants were not aware they had seen anything during the second lot of presentations, when the syllables which had previously been paired with electric shocks were shown again, they experienced anxiety, evidenced by their GSR.

Conclusion Lazarus and McCleary concluded that an effect known as subliminal or unconscious perception was taking place, as the participants had experienced perception without any conscious awareness. Perhaps, then, it is possible that our perceptual systems can screen out some undesirable material before we become consciously aware of it.

8.2.4 Culture and perceptual set

If perceptual set and expectation can be induced by immediate context, then it is likely that the enduring context of the culture in which we are raised and currently live will also influence our perception. Many studies from the 1960s suggest that people from different cultural backgrounds, with different visual experiences, perceive the world differently. For example, Turnbull (1961) studied people who lived in dense forest, taking them to the open plain to watch herds of buffalo. The forest dwellers thought the buffalo were ants and suspected witchcraft. Turnbull concluded they had not developed size constancy because of their restricted visual environment.

Many cross-cultural studies with illusions have suggested that westerners are generally much more susceptible to visual illusions.

Study

Aim Brislin (1993) set out to compare participants from different cultural backgrounds in their susceptibility to the Ponzo illusion (see Figure 8.14).

Method Using participants from the United States and Guam, Brislin compared susceptibility to the Ponzo illusion. Participants were asked to judge the length of the two horizontal lines, and it was noted whether they thought the top line was longer than the bottom one.

Results It was found that participants from rural and non-western environments were less likely to believe that the top horizontal line was longer than the bottom horizontal line than participants from western and urban environments. In other words, participants from rural and non-western backgrounds had an accurate perception of the length of lines, whereas participants from western and urban backgrounds were 'tricked' by the illusion.

Conclusion It seems that the cultural environment in which we live affects our interpretation of distortion illusions like the Ponzo illusion.

In order to explain such cultural differences, Segall et al. (1963) proposed the **carpentered-world hypothesis**, which suggested that westerners are tricked by line illusions because they live in an environment shaped by builders and carpenters, which is full of straight lines, right angles and level floors. As a result, we have a tendency to perceive any line drawings in terms of angular buildings. The carpentered-world explanation of the Müller-Lyer illusion can be seen in Figure 8.13.

Evaluation

- Critics argue that exposure to western culture, especially two-dimensional images such as pictures and TV screens, may be a confounding variable in many studies of cultural differences in perception. It could be that cultural differences in interpretation of illusions are not due to having been raised in different environments and exposure to a carpentered or non-carpentered world, but rather to differing experiences with two-dimensional images. In western art, interpretation of pictures involves inferring depth and distance, but not all cultures have art which requires the kind of interpretation we expect in the West. For example, Dziurawiec and Deregowski (1992) found that Australian Aborigines usually present drawings of a crocodile's trunk as it would be seen from above, while they tend to depict the head and tail as these would be seen from the side.

- Studies by Deregowski (1972) and Hudson (1960) appear to show that people who have no experience with two-dimensional pictures of three-dimensional scenes do not understand the need to make a three-dimensional interpretation. So, it may not be correct to assume from cross-cultural studies that surrounding environment determines our susceptibility to illusions and perception of depth; it might simply be due to the differing experiences of two-dimensional representations.

Here are some examples of how perceptual set might influence our perception in real life. Think about whether each example is mostly likely to be due to the effect of motivation, expectation, emotion or culture.

- Maria has stayed up late to watch a murder-mystery film on television. As she makes her way upstairs to bed, she notices what looks to be the shadowy outline of a figure in the doorway of the spare bedroom.

- Andrew and Bev go to the electrical store to buy a new vacuum cleaner. When they get home, Andrew, who loves watching football on TV, remarks how clear the pictures were on the TV screens in the store compared to their TV at home. 'Oh, were they?' says Bev, disinterestedly, 'I didn't notice.'

- Dionne decided to order her dessert from Today's Specials menu when she saw that it included her favourite: lemon mouse.

- Josie and her Italian boyfriend Roberto are on holiday in Italy. She is reading her book on the beach, but she keeps getting distracted by the noise. 'Why do Italian families talk so loudly?' she complains. 'What?' Roberto replies, puzzled.

8.3 Perceptual organisation: The Gestalt principles

The Gestaltists were a group of psychologists who argued that we perceive our world in an organised way. They proposed the Law of Pragnantz, which states that we are innately predisposed to perceive our world in the simplest way possible that requires us to make the least effort. Thus we would tend to perceive a flock of sheep in a field as a group (or flock) of sheep, rather than as one sheep, and another sheep, and another sheep, and so on.

According to the Gestalt theory of perceptual organisation, we perceive our world according to certain principles.

- The principle of figure–ground – We seek to distinguish objects from the background.

- The part–whole principle – We prefer to perceive the whole rather than separate constituent elements.

- The principle of symmetry – We seek out and prefer to experience symmetrical objects.

- The principle of continuity – We prefer to see objects as continuous rather than as separate fragments.

- The principle of similarity – We have a tendency to perceive similar objects as part of a larger group of objects rather than as single objects.

- The principle of proximity – Objects that are close together tend to be perceived as part of the same object.

- The principle of closure – We mentally complete incomplete figures.

- The principle of common fate – Elements of the visual array that move together are perceived as part of a single object.

Some of these Gestalt principles are illustrated in Figure 8.4.

An experimental study which supports the Gestalt theory of perceptual organisation was carried out by Navon (1977). Navon demonstrated our tendency to perceive wholes rather than parts, and a general preference to make the least effort when perceiving a stimulus.

Study

Aim Navon (1977) set out to demonstrate how we perceive wholes in preference to individual elements of a stimulus.

Method Participants were presented with letter stimuli, where a large letter was made up of smaller letters. In one condition, the large letter corresponded with the smaller component letters (for example, a large letter H made up of lots of small letter Hs), and in the other condition, the large letter did not correspond with the smaller component letters (for example, a large letter H made up of lots of small letter Ss). Participants had to identify either the large letter or the small letters in the stimulus as quickly as possible.

```
H    H   S     S
H    H   S     S
HHHHH   SSSSSS
H    H   S     S
H    H   S     S
```

Result Navon found that the time taken to identify the large letter was the same whether the small letters corresponded or not. However, the time taken to identify the small letters was longer in the non-corresponding condition than in the corresponding condition.

Conclusion Participants found it difficult to focus on the smaller elements of the figure and to disregard the whole, indicating a preference for wholes rather than parts, as the Gestalt theory would predict.

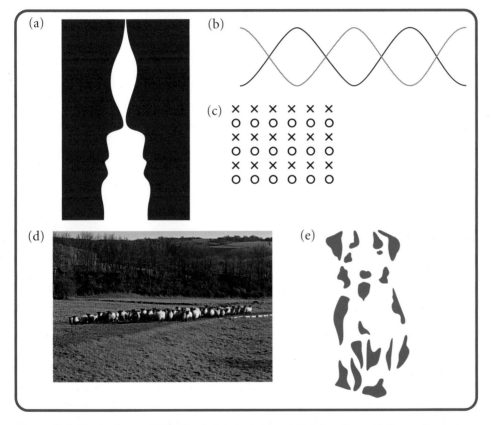

Figure 8.4. Illustrations of the Gestalt principles: a) the face/candle figure illustrates the principles of figure–ground and symmetry; b) seeing these intersecting lines as continuous rather than as three separate segments illustrates the principle of continuity; c) the way we tend to see alternating rows of crosses and circles illustrates the principle of similarity; d) here we see a flock of sheep rather than lots of separate sheep, illustrating the principles of similarity, proximity and a preference for wholes rather than parts; e) the unfinished picture illustrates the principle of closure – we fill in the gaps to perceive a dog.

Evaluation of the Gestalt theory

- The principles themselves are very appealing and seem to offer a useful interpretation of how we perceive visual stimuli.
- However, the Gestalt explanation for the neurological processes involved has been widely criticised. Gordon (1989) describes the Gestaltists' neurophysiological or brain-based explanation of the processes involved in perception as 'almost certainly incorrect'.
- Despite this criticism, he also applauds the Gestalt theory of perceptual organisation as 'a literate, enthusiastic and creative approach to the problems of perception'.
- The Gestaltists took what was described as a phenomenological approach, exploring the way that we experience real phenomena in our world, and, as such, Gestalt principles can be used to describe real-life instances of perception.
- Experimental research, such as that of Navon, supports the Gestalt principles of similarity and proximity, along with the general notion of preference for whole objects.

8.4 Theories of visual perception

As perception occurs early on in the processing of information, it is sometimes the focus for the debate about whether human information processing is **bottom-up** or **top-down**. By bottom-up, we mean that processing relies mostly on the sense information from the things we experience, like the shine and fruity smell of an apple, or the sparkle of light reflected on the surface of a lake. In contrast, top-down means that processing depends not just on the information coming to us from our senses, but also on our store of existing knowledge which comes from past experience. For example, our complete interpretation of an apple might depend on the sensory cues we get from it at the time, and also on our previous 'apple' experiences and our knowledge of the world in general. Although the apple in front of us may look shiny and smell fruity (bottom-up information), our previous knowledge might tell us that this type of apple is more suitable for baking (top-down information), and therefore we would perceive it as not a very good one to bite into.

8.4.1 Gibson's theory of visual perception

J.J. Gibson's (1966) theory of perception is an example of a bottom-up theory of information processing, and is sometimes known as a theory of **direct perception** or a theory of ecological perception. The term ecological is used to emphasise the import-ance of cues from the environment in Gibson's theory. The theory can be summarised as follows:

- Stimulus cues drive perception.

- The visual array contains visual cues, for example light reflected from objects and graded textures.

- As we move around our world, these cues change.

- The changes in visual cues allow us to perceive depth and objects.

- Properties afforded by objects are perceived instantly; for example, when we see a table, we instantly and automatically perceive its hardness, stability, and so on, from the visual cues. We can understand that objects may be placed on the table without having had any previous experience of tables. Gibson would say that the visual cues from the table indicate that the table 'affords' these properties. This is known as the theory of **affordances**.

- The human eye has evolved to be an acutely sensitive organ, able to detect very fine stimulus cues, like changes in light and texture. This extreme sensitivity enables bottom-up or **data-driven** perception.

Figure 8.5. Is this chair hard or soft, smooth or rough, warm or cold, stable or wobbly? What properties does it afford?

To consider Gibson's theory, look at an everyday object in your bedroom, kitchen or classroom, and imagine you have never seen the object before and have no knowledge that would enable you to understand what it is for. Look at it from different angles, but do not touch it. Does the visual information enable you to tell whether it is hard or soft, smooth or rough, warm or cold, stable or wobbly? If it were a completely unfamiliar object, made of unfamiliar materials, would you be able to tell what properties it affords?

Gibson studied the visual experience of Second World War pilots landing aircraft, referring to their entire view as the optic array. He said that factors like the optic-flow pattern and the changes in gradient of textures as pilots moved forward, enabled them to make correct judgement of distances. To understand what he meant by optic flow, imagine what it is like to travel fast in a car, and how, if you focus ahead of you, the rest of the visual information from the outer edges of your visual field appears at first to get larger and then flows past you, out of your field of vision. To understand what Gibson meant by gradient of textures, look closely at a carpet and observe how you can identify each tiny, individual tuft of material. Now look at the carpet from further away, and notice how the texture is much finer and individual tufts are no longer clear. Gibson thought the pilot would experience changes in the texture of grass and trees as the plane travelled along the runway. He called this flow of visual information and outward, radial expansion of textures from the point to which the pilot approached optic-flow patterns.

Figure 8.6. As a pilot approaches the runway, the visual information first expands and then flows out of sight – optic flow. The radial expansion of textures enables the judgement of distance.

Evaluation of Gibson's theory

- The theory is all about the way in which changes in visual cues occur with movement, and how our perception depends on these changes. As such, it is a really sensible theory, since people do move around as they perceive their world and do not see things from a static point.
- The theory stems from applied research with pilots and therefore shows how real-life perception occurs.
- It is quite unlikely that simple creatures, such as insects and fish, use past experience, for example, to perceive depth, so their perception is probably

entirely stimulus-driven. If we believe that all creatures are related, as in the theory of evolution, then perhaps human perception uses the same mechanisms as other, less complex creatures.

- Some infant research (see the study by Bower et al. 1970, on page 272) suggests that certain perceptual abilities may be innate and therefore cannot depend on the use of stored information.
- It is fairly obvious that stimulus information is a necessity for perception.
- Critics argue that it cannot be used to explain illusions and instances of mistaken perception, yet clearly we do make perceptual errors, as illustrated by the various examples of illusions later in this chapter (see pages 277–280). According to Gibson, all we need to perceive accurately is the stimulus information; but in illusions we often perceive the stimulus inaccurately, sometimes even to the extent that we think something is there when in fact it is not, as with fiction illusions (see Figure 8.7).

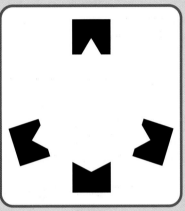

Figure 8.7. Richardson's pyramid is an example of a non-existent figure or fiction, where we perceive a figure that does not exist.

- The concept of affordances is difficult for many to accept, and of course it is hard to believe that we do not need or use past knowledge (or top-down information) to establish the properties of objects and what they might be used for.
- The theory implies that there is no distinction between sensation and perception, and yet from experience we know there is a distinction. This was demonstrated by looking at Figure 8.1, where we saw an array of black blobs on the white background, but we perceived a horse and rider.

8.4.2 Gregory's theory of visual perception

Richard Gregory (1966) proposed a top-down, **constructivist** theory of perception, stating that our perceptions of the world are hypotheses based on past experience and stored information. According to Gregory, our sensory receptors receive information from the environment, which is then combined with previously stored information about the world. Together, these two sets of information enable us to construct a hypothesis about what we are currently seeing. For example, if we are driving along a road through the woods at night, and we catch a glimpse of a small, reddish-brown creature running across the road, we would probably form the hypothesis that it is a fox. This hypothesis is formed not just on the available data, but also through the use of inference about what animals we might expect to see in the woods at night. The hypothesis is then tested and reformulated as we receive more information; for example, if we look through the trees as we pass, we might see a furry tail, enabling us to confirm our original hypothesis about the fox.

Thus the theory suggests that perception is active, constructive and requires some degree of inference. This means that we must go beyond the information given and add to stimulus information in order to make sense of it. Because Gregory's theory emphasises the role of stored information in perception, this type of top-down processing is sometimes referred to as **concept-driven processing**.

The top-down theory of perception emphasises the role of inference in interpreting our experience, and indeed we often use inference to help us perceive. Consider, for example, how we infer depth and distance in our mind when we look at two-dimensional or flat images in books and on TV screens. It is reasonable, then, to expect that we use inference all the time as part of our normal perception.

Many studies support the proposal that we use stored information in perception. Most of the studies involve the perception of visual information, but some research has been carried out on auditory (sound) perception.

Study

Aim Lieberman (1963) set out to show that the surrounding context and past experience influence the perception of single spoken words.

Method Participants listened to recordings of phrases such as 'A stitch in time saves nine' and had no difficulty perceiving the phrases when presented as a whole. In the experimental condition, however, participants heard single words spliced out of the phrases and presented on their own, for example the word 'time', without anything before or after it.

Results Words presented in isolation were much more difficult to perceive; for example, the word 'nine' was recognised only 50 per cent of the time in the isolation condition, but was never misperceived in the control condition.

Conclusion Lieberman concluded that participants were making use of previously stored information about the context to recognise single words within a phrase.

Use of context to enable perception has similarly been found in other work on auditory perception by Warren and Warren (1970), who discovered that participants 'heard' letters and even parts of words, even though they had been deleted from the tape recordings.

Evaluation of Gregory's theory

- Top-down theory is able to explain many of our perceptual activities, including the way we misperceive when we look at illusions (see pages 277–280) and perceptual set.
- It seems only logical that past experience influences our perception; after all, our store of personal experiences is what makes us who we are, so we cannot disregard its influence on our present experiences.
- It is often argued that empirical demonstrations, like experiments which use ambiguous figures, involve artificial stimuli which are deliberately misleading and not like our real, everyday perceptual experiences.
- In emphasising the use of already stored information, top-down theory neglects the richness of stimulus information.
- If perception relied solely on top-down information, how would a newborn baby, who has no stored information, ever be able to interpret any sensory experience and begin to build a mental model of the world? Studies with infants indicate that some perceptual abilities are present at birth, and therefore probably do not require top-down processing.

Study

Aim Bower et al. (1970) set out to show that very young babies were capable of perceiving distance.

Method Infants aged between 6 and 21 days were positioned facing an object suspended in front of them at a distance. As the object was released from the start position and loomed towards the infants' faces, the researchers observed their response.

Results As the object loomed closer, babies made a typical 'collision' response, pulling their heads upwards and away from the approaching object in an attempt to avoid collision. The babies' visual experience of a rapid expansion of the retinal image as the object moved closer enabled them to interpret this as a change in distance.

Conclusion Infants can perceive depth at just a few days old, as indicated by their avoidance response to the looming object. It is questionable whether six-day-old babies could have had sufficient visual experience to enable them to have learned about depth perception, so the study appears to contradict the top-down hypothesis. It seems, therefore, that nature endows us with certain abilities, such as depth perception.

Work with illusions seems at first sight to be good evidence for top-down processing, but some illusions still persist, even when we know we are making a perceptual error. For example, even when we are told that the horizontal lines in Figure 8.8 are straight and parallel, we continue to experience them as slightly curved or convex. According to top-down theory, once we know the lines are straight, we should no longer experience the illusion. Gregory's top-down theory of perception cannot adequately explain why such mistaken hypotheses still persist, even when we know they are wrong.

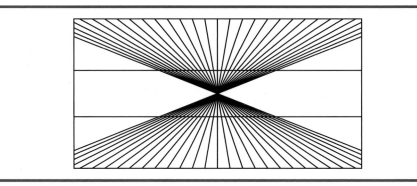

Figure 8.8. The two horizontal lines are parallel, although they don't look it.

8.4.3 Gibson and Gregory: A compromise

The theories of Gibson and Gregory represent two extreme views about how perception occurs. It is probably more sensible to take a combined approach, appreciating that both bottom-up and top-down perception can occur simultaneously and to varying degrees. As a compromise position, Eysenck and Keane (1995) suggest that perception is perhaps mostly bottom-up in clear viewing conditions, when the visual cues are obvious and easy to determine, but probably more dependent on top-down information when viewing conditions are not so clear and we need to fill in the missing bits.

An alternative compromise between Gibson and Gregory was proposed by Neisser (1976), who suggested a dynamic theory of perception which takes account of both bottom-up and top-down information. According to the **analysis-by-synthesis model**, past experience in the form of schemas leads us to look for particular features in the environment. A schema is an organised unit of knowledge about the world. The sensory data from the features we explore leads to a revision of our schema and an adjustment of what we expect, and therefore what sense data we notice and analyse. For example, a 'plant' schema might consist of information about the colour of flowers and leaves, so when you visit a garden, you seek out plants of a certain colour. As you inspect your chosen plants, you notice the aromatic smell of the lavender, which now becomes part of your plant schema. From now on, you will focus not only on colour and leaf texture, but also on the scent of the plants.

8.5 Depth cues

Depth cues are cues in the visual array that enable us to infer how far away things are from us. Monocular cues require the use of only one eye to enable perception of distance, whereas binocular cues require the use of both eyes working together to produce the effect of distance.

Monocular (one-eye) cues:

- Decreasing size: we learn that the size of an image made by an object is not constant. The image on our retina is smaller as the object moves away. Thus a person who makes a small image is assumed to be further away from us than a person who makes a larger image.

- Height in plane: things further away are higher up in two dimensions. For example, a faraway car in a level car park will appear higher up than a car that is closer to you.

- Gradient of texture: the finer the texture, the further the distance. Next time you are on a paved street, stand for a moment and look at the paving as it goes into the distance. You will see that the distant paving stones make a much smaller image than those close to you.

273

- Clarity/light: near objects are clearer/brighter, we can see details. For example, trees in the distance will be darker and will have blurred edges, as opposed to those in the foreground. Those that are near will be much brighter in colour, and you may be able to see fine details, such as individual leaves.

- Superimposition: close objects obscure those that are further away. This is sometimes referred to as occlusion.

- Linear perspective: parallel lines appear to converge as they go into the distance. Imagine standing on a straight road looking forward. It will seem as if the width of the road grows smaller and smaller, until eventually the sides of the road appear to meet in the far distance.

- Motion parallax: as we move, distant objects move more slowly across our visual field than near objects. You can experience this when you are on a train or in a car. If you look into the distance, trees, houses and flocks of sheep will stay in your field of vision for quite a few seconds as you move along. However, if you try to focus on the fencing at the side of the track or the road, you will see that it whizzes across your field of vision so rapidly that you can hardly see it at all.

Figure 8.9. How many monocular depth cues can you see in this photograph?

Artists are well-practised in the use of cues to enable depth perception. If you look at a picture of a scenic painting in a magazine or book, you will see the depth cues the artist has used to convey the illusion of depth in the painting. For example, if some things are higher up in the painting, that could be an indication that they are meant to appear further away. The photograph in Figure 8.9 contains a number of monocular depth cues. How many of those from the list above can you identify in the picture? (Note that motion parallax is dependent on movement, so will not occur when looking at a picture.)

Binocular (two-eye) cues:

- Retinal disparity: each eye receives a slightly different view because each sees the world from a slightly different angle. The nearer the object is to you, the greater the difference in the view each eye receives. The difference in the two images is analysed in the visual area of the brain and the distance of the object is computed (see below). The process of figuring out depth from retinal disparity is known as **stereopsis**. Stereopsis only works for objects up to about ten feet away. At any greater distance, the eyes can focus without having to cross, so there is no difference in the view received by each eye.

- Convergence: this is a cue from the eye muscles which feed back information to the brain about the angle of vision. The harder the muscles work to turn the eyes inwards, the greater the amount of muscle feedback. This would indicate the closeness of the object being viewed.

To understand the extent of the difference in the view from each eye, try the following exercise: close your right eye and hold your forefinger vertically in front of you at arm's length, lining up your finger with a vertical surface in the room, like the edge of the door. As you continue to look at the finger, switch eyes, closing the right and opening the left, but keep the finger quite still. Notice how the finger is no longer lined up with the door edge but appears to have jumped slightly to the left.

Now do the same again, this time with your hand quite close to your face. This time you will see the finger 'jump' dramatically to the left. This shows how retinal disparity (the difference in view from each eye) is much greater when things are close than when they are far away. When you look at your finger up close, you might also feel the muscles 'pulling' to turn your eyeballs inwards to focus on your finger; this convergence will provide the physical feedback which allows us to realise that the finger is close rather than further away.

8.6 Types of perceptual constancy

Although retinal images made by an object may vary according to how near or far away it is, or the angle from which it is viewed, our perceptual systems keep our mental representation of the object constant. For example, even though a person may walk away from us, or twirl round, with the image they make on our retina changing dramatically as a result, we perceive them as remaining the same size and shape. This is made possible by the automatic mental application of our perceptual constancies. The stabilising effect of perceptual constancies, which occurs in the brain, not in the eyes, enables us to live in a relatively predictable environment. In fact, the retinal images we receive from the environment change wildly as we move around our world, but our use of constancies allows us to have the subjective experience of a fairly unchanging world.

8.6.1 Size constancy

Size constancy refers to the ability to perceive the size of objects as constant, despite changes in the size of the retinal image with distance. We use depth cues from the visual field to determine the distance of objects, and once we determine that they are distant, we mentally enlarge them to make them appear normal-sized. Such a process is known as constancy scaling and is an integral feature in the working of many illusions.

8.6.2 Shape constancy

Shape constancy refers to the ability to perceive the shape of objects as constant, despite changes in the shape of the retinal image when they are viewed from different angles. When we look at objects or people from different angles, the image they make on our retina changes considerably, yet shape constancy means that we perceive the shape of the object or person as constant.

Figure 8.10. Even though objects or people in the distance make a much smaller retinal image, we perceive their size as constant.

Figure 8.11. Different retinal image, but we perceive the same object.

8.6.3 Colour constancy

Colour constancy refers to the ability to perceive colours of objects as constant, although the wavelengths of light reflected from them may change considerably as lighting conditions vary. Colour constancy can be demonstrated on a dull day when you have the lights on inside the house or classroom. Look round the room and focus on a brightly coloured object. It might be someone's jumper or a cushion. Look carefully at the colour of the object and think about your experience of it. Now turn off the light and view the object again in the semi-light. How do you experience its colour and brightness now? Do you still perceive the colour as you did previously? Your colour constancy should enable you to perceive the colour of the object as just the same, despite the changes in light conditions.

8.7 Distortion illusions

Living in a three-dimensional world, we have a natural tendency to convert a two-dimensional visual stimulus into a three-dimensional perception. In illusions, this tendency is triggered by intentional use of depth cues, such as linear perspective or height in plane. The presence of depth cues causes us to engage in **constancy scaling**, whereby our perceptual processes lead us to unconsciously mentally enlarge any stimulus we believe to be further away. Many distortion illusions work because we misapply size constancy scaling, falsely believing some parts of the stimulus to be further away than others.

8.7.1 The Müller-Lyer illusion

In the case of the famous distortion illusion known as the Müller-Lyer illusion (see Figure 8.12), the fins give linear perspective: the line with the ingoing fins, line (b), is unconsciously perceived as closer to us, and the line with outgoing fins, line (a), is unconsciously perceived as further away from us. Perhaps the most famous interpretation of this illusion is the **carpentered-world hypothesis** (see page 262 and Figure 8.13 below). According to this hypothesis, we unconsciously perceive the lines as either the outer edge of a building or the inner corner of a room: line (b) appears as the outer corner of the building, projecting towards us, and line (a) appears as the inner corner of a room, stretching far away from us. In this case, it is no wonder that we are tricked by the illusion into seeing line (a) as longer. If we believe it is further away, yet it still makes the same-sized retinal image as the other line, we are forced to conclude that it must be longer. Constancy scaling is 'misapplied' so that line (a) is mentally scaled up to compensate for its apparent perceived distance.

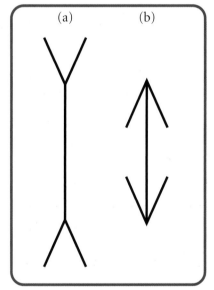

Figure 8.12. The Müller-Lyer illusion. The fins act as linear perspective, giving the illusion of 3D, so that the vertical line on the left appears longer than the one on the right.

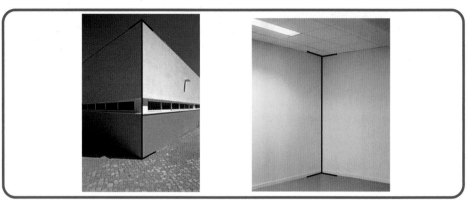

Figure 8.13. Here the linear perspective cues have been added to the outer edge of a building and the inner corner of a room. According to the carpentered-world hypothesis, this is how people from structured, or 'carpentered', cultures unconsciously perceive the Müller-Lyer illusion.

Evaluation

- Not all psychologists agree with the carpentered-world interpretation of the Müller-Lyer illusion; for example, Eysenck (1984) notes that the illusion persists when spheres are used in place of the fins. Without the fins, there are no depth cues, making it impossible to perceive the lines as the corner of a room or the edge of a building, yet people still experience the illusion.
- Others argue that the effect is due to different experiences of two-dimensional images, rather than different experiences of the built environment (see page 262).

8.7.2 The Ponzo illusion

In the Ponzo illusion (Figure 8.14), the viewer tends to perceive the top horizontal line as longer than the one below. This effect is so powerful that it even occurs when we know that the two lines are exactly equal in length. The distortion effect occurs because there are two depth cues in the drawing that lead us to believe the top horizontal line is further away from us than the bottom one. The first cue is linear perspective: the diagonal lines appear to converge in the distance like railway lines. The second cue is height in plane: the top line is higher up in the two-dimensional drawing.

Figure 8.14. The Ponzo illusion is a distortion illusion. Viewers normally perceive the top horizontal line as longer than the bottom one.

Together, these cues lead us to believe that the top line is further away from us than the bottom one, and, if it is further away, yet still makes the same-sized retinal image, we conclude that it must be bigger. Constancy scaling is unconsciously 'misapplied', so that the top line is mentally scaled up to compensate for its apparent perceived distance.

8.7.3 The Ebbinghaus illusion

In the Ebbinghaus illusion, the centre circle is surrounded either by larger circles or by smaller ones. When asked to judge the size of the centre circle, most people assume that the one surrounded by smaller circles is larger than the one surrounded by larger circles. This is because we are tricked into inferring distance by the surrounding circles. Where the surrounding circles are small, we unconsciously believe the whole array to be further away from us and so misapply size constancy scaling, such that the centre circle appears larger. Coren et al. (1999) point out that although the effect is greatest with circles, it also occurs with drawings of meaningful objects, such as dogs (see Figure 8.15).

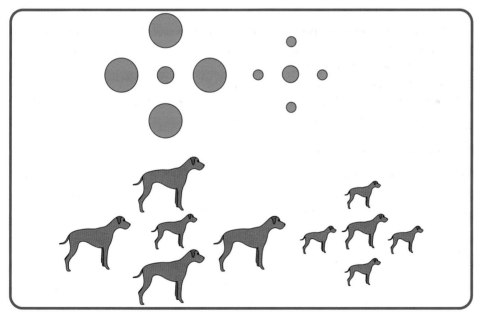

Figure 8.15. In the Ebbinghaus illusion, the centre circle on the left appears smaller than the centre circle on the right.

8.8 Ambiguous figures

Some illusions exist because there are two possible hypotheses in a stimulus, neither of which can be disconfirmed by the data. These illusions are known as ambiguous figures and include the rat-man drawing (see Figure 8.2, on page 256). Strictly speaking, ambiguous figures do not create an illusion as they do not lead us to make perceptual errors in the way that distortion illusions do. However, it is true that they do not allow for one single, accurate interpretation of the stimulus.

8.8.1 Rubin's vase

In Rubin's vase (Figure 8.16), there are two possible interpretations: either a central dark shape of a vase, or two light faces in profile at either side of the figure. Usually the perceiver can see one interpretation or the other at any given moment. According to the Gestalt laws of perception, we have a tendency to seek out and distinguish figures or shapes from the background and have a preference for symmetry. This preference for objects and for symmetry might lead us to perceive the vase more readily than the faces. The Rubin's vase illustrates Gregory's theory of hypothesis testing, as we are able to move readily from one possible interpretation, or hypothesis, to another.

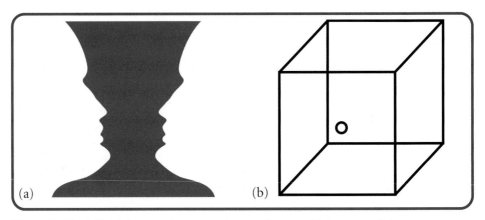

Figure 8.16. a) Rubin's vase is an ambiguous figure with two possible interpretations. b) The Necker cube is an example of an ambiguous figure where there is more than one perceptual hypothesis. If you find it difficult to perceive the cube at a different orientation, try blinking your eyes.

8.8.2 The Necker cube

The Necker cube (Figure 8.16) is another example of an ambiguous figure where there is more than one perceptual hypothesis. The figure is really a simple line drawing in two dimensions, but it is readily perceived as a cube. The cube can be perceived at different orientations, depending on which surface you understand to be the front or top of the figure and which you understand to be the back. Having settled on one way of perceiving the figure, it is often difficult to perceive it at a different orientation. If you blink you may find that it jumps from one orientation to another. The Necker cube is a two-dimensional drawing, yet we are inclined to perceive it as a three-dimensional object, perhaps because our real world consists of objects in three dimensions.

What distortion illusions and ambiguous figures tell us about perception

The way these types of illusions work can tell us a great deal about the normal processes of perception. In general, work involving illusions suggests that perception is based on past experiences of a world which has depth and where objects are perceived at different distances. As a result, we do not perceive stimuli accurately, but instead actively seek to form mental hypotheses and construct a representation of what we see, based on past experience. The observations above seem to confirm Gregory's view of perception as a top-down process based on past experience.

Distortion illusions such as the Müller-Lyer and Ponzo illusions also show how:

- we seek to perceive simple, two-dimensional drawings in terms of three dimensions;
- we use monocular depth cues, such as linear perspective and height in plane, to infer depth;
- we use size constancy scaling to mentally enlarge objects that we believe to be further away from us.

Ambiguous figures such as the Necker cube and Rubin's vase show how:

- we seek to perceive simple two-dimensional drawings in terms of three dimensions;
- we seek to identify objects, look for symmetry and distinguish figure from ground, as the Gestalt principles would suggest;
- we form mental hypotheses about what we are seeing and engage in hypothesis testing.

Evaluation – illusions

- Critics of illusion research point to the artificial nature of the stimuli and say that illusion research contributes little to our understanding of real-life perception.
- According to Gibson (1966), whose approach to perception was ecological and concerned with real-life perception in a dynamic and changing environment, studies involving illusions are of minimal importance and tell us very little about normal perceptual processes.
- The illusions explored above illustrate how the normal perceptual processes of depth-cue analysis, conversion of two dimensions into three dimensions, hypothesis testing, constancy scaling and object recognition are mistakenly applied in the processing of illusions. This, in turn, tells us quite a lot about normal perceptual processing.

How Psychology Works
Motivation and perception

Try your own version of the Gilchrist and Nesberg (1952) study (see page 255), using an abstract picture.

- Find some abstract pictures from the Internet, or prepare your own. You might want to assemble a set of five pictures in total.
- You are going to compare the responses of participants tested before they eat lunch with responses of participants tested after they have eaten lunch. It is necessary to use an independent design because once participants have seen the pictures, they will have been affected by the experience of the first condition.
- Write an appropriate experimental hypothesis for your study. According to past research, you would expect that hungry participants will be more likely to see food- or drink-related items in the ambiguous stimulus than participants who have just had food and drink. Remember to phrase your hypothesis so that it is absolutely clear what is being measured and what the two conditions involve.
- Prepare some standardised instructions and a suitable debrief. The instructions should make it clear that participants should say anything that comes into their mind when they look at each picture. The debrief should thank your participants and explain the purpose of the study in language that ordinary people would be able to understand.
- Select an opportunity sample of participants, brief them and ask for their consent.

- Show your pictures to your participants and ask them what they can 'see' in them. Ask some participants just before lunchtime when they are hungry, and ask other participants after lunch. Control presentation time by giving them a fixed time to look at each picture, 30 seconds for example.
- Use a tally chart to record how many times people mention food- or drink-related items in the two conditions.
- Calculate averages for each condition, and the range, and display your results in a table.
- Write up a summary conclusion of your investigation, stating whether or not the experimental hypothesis has been supported.

How Psychology Works

Perceptual set

Try your own version of the Bruner and Minturn (1955) study (see page 257), using your own handwritten stimulus.

- Experiment with writing words that could be seen in two different ways. Then set your ambiguous word into two different context groups. For example, if your ambiguous word was 'dog/clog', you could produce two lists like those below:
  - horse, cat, rabbit, clog
  - shoe, boot, slipper, clog
- Put the handwritten words on separate sheets of paper and check that each set has an identical version of the ambiguous word. You can photocopy it to make sure they are the same. The ambiguous word must be identical in each condition, otherwise you will have an uncontrolled variable.
- According to research into expectation and perceptual set, you should find that participants perceive your ambiguously written word in line with the surrounding context words. Write a suitable experimental hypothesis and a corresponding null hypothesis.
- Prepare a set of standardised instructions to use with your participants so that each person hears the same instructions beforehand. It will probably start out: 'I am going to show you a series of words. Please . . .'
- Select an opportunity sample of participants, brief them and ask for their consent.
- Present your stimulus words one at a time to your participants.
- On a tally chart, record the number of people perceiving each alternative of the ambiguous word. For each condition, calculate the percentages of participants who do and do not perceive the ambiguously written word in line with the surrounding context. Draw up a separate pie chart for each condition to display the results.

- Write up a summary conclusion of your investigation, stating whether or not the experimental hypothesis has been supported. If most people tend to read the ambiguous word in line with the surrounding context words, then your results are similar to those of Bruner and Minturn.

How Psychology Works

Wholes versus parts

- Try your own version of the Navon (1977) study (see page 264) to see whether people find it easier to perceive wholes rather than parts.
- Use cards with stimulus letters like the ones used by Navon, or you could devise a similar version, with large shapes made up of smaller shapes that correspond or do not correspond. For example, the large shape might be a square; in the corresponding condition it would be made up of little squares; and in the non-corresponding condition it would be made up of little circles.
- To make it simple, you should try just two conditions. In each condition, participants have to name the small component shape/letter out loud. According to Navon's findings and the Gestalt theory of perceptual organisation, it should take longer to name the small shapes/letters in the non-corresponding condition, because the large whole shape/letter will act as a distraction as it is easier to perceive.
- When you have decided on your materials, write a suitable experimental hypothesis and a corresponding null hypothesis.
- Prepare your stimulus cards – a set of eight cards will probably be sufficient.
- Write a set of standardised instructions, explaining to participants what they have to do, and a suitable debrief.
- Select an opportunity sample of participants, brief them and ask for their consent.
- As this is a repeated design with the same people in each condition, remember to counterbalance the conditions: half the participants do the corresponding condition followed by the non-corresponding condition, and the other half do the conditions in the opposite order.
- Collect the data by recording the time in seconds taken to name the full set of shapes.
- Calculate an average time for each condition and compare the findings for each condition.
- Draw a conclusion in relation to the experimental hypothesis.

Further reading

Introductory texts

Eysenck, M.W. (2001) *Principles of Cognitive Psychology*, 2nd edn, Hove: Psychology Press.

Eysenck, M.W. and Keane, M.T. (2005) *Cognitive Psychology: A Student's Handbook*, 5th edn, Hove: Psychology Press.

Gross, R. (2005) *Psychology: The Science of Mind and Behaviour*, 5th edn, London: Hodder Education.

Hill, G. (1998) *Advanced Psychology Through Diagrams*, Oxford: Oxford University Press.

Specialist sources

Block, J.R. and Yuker, H.E. (2002) *Can You Believe Your Eyes?* London: Robson Books.

Coren, S., Ward, L.M. and Ennis, J.T. (1999) *Sensation and Perception*, 5th edn, Orlando, FL: Harcourt, Brace and Co.

Gordon, I.E. (2004) *Theories of Visual Perception*, 3rd edn, Hove: Psychology Press.

Gregory, R. (1997) *Eye and Brain Psychology of Seeing*, 5th edn, Oxford: Oxford University Press.

Ninio, J. (2001) *The Science of Illusions*, Ithaca, NY: Cornell University Press.

Rookes, P. and Willson, J. (2000) *Perception: Theory, Development and Organisation*, London: Routledge.

Roth, I.A. and Bruce, V. (1995) *Perception and Representation*, 2nd edn, Milton Keynes: Open University Press.

Zakia, R.D. (2002) *Perception and Imaging*, 2nd edn, Woburn, MA: Butterworth-Heinemann.

Solution to Figure 8.1 (page 254)
The image is a horse and rider, facing the left-hand side of the page.

Anxiety disorders

9 Chapter

9.1 Introduction

Anxiety disorders are to do with feelings of fear, apprehension and tension that people experience. Anxiety disorders result in what appears to be irrational and strange behaviour. Everybody experiences anxiety at some time in their life. It is quite normal to do so and there are good biological reasons why feelings of fear and apprehension serve to help an animal survive. A threat will cause a person to be fearful and prepare them for the 'flight or fight' biological response. For some people, the level of anxiety experienced is very high and seriously affects their ability to function properly in everyday life.

Anxiety disorders are one of the most common forms of mental or psychological disorders, and they show themselves in three ways:

- **Cognitive effects** – Anxiety is in thoughts and can vary from mild feelings of worry to severe panic.

- **Behavioural effects** – A person may learn to avoid certain situations in order to prevent feelings of anxiety occurring in the first place. Avoidance behaviour is the most common behavioural response to anxiety.

- **Somatic effects** – A person experiences changes in their body, such as shallow breathing, a dry mouth, heart palpitations, perspiration, muscle tension and indigestion.

People who suffer from anxiety disorders are aware of the problem they have – this is called having 'insight' into their condition. This is different from people who suffer from psychotic disorders, such as schizophrenia, where the individual has a lack of insight into their condition. People with anxiety disorders do not lose touch with reality and can often go about their daily lives. But when the anxiety disorder is severe it is very debilitating for the individual; often it will stop the person from working or being able to sustain a relationship, and will dominate their thoughts and feelings. This can be destructive both for the individual suffering from the anxiety disorder and for friends and relatives.

In this chapter we will look at two of the main types of anxiety disorders: phobias and obsessive–compulsive disorders. Both these types of anxiety disorders are characterised by **panic attacks**. A panic attack is when there is a:

- rapid increase of intense anxiety – apprehension and fear;

- feeling of intense fear, with a pounding heart, dryness of the mouth and other extreme somatic effects;

- fear of losing control of everything and feelings of doom or dying.

People who experience severe panic attacks worry a lot about having another panic attack in the future. People who have panic attacks do not feel anxious all the time. The attack can be unpredictable and can happen when it is least expected. Panic attacks may last for just a few seconds, for many hours or even for days. While suffering a panic attack, the person is deeply distressed and unable to function at work or at home. Panic attacks affect women more than men, and are more common in teenagers and people in their twenties than in the middle-aged and the elderly (Robins and Regier 1991).

9.2 Phobias

The word 'phobia' comes from the Greek *Phobos*, who was the god of fear. People who have phobias are aware of what they fear.

9.2.1 Definition and symptoms

A **phobia** may be defined as follows: 'A persistent and unreasonable fear of a particular object, activity or situation' (Comer 2008). This definition highlights the fact that almost anything can become a phobia, including inanimate objects (for example, fear of rain), animals (for example, fear of snakes) and other people (for example, fear of crowds). Some people suffer from a phobia that is fear of fear (called phobophobia).

> The typical symptoms of a phobia are:
> - intense and irrational feelings of fear and anxiety, which may be a severe panic attack;
> - avoidance behaviour, where the person may engage in extreme and complicated behaviours in order to avoid the object or situation that causes panic attacks;
> - phobias may have a gradual onset or may happen very quickly as a result of a particular experience.

The condition tends to be a chronic one. Phobias typically last for many years, with a duration of over 20 years in some cases (Boyd et al. 1990). For some people, phobias may start from a general anxiety or panic attack that does not have an apparent cause. Subsequently, the anxiety comes to be focused on a particular object or situation.

The Diagnostic and Statistical Manual of Mental Disorders (DSM), which is a commonly used method for classifying mental disorders, divides phobias into three categories:

- agoraphobia – fear of open spaces;

- social phobias – fear of interacting and performing in front of people;

- specific phobias – fear of specific objects, animals or places.

9.2.2 Agoraphobia, social phobias and specific phobias

Agoraphobia

Agoraphobia is generally described as a fear of open spaces. The word *agora* comes from the Greek which means a place of assembly or marketplace. Agoraphobia, then, literally means fear of the marketplace. This is very apt, since many people who suffer from agoraphobia have an intense fear of going into busy shopping centres, supermarkets and high streets. Research has shown that agoraphobia develops as a result of severe panic attacks that the person does not expect to happen (Barlow 2002). A person who has an unexpected panic attack simply wants to be in a safe place, usually their home, so that the attack can be coped with better and the level of anxiety reduced. The first thoughts of a person having an unexpected panic attack while shopping, or in any kind of public place, are to get to somewhere that is safe. Being in a shopping mall, for example, while having a panic attack may cause the person to feel trapped, out of control and unable to get to a safe environment quickly. People who suffer panic attacks worry greatly about another one happening; therefore it seems rational to the individual not to place him or herself in a public place where escape and retreat to safety are difficult to achieve. The person then engages in **avoidance behaviour**, which results in staying at home, not going outside and becoming fearful at the simple thought of going out.

Barlow (2002) has identified the following situations which people who suffer from agoraphobia avoid:

shopping malls;	lifts;
being far from home;	restaurants;
cars;	escalators;
supermarkets;	wide streets;
trains;	queues.

Agoraphobic avoidance behaviour does result from panic attacks initially. However, a person who has not had a panic attack for many years may still be agoraphobic. In such instances, the person will still have a fear that going out will result in a panic attack. Avoiding going out to any kind of public place means that a panic attack will not occur. The person then stays at home, does not go outside and becomes regarded as eccentric by other people, rather than clinically ill. Some agoraphobics are able to cope with the feelings of panic that arise from going into public places. For example, some people force themselves to go to work each day, knowing that travelling to work and being at work with other people will cause them to experience high levels of anxiety. Such people are prepared to suffer and are able to do so. For others, the feeling of panic is so overwhelming that they are not able to cope with it at all while outside their home.

Social phobias

Comer (2008) defines a social phobia as: 'A severe and persistent fear of social or performance situations in which embarrassment may occur'. A social phobia is different from agoraphobia, as the fear is to do with being judged by others and/or intense and overwhelming feelings of embarrassment about performing in front of other people. Most us have to speak in front of other people, make a presentation to a group of people or be interviewed for a job by a panel of people. In all these situations, someone with a social phobia would experience high levels of anxiety or a panic attack when in such a situation. The high levels of anxiety or panic would result in the person performing poorly in front of other people. In an interview situation, for example, the person may perform so poorly that they are not offered the job. People with social phobias are often very able, but do not demonstrate this in front of other people because the anxiety is so debilitating.

> **Social phobias may be of three types (Sue et al. 2003):**
> - **performance** – anxiety about performing in public, for example public speaking, playing a musical instrument to an audience, eating with others in a restaurant;
> - **interaction** – anxiety about going out on a date or interacting with a person of high status, for example;
> - **generalised** – anxiety in any situation where other people are present.

The specific fears that social phobics report are to do with fear of criticism, fear of being in front of people, fear of blushing in front of others, fear of making mistakes and fear of the consequences of being assertive. Generally, people with a social phobia feel inadequate in comparison to other people and find relationships difficult. To compensate, such people may become workaholics or develop all-consuming hobbies.

Social phobias occur more in women than men, often start during adolescence and seem to be more common in families where parents and relatives use shame as a way of controlling a child or adolescent's behaviour (Bruch and Heimberg 1994).

Interestingly, social phobias seem not to be related to overprotective parents, lack of emotional warmth from the parents or parental rejection.

It is important to distinguish shyness from social phobias. People who suffer from shyness do not experience the high levels of anxiety and panic of social phobics.

Specific phobias

A specific phobia can have almost anything as its object. Most commonly we think of fear of spiders, fear of snakes, fear of flying and fear of strangers. There are literally hundreds of different types of specific phobias, and each has a particular name, as shown below:

Figure 9.1. Many people have a fear of spiders, which is a specific phobia.

- fear of beards – pogonophobia;

- fear of fear – phobophobia;

- fear of blood – hematophobia;

- fear of corpses – necrophobia;

- fear of fire – pyrophobia;

- fear of fur – doraphobia;

- fear of ghosts – phasmophobia;

- fear of marriage – gamophobia;

- fear of odours – osmophobia;

- fear of sleep – hypnophobia;

- fear of spiders – arachnophobia;

- fear of strangers – xenophobia.

Ost (1992) studied over 300 patients with a range of specific phobias and found that fear of animals tended to start in the child at about the age of seven years. In contrast, fear of closed spaces (claustrophobia) was much later, around the late teens. Research has shown that many children between the ages of five and ten years have a specific phobia (Muris and Merckelbach 2000). Many of these specific phobias either disappear or exist only very mildly as the child enters adolescence.

Fear of blood (hematophobia) is different from other specific phobias, since the person may actually faint at the sight of blood. People who suffer from this phobia may also avoid seeking medical care and be unable to care for someone who has had an accident and is bleeding profusely.

9.2.3 Explanations of phobias
Biological

Evidence for a straightforward genetic explanation in which a specific gene or set of genes is inherited has not been found. Agoraphobia has been shown to have some genetic basis. The most well-developed and researched biological explanation of phobias is the idea of **preparedness**. The claim here is that human beings have a genetic predisposition to develop certain fears (Scher et al. 2006) and, in consequence, certain types of phobias. It is argued that certain types of phobias are more common than others and have a biological basis which is concerned with survival of the organism. The phobias typically referred to here are fear of darkness, fear of heights, fear of open spaces and fear of strangers. The idea of preparedness states that human beings are physiologically and genetically 'prepared', or biologically ready, to acquire certain phobias and not others. The phobias that human beings are 'ready' to acquire on the basis of experience are those to do with survival and responding to threat.

> ### Study
>
> **Aim** Ohman et al. (1975) conducted a series of studies to investigate the preparedness explanation of phobia acquisition.
>
> **Method** Participants were shown pictures of houses, snakes, spiders and faces of people. Half the participants received an electric shock whenever they were presented with a picture of a house or a face. The other half received an electric shock whenever they were presented with a picture of a snake or a spider.
>
> **Results** Both groups of participants showed fear when subsequently shown pictures they had experienced with an electric shock. This was measured by their skin reaction called galvanic skin response (GSR). Following a period in which participants received no electric shocks it was found that the GSR was higher for those shocked when shown snakes and spiders.
>
> **Conclusion** Human beings may be more biologically prepared or ready to develop phobias for animals such as snakes and spiders, which may threaten survival.

Some psychologists argue that the idea of preparedness can be explained equally well from a biological and environmental perspective. From a biological perspective, one can see that a readiness to fear certain things could have evolved and then been passed on genetically. On the other hand, experience with certain animals, such as snakes or spiders, might have taught us to fear them and in some cases develop a phobia.

Another biological explanation for phobias is that some people are born with an autonomic nervous system (ANS) that reacts more strongly to stimuli in the environment. The ANS (see Chapter 2) is responsible for the body's reaction to threat and prepares the person to meet threat with a flight or fight response. People with a highly reactive ANS experience higher levels of fear when presented with a threat. This may result in such people developing phobias more readily and more strongly than people with a less reactive ANS.

Evaluation

- Overall, biological explanations for phobias have not been very convincing, and the research evidence is both weak and indirect.
- Biological explanations only cover a very limited number of phobias and many phobias cannot be explained by the idea of preparedness.

Behavioural

The two most common behavioural explanations for the acquisition of phobias are classical conditioning and observational learning (modelling).

Classical conditioning has been used to explain the acquisition of phobias by demonstrating that the pairing of a natural stimulus that causes fear with an initially neutral stimulus causes the neutral stimulus to be feared by the person. The neutral stimulus then becomes the object of the phobia. (See Little Albert, page 12.)

Case study

Bagby (1922) reported a case study of a young woman who developed a phobia of running water as a result of an experience she had when her feet became trapped in rocks near to a waterfall. The young woman had left her family to go for a walk and become trapped in some rocks. As time went on, the woman became more and more fearful that she would never escape. Her feelings of terror and panic increased. At the same time, the sound of running water from the waterfall became paired with these feelings of panic. The screaming young woman was eventually freed from the rocks by her family. Afterwards, the young woman showed a strong phobia for running water that lasted for many years.

In terms of classical conditioning, being trapped in the rocks (the unconditioned stimulus) elicited the fear response (unconditioned response). The running water of the waterfall is the conditioned stimulus, and the newly acquired fear of running water the conditioned response. This is shown in Figure 9.2.

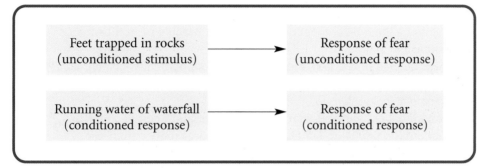

Figure 9.2. Classical conditioning explanation of the acquisition of phobias. The unconditioned stimulus is paired with the conditioned stimulus. When the unconditioned stimulus is removed, the conditioned stimulus produces the fear response.

Evidence that experience of a traumatic event can result in a person developing a phobia has been found. For example, DiGallo et al. (1997) found that nearly 20 per cent of people who had been in a bad traffic accident came to have a phobia about travel. This was shown by such people not wanting to travel in a car, and being frightened of travelling at medium speeds. They also preferred to stay at home rather than travel to see friends, and so on.

Case studies of children with strong phobias show the origin to be some unpleasant and upsetting experience (King et al. 1998). People often report a specific unpleasant experience as the origin of their phobia.

Observational learning

Social learning theory, or observational learning, explains the development of phobias as a result of an observer watching or observing another person (the model) experience pain or upset from an object or situation. If the observer is a young child, the model may be the mother or father. For example, if the mother has a fear of spiders and reacts in highly emotional and extreme ways when there is a large spider in the bath, the child may also develop a phobia for spiders. This is because the mother acts as a role model for the child, and because the strong emotions of the mother towards the spider may frighten the young child. Here, classical conditioning would operate to pair the spider with the fear reaction of the mother, resulting in fear of spiders in the young child.

Cognitive

The cognitive explanation of phobias focuses on the conscious thoughts of people with phobias. Clark (1996) developed an explanation based on the idea that phobics think in a distorted way and have **catastrophic thoughts**. Catastrophic thoughts are where the person thinks that something dreadful will happen to them. For example, a person with a phobia for snakes may think that any snake he or she comes across will attack and bite them, and that the bite will be fatal. Other typical catastrophic thoughts that people with phobias report having are:

● being out of control;

● being trapped and unable to escape to somewhere safe;

● suffocating because of shallow breathing when having a panic attack.

People with a phobia also have negative thoughts about how other people think about them. For example, those with a social phobia usually think that other people will think about them as uninteresting and boring to talk to. Generally, research has shown that people with phobias think that negative events are much more likely to happen to them than people who do not have a phobia (Menzies and Clark 1995).

Bodily sensations are monitored very closely by people with phobias. They are much more acutely aware of and think about their heartbeat, breathing, dryness of mouth, and so on, than people without a phobia. Clark (1996) described people with phobias as having a **cognitive vulnerability**. This means that bodily sensations are seen as dangerous and cause anxiety that might then lead to a panic attack.

Study

Aim Ehlers and Breuer (1992) conducted a study to show that people who suffer from panic attacks are much more aware of their heartbeat and other bodily functions than people who do not suffer panic attacks.

Method Participants who suffered panic attacks and participants who did not were asked to estimate how fast their heart was beating.

Results Participants who suffered panic attacks were much more accurate at estimating how fast their heart was beating than those who did not suffer panic attacks.

Conclusion People who have panic attacks monitor their bodily or somatic functions much more closely than those who do not have panic attacks.

Evaluation

- The cognitive explanation has proved valuable because psychologists can find out what type of thoughts people with phobias have. This has led to a treatment which tries to change how such people think.
- Psychologists can conduct experiments to identify the different thought processes of those who have a phobia and those who do not.

Psychodynamic

The psychodynamic explanation of phobias is based on Freud's idea that people have unconscious wishes and thoughts that cause unconscious conflict between the ego and the id or superego (see Chapter 1). The ego is threatened by unconscious conflict and fears that the anxiety caused by the conflicts will overwhelm it. This would result in the ego not being able to function at all. This is because all the ego's energy would be used up coping with the anxiety or feelings of panic. To cope with this, the ego uses a defence mechanism called **displacement** to displace these unconscious thoughts and conflicts onto something external. This results in a specific phobia. The psychodynamic explanation goes on to say that it is less threatening to the individual to have a phobia than it is to have the unconscious thoughts and conflicts without trying to do anything about them. Either way, from a psychodynamic perspective, the person is trapped in a no-win situation, since a phobia can be as debilitating as the original unconscious thoughts and desires. For the ego, though, a phobia is an acceptable compromise because the real source of anxiety resulting from unconscious thoughts has been avoided.

Case study: Little Hans

Freud's famous case study of Little Hans (Freud 1909) explained the boy's phobia of horses as resulting from the Oedipus complex and the ego's displacement of fear of castration onto fear of horses. Little Hans feared that horses would bite him. He displaced his fear that his father would harm him for having sexual thoughts about his mother. Instead of his unconscious fear that his father would harm him, Little Hans displaced the fear of being harmed onto horses biting him.

The psychodynamic approach explains agoraphobia as resulting from separation anxiety experienced by a young child. This is at the unconscious level and is to do with irrational thoughts that the young child has about separation from the mother and/or father, and the realisation of dependency on the caregivers. Agoraphobia serves the function of keeping the person at home, and for the unconscious, irrational mind this reduces separation anxiety. This is because, unconsciously, the person thinks that separation from either or both parents (or caregivers) is less likely if the person is at home all the time.

Evaluation

- All this is supposed to be happening at an unconscious level in the human mind. This makes scientific enquiry extremely difficult; for example, we cannot know directly about a person's unconscious thoughts in the way we can with conscious thoughts.
- Little evidence has been found to support the explanation that agoraphobia in adults is a result of separation anxiety during childhood (Barlow 2002). Psychologists do agree that separation in childhood may lead to more general psychological disorders.

9.2.4 Treatment of phobias

Not all people who suffer from a phobia seek treatment. Some people are able to lead almost normal lives, as long as they avoid situations that create anxiety and panic. For example, someone with a phobia of going in lifts may adjust to this by always walking up stairs. A person with a phobia of flying in aeroplanes may cope with this by not going on planes and travelling by car or on railways. For some people, however, their phobia prevents them from doing things they want to do in life and they seek treatment. Below we consider the main types of treatments that have been used on people with phobias.

Systematic desensitisation

Systematic desensitisation is a technique developed by Wolpe (1958). It has been found to be effective in the treatment of both social phobias and specific phobias. There are two key aspects to this technique:

- getting people to practise relaxation techniques when feelings of tension and anxiety arise;

- a stepped approach to getting the person to face the object or situation of their phobia.

For example, somebody with a fear of flying would first be taught relaxation techniques. This might involve the person listening to his or her favourite music, introducing relaxing smells (aromatherapy) and muscle relaxation techniques. There would then be a series of steps in which the person would be introduced to the real situation progressively. The next step might be to get the person to watch a plane take off. This could be followed by getting the person to sit in a plane seat and to fasten the seatbelt as if ready for take-off. If resources allowed, the step before actually going on a plane to fly could be to go in a flight simulator. To overcome fear of flying, the person would take a friend with them on the real flight who could help with relaxation techniques. The basic principle behind systematic desensitisation is to arrange the tasks in an ascending order of difficulty, a **hierarchy of fears**, finally leading to exposure to the real situation and the phobia itself.

Figure 9.3. Some people have a phobia about flying and may be treated successfully using systematic desensitisation.

The key to the success of this treatment is that the person must actually face their phobia. For example, someone with a fear of snakes has to end up actually holding a live snake. Someone with a social phobia must end up making a presentation to an audience, for example.

Study

Aim Lang and Lazovik (1963) conducted a controlled experiment to assess the effectiveness of desensitisation as a treatment for people with a phobia of snakes.

Method People with a phobia of snakes were divided into two groups. Group 1 received desensitisation therapy for their phobia. Group 2 were the control group and received no therapy.

Results Those in Group 1 showed less fear of snakes after receiving desensitisation therapy than the control group. The same people were followed up after six months and those in Group 1 still showed a reduced fear of snakes compared to the control group.

Conclusion Desensitisation therapy has both an immediate and a long-term effect in reducing fear associated with specific phobias, such as fear of snakes.

Flooding

The technique of flooding is very different from systematic desensitisation. This is because the treatment involves presenting the person with their phobia without relaxation techniques and without any step-by-step build-up. With flooding, a person is exposed repeatedly and in an intensive way to their phobia. For example, someone with a phobia of dogs (cynophobia) would first be asked to visualise a dog and then imagine picking it up (if not too big!) and stroking it. This would quickly be followed by presenting the person with a real dog to handle. The person with the phobia literally has their senses flooded with thoughts, images and actual experiences of the object of their phobia.

Flooding is also known as **exposure therapy**. The therapist's job is to keep their client motivated to continue with the therapy. This is because in the initial stages the therapy is very unpleasant for the client and produces high levels of anxiety, if not panic attacks. If the client can cope with the first few sessions of therapy, he or she is likely to be successful in overcoming their phobia. **In vivo exposure** is using the flooding technique with the real object of the phobia from the very start, that is, the first stage of imagining the object is missed out.

The principle underlying flooding therapy is that the client has to unlearn that a phobic object is associated with feelings of unpleasantness. The desired state is for the client to feel at least neutral, if not positive, about the once-phobic object.

Drug therapy

Numerous drugs are prescribed by medical doctors to treat phobias. The use of drugs is based on the view that the anxiety and panic attacks associated with phobias result from abnormal brain activities. The brain abnormalities identified are to do with **neurotransmitters**, especially norepinephrine, dopamine and serotonin (see Chapter 2). The drugs used change the levels of these neurotransmitters in the brain.

Agoraphobia is commonly treated with anti-anxiety drugs such as benzodiazepines and tricyclic antidepressants. These are powerful drugs which can have an adverse effect on the general activity level of the patient. These drugs also have undesirable side effects, such as weight gain, dry mouth and loss of memory. They often produce a dependency, and coming off a drug is a slow process in which the dosage has to be reduced gradually over a period of six months to a year.

Drug therapy does not actually remove the phobia, but treats the symptoms, the most common being high levels of anxiety and panic attacks.

Cognitive therapy

Cognitive therapy (Beck 1976) attempts to remove the conscious, distorted and catastrophic thoughts people with phobias typically have. One technique is **cognitive restructuring**, which has been developed from rational emotive therapy (Ellis 1970). With cognitive restructuring, the client is asked to tell the therapist exactly what unrealistic, distorted and catastrophic thoughts they have. The task then is to get the client to see that these thoughts are irrational and not based in reality. The therapist helps the client to change their thoughts to ones that are rational and more normal ways of thinking about objects or situations.

Another technique used in cognitive therapy is **cognitive rehearsal**. Here, the client with a social phobia, for example, is asked to think about being in front of a group of people and giving a presentation. The client is then asked to think about specific behaviours that are appropriate to the social situation – these are likely to be suggested by the therapist. The client then mentally rehearses the appropriate behaviours to perform, for example, clearly introducing themselves and saying what the topic of the presentation is, referring to notes when the different slides come up, looking at the audience and asking if anyone has any questions at the end of the presentation. Cognitive rehearsal helps the individual to think about and mentally rehearse appropriate behaviours, so that when it comes to the real thing these behaviours can be enacted. Cognitive rehearsal helps to stop the person thinking about the negatives.

Beck (1976) regarded people with phobias as having a negative view of their problem-solving abilities and exaggerating the extent to which a specific phobic object or situation is actually threatening. Beck's form of cognitive therapy is very task-focused and based on helping people to realise that they can solve problems successfully and that threats they see are not justified. The objective is to get the person thinking positively about themselves and to change how the phobic object or situation is thought about.

More recently, Turk et al. (2001) have developed cognitive behavioural group therapy (CBGT) for the treatment of social phobias. Here, a number of people with social phobias are brought together in a group and asked to role-play behaviours they find difficult. For example, if a person has a phobia about speaking in front of an audience, he or she would be asked to speak in front of the group of social phobics. This has been found to be very effective if, at the same time, individual cognitive therapy is provided to the person suffering from the social phobia.

Psychodynamic therapy

Psychodynamic therapy attempts to treat the root causes of the phobia rather than the symptoms. The causes are seen by psychodynamic therapists to be hidden deep in the unconscious. In order to find out about the unconscious conflict and disturbing thoughts, indirect techniques are used. The most common of these are **free association** and **dream analysis**. Free association involves first thinking consciously about the phobia and then reporting, without any censorship, all that comes to mind. The psychoanalyst then helps the client to see that the stream of seemingly unconnected thoughts make up some kind of pattern. This pattern is then interpreted to relate to certain unconscious thoughts and conflicts.

The most disturbing thoughts and conflicts, according to psychoanalysts, result from the Oedipus complex stage of psychosexual development (see Chapter 1). This occurs between the ages of three and five years. We have seen earlier that the psychodynamic explanation of phobias involves the use of a defence mechanism used by the ego, called **displacement**. The task of the psychoanalyst is to make the client aware that the phobia is a displacement from unconscious conflicts and disturbing thoughts. Once this has been achieved, the psychoanalyst helps the client to come to terms with their unconscious conflicts and thoughts and to accept them, no matter how painful the process.

Psychodynamic therapy may take years, and often the client will get worse, as they face their irrational thoughts, before getting better. The overall objective of psychodynamic therapy is to make the ego strong so that it is able to cope with irrational thoughts from the unconscious id and superego. A strong ego will feel in control at all times and be able to cope with feelings of anxiety without thinking that such feelings will become overwhelming.

Evaluation of treatments of phobias

Systematic desensitisation and flooding are techniques that aim to change the behaviour of the person suffering from a phobia. Both techniques are based on the exposure of the person to the phobia. These techniques have enjoyed a good deal of success in the treatment of phobias, with improvements lasting for a number of years (Barlow 2002). These techniques have proved most effective in treating specific phobias, but have been less effective with agoraphobia and social phobias. Research has shown that the longer the person is exposed to the phobic object or situation in therapy, the better the outcome and the longer the improvement lasts. Where a person does not improve, it is often because the client has not followed through the treatment instructions when not in therapy.

Drug therapy has proved effective in reducing feelings of anxiety and panic attacks in people suffering from phobias. However, on its own, drug therapy does not provide the person with any behavioural or cognitive strategies to cope and deal with the phobia. It has proved difficult to evaluate the effectiveness of drug therapy because it often allows the patient to develop their own behavioural therapy. The drug reduces anxiety, so allowing the person to better face their fears and phobia.

Cognitive therapy has proved a successful treatment for phobias, especially social phobias. Cognitive therapy has been successful in treating people with a phobia about speaking in public and claustrophobia more generally. Cognitive strategies, such as cognitive restructuring and cognitive rehearsal, can be practised by a person any time, outside the therapeutic situation. This means that once the therapy has ended, the person has been given cognitive strategies which can be developed further. This helps the individual to maintain his or her ability to cope with and reduce the phobia. As with systematic desensitisation and flooding, cognitive therapy has long-lasting benefits over a number of years.

Psychodynamic therapy is the most difficult to evaluate as a successful treatment for phobias. This is because the therapy may last many years and at times the client will seem to get worse rather than better. Smith and Glass (1977) analysed a large number of studies on the general effectiveness of psychodynamic therapy and found that this type of therapy was slightly less effective than other types. Since then, behavioural and cognitive therapies have been developed and have proved the most effective treatment of phobias.

Other points to note in the evaluation of treatments for phobias are:

- Psychodynamic therapy is the only treatment that attempts to get at the root cause of the phobia. The other therapies treat the symptoms of the phobia and help the person to develop cognitive behavioural strategies so that they can live as near to a normal life as possible.
- Therapies which combine two different types of treatments are also effective, for example combining drug therapy with systematic desensitisation or combining drug therapy with cognitive therapy.
- Drug therapy is often only effective when the person is taking the drug. Once the drug is stopped there may be a relapse. This may be prevented through combining drug therapy with cognitive therapy.

9.3 Obsessive–compulsive disorder

9.3.1 Definition and symptoms

An important distinction needs to be made between obsessions and compulsions. An **obsession** may be described as: 'A persistent thought, idea, impulse or image that is experienced repeatedly, feels intrusive and causes anxiety' (Comer 2008). Obsessive thoughts, ideas or images are not under the control of the individual. These occur repeatedly and endlessly in the person's mind when awake, and often have strong influence over the content of dreams. Obsessive thoughts are very disturbing for the individual, especially since they are uncontrollable much of the time. Sexual, aggressive and religious thoughts are the most common types of obsessive thoughts. Such obsessions often cause very high levels of anxiety and feelings of panic.

A **compulsion** may be described as: 'A repetitive and rigid behaviour or mental act that a person feels driven to perform in order to prevent or reduce anxiety' (Comer 2008). Compulsions are also largely uncontrollable for the person. He or she feels compelled to perform the act, and to perform it in a certain way, again and again and again. The compulsive repetition of the behaviour or mental act helps the individual to reduce their high level of anxiety to a more manageable level. The most common repetitive and compulsive behaviours are hand washing, showering, checking (for example, that you have turned the light switch off when you go to bed) and ordering (putting things neatly in order). The theme of uncleanliness or contamination is common. Mental acts are repeating the same phrase, poem or set prayer over and over again.

An **obsessive–compulsive disorder** is defined as: 'A disorder in which a person has recurrent and unwanted thoughts, a need to perform repetitive and rigid actions, or both' (Comer 2008). This definition highlights the key aspect of thoughts being unwanted by the person with an obsessive–compulsive disorder.

> The DSM describes the main symptoms of obsessive–compulsive disorder as:
>
> - recurrent obsessions and compulsions;
> - recognition by the individual that the obsessions and compulsions are excessive and/or unreasonable;
> - that the person is distressed or impaired, and daily life is disrupted by the obsessions and compulsions.

Additionally, if the person is prevented for some reason from performing the compulsion, feelings of dread and panic occur. People with obsessive–compulsive disorder also feel that they should resist the compulsion, but are unable to do so. Attempts are made to resist, but end in feelings of defeat and failure when the person gives in.

Obsessive–compulsive disorders are anxiety disorders because obsessive thoughts cause feelings of high anxiety and panic. Compulsive behaviour or mental acts are carried out in order to reduce the level of anxiety.

Most people have routines and little rituals in their lives, and performing them often provides feelings of reassurance to the person. Kanner (1998) conducted research to find out the most common rituals and routines that people have in their daily lives. These are shown in Figure 9.4.

Routine	Percentage of people reporting
Button shirt from top to bottom	75
Eat sweetcorn row by row	60
Brush teeth up and down	50
Sleep on left side	34
Sleep on right side	34
Sleep on stomach	25

Figure 9.4. Some normal routines of people. (Adapted from Kanner 1998)

Kanner (1998) also found that people often became agitated or felt uncomfortable if their normal routine was disrupted. Most people can adjust their lives if circumstances are such that they have to change their routine. For example, the time people get up on a weekday is usually dictated by the time they have to start work. A change of job may require a different start time and a change in the routine of getting up. The little routines and rituals that people have do not usually disrupt their lives or cause them distress. When the routine or ritual becomes compulsive, repetitive and very time-consuming, however, it becomes a psychological disorder.

Obsessive–compulsive disorder is equally common in males and females. It has a typical onset from late adolescence to early adulthood. Many people who have an obsessive–compulsive disorder do not go for treatment and manage to function well enough in their day-to-day life. People with obsessive–compulsive disorder are often secretive about their condition and attempt to hide it from other people. For example, someone who has an obsessive–compulsive disorder about not wanting to touch anybody because they might get contaminated with bugs and viruses will develop skills to avoid touching. Such a person may wear white gloves and explain this by saying they have a skin disorder.

For many sufferers of obsessive–compulsive disorder, their lives are so taken up with rituals that they are unable to function adequately or even hold down a job. For example, someone who feels compelled to keep washing may literally spend hours and hours in the shower and so not be able to get to work on time, or at all some days. A person who feels compelled to hoard and never throw anything away may find after some years that they simply cannot move in their home because every room is full.

Figure 9.5. Obsessive–compulsive disorder may result in a person not being able to live in their house!

Leckman et al. (1997) found that certain types of obsessions are related to certain types of rituals:

- Aggressive and sexual obsessions are often related to rituals of checking.

- Dirt or contamination obsessions are linked to washing rituals.

- Obsessions with symmetry are related to an obsession to order things.

9.3.2 Explanations of obsessive–compulsive disorder

The main explanations of obsessive–compulsive disorder are biological, behavioural, cognitive and psychodynamic.

Biological

Biological explanations of obsessive–compulsive disorder have identified genetic factors and abnormal brain activity. Bellodi et al. (2001) claim that genetic factors play a role in the disorder. Using evidence from twin studies and family studies, they showed that close relatives are more likely to have the disorder than more distant relatives. McKeon and Murray (1987) showed that obsessive–compulsive disorder was twice as common with relatives as in a control group.

The use of PET scans (see Chapter 2) has enabled researchers to identify abnormal brain activity. Two aspects of abnormal brain activity have been related to obsessive–compulsive disorder. These are:

- low levels of the neurotransmitter serotonin in the brain;

- high levels of activity in the orbital frontal cortex of the brain.

Serotonin is an important neurotransmitter that is responsible for communication between neurons. Drugs that increase the levels of serotonin in the brain have been found to reduce the symptoms of obsessive–compulsive disorder. These are anti-depressant drugs such as Prozac.

Results from PET scans show that people with obsessive–compulsive disorder have unusually high levels of activity in a part of the left frontal cortex of the brain called the orbital frontal cortex. High levels of glucose metabolism and blood flow have been found here. The frontal lobes are responsible for higher-level thought processes, and this particular area of the brain is involved with other parts of the brain that convert information from the senses into thoughts. What is difficult to determine is whether these high levels of activity are the cause of the disorder or a result of having the disorder.

Behavioural

The behavioural explanation uses classical conditioning to show how compulsive behaviour develops. Behaviourists claim that the specific obsessive behaviour has happened by chance.

- A person who has a high level of anxiety or is extremely fearful happens by chance and at the same time to wash their hands or put something in order, for example. The person finds that this reduces their level of anxiety.

- This behaviour is then performed again when the person is anxious. After performing the same action many times when anxious and finding that the level of anxiety is reduced, the behaviour becomes a learned response. The reduction in anxiety is **positively reinforcing**, so the behaviour is repeated.

Compulsive behaviour or mental acts are a result of many pairings of the behaviour with the lowering of anxiety. Having learned this, the person then engages in the compulsion to prevent a high level of anxiety developing in the first place. This is shown in Figure 9.6.

1. **Initial learned response**
   High level of anxiety ———→ Hand washing reduces anxiety

2. **Established response**
   Hand washing ———→ Prevents anxiety reaching high level

Figure 9.6. Behavioural explanation of how a compulsive behaviour is acquired.

Study

Aim Hodgson and Rachman (1972) conducted a study to show that compulsive behaviour reduced anxiety in people suffering from obsessive–compulsive disorder.

Method Participants suffering from hand-washing obsessive–compulsive disorder were put in a room with objects that they regarded as dirty or contaminated.

Results It was found that participants showed ritual hand-washing behaviour and reported that this lowered their anxiety on seeing the dirty objects.

Conclusion Ritual behaviour, such as hand washing, lowers anxiety in people with obsessive–compulsive disorder.

Evaluation

- The behavioural approach has focused on the compulsion, but has not been able to adequately explain the origins and maintenance of the obsessive thoughts that are characteristic of obsessive–compulsive disorder.
- The behavioural approach is limited because it cannot explain why some people have obsessions but not compulsive behaviour.

Cognitive

The cognitive explanation of obsessive–compulsive disorder starts from the observation that everybody at some time has undesirable thoughts that they would be ashamed to admit to other people. For example, most of us worry at times about touching something dirty or being unsure if we have turned the light off in the living room before going to bed. Cognitive psychologists claim that people with obsessive–compulsive disorder have the following characteristics:

- They are more likely to suffer from depression.

- They have very high moral standards and standards of conduct.

- They believe that their obsessive thoughts are just like actually performing the behaviour. That is, they believe their thoughts are harmful to other people.

- They believe that they should be able to have total control over their thoughts and behaviours.

The cognitive approach regards the compulsive behaviour as having a **neutralising** effect on obsessive thoughts and images. Neutralising may be defined as: 'A person's attempt to eliminate unwanted thoughts by thinking or behaving in ways that put matters right internally, making up for unacceptable thoughts' (Comer 2008).

The idea that the obsessive–compulsive has to 'put matters right internally' is to do with making up to oneself for having unacceptable thoughts in the first place. The neutralising effect of the behaviour makes the person feel better. It is then repeated and becomes a compulsion.

Another cognitive approach to explaining the disorder has been developed by Rachman (1997). This is based on the idea that people with obsessive–compulsive disorder make **catastrophic misinterpretations** of their thoughts.

> Rachman sees this as a four-step process:
> - Step 1: Presence of obsessional thoughts or images, for example images of harming another person.
> - Step 2: Catastrophic misinterpretation of the thought – 'I am a bad person and may end up murdering somebody.'
> - Step 3: Fear and high level of anxiety.
> - Step 4: Attempts to resist and avoid the thoughts.

> ## Evaluation
>
> - Rachman's four-step model does help to explain how an obsessive–compulsive disorder is maintained. What it does not explain, however, is why the person has obsessional thoughts and images in the first place.
> - Perhaps the combination of the four characteristics given above and the four-step model offers an explanation of both the establishment and maintenance of the disorder.

Psychodynamic

The Freudian explanation of obsessive–compulsive disorder is to do with conflict between the id, ego and superego. The conflict is said to date back to early childhood, especially the anal and phallic stages of psychosexual development (see Chapter 1).

The conflict between the id, ego and superego arises as follows:

- The id produces obsessive and disturbing thoughts that are either aggressive or sexual in nature.

- The superego is the moral part of the person and so causes feelings of guilt and badness in the person for having such thoughts.

- The ego tries to reduce the feelings of anxiety caused by the id and superego by using defence mechanisms.

The most common defence mechanisms used by the ego in an attempt to get rid of unacceptable obsessive thoughts include:

- **Reaction formation** – behaviour is the opposite of that of the obsessive thoughts. For example, thoughts of aggression result in a person being kind and giving to charity.

- **Isolation** – the ego tries to isolate the obsessive thought and not to respond emotionally. This might result in someone becoming highly intellectual and aloof from other people.

- **Undoing** – the person behaves in ways that attempt to undo the thoughts. Compulsive washing will 'undo' unacceptable, dirty, sexual thoughts.

The ego employs these defence mechanisms to cope with the conflict and the anxiety that it produces. The ego does not get rid of the conflict by doing this. The conflict remains for the individual, resulting in the obsessive–compulsive disorder.

The anal and phallic psychosexual stages of development are seen as the origins of the conflict. This is because the anal stage is concerned with cleanliness as a result of toilet training. The phallic stage is about unconscious sexual thought from the Oedipus complex. Freud claimed that the anal stage in particular, which occurs around the age of two years, can cause unconscious aggression, resulting from negative emotions about toilet training. This makes the id aggressive and will dominate a weak ego as the child becomes a teenager or young adult. Freud called this 'anal fixation'.

Freud clearly saw the origins of obsessive–compulsive disorder in early childhood and from the two psychosexual stages of development. Other psychodynamic psychologists, such as Erickson, agree that aggressive id thoughts originate in childhood. However, they propose that these come from feelings of insecurity and separation anxiety rather than from psychosexual origins.

Evaluation

- Psychodynamic explanations are difficult to examine from a scientific perspective, especially since so much is said to be going on at the unconscious level of the mind.
- The psychodynamic explanation is negative about being able to do anything to remove the conflict that causes the disorder.

9.3.3 Treatment of obsessive–compulsive disorder

People with obsessive–compulsive disorder are likely to seek treatment only when the disorder becomes very disruptive to their life. The disruption may be to do with being unable to go to work, being unable to sustain an intimate relationship, or being socially isolated and without friends. Many people with a mild form of obsessive–compulsive disorder may not seek treatment because they are able to adapt their daily life to accommodate the disorder.

Behavioural treatments

The most successful form of behavioural treatment of obsessive–compulsive disorder is a technique called **exposure and response prevention (ERP)**, sometimes called exposure and ritual prevention (Meyer 1966). ERP can be used both by flooding, where the anxiety is very high, and by systematic desensitisation, where anxiety levels are kept low through gradual exposure. ERP focuses on the compulsive behaviour rather than the obsessive thoughts, and is not used with people who have only obsessive thoughts or images.

Exposure and response prevention deliberately exposes clients to objects or situations that cause anxiety and requires the client to resist performing the compulsive behaviour. The role of the therapist is to help the person develop ways in which they can resist performing the compulsive behaviour.

A number of steps are usually involved (Franklin et al. 2000):

- informing the client about exposure and response prevention, and what the therapy will involve;
- using what is called an **exposure hierarchy,** which starts with mildly anxiety-raising situations and goes through to the highest level of anxiety (this is similar to systematic desensitisation);
- repeated exposure to situations that cause high anxiety, until the level of anxiety reduces;
- getting the client to resist and refrain from performing the compulsive behaviour.

ERP has been used in both one-to-one and group therapy sessions. Outside the therapy session, clients are asked to practise exposing themselves to feared situations and refraining from the compulsive behaviour.

Research which has followed up clients after ERP therapy has shown that between 55 and 75 per cent show improvement and that the improvement lasts for five or six years (Franklin et al. 2005). Sometimes the person will need a small number of additional therapy sessions to prevent relapse.

Drug therapy

Obsessive–compulsive disorder is classified as an anxiety disorder by the DSM. Treatment of the disorder using tranquillisers has been found not to be effective. Drugs that increase the levels of the neurotransmitter serotonin have been found to be effective. The most commonly prescribed drugs are clomipramine (Anafranil) and fluoxetine (Prozac). These drugs not only increase the levels of serotonin in the brain generally, but also cause the orbital frontal cortex to operate at more normal activity levels.

Improvement is found in between 50 and 80 per cent of cases (Julien 2005). The obsessions and compulsive behaviours do not fully disappear, but are greatly reduced. This allows the person to adopt a much more normal life, where obsessive thoughts and compulsive behaviours do not dominate on a regular, daily basis.

People with obsessive–compulsive disorder who are only being treated by drug therapy relapse to the full-blown disorder if they stop taking the drug. The most common approach is to combine drug therapy with a psychological therapy such as exposure and response prevention. With this dual approach, people are far less likely to revert to the obsessive–compulsive disorder once drug treatment is stopped.

In very extreme circumstances, where drug therapy and psychological therapies have little effect, and the disorder is very debilitating for the individual, **neurosurgery** may be used. Jenike et al. (1991) reviewed 33 cases where neurosurgery had been used and found that about one-third improved significantly following the operation. Neurosurgery is a radical treatment and one that doctors are very reluctant to recommend. Modern drug therapy combined with psychological therapy has reduced the need to resort to neurosurgery.

Cognitive therapy

Cognitive therapy attempts to change the conscious thought processes. There are two initial steps involved:

- helping people to understand that they are **misinterpreting their thoughts** – misinterpretations include thinking that the thought will become an actual behaviour, and feeling guilty and ashamed about having obsessive thoughts;
- making people aware of how they try to neutralise the obsessive thoughts by attempting to make amends for having such thoughts.

Once these two steps have been achieved, the cognitive therapist moves on to helping the person to change their distorted cognitive processes. The most important aspect here is to stop the person from making catastrophic interpretations. The approach attempts either to remove the obsessive thoughts or get the person to think about them in a different way. Both approaches are done to help the person stop performing the compulsive behaviours.

An additional technique used in cognitive therapy is **habituation training** (Franklin et al. 2000). Here the client is asked to think repeatedly about their obsessive thoughts. The idea is that by deliberately thinking about obsessions, they will become less anxiety-raising, with the consequence that compulsive behaviour is not required to reduce high levels of anxiety.

Research has shown that cognitive therapy is successful in reducing the frequency with which people have obsessive thoughts. It has also been found to be effective in reducing both the frequency and the duration of compulsive behaviours (Rufer et al. 2005).

Psychodynamic therapy

Psychodynamic treatment of obsessive–compulsive disorder is similar in many ways to psychodynamic treatment for phobias. The techniques of free association and dream analysis are used in an attempt to uncover the unconscious conflicts that have occurred during the anal and phallic psychosexual stages of development. Psychodynamic therapy tries to get at the underlying cause of the disorder. It is assumed that the obsessive–compulsive symptoms will disappear once the conflicts have been brought to consciousness and analysed.

One of Freud's most famous case studies was of an obsessive–compulsive disorder. This was the 'rat man' case study (Freud 1909), in which a man of 29 years of age sought help from Freud because he suffered from obsessional thoughts which he found very distressing.

Case study: Freud's rat man

The rat man was a young lawyer who first saw Freud in October 1907. His real name was Ernst Lanzer. Ernst told Freud that he had disturbing thoughts about harm coming to his father and a young woman that he liked. The disturbing thoughts centred around a punishment he had been told about when in the army. This punishment involved tying a pot of rats to a person's buttocks and the rats entering the person through the anus. Ernst reported that he thought about this happening to his father and the young lady.

Freud treated the rat man for about a year, using psychoanalysis. Freud traced the obsessional thoughts to conflicts that Ernst had between love and hate. Using free association, Freud analysed the conflict with Ernst. Freud reported that after a year the obsessive thoughts had been removed and Ernst was cured.

It is not known whether or not the rat man remained free of his disturbing obsessive thoughts about rats, since no follow-up study took place after the year in psychoanalysis with Freud.

Traditional psychodynamic treatment of obsessive–compulsive disorder would take between two and five years. These days, psychodynamic therapists offer much shorter therapy, over just a number of months. This therapy concentrates on helping the person take actions to lessen the impact of the disorder on daily life. Less attention is paid to the underlying causes buried in the unconscious and originating in early childhood.

Case study: Combined behaviour and cognitive therapy

O'Kearney (1993) reports a case study of a woman who had obsessive thoughts about stabbing her mother and sister. The woman also had obsessive thoughts about stabbing her own eyes out. O'Kearney asked the woman to record her obsessive thoughts on audiotape and play them back to herself. This is the 'exposure' part of the behavioural treatment. The woman was also helped to identify her catastrophic thoughts and to change these to realistic thoughts. She was taught how to do this in the therapy sessions and then asked to practise when listening to the tape of her thoughts. This combined approach reduced both the frequency of the obsessive thoughts and the associated compulsive behaviours.

Evaluation of treatments

We have seen that the most effective treatments for obsessive–compulsive disorder are behaviour therapy, drug therapy and cognitive therapy. Little evidence has been found to show that long-term psychodynamic therapy is very effective in treating this type of anxiety disorder (Foa and Franklin 2004).

The most effective treatments for this disorder have been found to be a combination of:

- drug therapy with either behavioural or cognitive therapy;
- behaviour therapy and cognitive therapy.

Combining exposure and response prevention (behaviour therapy) with cognitive therapy has been found to be particularly effective.

Treatments that combine drug therapy with behavioural and/or cognitive therapy have been found to result in improvements that last a number of years (Kordon et al. 2005).

Whichever treatment or combination of treatments is used for obsessive–compulsive disorder, rarely is the person completely cured. Successful treatment is usually seen to be when the person reports a major decrease in obsessive thoughts and a dramatic reduction in compulsive behaviour. Success is also measured by the extent to which the person is able to function well in everyday life, by holding down a job, having a stable intimate relationship and having a group of friends. People suffering from obsessive–compulsive disorder may never be free of obsessive thoughts and compulsive behaviour. Cognitive therapy helps them to become aware of this and manage expectations accordingly.

How Psychology Works

A structured interview into daily rituals

In this chapter we have looked at obsessive–compulsive disorders, which thankfully affect relatively few people. In contrast, we have noted that many of us have daily rituals when it comes to the performance of everyday behaviours like brushing our teeth. A ritual is a behaviour which an individual always performs in a particular way. Figure 9.4 (page 303) shows a number of common ritualised everyday behaviours.

- You are going to design a structured interview to investigate people's daily rituals. Remember that a structured interview is one where all the questions are predetermined and asked in a specific order. As you are not allowed to ask supplementary questions, your questions should cover as many relevant aspects of the target behaviour as possible.
- Fully structured interviews are ones where there is a fixed set of options and the interviewee has to choose one of the answers. Decide whether to use fixed options in your interview. This would make analysis easier.
- Make a list of the everyday behaviours to ask questions about. Use Figure 9.4 as a starting point and then add any others that you think might be interesting.
- Write down the questions you are going to ask in relation to each of the behaviours. For example, a series of questions about brushing teeth might go as follows:
  When it comes to brushing your teeth, do you have a specific way of doing it?
  When did you first become aware that you brushed your teeth that way?
  How long do you usually spend brushing your teeth?
  Is there anything that you always do immediately after you have brushed your teeth?
- Decide how to record the responses. If your interview is fully structured, you can tally the answers using a frequency table. If it is not fully structured, you will probably need to note down people's answers.
- Pilot your interview using a few friends and relatives.
- Review the outcome of your pilot study. Were there any questions that did not yield much useful information? Would you amend these if you were to carry out a full-scale investigation, or would you omit them altogether? On reflection, are there any other questions that you should have included?
- Write a paragraph summarising your activity. Include in this paragraph a review of ethical issues to be considered if you were to carry out a full-scale investigation on this topic.

How Psychology Works

A phobia of fur

A psychologist treating a patient with a phobia of fur (doraphobia) uses a toy kitten as a stimulus to test the patient's anxiety levels before treatment begins. She uses a rating scale to measure the patient's levels of anxiety at different proximities to the toy kitten. A low score on the scale indicates a low level of anxiety and a high score indicates a high level of anxiety.

The results are shown in the table below.

Distance from toy kitten stimulus (in metres)	Anxiety rating
10	2
8	2
6	3
5	3
4	4
3	6
2	8
1	9
0.5	10

- Draw a scattergram to illustrate the relationship between distance and anxiety level. Make sure the scattergram has a full title and is fully labelled.
- Write a sentence to describe the relationship between the two variables that is shown on the scattergram.
- Explain how a correlation study differs from an experiment.
- Devise a suitable rating scale that the psychologists could have used to find the patient's anxiety level. Include instructions for the patient at the top of the rating scale to explain how the scale is to be used. Type up your rating scale using a computer.
- The psychologist decides to treat the patient using systematic desensitisation. In order to do this, she must first devise a 'hierarchy of "fur" fears'. Devise a suitable ten-stage hierarchy using various 'fur' stimuli. Now arrange your ten stimuli in rank order, from lowest fear-provoking stimulus to highest fear-provoking stimulus.
- Write a few paragraphs to discuss how the psychologist should take account of ethical considerations in this situation.

Further reading

Introductory texts

Comer, R.J. (2008) *Fundamentals of Abnormal Psychology*, 5th edn, New York: Worth Publishers.

Sarason, I.G. and Sarason, B.R. (2002) *Abnormal Psychology: The Problem of Maladaptive Behaviour*, 10th edn, Upper Saddle River, NJ: Prentice Hall.

Sue, D., Sue, D.W. and Sue, S. (2003) *Understanding Abnormal Behaviour*, 7th edn, Boston, MA: Houghton Mifflin Company.

Specialist sources

Freud, S. (1909) *Notes upon a Case of Obsessional Neurosis (the 'Rat Man')*, Penguin Freud Library, Volume 9, Case Histories 2, Harmondsworth: Penguin Books.

Ledley, D.R. and Heimberg, R.G. (2005) *Improving Outcomes and Preventing Relapse in Cognitive-Behavioural Therapy*, New York: Guildford Press.

Autism

10 Chapter

10.1 Definition and symptoms

According to The National Autistic Society, autism is defined fairly generally as 'a complex, lifelong disability which affects a person's social and communication skills'. The extent to which a sufferer's social and communication skills are affected is indicated by the description of autism in the Diagnostic and Statistical Manual IV (DSM-IV) for mental disorders. DSM-IV is used by psychiatrists to diagnose mental disorders and conditions. It refers to autism as a **pervasive mental disorder**, suggesting that children with autism show severe and extensive developmental problems, with disturbances in almost every aspect of functioning, including relationships, thinking and language.

Diagnostic criteria for autism (after DSM-IV 2000) Diagnosis requires at least two items from Category 1, and one each from Categories 2 and 3, with a total of six or more items.		
Category 1	**Category 2**	**Category 3**
• Problems with non-verbal communication (e.g. eye contact) • Problems with peer relationships • Lack of interest in other people • Not responding to others	• Delayed language • Problems in conversation • Repetitive language • Lack of make-believe or pretend play	• Very restricted range of interests • Extreme preference for routine • Stereotyped movements (e.g. hand-flapping) • Fascination with parts of objects

Figure 10.1. The diagnostic criteria for autism.

The term autism stems from the Greek word 'autos', meaning self, and children with autism certainly appear to be very self-absorbed, or 'in their own little world'.

Here are some examples of behaviours shown by children with autism (Carson and Butcher 1992):

• 'A child seems apart or aloof from others, even in the earliest stages of life.'

- 'If speech is present, it is almost never used to communicate except in the most rudimentary fashion.'

- 'Mothers often remember such babies as never being "cuddly", never reaching out when being picked up.'

- 'Autistic children are said to be obsessed with the maintenance of sameness.'

- 'He ... collected objects such as bottle tops, and insisted on having two of everything, one in each hand.'

Estimates of the frequency of autism vary considerably. Rates of 4.5 per 10,000 have been found in two large-scale independent studies in the UK cited by Kendall (2000). More recently, rates have been found to be higher, perhaps because the definition is often broadened to include individuals who show mild symptoms of autism. The disorder is usually identified before 30 months of age and is three or four times more common in males than in females (Bryson 1996). Cross-cultural evidence suggests different rates in different countries. Autism is hardly ever found in China, with only two cases reported in Nanjing in 1987, despite an estimated population at the time of 4.5 million people. Autism is reported much more frequently in Japan, at 16 per 10,000 (Kendall 2000). These differences might suggest that different cultures use different criteria to diagnose the disorder, or that the disorder is somehow culturally determined. As we shall see later, most modern-day explanations for autism do not normally consider social or cultural influences to be key factors in the development of the disorder.

10.1.1 Kanner's early description of autism

The earliest accounts of autism were published separately by Kanner (1943) and Asperger (1944). (Note that Asperger's syndrome is often referred to as a mild form of autism.) In his paper, Kanner referred to the cases of nine boys and two girls, describing their striking symptoms:

- **Autistic aloneness:** Kanner described how children with autism seemed completely unable to relate to other people, and therefore might as well be entirely 'alone', even when surrounded by others.

- **Desire for sameness:** Kanner noted that the child showed very little variety in either speech or actions, tending to repeat the same sound or activity over and over again, without any sign of boredom.

- **Islets of ability:** Kanner used this term to refer to the very specific and sometimes incredible talents shown by some people with autism. Now known as **autistic savants**, such people exhibit amazing intellectual ability or artistic talent, for example performing feats of mental arithmetic, or producing minutely detailed images from memory.

Kanner's work seemed to suggest that many children with autism have a high level of cognitive functioning. More recent research shows that many children with autism have a general intellectual impairment, and many have an IQ test score of below 70 points (Prior and Wherry 1986), which is the determining level for diagnosis of mental retardation, according to DSM-IV.

Figure 10.2. Autistic savant Stephen Wiltshire displays an extraordinary artistic talent. He adds or subtracts details according to his impressions of the scene, as well as using his own style, to produce a wide range of drawings, including caricatures and intricately detailed scenes of the human form.

Initially, it was suggested by Kanner (1943) that five types of behaviour were typical in cases of autism:

- poor communication;

- poor social interaction;

- preference for routine;

- preference for objects rather than people;

- occasional extreme ability or special talent.

More recently, researchers and clinicians have reorganised and refined Kanner's original characteristics into three groups, each containing a number of specific behaviours. These three groups of characteristics and symptoms have become known as the **triad of impairments** (Frith 2003).

10.1.2 Autism as a syndrome

A landmark population study of autism was carried out by Wing and Gould in 1979. Rather than look at all children with possible symptoms of autism, they started by looking at children who had been identified with any form of physical or mental disorder or problem. They then looked to see what traits they had, and which of these tended to occur together.

Study

Aim Wing and Gould (1979) set out to discover the number of children suffering from autism in a large population.

Method Health or education service data were gathered for 914 children between the ages of 0 and 14 years, living in Camberwell, London. All the children were known to be suffering from some form of mental or physical handicap. Most of these children had IQs below 70. From the original sample, 173 children were chosen for further investigation. Each of the 173 children showed at least one of the following symptoms: severe social impairment; severe communication impairment; repetitive behaviour. Each child was observed and tested repeatedly over the next few years, and there were extensive interviews with parents. When the children were aged between 16 and 30 years, a follow-up study was conducted.

Results Wing and Gould found that severe social impairment takes different forms and affects children with varying levels of intellectual ability. They then separated the children out on the basis of their intellectual ability. They found that if children of higher intellectual ability (with a mental age of 20 months or more) showed social impairment, they also showed the other key features of autism: severe communication impairment and repetitive and stereotyped behaviour. At the same time, they found that none of the sociable children in the higher ability sample demonstrated the other two features of autism.

Conclusion The symptoms of autism should be seen as a triad (or threesome) of connected impairments.

The triad of impairments

Frith (2003) suggests that the following three features occur so regularly together in cases of autism that they cannot simply be a chance combination of symptoms: impairment in social interaction, impairment in communication, and repetitive and stereotyped behaviours. Instead, she proposes that they should be seen as a 'triad' or threesome that is present in sufferers of a specific disorder or syndrome. For this reason, she says: 'We can now be sure that when we speak of autism, we are speaking of a syndrome.'

Impairment in social interaction

There is a noticeable lack of responsiveness to other people, with impaired use of non-verbal behaviours such as eye contact and facial expression. Sufferers prefer objects to people and avoid games and joint activities with other children. Autistic children seem unable to engage in pretend play and show a lack of empathy, meaning they have no understanding of the feelings of others.

Impairment in communication

Children with autism often show an absence of speech, or severely restricted speech. They are reluctant to start a conversation or join in with any conversation. Any language they do show is often repetitive and stereotypical, for example where the child repeats a word or sound over and over (**echolalia**).

Repetitive and stereotyped behaviours

Children with autism have limited interests and will become preoccupied with and attached to unusual objects (e.g. rocks, keys). Routine and ritual are so important that any change from the usual activities or routine can cause the child to have a violent temper outburst. Repetitive behaviours such as head banging and rocking backwards and forwards are quite common.

The nature of impairment in social interaction can vary enormously. Frith (2003) identifies three types of social impairment which she refers to as the aloof, the passive and the odd.

Aloof

Danny is totally withdrawn. He does not speak or use eye contact. He will not be cuddled or held. He will play for hours with a toy or computer game, but will not play with other children at all. He will look and sometimes stare at other people, but never appears to recognise them, or even acknowledge that they are people. He shows no expression.

Passive

Ben is a very obedient child, doing exactly what he is told by anyone. Other children sometimes get him into trouble when they tell him to do naughty things. He is often teased and bullied. He will speak and is always completely honest, showing no awareness of people's feelings when he says things.

Odd

Angie is overly familiar with people, including complete strangers. She makes inappropriate approaches, touching or stroking people she does not even know. She chatters continually, asking questions one after another. Although initially fascinated by her strangeness, people soon come to perceive her as a nuisance when she will not leave them alone.

10.1.3 Lack of joint attention

One specific difficulty that has recently become the focus of investigation for researchers interested in autism is the lack of joint attention. Even very young babies will show an interest in what other people are looking at. If a mother is watching a cat playing on the rug, a young infant will look where the mother is looking and watch the cat with her, glancing back to the mother's face now and again, watching her expression, laughing when she does. Similarly, a child will watch a mother's reaction to a stranger who is at the door, observing and sharing her reaction to the unfamiliar person. Such joint attention, which is common in normally functioning children, shows that the child is interested in other people, and in what they are thinking and experiencing. It shows that the child is aware of other people's mental states. A child showing joint attention is sharing the adult's experience of the world and learning how to react appropriately to new and different experiences.

One activity that children use very cleverly to attract the attention of other people and engage with them is 'pointing'. A little boy pointing to a toy is not necessarily interested in the toy very much at all, but is rather hoping to get a response from his father: 'Yes, there's teddy. You love teddy, don't you?' Another social behaviour often seen in young children is 'showing' objects to another person. A little girl building bricks will frequently turn to her parent or another child and hold up the bricks to show them what she has made, expecting to get a reaction from them: 'Ooh! That's a big tower. You are a clever girl.'

Figure 10.3. Normally functioning children show 'joint attention'. This is lacking in children with autism.

For normally functioning children, pointing and showing are frequently used as a way of engaging the adult in a joint, two-way, shared communication. Children with autism tend to show a lack of joint attention; they are less likely to point to objects or use objects to engage the attention of another person.

Study

Aim Sigman et al. (1986) set out to investigate joint attention activities, such as pointing and showing, in children with autism.

Method Three groups of children were observed: children with autism; children with an intellectual impairment other than autism; and controls with no impairment. Each child was observed in a playroom, with toys, in the presence of his or her mother. Various behaviours were recorded, including instances of showing objects, pointing at objects, keeping proximity to mother, looking and vocalising.

Results The children with autism showed significantly fewer instances of pointing and showing than did the other two groups of children. There were no significant differences observed in the other behaviours.

Conclusion Children with autism do not tend to demonstrate behaviours likely to involve and encourage joint attention.

More recent studies have focused on the link between lack of joint attention and language problems in children with autism. Since joint attention is an important shared activity, it is likely that problems in joint attention will be related to problems in communication.

Study

Aim Dawson et al. (2004) set out to investigate the relationship between various forms of social impairment and language ability.

Method Three groups of children were compared on tasks involving the following:

1 social orientation – the ability to attend to social communication (e.g. someone making verbal sounds);
2 joint attention (e.g. following an adult's gaze);
3 attention to another person's distress (e.g. seeing the experimenter apparently bang their finger with a toy hammer).

The first group consisted of 72 children with autism, aged 36–48 months. The second group consisted of 34 children, aged 36–48 months, who were developmentally delayed, but matched for mental age. There was also a control group of 39 typically developing children, aged 12–46 months, again matched for mental age. Language ability was assessed using both the Vineland and Mullen scales of verbal ability.

Results The children with autism performed significantly worse than children in both the other groups on all three types of task. Further analysis showed that poor performance on the joint attention task was significantly linked to poor performance on the language ability scales.

Conclusion Impairment in joint attention is related to other symptoms of autism, including communication problems.

10.2 Explanations of autism

Given that there are many different symptoms of autism, and that some autistic children show high levels of cognitive ability, while others are quite severely impaired, there are problems identifying a single cause of autism.

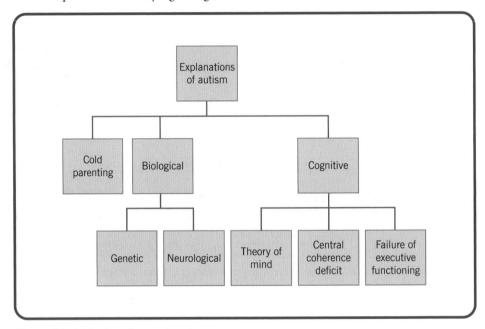

Figure 10.4. Explanations of autism.

10.2.1 The cold parenting hypothesis

The 'cold parenting' hypothesis was originally proposed by Kanner (1943). He suggested that what might be an innate or inborn disorder in the child would be made worse by the behaviour of a cold, unresponsive mother, or **refrigerator mother**. This idea was supported by the work of Bettleheim (1967). Bettleheim had been partially successful in treating some cases of autism at the Orthogenic School of the University of Chicago. The treatment he devised involved a programme of warm acceptance and reinforcement, and seemed to help with some of the problems in some autistic children. It therefore seemed possible that the mother's cold behaviour might have been responsible for the autistic behaviour in the first place.

In some ways, particularly in their reluctance to engage in social interaction and communication, the behaviour of children with autism appears similar to that of emotionally neglected or abused children. Bettleheim noted how autistic behaviour was like the withdrawn and hopeless behaviour demonstrated by survivors of Second World War concentration camps. This observation led some mental health professionals to conclude that autism could have been a consequence of child abuse. However, although it is clear that early socialisation does affect later social behaviour, much evidence suggests that cold parenting is not a cause of autism. McAdoo and De Myer (1978) found no significant differences in the personality traits shown by parents of autistic children and parents of children suffering from other developmental disturbances. In an extension study, they also found that mothers of autistic children had fewer psychological problems than mothers who were being treated for mental health difficulties. Cox et al. (1975) showed that parents of autistic children are no less warm or responsive than other parents.

Study

Aim Koegel et al. (1983) investigated the personality characteristics of parents of children with autism.

Method Parents of children with autism were tested using several psychometric measures: the Minnesota Multiphasic Personality Inventory (MMPI), which is a personality test; the Dyadic Adjustment Scale (DAS), which assesses marital relationships; and the Family Environment Scale (FES), which assesses relationships between family members.

Results On the MMPI, the parents' scores were within the normal range. On the DAS and FES, their scores were similar to those of a control group.

Conclusions It was concluded that parents of children with autism do not show personality characteristics that are significantly different to normal. It was also concluded that relationships in families with an autistic child are not significantly different to those in other families.

Evaluation

- The cold-parenting explanation for autism had serious negative effects on parents of autistic children because it made them feel responsible for their child's condition. Frith (2003) criticises the refrigerator-mother hypothesis as an 'evil myth'.
- Several studies show that the personalities of parents of autistic children are not significantly different to normal.
- The theory that parental behaviour causes autism is not really testable. A child who is emotionally withdrawn and has severely impaired communication would be a very difficult child to look after. Having such an unrewarding, difficult child may cause a parent to be less affectionate. It is

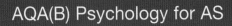

therefore very difficult to demonstrate a one-way cause-and-effect relationship between the behaviour of parent and child.
- According to Messer and Millar (1999), video analysis of a child's early years can sometimes reveal that parents behave differently with their child with autism. However, they suggest that these behaviours are a result of the autism, rather than a cause of it.

10.2.2 Biological explanations

Genetics

We inherit our genetic material from our parents, normally receiving 23 chromosomes from our mother and 23 chromosomes from our father. How much our genetic material contributes to our behaviour has been a topic of interest for psychologists for many years.

Concordance studies are often used to determine the extent to which a condition is inherited. They involve calculating the percentage likelihood of someone suffering from a disorder if they have a relative who is also a sufferer. Folstein and Piven (1991) reported a concordance rate for autism of between 2 and 3 per cent for siblings. This rate is much higher than the frequency of autism in the general population, indicating a substantial genetic component. However, the strongest evidence for genetic factors in autism comes from twin studies, some of which indicate that the concordance rate for **monozygotic** (identical) twins is as high as 96 per cent, with a concordance rate for **dizygotic** (fraternal or non-identical) twins similar to that of ordinary siblings (Folstein and Piven 1991).

Although concordance rates vary from study to study, Rutter et al. (1999) are convinced that autism has a strong genetic component and that several different genes may be involved.

The first twin study of autism was carried out by Folstein and Rutter (1977).

Study

Aim Folstein and Rutter (1977) set out to investigate a possible genetic basis for autism.

Method The researchers carried out a concordance analysis, using identical and non-identical twin pairs. Identical twin pairs share 100 per cent of their genes, whereas non-identical twin pairs share 50 per cent of their genes. Concordance is the percentage likelihood of one twin in a pair having autism if the other twin has the condition. Twenty-one same-sex pairs of twins were recruited for the study. The participants were aged between 5 and 23 years. Eleven pairs were identical and ten were non-identical. One of each pair had autism.

Results In four out of the eleven identical pairs, both twins had autism. In the non-identical pairs there were no cases where both twins had autism. The percentage concordance rate for identical pairs was 36 per cent, compared to 0 per cent for non-identical twin pairs. When the researchers broadened their study to include milder signs of autism – referred to as autistic spectrum signs – the concordance rate for the identical pairs was 90 per cent.

Conclusion The higher rate of concordance in the identical twins indicates that autism has a genetic component.

The higher concordance rate for identical twins has been replicated in other studies. For example, Ritvo et al. (1985) studied 23 sets of identical twins and 17 sets of non-identical twins. All but one of the 23 identical twin pairs were concordant (96 per cent concordance rate), whereas only 4 of the non-identical twin pairs were concordant (23 per cent concordance rate). Again, this seems to be extremely strong evidence for the genetic basis of autism. However, non-identical twins are no more similar genetically than ordinary brothers and sisters, who typically show only 2 per cent concordance for the disorder. This suggests that environmental factors might also have some influence on autism, since the environment for twins is likely to be more similar than it is for ordinary siblings.

Several researchers have attempted to find specific genes responsible for the autism. These studies usually involve comparing the chromosomes of affected and unaffected family members in minute detail. Frith (2003) noted that several large studies have identified sites on four different chromosomes (2, 7, 15 and 16) as being involved. Roder (2000) has suggested that the HOSA1 gene may have a role in the cause of autism. Work in this area is continuing.

Evaluation

- Twin study evidence suggests a strong genetic basis for autism.
- Twins share the same environment and therefore any similarities may be a result of similar environments rather than genetic similarity.
- The suggestion that autism has a genetic cause is consistent with findings showing a link between autistic symptoms and other genetic disorders. For example, it has been found that approximately 10 per cent of children with autism have a chromosomal abnormality known as **fragile X syndrome** (Bee 1989).
- Autism has also been associated with other genetic disorders, such as **Tourette's syndrome**. Comings and Comings (1991) noted that sufferers

of Tourette's syndrome and autism share many symptoms, including obsessive and ritualistic behaviours, adherence to routine, stereotypical movements, and so on.
- Chromosomal analysis studies are as yet inconclusive.
- Consider the consequences if a particular gene, or a combination of genes, is found to be responsible for autism. Perhaps couples who have relatives with autism will choose not to have a child, or perhaps they will ask to have antenatal screening.

Neurological correlates

When psychologists talk of neurological correlates, they are referring to the characteristic patterns of brain structure and function that are seen in people suffering from autism.

In one study using a **double-blind** procedure, Leboyer et al. (1992) found that injecting patients with naltrexone, a drug that blocks the activity of the body's natural opiates or **endorphins**, dramatically reduced autistic symptoms. This and similar findings have led to the suggestion that abnormal levels of the body's own endorphins could be responsible for the symptoms of autism (Kalat 1992).

Recent neurological research has explored differences in brain structure and function between sufferers of autism and non-sufferers. Differences have been found in several areas of the brain (see Figure 10.5).

Brain structure/function	Researchers
Cerebellum size	Courchesne 1991
Overall brain enlargement	Fombonne et al. 1999
Blood flow abnormalities in the brain	Ohnishi et al. 2000
Abnormal development of the brain stem	Roder 2000
Amygdala function	Baron-Cohen et al. 2000

Figure 10.5. Differences in brain structure and/or function between sufferers of autism and non-sufferers.

Study

Aim Allen et al. (2004) set out to study differences in cerebellum activity between autistic and non-autistic participants.

Method The researchers used a functional magnetic resonance image (fMRI) scanner to observe brain structure and activity in eight sufferers of autism and eight matched controls. Each participant's brain activity was scanned as they performed a simple motor task. Areas of the brain which are active during performance of a task have increased blood flow, which can be seen in the scan.

Results The participants with autism showed increased motor activity in a specific area of the cerebellum, compared to the controls. This increase in activity was also found to be correlated with the amount of structural abnormality in the cerebellum.

Conclusion The findings strongly suggest abnormal structure and function of the cerebellum in cases of autism.

Frith (2003) suggests that the enlarged head circumference and increased brain weight commonly seen in people with autism may be due to an exceptionally large number of brain cell connections or synapses. She proposes that people with autism do not appear to have the same kind of natural 'pruning' system for cell connections that exists in normally functioning brains. This means they have an excessive number of cell connections, possibly in some specific areas of the brain and not others.

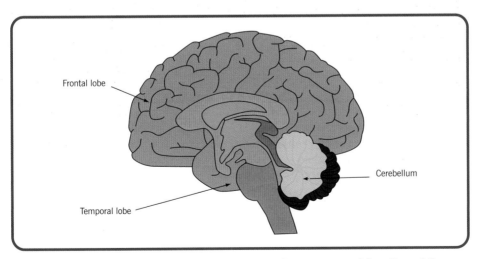

Figure 10.6. Some studies suggest that abnormal structure and function of the cerebellum are related to autism.

Evaluation

- The theory that autism is inherited might be supported by biological evidence for differences in brain structure or brain chemistry between autistic people and non-sufferers.
- However, biological differences in themselves do not necessarily confirm that a disorder is inherited.
- Biological differences may be a result of the disorder rather than a cause.
- Autism is extremely complex, so any differences in brain anatomy or function between people with autism and non-sufferers are likely to be substantial and non-localised (Happé 1999).
- Scans are difficult to conduct and the participant has to remain still for a long time. This means that most studies use only small samples, so it is inappropriate to generalise the results to all cases of autism.
- Most evidence is correlational and we cannot assume cause and effect on the basis of correlation.
- Knowledge about the neurological factors involved in autism may help in understanding the disorder and may lead to more effective therapies.
- At present, many of the findings are contradictory (Frith 2003), but as imaging techniques become more sophisticated, there are likely to be advances in our understanding in this area.

10.2.3 Cognitive explanations
Theory of mind

The social and communication problems observed in people with autism suggest that sufferers do not understand the world from another person's point of view. For example, if someone asks, 'Can you open the door?' we would normally assume that they want to come in and would open the door for them. However, an autistic person who hears that question might just answer, 'Yes', as if responding to a request for information. This everyday example illustrates a profound lack of ability to understand another person's point of view or intention. The apparent failure of people with autism to understand that other people – or indeed themselves – have a mental state was proposed by Frith (1989). Frith suggested that people with autism seriously lack the ability to 'mentalise' or mind-read, to guess what people around them are thinking. In effect, people with autism have **mind-blindness**. This idea was put forward as a **theory of mind** by Baron-Cohen et al. (1993).

The theory of mind hypothesis (Baron-Cohen et al. 1993) accounted neatly for the highly selective nature of problems in autistic children. These children have severe difficulty with tasks requiring an understanding of another person's mind

(mind-reading), and yet are largely unaffected in their ability to perform many cognitive tasks. Leslie (1987) extended the theory of mind hypothesis, proposing that there is an innate **theory of mind mechanism** (ToMM), which is normally fully matured by about two years of age. According to Leslie, biological damage, either before or shortly after birth, might interfere with the development of this mechanism, leading to the cognitive impairments typically seen in children with autism.

Evaluation

- Many studies support the notion of mind-blindness in children with autism. (See pages 337–340.)
- Understanding of autism in terms of a lack of theory of mind is helpful for sufferers. If the reason for the social and communication problems is understood, then it is possible to make allowances for people who cannot read minds.
- The theory of mind hypothesis is criticised for being an incomplete account of autism. It explains the problems seen in autistic children, but does not explain the exceptional abilities, or islets of ability, often demonstrated by people with autism. Accounts of autistic savants are often presented in literature, and there are some fascinating cases of people with autism who can perform amazing mathematical feats or play any tune from beginning to end after hearing it just once. At a more general level, it is not unusual to see a child with autism complete a complex jigsaw at incredible speed, even with the puzzle upside down.

Central coherence deficit

Frith (1989) elaborated on the theory of mind hypothesis, proposing that both the deficits and the exceptional skills shown in autism can be explained through a lack of **central coherence**. Central coherence is the tendency to process information for its general meaning rather than for the specific meaning of each element. For example, when we are presented with a story, we process the overall meaning of the content rather than recall exactly the word-for-word content. Similarly, when listening to a piece of music, we notice the melody and sing along to the tune rather than identifying every single note on each individual instrument. Thus, in any normal processing situation, we take account of the context and the purpose of the activity, processing for general meaning or gist, and do not get sidetracked by minute details which are often of little overall importance.

The concept of central coherence can be easily demonstrated. Complete each sentence below by choosing the appropriate word from the words shown in brackets:

The father was delighted to see his long-lost _____.	(son/sun)
Carrie hungrily ate the juicy, ripe _____.	(pair/pear)
The car stopped suddenly as he put his foot on the _____.	(break/brake)

This task should present no difficulties for most people because they use the context of the sentence to decide which of the two words is correct. In other words, using central coherence means using our general understanding of the world to help us choose the right word.

If people with autism lack central coherence, this would account for many detail-focused autistic behaviours, and the apparent inability of people with autism to understand events and information in terms of global meaning and significance. For example, an autistic person might be able to identify and reproduce every note from a piece of music, but would not be able to say whether it was a 'jolly' or a 'sad' piece.

A number of investigations confirm the tendency for people with autism to process without central coherence, focusing instead on the small details. For example, lack of perceptual central coherence has been shown in the decreased tendency for autistic people to be fooled by visual illusions which rely on the surrounding context, such as the Titchener circles illusion (see Figure 10.7).

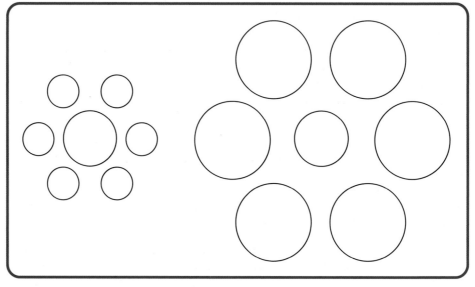

Figure 10.7. The Titchener circles: most people perceive the middle circle on the right to be smaller than the middle circle on the left, but people with autism tend to perceive the two middle circles as the same size.

The lack of perceptual central coherence has also been demonstrated in studies of face recognition in autistic people. Normal-functioning people tend to recognise faces by analysing the whole face, including the person's expression. However, Hobson et al. (1988) found that autistic children seem to process faces through analysis of individual features rather than analysis of the whole face. Since interpretation of emotional expression depends largely on the overall look of the face, Hobson's finding could account for the inability to determine emotional expression that is so typical of autistic people.

Study

Aim The role of central coherence in visuospatial processing was investigated by Shah and Frith (1993).

Method A group of people with autism and a control group were required to produce a geometric design using a number of small patterned blocks. This is an example of a visuospatial task because it requires the coordinated use of visual ability and the ability to manipulate the pieces. Such tasks are commonly used in intelligence tests.

Results The autism group performed exceptionally well in the block task, completing the puzzle correctly in less time than the control group.

Conclusions The poor performance of the control group occurred because they focused on and were distracted by the final overall pattern. This meant that they paid less attention to the features of each separate block. Participants with autism, on the other hand, focused on the detail rather than the whole because they lacked central coherence. Whereas this would normally be a disadvantage, in this task it was helpful.

Memory research indicates that people with autism do not use meaning in memory tasks in the same way that other people do. For example, Hermelin and O'Connor (1967) showed how autistic people could recall lists of unconnected words just as well as they could recall sentences, whereas control groups fared much better with sentences than unconnected words. As Happé (1999) points out, this and findings from other verbal studies seems to indicate that reading a sentence may, for people with autism, be like reading a set of unconnected words.

Happé (1999) suggests that central coherence is best seen in terms of cognitive style or style of thought. She says that we are all on a scale, with some people very strong on central coherence, others very weak, and most people somewhere in the middle. She points out that all people vary in the degree to which they use central coherence to process information, and that weak central coherence does not in itself determine autism.

Evaluation

- Several studies show that people with autism lack central coherence.
- A lack of central coherence might explain some of the typically autistic behaviours that theory of mind alone cannot: for example, excessive attention to minute details and the inability to read facial expression.
- It is likely that weak central coherence *coupled with* a lack of theory of mind would result in autistic behaviours (Happé 1999).

Failure of executive functioning

Executive functions can be described as the higher-order mental functions that allow us to plan activities, and pay attention to some things and not others. We do not need them to perform well-learned everyday actions, such as walking and eating, but we do need them to consciously organise our behaviour. If we did not have executive functioning, we would not be able to switch our attention when necessary or solve problems methodically. We would be limited to routine responses and would not be able to plan or initiate any new behaviours.

Frith (2003) draws parallels between the behaviour of people with poor executive functioning ability and behaviours typically associated with old age. Elderly people are often forgetful and cannot deal with more than one thing at a time. If their attention is momentarily distracted from a task, they forget what they were doing. They are constantly distracted by incoming stimuli. Neuropsychologists have discovered that problems in executive functioning can sometimes be linked to damage in the area of the frontal lobe, although a clear link between frontal lobe damage and autism has not been established.

Studies have shown that people with autism behave quite distinctively in certain types of task which involve the learning of a rule. In the Wisconsin card-sorting task, for example, participants are asked to sort a set of cards of varying sizes, colours and shapes. The researcher rewards the participant for carrying out the sorting correctly. Let's say the participant starts by sorting the cards into piles according to colour, and each time they sort them correctly they receive a reward. However, after a few trials, the researcher ceases to reward for sorting by colour, and, unknown to the participant, establishes a new rule – reward for sorting by shape. People with autism find it particularly difficult to learn this new rule and they persevere in sorting by colour, even though they no longer get rewarded. They continue to make what are known as **perseverative errors**. It appears that their higher-level decision-making and thinking processes do not register the failure of the old rule and the need to devise a new rule.

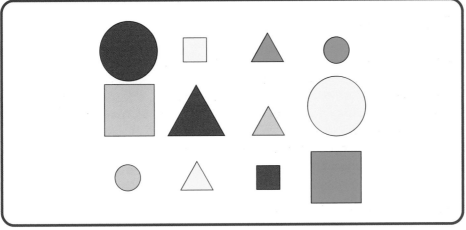

Figure 10.8. People with autism find it difficult to switch from one rule to another, for example, continuing to sort by colour even though they are no longer rewarded. People without autism will quickly switch strategies and solve the problem by starting to sort by another feature, such as shape or size.

Study

Aim Turner (1999) set out to study the ability of autistic people to generate words, ideas and abstract designs.

Method Turner compared the performances of autistic participants with the performances of learning-disabled participants on several tasks. She matched the groups for verbal IQ. All participants were tested for word fluency, fluency of ideas (for uses of objects and interpretation of abstract line drawings) and the ability to produce abstract designs.

Results Turner found that the autistic participants showed significantly impaired word fluency and produced significantly fewer responses on the ideas task. In fact, the performance of high-functioning autistic participants (verbal IQ of 76 or above) on the ideas task was worse than that of learning-disabled controls (verbal IQ of 74 or below). On the design task, participants with autism produced significantly more 'disallowed' designs. In other words, they made more perseverative errors, continuing to offer the same designs even though they had been told they were not appropriate.

Conclusions People with autism are less able to generate novel ideas and behaviours, and lack the executive function to override repetitive or practised actions.

Evaluation

- The theory of failure of executive functioning explains some of the symptoms demonstrated by people with autism, particularly the stereotyped and repetitive behaviours.
- The theory is supported by research findings such as Turner (1999), explored above.
- The notion of executive functioning fits well with our understanding of working memory. It seems that people with autism may have problems with the functioning of the central executive, which supervises and controls the other components of the working memory (see page 220).
- This explanation does not contradict biological explanations, as it may well be that failure of executive function originates in some malfunction of the frontal lobe yet to be determined.

An overview of cognitive explanations

Cognitive explanations account for the various symptoms typically shown by people with autism.

- **Lack of theory of mind** explains the lack of responsiveness to others and an inability to empathise.

- **Central coherence deficit** explains the tendency to focus on detail rather than the whole picture.

- **Failure of executive functioning** explains the stereotyped and repetitive behaviours, and the preference for routine.

However, cognitive explanations for autism are not really explanations of cause, as they merely elaborate on the precise nature of the cognitive differences between people with autism and people without. While knowing exactly what information-processing deficits and special talents are involved in autism is interesting, it remains for further research to determine the cause of these differences in processing. Given the above, cognitive explanations coupled with biological explanations can perhaps provide a fuller account of autism.

10.3 Studying autism

10.3.1 The Sally–Anne experiment

One of the most well-known studies of thinking in autistic children is an experiment used to test theory of mind. In the Sally–Anne experiment, children have to understand what another person might be thinking in order to answer the question correctly at the end.

This is Sally   This is Anne

Sally has a basket   Anne has a box

Figure 10.9. The stages of the Sally–Anne experiment: 1) Sally has a basket, Anne has a box. 2) Sally puts a marble in her basket. 3) Sally goes out for a walk. 4) Anne takes the marble out of Sally's basket and puts it in her own box. 5) Sally comes back. She wants the marble. Where does she look for it?

Study

Aim Baron-Cohen et al. (1985) set out to demonstrate differences in mind-reading ability between children with autism, Down's syndrome children and ordinary children.

Method Children observed a scenario involving two puppet dolls, Sally and Anne. As the scenario developed Sally left her marble in a basket and went out. While Sally was out, Anne moved Sally's marble from the basket to the box. Children were then questioned about where Sally would look for the marble when she returned. The correct answer, 'Sally will look in the basket', requires an understanding of what Sally knows, or, more importantly, what she does not know. The sample of autistic children ranged between 6 and 16 years of age, with a mean verbal age of 5½ years; the Down's syndrome children were approximately the same chronological age, but had lower verbal ability; and the ordinary children had a mean age of 4½ years.

Result The researchers recorded the percentage of correct answers for each group of participants. The Down's syndrome group and the ordinary children gave the correct answer 85 per cent of the time, whereas the

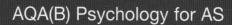
children with autism gave the correct answer on only 20 per cent of trials.

Conclusion The autistic children's understanding of the scenario was quite different to that of the other two groups of children. Children with autism were much less able to put themselves in Sally's place and understand the way she represented the situation in her mind, supporting the view that children with autism do not have a theory of mind.

10.3.2 The 'Smartie tube' test

Autism researchers thought that perhaps children make a mistake in the Sally–Anne experiment because of the type of task. Maybe their difficulty in understanding is due to that fact that they have not actually experienced Sally's problem and made the mistake themselves. In the next experiment, Perner et al. (1989) let the children with autism have the experience of a mistaken or false belief themselves, and then tested whether they could understand what another person would be thinking in the same position.

Study

Aim The researchers wanted to test whether children with autism could understand things from another person's point of view.

Method They showed autistic children a very distinctive 'Smartie tube' that would normally contain little candy-coated chocolate sweets (Smarties). They then opened the tube and tipped out the contents. Out fell a pencil – not what was expected at all. Not surprisingly, the children were disappointed not to have any Smarties. Then a new child, let's call him 'Tom', came into the room, and the autistic child was asked: 'What does Tom think is in the tube?'

Results Normally functioning children over the age of four years tend to give the correct answer in this test because they can put themselves in the place of the other person. Of the children with autism, 80 per cent gave an incorrect answer. They wrongly replied, 'A pencil', failing to understand that the new child would expect there to be Smarties inside the tube as they had not seen that the pencil was in there. When the autistic children were interviewed about their answers, they did remember making the mistake themselves at the start of the experiment. Despite this, they still could not give a correct answer when asked about what the new child was thinking.

Conclusion Perner et al. (1989) concluded that children with autism cannot guess what other people are thinking, even when they have had the same experience themselves. This study supports the theory of mind hypothesis.

10.3.3 Comic-strip stories

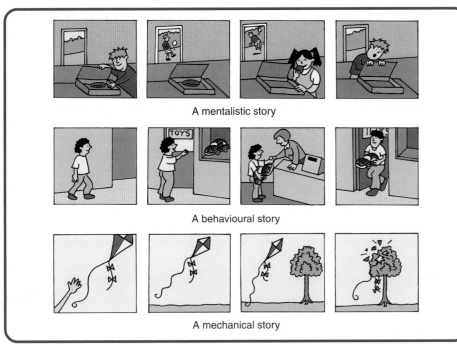

A mentalistic story

A behavioural story

A mechanical story

Figure 10.10. A further experiment tested the ability to understand the point of view of other people. Children with autism were presented with stories in a set of picture cards (similar to these above) which needed to be put into order (Baron-Cohen et al. 1986).

Study

Aim Baron-Cohen et al. (1986) carried out a further experiment to test children's understanding of sequences of events, using the same participants as in the Sally–Anne experiment.

Method The task involved arranging sequences of comic-strip pictures in the right order. The children then had to explain to the researcher what was happening in the stories. There were three types of story: a 'mechanical' story, where the images depicted a series of physical events; a 'behavioural' story, where the pictures showed a series of actions; and a 'mentalistic' or 'belief' story, where the pictures could only be put into the correct order if the child understood the thoughts of the characters in the story.

Results Baron-Cohen et al. found that the autistic children performed significantly worse than the normal and Down's syndrome children on the mentalistic story, although they performed better than both these groups on the mechanical story. For the behavioural story, the children with autism performed about the same as the normal children and better than the Down's syndrome group. Furthermore, when the children with autism explained the events in the stories to the researcher, their explanations lacked reference to the thoughts of the story characters.

Conclusions The study shows that children with autism lack a theory of mind and are unable to mentalise, lacking the ability to put themselves in the place of other people. Their competent performance on the first two types of story suggests that they have no problem with logical thinking in general, but only with one type of thinking. Frith (2003) suggests that the results show how 'children with autism appear to be better "physicists", and equally able "behaviourists", but poorer "psychologists"'.

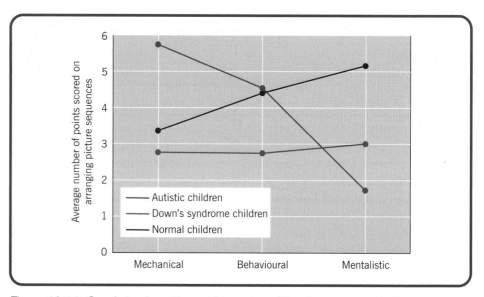

Figure 10.11. Graph to show the performance of the three groups in the comic-strip story experiment. (Adapted from Baron-Cohen et al. 1986)

10.4 Therapeutic programmes for autism

10.4.1 Drug therapy

Various drugs have been used to treat the different symptoms of autism. None of these drugs offers a cure, but they may make the disorder more manageable by reducing the symptoms.

Antipsychotics like haloperidol and, more recently, risperidone, have been used to treat the stereotypical movements and fidgetiness typical of autism. Also used in the treatment of schizophrenia, these antipsychotics are not recommended for treatment of autism unless a child's behaviour is unmanageable through other means (Sloman 1991). However, several studies show that they are effective in reducing repetitive behaviours, social withdrawal and self-abusive behaviours.

Study

Aim McCracken et al. (2002) set out to compare the effectiveness of risperidone as a treatment for behavioural disturbances in young people with autism.

Method A large team of researchers carried out a multi-site, double-blind trial, using 101 children aged between 5 and 17 years. There were 82 boys and 19 girls. The children were randomly assigned to receive either risperidone or a placebo. For eight weeks, the participants in the risperidone condition received doses varying between 0.5 and 3.5mg per day. Before starting treatment, and at the end of the treatment period, all the children were assessed on two measures: an irritability scale and an improvement scale.

Results The reduction in irritability score was 56.9 per cent for the risperidone condition and 14.1 per cent for the placebo condition. On the improvement scale, 69 per cent of the treatment group were categorised as 'much improved' or 'very much improved', as opposed to 12 per cent of the placebo group. After six months, two-thirds of those who showed a positive response to the drug continued to show beneficial effects.

Conclusion Risperidone is effective in reducing tantrums, aggression and self-injurious behaviour in young people with autism.

Antidepressants like fluoxetine (Prozac), which affect the activity of the neurotransmitter serotonin, are frequently used to treat high-functioning people with autism. They appear to be successful in reducing the repetitive behaviours and anxiety-type symptoms.

Stimulants such as Ritalin, frequently used in the treatment of attention deficit hyper-activity disorder (ADHD), seem to be effective in reducing the hyperactivity and improving the focus of patients with autism.

A **synthetic hormone**, secretin, was thought to alleviate symptoms of autism and lead to improved language skills; however, controlled studies have failed to show any benefit. Chez et al. (2000), using a double-blind procedure, found there to be no significant improvement in the group treated with secretin when compared to a placebo group.

Evaluation

- Drugs are generally given to control the symptoms of autism and are not in themselves a cure.
- Many of the drugs have unpleasant side effects. For example, in the McCracken et al. (2002) study of the effects of risperidone, drowsiness, dizziness and drooling were found to be significantly more common in the drug treatment group than in the placebo group.
- On the positive side, the drugs may improve the overall quality of life for sufferers and their families.

10.4.2 Behavioural techniques
Behaviour modification

Behaviour modification involves the use of reward for appropriate behaviour and is a technique based on the theory of operant conditioning (Skinner 1953). According to Skinner, behaviours that are followed by pleasant consequences are more likely to be repeated. Skinner used the term **reinforcement** to refer to the strengthening of a response or behaviour that occurs when it is followed by a pleasant consequence. A positive reinforcer is something pleasant that is given for performance of desired behaviour.

Study

Aim Wolf et al. (1964) carried out a case study of a young boy with autism who had problems with verbal and social behaviour, and engaged in self-destructive head-banging behaviour.

Method The researchers monitored and documented the boy's progress as he underwent a behaviour-shaping programme. A particular problem was his refusal to wear glasses, without which his sight would not develop normally. The behaviour-shaping programme involved giving a sweet as a reward, first for inspection of a toy, and then for inspection of the spectacle frames. Each time, the child had to hold the frames nearer to his face for the reward, and finally he was rewarded only if the frames were on his head.

Result Through reward for successive approximations to the desired behaviour, the child eventually learned to wear his glasses.

Conclusion Operant conditioning techniques in the form of behaviour shaping can be used to successfully condition desired behaviour in children with autism.

Aversion therapy

Lovaas (1977) used electric shocks as an aversive stimulus in the case of extreme head-banging behaviour in a seven-year-old boy with autism. The boy, who had been diagnosed as severely mentally retarded, was normally restrained for 24 hours a day to avoid injuring himself. After just a few sessions of aversion therapy, the maladaptive behaviour ceased. While there are obvious ethical issues related to the use of electric shocks in therapy, it could be argued that the therapeutic procedure was necessary if it led to a reduction in self-injurious behaviour. According to a review by Favell et al. (1982), use of electric shock can effectively reduce the amount of self-injuring behaviour, but should be applied only in extreme cases and by trained professionals.

Language training and the Lovaas technique

Positive reinforcers have been used to successfully shape desired behaviour in children suffering from autism. The **Lovaas technique** is a well-known procedure used to elicit communication or language through the use of operant conditioning. Lovaas (1967) used behaviour-shaping principles, rewarding successive approximations to desired language in children with autism. Using food as positive reinforcement, the child would be rewarded first for making eye contact, then for any speech sound, then for particular vowel or consonant sounds, and finally for the desired word or phrase. Although time-consuming, this technique has been used frequently, both by therapists and by parents of children with autism.

Early critics of the Lovaas technique pointed out that improvements in behaviour tended to cease once the reinforcement therapy stopped. As a result of these criticisms, Lovaas went on to develop a more intensive version of the original technique. This reinvention of the Lovaas technique became known as **applied behavioural analysis** (ABA) and has been used extensively in the USA. Another similar intensive therapy is known as **early intensive behavioural intervention** (EIBI). The key differences between ABA or EIBI and the original Lovaas method are the intensity of application and the rigorously structured approach. Using the more intensive training methods, children with autism undergo long periods of behaviour therapy, sometimes with several trainers working in shifts, so that the child is being treated more or less continuously. New skills or behaviours are taught using direct instruction, repetition and what is known as the hand-over-hand method, to keep the child's attention. Reinforcers can be social praise, edible treats or some other tangible reinforcement, such as a toy. Incorrect or undesired behaviour receives a monotone 'No' from the trainer. Desired speech can also be taught through imitation of mouth movement, and intensive therapy can form part of a **token economy** programme. In a token economy programme, appropriate behaviour is rewarded with tokens which can later be exchanged for treats. Family participation is also seen as important so that the new behaviours and skills continue to be produced in the home environment.

Study

Aim In 1987, Lovaas carried out a study to investigate the effectiveness of the new intensive programme.

Method Three groups of 20 children were compared: the intensive treatment group received 40 hours of treatment per week; a first control group received 10 hours of treatment per week, plus some special education; and a second control group received no treatment.

Results Lovaas reported that of the intensive treatment group, 47 per cent achieved normal functioning by the time they entered full-time schooling at the age of seven years, and 40 per cent showed substantial improvements. On average, the intensive treatment group showed an increase in IQ of 30 points after two years of training, compared to no IQ gains for the other two groups.

Conclusion A structured intensive programme of behaviour therapy can be effective in cases of autism.

The following key features are typical of an intensive behaviour therapy programme for autism:

- use of positive reinforcement;
- customised programme according to individual child's needs;
- addresses all skill domains;
- frequent monitoring of progress;
- parents act as co-therapists;
- directed and supervised by trained practitioners.

Study

Aim Cohen et al. (2006) aimed to investigate the effectiveness of an intensive, community-based behavioural treatment for autism.

Method Over three years, the researchers compared two groups of 21 children. One group received 35–40 hours of early intensive behavioural treatment (EIBT) from a community agency. A control group, matched for age and IQ, attended special education classes at local schools. The children were tested periodically on a variety of measures for IQ, language development, non-verbal skills and adaptive behaviour.

Results The treatment group showed significantly higher IQ and adaptive behaviour scores than the control group. There were no notable differences on either the language or non-verbal test scores. After three years, 17 children from the treatment group went into ordinary teaching classes, either with or without special support. In comparison, only one child from the control group was able to be integrated into mainstream schooling.

Conclusion Early intensive behavioural treatment can be successful in treating some symptoms of autism and can lead to favourable long-term outcomes.

Evaluation of behavioural techniques

- Many people consider aversion therapy and behaviour modification techniques to be unethical because they involve control and manipulation.
- Gross (2001) points out that children treated using these methods are not magically transformed into 'normal' children, and their behaviour often regresses once the treatment stops.
- Behavioural treatments might help children with autism and their parents to live easier lives than without the treatment. For that reason alone they might be considered successful.
- Although popular with many parents, there is controversy about the use of intensive therapy. Critics argue that children may produce appropriate behaviours without understanding what they are doing. For example, a child may learn to respond by smiling and saying 'thank you', but may not have any understanding of how or why these actions are appropriate.
- Many studies are small-scale and do not involve random allocation to conditions.
- Summarising the research, Kendall (2000) suggests that progress is often slow, not always successful and that the greatest improvements occur when the therapy is intensive and involves the parents.

Parental involvement

Early therapy for autism reflected the early suggestion by Bettleheim that the condition might be due to the cold and unresponsive attitude of the mother. The treatment involved a programme of warm acceptance and reinforcement, and seemed to help with some of the problems in some autistic children. An extreme version involved 'holding therapy', where the child was forced to have close physical contact with the mother, in the hope that the protesting child would eventually relax and begin to respond positively.

More recently, parents have been successfully involved in behavioural treatments. In the 1960s and 1970s, it was noted how any benefits from these treatments tended to be lost when the treatment stopped. The need for consistency was recognised: only with consistent application of reinforcement can the child make a clear association between the desired behaviour and the reward. Because of this need for consistency, efforts are now made to encourage families of children with autism to be involved in the therapy themselves. Therapists work with the family so that family members learn how to apply the therapy in the home environment. Involving the family also means that they feel they have some control over what is happening and usually results in greater enthusiasm for the project.

Impressive results have been found in projects that involve parents. Howlin and Rutter (1987) studied 16 families with high-functioning boys with autism. The average age of the boys was six years. Over an 18-month period, mothers were trained to teach language and cope with behaviour problems by using behaviour therapy techniques. The parents were visited by the researchers for several hours each month and counselling was made available. Compared with a control group who received treatment as outpatients, the parental group showed improvements in social responsiveness and had fewer temper outbursts. Tape recordings of verbal interactions showed that the parental group children also had improvements in the amount and quality of speech.

How Psychology Works

An autistic boy

The text below is an extract from a transcript of an interview with the parent of an autistic child. You should carry out a **content analysis** of the text. Content analysis involves looking for themes. You might want to quantify the number of times the parent mentions certain types of symptoms. Think about how individual symptoms might be grouped together. Before you start, refresh your knowledge of the diagnostic criteria and symptoms mentioned on pages 317–323, and then draw up a table to record the frequency of symptoms. You could check for **reliability** by working alongside another student. Discuss the categories beforehand and then record independently; afterwards check to see whether you have got the same or similar results in each category.

Jamie

When Jamie was a baby he was no trouble really. When he was about two and a half I began to think that he was not like other children. He didn't say baby words like other children did and he played always on his own. Well, there might be others there, but he didn't bother with them, or when he looked at them there was no communication. You know, he didn't smile or use his eyes to ask what they were up to. It was hard for me because he didn't like cuddles, he never snuggled up to you like babies usually do and he always looked at you blankly if you tried to talk and play – as if he thought I was stupid; as if he was looking right through me at something else.

He didn't show much interest in toys, and he certainly was never excited about playing with anything, well, except bunches of keys. He loved winding keys around on the key ring. Not counting or anything like that, but just winding. He wanted his own keys so I gave him a bunch and then we added extra ones whenever there were any old ones about. In the end it was a huge bunch. He could hardly lift it but wouldn't go anywhere without it. If I tried to carry them, or moved them out of the way he would go crazy. Yelling and screaming till I put them back just where they were. When people came to the house he wanted their keys and didn't understand that he couldn't have them. He would throw a real tantrum, shouting and tearing at his hair. Once it came out in tufts and he scratched the back of his neck. Then he got the keys and ran to his room. He wouldn't let anyone near for hours. When I finally got inside he was rocking and winding the keys, almost like in a trance. After that the rocking started to become quite frequent.

When people ask him questions he can answer but mostly doesn't. He will ask questions about certain things, always objects. He never wants to talk about people. When we meet anyone he will ask them if they have any keys, where they are, what make they are. He knows all the makes and shapes of different sorts of keys. Is he happy? I don't know. I don't really know him at all. He never laughs and he has no friends.

How Psychology Works

An experimental study of false belief, based on the 'Smartie tube' study (see page 338).

A study was carried out to investigate false beliefs in children with autism. A group of 20 children with autism were compared with a control group of 20 typically developing children with the same average mental age as the autism group.

The children were tested to see whether they could understand what someone else might believe. The researcher used a box of chocolates and a stooge child or actor. Participants were tested individually. Each participant was shown the box of chocolates and watched the researcher take out the chocolates and hide them in the desk. A toy car was then placed inside the box. Then the stooge child entered the room. The researcher then asked the participant what the stooge child would think was in the box. The correct answer would be 'Chocolates', as the stooge child would not know the chocolates had been replaced by the toy car. The researcher recorded the participants' responses as either correct or incorrect. The table below shows the results of the study.

	Children with autism	Typically developing children
Number of correct answers	7	15
Number of incorrect answers	13	5

- Write a suitable hypothesis for this study.
- Calculate the frequencies in the table above as percentages.
- Draw a bar chart to display the percentages you have calculated. Label and title your bar chart.
- Write a brief summary of the outcome in your own words.
- What was the independent variable in this study?
- What was the dependent variable in this study?
- What experimental design did the researcher use?
- Why was it important to use normally developing children of the same mental age as the children in the autism group?
- What ethical issues should the researcher have considered before carrying out this study?

Further reading

Introductory texts

Bee, H. and Boyd, D. (2003) *The Developing Child*, 10th edn, Boston, MA: Allyn & Bacon.

Gross, R. (2005) *Psychology: The Science of Mind and Behaviour*, 5th edn, London: Hodder Education.

Harris, M. and Butterworth, G. (2002) *Developmental Psychology: A Student's Handbook*, Hove: Psychology Press.

Messer, D. and Millar, S. (1999) *Exploring Developmental Psychology*, London: Hodder Education.

Smith, P.K., Cowie, H. and Blades, M. (2003) *Understanding Children's Development*, 4th edn, Oxford: Blackwell.

Specialist sources

Frith, U. (2003) *Autism: Explaining the Enigma*, Oxford: Blackwell.

Kendall, P.C. (2000) *Childhood Disorders*, Hove: Psychology Press.

The AS Examinations

In Unit 1 there are three compulsory questions:

Question 1 Approaches (including the biological approach)
Question 2 Gender development
Question 3 Research methods

In Unit 2 there are six questions in total. Students choose one question on social psychology, one question on cognitive psychology and one question on individual differences. Choices are as follows:

Social influence	OR	Social cognition
Remembering and forgetting	OR	Perceptual processes
Anxiety disorders	OR	Autism

Question Structure

Each examination is 1hour 30mins and all questions carry the same number of marks. Questions are structured, meaning that there are several subsections to each question. There are usually some short answer questions worth 1, 2, 3 or 4 marks, plus one subsection which requires extended writing for 10 marks.

1. Short answer questions

These vary enormously. Here are some examples:

- 'Explain what is meant by ...'

- 'Identify two types of ...'

- 'State two reasons why ...'

- 'Give an example of how a person might demonstrate ...'

- 'Outline what psychologists mean by the term ...'

- 'Describe a study of ...'

These questions require students to demonstrate knowledge of psychological concepts, theories or studies. Some require application of that knowledge or brief explanation, comment or discussion.

2. Long answer questions

These are normally worth 10 marks. A typical 10-mark question would ask the student to 'describe and evaluate' a theory or a piece of research. Here, knowledge of psychology would be demonstrated in the description – for example, a description of a theory of memory. However, the skill of evaluation is also being tested here. For this, the student would have to present an analysis of strengths and limitations of the theory in addition to the description. In these 10-mark questions, it is usual to expect that half the marks are for description and half are for evaluation. You should expect to spend quite a long time on this subsection of the question in the examination.

3. Scenario questions

Some questions are designed so that students can use their knowledge of psychology by applying what they know to a novel situation. For example, a question might include a scenario about a person who forgets different types of information in a number of different circumstances. In this case, students would need to use their knowledge of theories of forgetting to explain probable reasons for forgetting in the scenario. This sort of question tests the application of knowledge.

4. Research methods questions

Unit 1 has one full question on research methods. This is more heavily structured than the other questions, consisting of many subsections requiring short answers. There is no 10-mark subsection in the research methods question.

In addition, questions assessing knowledge and understanding of research methods in psychology will appear in some other questions in both Unit 1 and Unit 2. In Unit 2 this will be confined to knowledge of the experimental method only. As an example of how this would work, a question on remembering and forgetting in Unit 2 might include description of a memory experiment and ask about some aspect of the experimental method. **For this reason, it absolutely essential that students planning to sit Unit 2 before Unit 1 cover the Experimental Methods section of Research Methods in Unit 1 as part of their preparation for Unit 2.**

Glossary

Acetylcholine: A *Neurotransmitter* playing a significant role in the consolidation of memories.

Action potential: Spike of electrical activity that moves down a *Neuron*.

Actor–observer effect: A bias towards making more *Situational attributions* of some behaviour when you are doing it yourself than when you see another person doing it.

Adoption studies: Compare characteristics of adopted children with those of their biological and adoptive parents.

Adrenal glands: Located above the kidneys, these secrete a number of hormones, the most important being adrenalin.

Affordances: Aspect of Gibson's theory of perception which states that visual information alone is sufficient to enable perception of properties of objects.

Agoraphobia: Fear of open spaces.

Alternative hypothesis: Also known as the experimental or research hypothesis. This states that there is a relationship (association or difference) between the two variables being studied. Often shown as H1.

Ambiguous figure: Figure with two or more possible interpretations.

Amnesia: Partial or complete loss of memory, often as a result of damage to the brain.

Anal stage: The second stage of development, when the sexual energy is mainly focused in the anal region and the child receives sexual gratification from urination and defecation.

Analysis by synthesis: Neisser's theory of perception in which the *Bottom-up approach* and the *Top-down approach* are combined.

Androgyny: The appearance of both typically masculine and typically feminine traits within one individual's personality.

Anomalous score: A score which is inconsistent with other scores in a set of scores.

Anthropology: The study of different cultures that exist across the world, including their historical origins and development.

Antipsychotics: A class of drugs used to reduce psychotic symptoms such as hallucinations.

Anxiety: Negative mood state with feelings of fear and apprehension. See *Panic attacks*.

Articulatory loop: A component of *Working memory* which acts as a verbal rehearsal system.

Asch's line study: Asch used an unambiguous and clear task whereby participants were shown a target line and three comparison lines.

Asperger's syndrome: A condition similar to autism but of a milder form.

Attitude: A general evaluation people make about themselves, others, objects or issues which is developed from past experience and which guides behaviour.

Attribution: Perceived cause of a person's own or another's behaviour.

Attributional bias: A source of bias in making inferences about the causes of a person's behaviour.

Authoritarian personality: Characterised as upholding convention, conforming and obeying those in authority, but being authoritarian to subordinates. Linked to *Prejudice* and *Discrimination*.

Autism: A mental disorder resulting in wide-ranging and severe deficits, including problems in social interaction, language and communication, and repetitive or stereotyped behaviours.

Autistic savant: A person with autism who displays a remarkable skill or ability, for example, the ability to produce detailed drawings from memory.

Autobiographical memory: Memory for events that have happened in one's own life.

Autokinetic effect: The apparent movement people see with a stationary spot of light in a darkened room. Used by Sherif to investigate *Conformity*.

Autonomic nervous system: This consists of two subsystems: the *Sympathetic nervous system* and the *Parasympathetic nervous system*.

Aversion therapy: A form of behaviour therapy which involves pairing an unpleasant stimulus with an undesired behaviour.

Baby X study: A study where participants are led to believe that a baby is either male or female.

Behaviour genetics: Concerned with how our genetic make-up (*Genotype*) influences characteristics such as personality, intelligence and mental disorder (schizophrenia).

Behaviour modification: A therapy to change behaviour that uses some form of reward for appropriate behaviour.

Behaviour shaping: Reinforcement is given for successive approximations to the desired behaviour until a long sequence of behaviours is performed for a single reward.

Behavioural sciences: See *Social sciences*.

Behaviourism: An approach in psychology which states that only the objective measurement of behaviour is scientific, and that all learning comes from reinforcement or punishment of responses. See also *Classical conditioning* and *Operant conditioning*.

Binocular cues: Cues to depth or distance perception that require the use of both eyes.

Biological approach: An approach which is interested in how physical structures (especially the *Central nervous system*) and our genes influence thought and behaviour.

Biology: Concerned with understanding the structure and function of the physical aspects of the body.

Bisexual: Possessing the characteristics of both sexes and finding attraction in the qualities of both the same and the opposite sex.

Bottom-up approach: An approach which suggests that our cognitive processes are mainly influenced by incoming stimuli rather than previously stored information. Sometimes known as *Data-driven approach*.

Broca's area: An area of the frontal cortical lobe responsible for the function of speech. If damaged, it results in Broca's aphasia: speech will be slow, laborious and hesitant.

Brown–Peterson task: A method developed to investigate the characteristics of *Short-term memory*. It typically involves the use of lists of three-letter sequences which participants are required to learn and recall.

Carpentered-world hypothesis: Suggestion that people from western cultures, where buildings are structured, or carpentered, with right angles and level floors, perceive the world differently to people from less structured environments.

Case study: An in-depth or detailed study of one individual or a small group of individuals.

Catastrophic thoughts: Where a person thinks something terrible will happen to them.

Causal attribution: An inference about whether the cause of a person's behaviour is dispositional or situational.

Cell assemblies: Hebb's suggestion that groups of *Neurons* are activated in response to new information, forming the basis for the formation of permanent memories.

Central coherence: The tendency to process information for its general meaning or gist rather than processing the specific individual elements.

Central executive: The part of Baddeley and Hitch's *Working memory* model responsible for controlling the operation of the other components.

Central nervous system: Made up of the brain and the spinal cord. The human brain has three major parts: the brain stem, cerebellum and cerebral cortex.

Central traits: Descriptions of personality which have a strong influence on impression formation. See also *Peripheral traits*.

Chunking: A way of increasing the capacity of *Short-term memory* by grouping individual items together in chunks.

Classical conditioning: The pairing of a neutral stimulus with a stimulus that automatically elicits a response, so that the neutral stimulus comes to elicit a response. First developed by Ivan Pavlov.

Client-centred therapy: Humanistic therapy based on the principle that the therapist must show unconditional positive regard to the client.

Closed questions: Questions with a fixed number of optional answers.

Cognitive approach: The dominant approach in contemporary psychology which studies thought and mental processes. Areas of study include perception, memory and thought. See also *Information-processing approach*.

Cognitive neuropsychology: Study of brain processes, especially in people who have suffered brain damage.

Cognitive science: Theoretical approach to understanding how we think.

Cognitive therapy: Treatment of phobias and obsessive–compulsive disorder by attempting to change negative thoughts.

Cold-parenting hypothesis: A theory of autism according to which the disorder is due to cold and unresponsive parenting. See also *Refrigerator mother*.

Collectivistic cultures: Cultures where the good of the group and the achievement of the group is valued over individual achievement, for example in China and Asian countries. See also *Individualistic cultures*.

Colour constancy: The ability to perceive colours as constant, despite changes in the retinal cues with varying light conditions.

Compliance: A type of *Social influence* whereby direct requests are made from one person to another.

Compulsion: Repetitive behaviour which a person performs in an attempt to reduce *Anxiety*. See also *Obsession*.

Concept-driven processing: See *Top-down approach*.

Concordance: The percentage likelihood that if one individual in a pair has a trait, the other individual also possesses the same trait.

Conditional positive regard: Humanistic concept in which a person is loved with certain conditions attached.

Conformity: A type of *Social influence* in which a person changes their attitudes, beliefs or behaviours to adhere to social norms. Usually seen as *Majority influence*.

Confounding variable: A variable that has not been controlled in an experiment and hence has influenced the *Dependent variable*.

Consolidation: The process by which memories become permanent. Lack of consolidation is one explanation that has been used to try to account for forgetting.

Constancy scaling: The process by which we mentally enlarge our perception of a distant object to compensate for its distance from us.

Constructivist theory: A theory which suggests that

knowledge and understanding are constructed or built up as a result of experience.

Content analysis: A systematic method for quantifying the content of media communication.

Continuous recording: An observational recording technique where observers record all instances of target behaviour as they occur.

Controlled observation: An observation carried out in a controlled, laboratory setting.

Correlation: A statistical technique used to determine whether or not there is a relationship between two variables. A correlation statistic can range from positive, through zero, to negative.

Counterbalancing: A procedure used in a repeated design experiment to balance out the effects of order of conditions.

Covert observation: An observation where the researcher's presence is not apparent to those being observed.

Cross-cultural study: A study involving the comparison of different cultures.

Cued recall: Participants learn some information, usually a list of words. In the recall phase, participants are given cues, such as parts of words or categories, to aid their recall.

Data-driven approach: See *Bottom-up approach.*

Decay: The idea that memories are lost because the memory trace fades away as a result of the passage of time.

Declarative memory: Memory that can be put into words.

Defence mechanisms: Proposed by Freud, these are unconscious mechanisms which act to protect the conscious self from unpleasant memories or thoughts, e.g. *Repression.*

Demand characteristics: Cues as to the aim of research which may cause participants to behave in a way that they would not have done otherwise.

Denial: An unconscious defence mechanism where the existence of something unpleasant is denied.

Dependent variable (DV): The measure or measures taken by the psychologist of people's behaviour in an experiment.

Depth cues: Visual cues that enable us to infer distance. See also *Binocular cues* and *Monocular cues.*

Descriptive statistics: Used to summarise and present the findings of *Quantitative data* or raw data. Descriptive statistics include *Measures of central tendency* and *Measures of dispersion.*

Determinism: The idea that behaviour (and thought) is determined by either or both genetic inheritance and the environment; the belief that behaviour is programmed for an individual and that the person has no *Free will* to choose their behaviour.

Digit span test: Participants repeat back sequences of digits presented aurally. The maximum number of digits to be recalled correctly in sequence indicates the *Short-term memory* capacity.

Discrimination: Behaviour or actions, usually negative, towards individuals or groups of people.

Displacement: Theory of forgetting from *Short-term memory* which states that forgetting occurs when the capacity of *Short-term memory* is exceeded.

Dispositional attribution: Explains behaviour in terms of the person rather than the situation.

Dissociative amnesia: A condition in which the sufferer is unable to recall a specific unpleasant event.

Distortion illusions: Where the viewer mistakenly believes that part of the illusion is nearer or further away, and therefore larger or smaller than it really is.

Distracter task: Task given to participants in memory experiments to prevent rehearsal.

Dizygotic twins: Also known as fraternal twins. They are no more alike than ordinary brothers and sisters, since they come from two different fertilised eggs.

Dominant response: What an individual is most likely to do when asked to perform a task. The person may be highly skilled at a task or have little previous experience – either is a dominant response.

Double-blind research: Where neither the participant nor the researcher dealing directly with the participant is aware of the purpose of the study.

Echoic memory: A *Sensory memory* store specialised for holding sounds for a very brief period.

Echolalia: Repetitive language, usually where a speech sound or word is repeated over and over.

Ecological validity: The extent to which a behaviour has been measured in circumstances similar to the way in which that behaviour occurs in real life.

Ego: One of the aspects of personality identified by Freud; it serves to satisfy the needs of the *Id.*

Elaborative rehearsal: Involves the deep and meaningful analysis of information, rather than simply repeating it over and over. See also *Maintenance rehearsal.*

Electra complex: Freudian theory that girls develop *Penis envy,* which finally leads to adoption of the female role.

Encoding: The process by which information is stored in memory in a form in which it can be used.

Encoding-specificity principle: Our ability to recall memories is dependent on the extent to which the information held in a memory trace matches the information available at retrieval.

Endocrine system: Network of glands that secrete chemicals called hormones into the bloodstream.

Endorphins: Opium-like substances released when the body is stressed or aroused.

Episodic memory: A memory system proposed by Tulving which stores our memories of personal experiences and events.

Evaluation apprehension: Occurs when performing a task in the presence of others. It causes arousal, which, in turn, increases the likelihood of the dominant response.

Evolutionary psychology: An area of psychology which uses evolutionary mechanisms and explanations for human thought, behaviour and culture.

Executive functioning: Higher-order mental functioning which allows for supervision, attention and direction of mental activities.

Experimental design: Way of using participants in an experiment: *Repeated design, Independent design* and *Matched pairs design.*

Experimental hypothesis: See *Alternative hypothesis.*

Experimenter bias: Where an experimenter treats some participants differently to others, either intentionally or unintentionally.

Exposure and prevention therapy: Behavioural treatment used to treat obsessive–compulsive disorder.

External attribution: See *Situational attribution.*

Extraneous variable: See *Confounding variable.*

Family studies: See *Twin studies.*

Fatigue effect: In a repeated design experiment, where a participant's performance is worse in the second condition after taking part in the first condition.

Field experiment: An experiment carried out in a natural setting or real-life situation, but where the psychologist has control over some variables.

Flashbulb memory: Vivid memory of a significant event.

Flooding: Therapy where a person is exposed to what they fear. Used to treat phobias and obsessive–compulsive disorder.

Fragile X syndrome: A genetic disorder caused by a defective gene in the X chromosome which results in mental retardation.

Free association: A technique where participants are encouraged to respond to a stimulus with the first thing that occurs to them.

Free recall: A technique used in memory research. After learning some information, participants are instructed to recall as much of the information as they can, in any order.

Free will: The idea that people are free to choose and that their behaviour is not predetermined by either *Genetics* or the environment. See also *Determinism.*

Fully structured interview: An interview in which there are fixed questions to be asked in a fixed order, with a fixed set of optional answers. See also *Structured interview.*

Functional approach to attitudes: Suggests that a person's general wellbeing is promoted through attitudes serving four functions: adaptive, knowledge, ego-expressive and ego-defensive.

Fundamental attribution error: A source of bias in causal attribution which leads to more *Dispositional attributions* than *Situational attributions* being made.

Galvanic skin response (GSR): Method for detecting emotion or stress which involves placing electrodes on the surface of the skin to record minute changes in surface moisture.

Gender: This refers to the social and cultural interpretation of behaviour expected of men and women.

Gender constancy (consistency): The third of Kohlberg's stages of gender development, where a child realises that gender remains stable over time, across situations and despite superficial changes in appearance.

Gender identity: The first of Kohlberg's stages of gender development, when a child can label his or her sex and the sex of others correctly.

Gender schema: An organised unit of knowledge about the characteristics and behaviours associated with a specific gender.

Gender stability: The second of Kohlberg's stages of gender development, when a child realises that sex remains stable over time.

Genetics: The study of the genetic make-up of organisms and how this influences physical and behavioural characteristics.

Genotype: The actual genetic make-up of a person, as represented in the 23 pairs of human chromosomes. See also *Phenotype.*

Gestalt approach: An approach to psychology originating in Germany. Gestalt psychologists were interested primarily in perception and problem solving, proposing that organisation of perceptual information was determined by the least effort needed to interpret the sense data; an approach which emphasises the 'wholeness' of experience and thinking.

Hemispheric specialisation: See *Lateralisation of function.*

Heredity: The traits, tendencies and characteristics inherited from a person's parents and their ancestors.

Humanistic psychology: Also known as the 'third force' in psychology, this is an approach which places value on human experience and sees each person as unique; also known as a phenomenological or idiographic approach.

Huntington's disease: An inherited disorder which causes damage to the motor areas of the brain. Patients experience increasing problems with their motor skills, but retain the ability to acquire declarative knowledge.

Iconic memory: A *Sensory memory* store specialised for holding visual information for about a quarter of a second.

Id: Also known as 'das est' (the it), this refers to the fact that the child at birth only contains instinctive needs which require gratification at any cost. An aspect of personality identified by Frend.

Identification: A form of attachment to a specific person which leads to the desire to imitate that person and assume their traits. See also *Oedipus complex* and *Electra complex* for Freudian identification.

Imitation: Copying the behaviour of another person.

Impression formation: The process of making inferences about another person's character, mood, abilities and intentions.

Impression management: Attempting to influence the impressions which other people form of you.

Incidental learning: Participants are presented with information, but they are not aware that they are going to be asked to recall it; used in research investigating the levels of processing approach to memory.

Independent design: Where different people take part in each experimental condition.

Independent variable (IV): The variable which is manipulated and controlled by the psychologist in an experiment.

Individualistic cultures: Cultures where individual achievement and personal choice are highly valued, for example in the USA and UK. See also *Collectivistic cultures*.

Infantile amnesia: Loss of memory for events that took place in early childhood.

Information-processing approach: An approach to cognition popularised in the 1960s and 1970s, which likens the human mind to the operation of a computer where information is coded, stored, retrieved and used to make a response. See also *Cognitive approach*.

Informational influence: Where conformity to the majority view results from new information or reasoned arguments presented to a minority by a majority in the group. This form of *Social influence* results in private acceptance of the view.

Informed consent: Where those consenting know and understand what it is that they are consenting to.

Intelligence: A person's ability to learn and remember, recognise concepts and their relationships, and apply information to behaviour in an adaptive way.

Interactionist approach: The view that behaviour is determined by a combination of inherited and environmental influences.

Interference: Proposes that forgetting is the result of our memories being disrupted or interfered with by other information.

Inter-group conflict: Where two groups or teams compete with each other for the same prize or resource; as a result, competition and conflict develop between the two teams.

Internal attribution: See *Dispositional attribution*.

Inter-observer reliability: Consistency in observational recordings made by two observers recording at the same time but working independently.

Introspection: Technique first used by Wilhelm Wundt to establish psychology as a science, which requires a person to report on conscious experience; Wundt realised that introspection is subjective and not scientific.

Islets of ability: A term used by Kanner to describe special talents shown by people with *Autism*.

Klinefelter's syndrome: A disorder caused by the presence of an extra X chromosome in a male.

Laboratory experiment: A type of experiment that is carried out in a highly controlled environment. This is often, but not always, in a psychology laboratory.

Lack of joint attention: Failure to attend to the focus of interest for others, seen in cases of *Autism*.

Lateralisation: The division of the brain into two distinct hemispheres, each having specific functions.

Lateralisation of function: Also known as hemispheric specialisation. This refers to the finding that the left hemisphere in most people is dominant for language and logical thought, while the right hemisphere is dominant for artistic creativity, music and intuition.

Law of disuse: As in the *Decay* theory of forgetting, the law states that forgetting occurs when information is not used for a period of time.

Law of effect: Proposed by Thorndike, this states that the tendency of an individual to produce behaviour depends on the effect the behaviour has on the environment.

Laws of Pragnanz: Laws of perceptual organisation proposed by the Gestalt psychologists. The laws govern the interpretation of sensory information and suggest we make the simplest interpretation of a given stimulus.

Levels of processing: An alternative to the *Multi-store model* of memory which proposes that deep processing is more likely to lead to successful recall than shallow processing.

Libido: A form of sexual energy which the person is born with and which forms the motivation for behaviour.

Localisation of (cortical) function: The idea that different parts or areas of the brain are specialised at certain tasks or activities. See also *Broca's area* and *Wernicke's area*.

Long-term memory: Our permanent store of knowledge, which has a more or less infinite capacity and can retain information for a lifetime.

Lovaas technique: A technique involving *Positive reinforcement* which is used to encourage speech in children with *Autism*.

Magnetic resonance image (MRI): An image from an MRI scan which shows activity in the living brain.

Maintenance rehearsal: Involves retaining information by repeating it over and over again. See also *Elaborative rehearsal.*

Majority influence: The influence of a majority view on a minority, with the result that the minority conform to the view of the majority.

Matched pairs design: Where different people take part in each experimental condition, but they are matched in ways that matter for the experiment, e.g. sex, age.

Mean: The sum of all the raw scores divided by the number of raw scores.

Measures of central tendency: Commonly used to describe data and include the *Mean, Median* and *Mode.*

Measures of dispersion: Describe the spread of scores; the most commonly used measures of dispersion are the *Range* and *Standard deviation.*

Median: The central or middle value of a set of raw scores.

Mind-blindness: The inability to understand what other people are thinking.

Mode: The most commonly occurring score or value in a set of data.

Modelling: Imitation of a (role) model.

Monocular cues: Cues to depth or distance perception that require the use of only one eye.

Monozygotic twins: Also known as identical twins, they share exactly the same genetic make-up, since they both come from the same fertilised egg. See also *Dizygotic twins.*

Motivated forgetting: See *Repression.*

Multi-store model: A model of memory which proposes three types of memory store, each with different characteristics: *Sensory memory, Short-term memory* and *Long-term memory.*

Natural observation: An observation carried out in a natural setting.

Natural selection: An evolutionary process in which genetically influenced characteristics either benefit a species and help individuals to survive better in their environment, or do not aid survival; an important concept in Darwin's *Theory of evolution.* See also *Survival of the fittest.*

Nature–nurture debate: The debate about the relative extent to which behaviour is determined by inherited and environmental influences.

Negative correlation: A relationship between two variables where, as one variable increases, the other variable decreases.

Negative reinforcement: Desired behaviour is performed to avoid an unpleasant stimulus.

Neo-Freudian: A follower of Freud who generally adheres to Freud's ideas, but has reinterpreted some aspect of Freudian theory.

Neuron: The basic building block of the nervous system. The neuron, or nerve cell, transmits and receives information in the form of electrical impulses in the nervous system.

Neurotransmitters: Chemicals found in the vesicles at the *Synapse.* These chemicals may increase or decrease the firing of a *Neuron.*

Non-declarative memory: Memory that cannot be put into words.

Non-participant observation: Where the researcher observes the behaviour of other people but does not become a member of the group. See also *Participant observation.*

Normative social influence: Where people conform to the majority view in order to maintain group harmony, avoid rejection by the group or gain approval from other group members.

Null hypothesis: States that there is no relationship (association or difference) between the two variables being studied. Often shown as H0.

Obedience to authority: A type of *Social influence* in which one or more people follow the instructions of an authority figure.

Objective: This is what science aspires to be: value-free and lacking in subjectivity.

Observer bias: The outcome of an observation is influenced by the observer's expectations.

Observer effect: The behaviour of those being observed is altered by the presence of an observer.

Obsession: Persistent unwanted idea or image that causes *Anxiety.* See also *Compulsion.*

Obsessive–compulsive disorder: *Anxiety* disorder in which person has undesirable thoughts and repetitive actions.

Oedipus complex: Freud's theory that, at a certain stage in their development, boys develop a sexual attachment to their mother.

Open questions: Questions where respondents can give any answer they choose.

Operant conditioning: Skinner's theory that learning depends on consequences.

Operationalisation: Process of defining precisely how variables will be realised in a study.

Opportunity sampling: Where a sample is selected according to availability or convenience.

Optic array: All the visual information currently in our field of vision.

Optic-flow patterns: Flow of visual information across the visual field and radial expansion of textures that occurs as we move forward.

Oral stage: The first of Freud's stages of development, when the sexual energy of the libido is located around the mouth and the child finds sexual satisfaction from objects placed in this area.

Order effects: Where performance in one condition of an experiment is affected by performance in the other condition (occurs in repeated design experiments).

Overt observation: An observation where those being observed are aware of the observer's presence.

Panic attacks: Rapid increase of intense *Anxiety*, with pounding heart and dryness of mouth.

Parasympathetic nervous system: Maintains normal bodily activity, by regulating breathing and heart rate, for example; reduces the activity of the *Sympathetic nervous system*.

Participant observation: Where the researcher takes part in the action. See also *Non-participant observation*.

Penis envy: Experienced by girls during the *Phallic stage*, when they realise that they do not have a penis.

Perceptual accentuation: Heightened or increased awareness, usually in relation to something we want or need.

Perceptual defence: Decreased perceptual awareness or reluctance to perceive, due to the use of unconscious Freudian defence mechanisms. Perceptual defence supposedly prevents us from perceiving a stimulus we would find unpleasant or upsetting.

Perceptual set: Predisposition to perceive and attend to certain aspects of a stimulus rather than others.

Peripheral nervous system: Has two subsystems: the *Somatic nervous system* and the *Autonomic nervous system*. The peripheral nervous system transmits and conveys information to and from the *Central nervous system*.

Peripheral traits: Descriptions of personality which have little influence on impression formation.

Perseverative errors: Errors which continue to be made even when there is evidence that the strategy being used is not successful.

Pervasive mental disorder: A severe childhood disorder, affecting many aspects of behaviour and functioning.

Phallic stage: The third psychosexual stage in development, when the libido transfers itself to the genitals. This results in sexual desire of the boy child for the mother, and *Penis envy* in the young girl.

Phenotype: The expression of a person's genetic make-up: physical appearance, behavioural characteristics, personality, and so on.

Phenylketonuria (PKU): A disorder resulting from a double recessive gene which can cause severe learning difficulties, due to the inability to synthesise the amine phenylalanine. Special diets can result in normal development.

Phobia: An irrational fear of an object or situation.

Phonological store: A component of *Working memory*, responsible for the processing of sound-based information.

Pilot study: A small-scale study conducted before an investigation to check for any problems in the design.

Pituitary gland: Master gland of the endocrine system. Located in the middle of the brain.

Placebo group: A group of participants who receive a 'dummy' treatment; used as a control group in research.

Positive correlation: A relationship between two variables where, as one variable increases, the other variable increases.

Positive reinforcement: A pleasant stimulus for the performance of desired behaviour.

Positron emission tomography (PET): A computerised brain-scanning technique which enables researchers to monitor the activity of different parts of the brain.

Post-traumatic stress disorder (PTSD): An *Anxiety* disorder that occurs following a severely distressing event.

Practice effect: In a repeated design experiment, where participants perform better in the second condition after having taken part in the first condition.

Prejudice: An unjustified or incorrect negative (or positive) attitude towards an individual, based solely on the individual's membership of a group.

Primacy effect: The tendency for the first few items on a list to be remembered better than the items which appear in the middle of the list; may cause bias in impression formation.

Primary acoustic store: A component of *Working memory* which acts as a verbal rehearsal system.

Proactive interference: Where old memories which have already been stored interfere with the storage and retrieval of new information.

Procedural memory: Motor-based *Long-term memory* for motor skills and abilities. The memory for knowing how to do something that is difficult to express verbally.

Psychoanalysis: Theory and therapy developed by Freud, emphasising the importance of the unconscious, sexual instinct and psychosexual development in childhood. See also *Psychodynamics*.

Psychodynamics: An approach in psychology, originating with Freudian theory, which emphasises the importance of unconscious conflicts; therapies based on a psychodynamic approach may analyse dreams to uncover and help resolve mental conflicts.

Psychology: The scientific study of mind and behaviour;

derived from the Greek words 'psyche' (mind) and 'logos' (study of).

Psychosexual stages: Oral, anal and phallic stages of development in Freudian theory, which take place over the first five or six years of life. The final stage is the genital stage, which is around the age of puberty.

Qualitative data: Non-numerical data.

Quantitative data: Numerical data.

Quasi-experiment: An experiment where there is no random allocation to conditions and no direct manipulation of the *Independent variable*.

Questionnaires: Can be used to obtain people's views and attitudes about a topic or to measure a specific aspect of personality; can use both *Open questions* and *Closed questions*.

Racism: Prejudice and discrimination aimed at one group of people by another group of people; racism can be both subtle and blatant.

Radical behaviourism: See *Behaviourism*.

Random allocation: A procedure for allocating participants to conditions where every participant has an equal chance of being allocated to any one of the conditions.

Random sampling: Where each person in the target population has an equal chance of being selected for a sample.

Range: The difference between the highest and the lowest scores in a set of data.

Rational emotive therapy: Developed by Albert Ellis, attempts to change the way people think, to remove negative thoughts and replace them with positive ones.

Recency effect: The tendency for the last few items on a list to be remembered better than those in the middle of the list. See also *Primacy effect*.

Refrigerator mother: A type of mother who is cold and unaccepting of her child. See also *Cold-parenting hypothesis*.

Reinforcement: A stimulus that acts to strengthen learning. See *Operant conditioning*, *Positive reinforcement* and *Negative reinforcement*.

Reliability: The extent to which a measure is consistent.

Reminiscence bump: The increased ability to remember information from a specific point in one's life, usually from between the ages of 11 and 30 years.

Repeated (or related) design: Where the same participants perform in each experimental condition.

Repression: Freudian defence mechanism which suggests that forgetting has an emotional basis; according to Freud's theory of motivated forgetting, unpleasant memories are held in the unconscious because they are so distressing.

Researcher bias: See *Experimenter bias*.

Retrieval: Remembering information by bringing it from

Long-term memory, *Working memory* or *Short-term memory*.

Retrieval cues: Stimuli or thoughts that can be used as an aid to the retrieval of information from *Long-term memory*.

Retrieval failure: Information is available in memory but cannot be retrieved because the retrieval cues are inadequate.

Retroactive interference: Where new information interferes with the retrieval of older information already stored in *Long-term memory*.

Sample: Group of people (individually known as participants) used in research.

Sampling: Where a psychologist selects a sample of people to take part in a study or experiment.

Sampling bias: Where a subsection of the target population is over-represented in the sample.

Schema (plural schemata): An organised unit of knowledge, a schema helps to structure and interpret new information and is stored in *Long-term memory*.

Science: The use of theory to generate hypotheses, which can then be tested in controlled, laboratory conditions; empirical evidence is used to provide support for or refute a theory/hypothesis.

Self-esteem: How favourably a person evaluates themselves.

Self-fulfilling prophecy: A prediction or statement that becomes true simply because it is expected to.

Self-image: The set of perceptions a person has about themselves; the complete set of a person's self-schemas.

Self-report method: Method of research where participants report on their own behaviour, attitudes and so on.

Self-serving bias: A type of attribution bias in which you attribute your successes dispositionally, but your failures situationally.

Semantic memory: A *Long-term memory* system which contains our general knowledge about the world, including the rules of language and the meaning of words.

Sensory memory: The memory store that holds sensory information for brief periods of time; each of our senses (vision, hearing, touch, taste, smell) has a separate store.

Serial position curve: The U-shaped curve produced when people remember the first few and last few items from a list of words.

Sex: This refers to the biological distinction between males and females, based on chromosomes. See also *Gender*.

Sex-role (gender) stereotype: An organised belief about the behaviour and characteristics expected of males and females.

Sexually dimorphic nucleus: A region of the hypothalamus which is larger in males than in females.

Shape constancy: The ability to perceive objects as having a constant shape, despite changes in the retinal image when viewed from different angles.

Short-term memory: A component of the *Multi-store model* of memory which holds information for a short time if rehearsal is prevented.

Situational attribution: Explains behaviour in terms of the situation rather than the person.

Size constancy: The ability to perceive the size of objects as constant, despite changes in the size of the retinal image with distance.

Social cognition: The thought processes, knowledge and beliefs which people use in order to understand the character and behaviour of other people.

Social desirability: How consistent an action is with group or cultural norms.

Social facilitation: The enhancement of task performance caused by the mere presence of other people.

Social identity theory: States that we divide the world into groups of people, 'us' and 'them', through a process called social categorisation.

Social influence: Efforts by one or more people to change the attitudes, beliefs, perceptions or behaviours of one or more other people.

Social learning theory (SLT): A theory of learning stating that behaviour is learnt through observation and imitation.

Social norms: Written or unwritten rules guiding how people are expected to behave in social situations. Social norms often reflect majority view and are a source of *Social influence*.

Social perception: Observing other people and making inferences about them.

Social phobia: Irrational fear and avoidance of social or performance situations.

Social schema: Cognitive structure representing knowledge and beliefs about individuals or groups.

Social sciences: A family or cluster of related disciplines, including psychology, sociology, anthropology and biology; also called behavioural sciences.

Sociology: The study of groups and institutions within society, or of different societies; includes study of the family, ethnic groups, subcultures, religious institutions and the workplace.

Somatic nervous system: Transmits information from our senses, through receptors, to the central nervous system.

Specific phobias: Irrational or unreasonable fear of a specific object or situation.

Standard deviation: A measure of dispersion which tells you how the scores spread around the *Mean*.

Stereogram: Where two different images are presented simultaneously, one to the left eye and one to the right eye.

Stereopsis: The unconscious process of figuring out depth from the difference in the images received by each eye.

Stereotype: A highly simplified, gross overgeneralisation of a group of people that is then applied to an individual seen to be a member of that group; often based on a single attribute, such as race, *Gender*, disability or social class.

Stereotyping: A source of bias in impression formation in which shared beliefs about a specific group of people lead to overgeneralised and often inaccurate inferences about a member of that group.

Storage: The process of keeping memories for retrieval.

Stratified sampling: A combination of quota and *Random sampling*; the different strata or types of people in the population are identified, and a random sample taken from each of the strata.

Structural approach: An approach to attitudes which consists of three components: cognitive, affective and behavioural aspects of attitudes.

Structured interview: An interview in which fixed questions are asked in a fixed order. See also *Fully structured interview*.

Subliminal perception: Perception without conscious awareness.

Subjective: Where the interpretation can vary, depending on the point of view of the observer.

Superego: The third aspect of personality identified by Freud, representing a person's conscience and ideal self.

Survival of the fittest: Characteristics which help an individual to survive better will be passed on to future generations, and hence will help the species to adapt better to its environment.

Sympathetic nervous system: This responds to threat by preparing the body for flight or fight; it works in opposition to the *Parasympathetic nervous system*.

Synapse: A small gap between *Neurons* through which neurons communicate. See also *Neurotransmitters*.

Syndrome: A collection of symptoms associated with a particular disease or disorder.

Systematic desensitisation: Therapy using relaxation and exposure to treat an *Anxiety* disorder.

Systematic sampling: Where every nth member of the target population is selected, for example, every fifth person on a register.

Tachistoscope: A machine which displays a visual stimulus for a very brief time.

Target population: The (larger) group of people from which the sample is drawn.

Test-retest reliability: Where a measure produces the same or similar results on more than one occasion.

Theory of evolution: First proposed by Charles Darwin, it states that all creatures, including human beings, have evolved biologically and share common ancestors.

Theory of mind (ToM): An explanation for *Autism* according to which the disorder results from the inability to understand the minds of others.

Theory of mind mechanism (ToMM): An extension of the *Theory of mind* explanation for *Autism* according to which an innate maturational mechanism underlies the development of a theory of mind.

Theory of neutrality: A theory of *Gender* which states that children are born gender-neutral.

Time sampling: An observational recording technique where recordings are made at predetermined time intervals.

Tip-of-the-tongue state: When people are attempting to recall information from *Long-term memory*, but failing; they know the information is 'in there', but they are unable to retrieve it.

Token economy programme: Token rewards are given for desirable behaviour; these can then be exchanged for primary rewards, such as food or treats.

Top-down approach: An approach which suggests that our cognitive processes are mainly influenced by previously stored information rather than incoming data; sometimes known as concept-driven processing.

Tourette's syndrome: A disorder in which an individual shows uncontrollable motor tics/mannerisms and verbal outbursts.

Triad of impairments: The combination of three impairments, typically seen in cases of *Autism*: impairment in social interaction; impairment in communication; repetitive and stereotyped behaviours.

Turner's syndrome: A disorder caused by the absence of an X chromosome in a female.

Twin studies: The use of identical (monozygotic) and/or fraternal (dizygotic) twins to investigate the heritability of psychological characteristics such as intelligence.

Unconditional positive regard: Humanistic concept of loving somebody for what they are and without conditions attached. See also *Conditional positive regard*.

Unstructured interview: An interview where the researcher has a general aim, but there are no fixed questions.

Validity: The extent to which a measure tests or measures what it is supposed to.

Vicarious reinforcement: Where a behaviour is learnt through observation of the consequences for others of their actions.

Visuospatial scratch pad: A component of *Working memory* which acts as a visual and spatial rehearsal system.

Wernicke's area: An area of the left temporal lobe, responsible for the language function of comprehension or word recognition; damage to this area results in Wernicke's aphasia – a person will have difficulty understanding what others say and speech will be meaningless.

Working memory: A version of *Short-term memory* proposed by Baddeley, it consists of a 'central executive', which controls and coordinates the operation of a number of subcomponents.

References

AAKER, J.L. and SMITT, B. (2001) Culture-dependent assimilation and differences of the self: Preferences for consumption symbols in the United States and China. *Journal of Cross-Cultural Psychology*, 32: 561–76.

ADORNO, T.W., FRENKEL-BRONSWICK, E., LEVINSON, D.J. and SANFORD, R.N. (1950) *The Authoritarian Personality*, New York: Harper.

AIELLO, J.R. and KOLB, K.J. (1995) Electronic performance monitoring: Impact on productivity and stress. *Journal of Applied Psychology*, 80: 339–53.

AIELLO, J.R. and DOTHITT, E.A. (2001) Social facilitation from Triplett to electronic performance monitoring. *Group Dynamics*, 5: 163–80.

ALLEN, G., MULLER, R.A. and COURCHESNE, E. (2004) Cerebellar functioning in autism: Functional magnetic resonance image activation during a simple motor task. *Biological Psychiatry*, 56(4): 269–78.

ALLPORT, F.H. (1924) *Social Psychology*, Cambridge, MA: Houghton Mifflin.

ALTEMEYER, B. (1996) *The Authoritarian Spectre*, Cambridge, MA: Harvard University Press.

ANDERSON, J.L., CRAWFORD, C.B., NADEAU, J. and LINDBERG, T. (1992) Was the Duchess of Windsor right? A cross-cultural review of the socioecology of ideals of female body shape. *Ethology and Sociobiology*, 13: 197–227.

ANDERSON, J.R. (2000) *Cognitive Psychology and its Implications*, 5th edn, New York: Worth.

ANDERSON, J.R. (2000) *Learning and Memory*, New York: John Wiley and Sons.

ASCH, S. (1951) Effects of group pressure on the modification and distortion of judgements. In H. Gretzikow (ed.) *Groups, Leadership and Men*, Pittsburgh, PA: Carnegie Press.

ASCH, S. (1955) Opinions and social pressure. *Scientific American*, 193: 5, 31–35.

ASCH, S.E. (1946) Forming impressions of personality. *Journal of Abnormal and Social Psychology*, 4: 258–290.

ASPERGER, H. (1944) Die 'aunstisehen Psychopathen' im Kindesalter. *Archiv fur psychiatrie und Nerverkrankheiten*, 117: 76–136.

ATKINSON, R.C. and SHIFFRIN, R.M. (1968) Human memory: A proposed system and its control processes. In K.W. Spence (ed.) *The Psychology of Learning and Motivation: Advances in Research and Theory*, vol. 2, New York: Academic Press.

BADDELEY, A.D. (1966a) Short-term memory for word sequences as a function of acoustic, semantic and formal similarity. *Quarterly Journal of Experimental Psychology*, 18: 362–5.

BADDELEY, A.D. (1966b) The influence of acoustic and semantic similarity on long-term memory for word sequences. *Quarterly Journal of Experimental Psychology*, 18: 302–9.

BADDELEY, A.D. (1986) *Working Memory*, Oxford: Oxford University Press.

BADDELEY, A.D. (1997) *Human Memory: Theory and Practice*, Hove: Psychology Press.

BADDELEY, A.D. (1999) *Essentials of Human Memory*, Hove: Psychology Press.

BADDELEY, A.D. and HITCH, G.J. (1974) Working memory. In G. Bower (ed.) *Recent Advances in Learning and Memory*, vol. 8, New York: Academic Press.

BADDELEY, A.D. and HITCH, G.J. (1977) Recency re-examined. In S. Dornic (ed.) *Attention and Performance*, vol. VI, Hillsdale, NJ: Lawrence Erlbaum Associates.

BADDELEY, A.D., GATHERCOLE, S. and PAPAGNO, C. (1998) The phonological loop as a language learning device. *Psychological Review*, 105: 158–73.

BAGBY, E. (1922) The etiology of phobias. *Journal of Abnormal Psychology*, 17: 16–18.

BAHRICK, H.P., BAHRICK, P.O. and WITTLINGER, R.P. (1975) Fifty years of memory for names and faces: A cross-sectional approach. *Journal of Experimental Psychology: General*, 104: 54–75.

BANDURA, A. (1965) Influence of model's reinforcement contingencies on the acquisition of imitative responses. *Journal of Personality and Social Psychology*, 1: 589–95.

BANDURA, A. (1977) *Social Learning Theory*, Englewood Cliffs, NJ: Prentice Hall.

BANDURA, A. (1986) *Social Foundations of Thought and Action: A Social-Cognitive Theory*, Englewood Cliffs, NJ: Prentice Hall.

BANDURA, A., ROSS, D. and ROSS, S. (1961) Transmission of aggression through imitation of aggressive models. *Journal of Abnormal and Social Psychology*, 63(3): 575–82.

BARJONET, P.E. (1980) L'influence sociale et des représentations des causes de l'accident de la route. *Le Travail Human*, 20: 1–14.

BARLOW, D.H. (2002) *Anxiety and its Disorders: The Nature and Treatment of Anxiety and Panic*, 2nd edn, New York: Guilford Press.

BARLOW, D.H. and DURAND, V.M. (2002) *Abnormal Psychology*, 3rd edn, Belmont, CA: Wadsworth.

BARON, R.A., BYRNE, D. and BRANSCOMBE, N.R. (2006) *Social Psychology*, 11th edn, London: Allyn & Bacon.

BARON, R.S., VANDELLO, U.A. and BRUNSMAN, B. (1996) The forgotten variable in conformity research: Impact of task importance on social influence. *Journal of Personality and Social Psychology*, 71: 915–27.

BARON-COHEN, S., LESLIE, A.M. and FRITH, U. (1985) Does the autistic child have a theory of mind? *Cognition*, 21: 37–46.

BARON-COHEN, S., LESLIE, A.M. and FRITH, U. (1986) Mechanical, behavioural and intentional understanding of picture stories in autistic children. *British Journal of Developmental Psychology*, 4: 113–25.

BARON-COHEN, S., TAGER-FLUSBERG, H. and COHEN, D.J. (eds) (1993) *Understanding Other Minds: Perspectives from Autism*, Oxford: Oxford University Press.

BARON-COHEN, S., RING, H., BULLMORE, E., WHEELWRIGHT, S., ASHWIN, C. and WILLIAMS, S. (2000) The amygdala theory of autism. *Neuroscience and Biobehavioural Reviews*, 24: 355–64.

BARTIS, S., SZYMANSTIC, K. and HARKINS, S.G. (1988) Evaluation and performance: A two-edged knife. *Personality and Social Psychology Bulletin*, 14: 242–51.

BAUMRIND, D. (1964) Some thoughts on ethics of research: After reading Milgram's 'Behavioural study of Obedience'. *American Psychologist*, 19: 421–3.

BAUMRIND, D. (1985) Research using intentional deception: Ethical issues revisited. *American Psychologist*, 40: 165–174.

BECK, A.T. (1976) *Cognitive Therapy and Emotional Disorder*, New York: International Universities Press.

BEE, H. (1989) *The Developing Child*, 5th edn, New York: HarperCollins.

BELLODI, L., CAVALLINI, M.C., BERTELLI, S. et al. (2001) Morbidity risk for obsessive–compulsive spectrum disorders in first degree relatives of patients with eating disorders. *American Journal of Psychiatry*, 158: 563–9.

BEM, S. (1974) The measurement of psychological androgyny. *Journal of Consulting and Clinical Psychology*, 42: 155–62.

BEM, S. (1989) Genital knowledge and gender constancy in preschool children. *Child Development*, 60: 649–62.

BERENBAUM, S.A. and HINES, M. (1992) Early androgens are related to sex-typed toy preferences. *Psychological Science*, 3: 202–6.

BERGER, D. and WILLIAMS, J. (1991) Sex stereotypes in the United States revisited: 1972–1988. *Sex Roles*, 24: 413–23.

BETTLEHEIM, B. (1967) *The Empty Fortress*, New York: Free Press.

BICKMAN, L. (1974) The social power of a uniform. *Journal of Applied Social Psychology*, 7: 47–61.

BJORK, R.A. and BJORK, E.L. (1992) A new theory of disuse and an old theory of stimulus fluctuation. In A. Healey, S. Kosslyn and R. Shiffrin (eds) *From Learning Processes to Cognitive Processes: Essays in Honour of William K. Estes*, vol. 2, Hillsdale, NJ: Lawrence Erlbaum Associates.

BOBO, L. (1988) Group conflict, prejudice, and the paradox of contemporary racial attitudes. In P.A. Katz and D.A. Taylor (eds) *Eliminating Racism: Profiles in Controversy*, New York: Plenum.

BOGELS, S.M., van OOSTEN, A., MURIS, P. and SMULDERS, D. (2001) Family correlates of social anxiety in children and adolescents. *Behaviour Research and Therapy*, 39: 273–87.

BORD, J.H., RAE, D.S., THOMPSON, J.W., BURNS, B.J., BOURDON, K., LOCKE, B.Z. and REIGER, D.A. (1990) Phobia: Prevalence and risk factors. *Social Psychiatry and Psychiatric Epidemiology*, 25: 314–23.

BOSTON, M.B. and LEVY, G.D. (1991) Changes and differences in pre-schoolers' understanding of gender scripts. *Cognitive Development*, 6: 417–32.

BOUCHARD, T.J., LYKKEN, D.T., McGUE, M., SEGAL, N.L. and TELLEGEN, A. (1990) Sources of human psychological differences: The Minnesota Study of twins reared apart. *Science*, 250: 223–8.

BOWER, G.H., CLARK, M., LESGOLD, A. and WINZENZ, D. (1969) Hierarchical retrieval schemes in recall of categorised word lists. *Journal of Verbal Learning and Verbal Behaviour*, 8: 323–43.

BOWER, T.G.R., BROUGHTON, J.M. and MOORE, M.K. (1970) The coordination of visual and tactual input in infants. *Perception and Psychophysics*, 8: 51–3. In G. Butterworth and M. Harris, *Principles of Developmental Psychology*, Hove: Lawrence Erlbaum Associates.

BOYD, J.H., RAE, D.S., THOMPSON, J.W., BURNS, B.J., LOCKE, B.Z. and REGIER, D.A. (1990) Phobia: Prevalence and risk factors. *Social Psychiatry and Psychiatric Epidemiology*, 25: 314–23.

BRISLIN, R. (1993) *Understanding Culture's Influence on Behaviour*, Fort Worth, TX: Harcourt Brace Jovanovich.

BRITISH PSYCHOLOGICAL SOCIETY (2006) Code of Ethics and Conduct, Leicester: BPS Publications.

BROVERMAN, I., VOGEL, S., BROVERMAN, D., CLARKSON, F. and ROSENKRANTZ, P. (1972) Sex-role stereotypes: A current appraisal. *Journal of Social Issues*, 28(2): 59–78.

BROWN, J. (1958) Some tests of the decay theory of immediate memory. *Quarterly Journal of Experimental Psychology*, 10: 12–21.

BROWN, R. and McNEILL, D. (1966) The 'tip-of-the-tongue' phenomenon. *Journal of Verbal Learning and Verbal Behaviour*, 5: 325–37.

BROWN, R.J. (1995) *Prejudice and its Social Psychology*. Oxford: Blackwell.

BRUCH, M.A. and HEIMBERG, R.G. (1994) Differences in perceptions of parental and personal characteristics between generalised and nongeneralised social phobics. *Journal of Anxiety Disorders*, 8: 155–68.

BRUNER, J.S. and GOODMAN, C.C. (1947) Value and need as organizing factors in perception. *Journal of Abnormal and Social Psychology*, 42: 33–44.

BRUNER, J.S. and MINTURN, A.L. (1955) Perceptual identification and perceptual organisation. *Journal of General Psychology*, 53: 21.

BRYSON, S.E. (1996) Brief report: Epidemiological study of autism. *Journal of Autism and Developmental Disorders*, 26: 165–7.

BUGELSKI, B.R. and ALAMPAY, D.A. (1962) The role of frequency in developing perceptual sets. *Canadian Journal of Psychology*, 15: 205–11.

BUSS, D.M. (1995) Evolutionary psychology: A new paradigm for psychological science. *Psychological Inquiry*, 6: 1–49.

BYRNE, D. (1992) The transition from controlled laboratory experiment to less controlled settings:

Surprise. Additional variables are operative. *Communications Monograph*, 59: 190–8.

CARLSON, N.R. and BUSKIST, W. (1997) *Psychology: The Science of Behaviour*, 5th edn, Boston, MA: Allyn & Bacon.

CARSON, R.C. and BUTCHER, J.N. (1992) *Abnormal Psychology and Modern Life*, 9th edn, New York: HarperCollins.

CHEZ, M.G., BUCHANAN, C.P., BAGAN, B.T. et al. (2000) Secretin and autism: A two-part clinical investigation. *Journal of Autism and Developmental Disorders*, 30(2): 87–98.

CHODOROW, N. (1978) *The Reproduction of Mothering*, Berkeley, CA: University of California Press.

CHRISTIE, R. and COOK, P. (1958) A guide to the published literature relating to the authoritarian personality. *Journal of Psychology*, 45: 171–99.

CLARK, D.M. (1996) Panic disorder: From theory to therapy. In P. Salkovskis (ed.) *Frontiers of Cognitive Therapy*, New York: Guilford Press.

CLARY, E.G., SNYDER, M., RIDGE, R.D., MIENE, P.K. and HAUGEN, J.A. (1994) Matching messages to motives in persuasion: A functional approach to promoting volunteerism. *Journal of Applied Social Psychology*, 24: 1129–49.

CLEARE, A. and BOND, A. (1997) Does central serotoninergic function correlate inversely with aggression? A study using d-fenfluramine in healthy subjects. *Psychiatry Research*, 69: 89–95.

CLONINGER, C.R. (1987) Neurogenetic adaptive mechanisms in alcoholism. *Science*, 236: 410–16.

COHEN, H., AMERINE-DICKENS, M.M.S. and SMITH, T. (2006) Early intensive behavioural treatment: Replication of the UCLA model in a community setting. *Journal of Developmental and Behavioural Pediatrics*, 27(2): 145–55.

COHEN, N.J. (1984) Preserved learning capacity in amnesia: Evidence for multiple memory systems. In L.R. Squire and N. Butters (eds) *The Neuropsychology of Memory*, New York: Guilford Press.

COHEN, N.J. and SQUIRE, L.R. (1980) Preserved learning and retention of pattern analyzing skill in amnesia: Dissociation of knowing how and knowing that. *Science*, 210: 207–10.

COMER, R.J. (2008) *Fundamentals of Abnormal Psychology*, 5th edn, New York: Worth Publishers.

COMINGS, D.E. and COMINGS, B.G. (1991) Clinical and genetic relationships between autism-pervasive developmental disorder and Tourette syndrome: A study of 19 cases. *American Journal of Medical Genetics*, 39: 180–91.

COON, D. (1983) *Introduction to Psychology*, 3rd edn, St Paul, MN, West Publishing Co.

CORDUA, G.D., McGRAW, K.O. and DRABMAN, R.S. (1979) Doctor or nurse: Children's perceptions of sex-typed occupations. *Child Development*, 50: 590.

COREN, S., WARD, L.M. and ENNS, J.T. (1999) *Sensation and Perception*, 5th edn, Fort Worth, TX: Harcourt Brace.

CORKIN, S. (1968) Acquisition of motor skill after bilateral medial temporal lobe excision. *Neuropsychologia*, 6: 255–65.

COTTRELL, N.B. (1972) Social facilitation. In C. McClintock (ed.) *Experimental Social Psychology*, New York: Holt, Rinehart & Winston.

COURCHESNE, E. (1991) Neuroanatomic imaging in autism. *Pediatrics*, 87: 781–90.

COX, A., RUTTER, M., NEWMAN, S. and BARTAK, L. (1975) A comparative study of infantile autism and specific developmental language disorders: Parental characteristics. *British Journal of Psychiatry*, 126: 146–59.

CRAIK, F.I.M. and LOCKHART, R.S. (1972) Levels of processing: A framework for memory research. *Journal of Verbal Learning and Verbal Behaviour*, 11: 671–84.

CRAIK, F.I.M. and WATKINS, M.J. (1973) The role of rehearsal in short-term memory. *Journal of Verbal Learning and Verbal Behaviour*, 12: 599–607.

CRAIK, F.I.M. and TULVING, E. (1975) Depth of processing and the retention of words in episodic memory. *Journal of Experimental Psychology: General*, 104: 268–94.

CRUTCHFIELD, R.S. (1955) Conformity and character. *American Psychologist*, 10: 191–8.

DABBS, J.M., CARR, T.S., FRADY, R.L. et al. (1995) Testosterone, crime and misbehaviour among 692 male inmates. *Personality and Individual Differences*, 18(5), 627–33.

DAMON, W. (1977) *The Social World of the Child*, San Francisco, CA: Jossey-Bass.

DARWIN, C. (1859) *The Origin of the Species by Means of Natural Selection*, London: John Murray.

DARWIN, C. (1871) *The Descent of Man and Selection in Relation to Sex*, London: John Murray.

DARWIN, C. (1872) *The Expression of Emotion in Man and Animals*, London: John Murray.

DASHIELL, J.E. (1930) An experimental analysis of some group effects. *Journal of Abnormal and Social Psychology*, 25: 190–9.

DAVIS, D.M. (1990) Portrayals of women in prime-time network television: Some demographic characteristics. *Sex Roles*, 23: 325–32.

DAWSON, G., TOTH, K., ABBOTT, R., OSTERLING, J., MUNSON, J., ESTES, A. and LIAW, J. (2004) Early social attention impairments in autism: Social orienting, joint attention and attention to distress. *Developmental Psychology*, 40(2): 271–83.

DELOACHE, J., CASSIDY, D.J. and CARPENTER, J.C. (1987) The three bears are all male: Mothers' gender labelling of neutral picture book characters. *Sex Roles*, 17: 163–78.

DEREGOWSKI, J. (1972) Pictorial perception and culture. *Scientific American*, 227: 82–8.

DEUTSCH, M. and GERARD, H.B. (1955) A study of normative and informational influence upon individual judgement. *Journal of Abnormal and Social Psychology*, 51: 629–39.

DIAMOND, M. (1982) Sexual identity, monozygotic twins raised in discordant roles, and a BBC follow-up. *Archives of Sexual Behaviour*, 11: 181–6.

DiGALLO, A., BARTON, J. and PARRY-JONES, W.L. (1997) Road traffic accidents: Early psychological consequences in children and adolescents. *British Journal of Psychiatry*, 170: 358–63.

DRACHMAN, D.A. and SAHAKIAN, B.J. (1979) Effects of cholinergic agents on human learning and memory. In R. Barbeau et al. (eds) *Nutrition and the Brain*, vol. 5, 351–66, New York: Raven Press.

DURKIN, K. (1995) *Developmental Social Psychology*, Oxford: Blackwell.

DWECK, C.S., DAVIDSON, W., NELSON, S. and ENNA, B. (1978) Sex differences in learned helplessness: II The contingencies of evaluative feedback in the classroom and III An experimental analysis. *Developmental Psychology*, 14: 268–76.

DZIURAWIEC, S. and DEREGOWSKI, J. (1992) 'Twisted perspective' in young children's drawings. *British Journal of Developmental Psychology*, 10: 35–49.

EASTEAL, D. (1991) Women and crime: Pre-menstrual issues. *Trends and Issues in Crime*, 31, Canberra: Australian Institute of Criminology.

EBBINGHAUS, H. (1885/1964) *Memory*, New York: Columbia University/Dover Press.

EDWARDS, K. (1990) The interplay of affect and cognition in attitude formation and change. *Journal of Personality and Social Psychology*, 59: 202–16.

EDWARDS, K. and von HIPPEL, W. (1995) Hearts and minds: The priority of affective versus cognitive factors in person perception. *Personality and Social Psychology Bulletin*, 21: 996–1011.

EHLERS, A. and BREUER, P. (1992) Increased cardiac awareness in panic disorder. *Journal of Abnormal Psychology*, 101: 371–82.

ELLIS, A. (1962) *Reason and Emotion in Psychotherapy*, New York: Lyle Stuart.

ELLIS, A. (1970) Rational-emotive therapy. In L. Hersher (ed.) *Four Psychotherapies*, New York: Appleton-Century-Croft.

ELLIS, A. (1989) *Inside Rational-Emotive Therapy: A Critical Appraisal of the Theory and Therapy of Albert Ellis*, New York: Academic Press.

ERICCSON, K.A., CHASE, W.G. and FALOON, S. (1980) Acquisition of a memory skill. *Science*, 208: 201–4.

ERIKSON, E. (1968) *Identity: Youth and Crisis*, New York: Norton.

ERIKSON, E. (1968/1974) *Womanhood and Inner Space*. Reprinted in J. Strouse (ed.) *Women and Analysis*, New York: Grossman.

ERRINGTON, F. and GEWERTZ, D. (1989) *Cultural Alternatives and a Feminist Anthropology*, Cambridge: Cambridge University Press.

ESTGATE, A. and GROOME, D. (2005) *An Introduction to Applied Cognitive Psychology*, Hove: Psychology Press.

EYSENCK, M.W. (1984) *A Handbook of Cognitive Psychology*, London: Lawrence Erlbaum Associates.

EYSENCK, M.W. (1993) *Principles of Cognitive Psychology*, Hove: Lawrence Erlbaum Associates, chapter 4.

EYSENCK, M.W. and KEANE, M.J. (1995) *Cognitive Psychology: A Student's Handbook*, 3rd edn, Hove: Lawrence Erlbaum Associates.

EYSENCK, M.W. and KEANE, M.T. (2000) *Cognitive Psychology: A Student's Handbook*, 4th edn, Hove: Psychology Press.

FAGOT, B.I. (1978) The influence of sex of child on parental reactions to toddler children. *Child Development*, 49: 459–65.

FAVELL, J.E., AZRIN, N.H., BAUMEISTER, A.A. et al. (1982) The treatment of self-injurious behaviour. *Behaviour Therapy*, 13: 529–54.

FAZIO, R.H., ROSKOS-EWOLDSEN, D.R and POWELL, M.C. (1994) Attitudes, perception and attention. In P.M. Niedenthal and S. Kitayama (eds) *The Heart's Eye: Emotional Influences in Perception and Attention*. New York: Academic Press.

FELDMAN, R.S. and SCHEIBE, K.E. (1972) Determinants of dissent in a psychological experiment. *Journal of Personality*, 40: 331–48.

FEMINA, D.D., YEAGAR, C.A. and LEWIS, D.O. (1990) Child abuse: Adolescent records vs adult recall. *Child Abuse and Neglect*, 14: 227–31.

FIEZ, J.A. (1996) Cerebellar contributions to cognition. *Neuron*, 16: 13–15.

FISHBEIN, M. and AJZEN, I. (1975) *Belief, Attitude, Intention and Behaviour*, Reading, MA: Addison-Wesley.

FISKE, S.T. and TAYLOR, S.E. (1991) *Social Cognition*, 2nd edn, New York: McGraw-Hill.

FOA, E.B. and FRANKLIN, M.E. (2004) Psychotherapies for obsessive–compulsive disorder: A review. In M. May., N. Sartorius, A. Okashi and J. Zohar (eds) *Obsessive–Compulsive Disorder*, New York: John Wiley and Sons.

FOLSTEIN, S. and RUTTER, M. (1977) Infantile autism: A genetic study of 21 twin pairs. *Journal of Child Psychology and Psychiatry*, 18: 297–321.

FOLSTEIN, S.E. and PIVEN, J. (1991) Etiology of autism: Genetic influences. *Pediatrics*, 87: 767–73.

FOMBONNE, E., ROGE, B., CLAVERIE, J., COURTY, S. and FREMOLLE, J. (1999) Microcephaly and macrocephaly in autism. *Journal of Autism and Developmental Disorders*, 29: 113–119.

FRANKLIN, M. E., ABRAMOWITZ, J.S., KOZAK, M.J., LEVITT, J.T. and FOA, E.B. (2000) Effectiveness of exposure and ritual prevention for obsessive–compulsive disorder: Randomised compared with nonrandomised samples. *Journal of Consulting and Clinical Pschology*, 68: 594–602.

FRANKLIN, M.E., RIGGS, D.S. and PAI, A. (2005) Obsessive–compulsive disorder. In M.M. Anthony and R.G. Heimberg (eds) *Improving Outcomes and Preventing Relapse in Cognitive Behavioural Therapy*, New York: Guilford Press.

FRENCH, J.R.O. and RAVEN, B.H. (1959) The bases of social power. In D. Cartwright (ed.) *Studies in Social Power*, Ann Arbor, MI: Institute for Social Research.

FREUD, S. (1900/1976) *The Interpretation of Dreams*, Pelican Freud Library, vol. 4, Harmondsworth: Penguin.

FREUD, S. (1901/1976) *The Psychopathology of Everyday Life*, Pelican Freud Library, vol. 5, Harmondsworth: Penguin.

FREUD, S. (1909/1977) *Analysis of a Phobia in a Five-Year-Old Boy*, Pelican Freud Library, vol. 8, Harmondsworth: Penguin.

FREUD, S. (1933/1973) *New Introductory Lectures on Psychoanalysis*, Pelican Freud Library, vol. 2, Harmondsworth: Penguin.

FRITH, U. (1989) *Autism: Explaining the Enigma*, Oxford: Blackwell.

FRITH, U. (2003) *Autism: Explaining the Enigma*, 2nd edn, Oxford: Blackwell.

GALTON, F. (1869) *Hereditary Genius: An Inquiry into its Laws and Consequences*, Cleveland, OH: World Publishing.

GANNON, P.J., HOLLOWAY, R.L., BROADFIELD, D.C. and BRAIN, A.R. (1998) Asymmetry of chimpanzee planum temporale. *Science*, 279: 220–2.

GAZZANIGA, M. (1967) The split brain in man. *Scientific American*, 217: 24–9.

GIBSON, J.J. (1966) *The Senses Considered as Perceptual Systems*, Boston, MA: Houghton Mifflin.

GILBERT, D.T. (1998) Ordinary personology. In D.T. Gilbert, S.T. Fiske and G. Lindzey (eds) *Handbook of Social Psychology*, 4th edn, vol. 2, 89–150, Boston, MA: McGraw-Hill.

GILBERT, D.T. and MALONE, P.S. (1995) The correspondence bias. *Psychological Bulletin*, 117: 21–38.

GILCHRIST, J.C. and NESBERG, L.S. (1952) Need and perceptual change in need-related objects. *Journal of Experimental Psychology*, 44: 369.

GLANZER, M. and CUNITZ, A.R. (1966) Two storage mechanisms in free recall. *Journal of Verbal Learning and Verbal Behavior*, 5(4): 351–60.

GODDEN, D. and BADDELEY, A.D. (1975) Context-dependent memory in two natural environments: On land and under water. *British Journal of Psychology*, 66: 325–31.

GOLOMBOK, S. and FIVUSH, R. (1994) *Gender Development*, Cambridge: Cambridge University Press.

GORDON, I.E. (1989) *Theories of Visual Perception*, Chichester: John Wiley and Sons.

GORSKI, R.A., GORDON, J.H., SHRYNE, J.E. and SOUTHAM, A.M. (1978) Evidence for a morphological sex difference within the medial preoptic area of the rat brain. *Brain Research*, 148: 333–46.

GOTTESMAN, I.I. (1991) *Schizophrenia Genesis*, New York: W.H. Freeman.

GOTTESMAN, I.I. and BERTELSEN, A. (1989) Confirming unexpressed genotypes for schizophrenia. *Archives of General Psychiatry*, 46: 867–72.

GREEN, R. (1978), Sexual identity of 37 children raised by homosexual or transsexual parents. *American Journal of Psychiatry*, 135: 692–7.

GREGORY, R.L. (1966) *Eye and Brain*, London: Weidenfeld and Nicholson.

GROEGER, J.A. (1997) *Memory and Remembering: Everyday Memory in Context*, New York: Addison Wesley Longman.

GROOME, D. (1999) *An Introduction to Cognitive Psychology: Processes and Disorders*, Hove: Psychology Press.

GROOME, D.H. and SOURETI, A. (2004) PTSD and anxiety symptoms in children exposed to the 1999 Greek earthquake. *British Journal of Psychology*, 95: 387–97.

GROSS, R. (2005) *Psychology: The Science of Mind and Behaviour*, 5th edn, London: Hodder Education.

HAMILTON, G.V. (1978) Obedience and responsibility: A jury simulation. *Journal of Personality and Social Psychology*, 36: 126–46.

HAPPÉ, F. (1999) Understanding assets and deficits in autism. Why success is more interesting than failure. *The Psychologist*, 12(11): 540–6.

HEBB, D.O. (1949) *Organization of Behaviour*, New York: John Wiley and Sons.

HEIDER, F. (1944) Social perception and phenomenal causality. *Psychological Review*, 51: 358–74.

HEIDER, F. (1958) *The Psychology of Interpersonal Relations*. New York: John Wiley and Sons.

HEINDEL, W.C., BUTTERS, N. and SALMON, D.P. (1988) Impaired learning of a motor skill in patients with Huntington's disease. *Behavioural Neuroscience*, 102: 141–7.

HENCHY, T.P. and GLASS, D.C. (1968) Evaluation apprehension and social facilitation of dominant and subordinate responses. *Journal of Personality and Social Psychology*, 10: 446–54.

HENDERSON, N.D. (1982) Human behaviour genetics. *Annual Review of Psychology*, 33: 403–40.

HEREK, G.M. (1987) Can function be measured? A new perspective on the functional approach to attitudes. *Social Psychology Quarterly*, 50: 285–303.

HERMELIN, B. and O'CONNOR, N. (1967) Remembering of words by psychotic and sub-normal children. *British Journal of Psychology*, 58: 213–18.

HINES, M. (2004) *Brain Gender*, Oxford: Oxford University Press.

HOBSON, R.P., OUSTON, J. and LEE, T. (1988) What's in a face? The case of autism. *British Journal of Psychology*, 79: 441–53.

HODGSON, R.J. and RACHMAN, S. (1972) The effects of contamination and washing in obsessive patients. *Behaviour Research and Therapy*, 10: 111–17.

HOFFMAN, S.G. (2000) Self-focused attention before and after treatment of social phobia. *Behaviour Research and Therapy*, 38: 717–25.

HOGG, M.A. and VAUGHAN, G.M. (2002) *Social Psychology*, 3rd edn, London: Prentice Hall.

HORNEY, K. (1933/1967) *The Denial of the Vagina*. Reprinted in H.M. Ruitenbook (ed.) *Psychoanalysis and Female Sexuality*, New Haven, CT: College and University Press.

HOWLIN, P.A. and RUTTER, M. (1987) *Treatment of Autistic Children*, New York: John Wiley and Sons.

HUBEL, D.H. and WEISEL, T.N. (1979) Brain mechanisms of vision. *Scientific American*, 241: 150–62.

HUDSON, W. (1960) Pictorial depth perception in sub-cultural groups in Africa. *Journal of Social Psychology*, 52: 183–208.

HUGUET, P. GALVAIANG, M.P., MONTEIL, J.M. and DUMAS, F. (1999) Social presence effects in the Stroop task: Further evidence for an attentional view of social facilitation. *Journal of Personality and Social Psychology*, 77: 1011–25.

HYMAN, H.H. and SHEATSLEY, P.B. (1954) The authoritarian personality: A methodological critique. In R. Christie and M. Jahoda (eds) *Studies in the Scope of the Authoritarian Personality*, New York: Free Press.

IMPERATO-MCGINLEY, J., PETERSON, R.E., STOLLER, R. and GOODWIN, W.E. (1979) Male pseudohermaphroditism secondary to 17-beta-dehyroxysteroid dehydrogenase deficiency: Gender role change with puberty. *Journal of Clinical Endocrinology and Metabolism*, 49: 391–5.

JENIKE, M.A. et al. (1991) Cingulotomy for refractory obsessive compulsive disorder: A long-term follow-up of 33 patients. *Archives of General Psychiatry*, 48: 548–55.

JENKINS, J.G. and DALLENBACH, K.M. (1924) Obliviscence during sleeping and waking. *American Journal of Psychology*, 35: 605–12.

JENNESS, A. (1932) The role of discussion in changing opinion regarding matter of fact. *Journal of Abnormal and Social Psychology*, 27: 279–96.

JOHNSON, L.A. (2005) Lobotomy back in the spotlight after 30 years. *Netscape News*.

JONES, E.E. and NISBETT, R.E. (1971) *The Actor and the Observer: Divergent Perceptions of the Causes of Behaviour*, Morristown, NJ: General Learning Press.

JONES, E.E. and GOETHALS, G.R. (1972) Order effects in impression formation: Attribution context and the nature of the entity. In E.E. Jones et al. (eds) *Attribution: Perceiving the Causes of Behaviour*, Morristown, NJ: General Learning Press.

JULIEN, R.M. (2005) *A Primer of Drug Action*, New York: Worth Publishers.

KALAT, J.W. (1992) *Biological Psychology*, 4th edn, Pacific Grove, CA: Brooks/Cole.

KANNER, B. (1998) Are you normal? Creatures of habit. *American Demography*.

KANNER, L. (1943) Autistic disturbance of affective contact. *Nervous Child*, 12: 17–50.

KATZ, D. (1960) The functional approach to the study of attitudes. *Public Opinion Quarterly*, 24: 163–204.

KELLEY, H.H. (1950) The warm-cold variable in first impressions of persons. *Journal of Personality*, 18: 431–9.

KELMAN, H.C. (1958) Compliance, identification and internalisation: Three processes of attitude change. *Journal of Conflict Resolution*, 2: 51–60.

KELMAN, H.C. (1967) Human use of human subjects: The problem of deception in social psychology. *Psychological Bulletin*, 67: 1–11.

KELMAN, H.C. and HAMILTON, V.L. (1989) *Crimes of Obedience*, New Haven, CT: Yale University Press.

KENDALL, P.C. (2000) *Childhood Disorders*, Hove: Psychology Press.

KENDLER, K.S. and DIEHL, S.R. (1993) The genetics of schizophrenia: A current genetic-epidemiologic perspective. *Schizophrenia Bulletin*, 19: 261–85.

KERR, N.L. and PARK, E.S. (2001) Group performance in collaborative and social dilemma

tasks: Progress and prospects. In M.A. Hogg and R.S Tindale (eds) *Blackwell Handbook of Social Psychology: Group Processes*, Oxford: Blackwell.

KETY, S.S. (1988) Schizophrenic illness in the families of schizophrenic adoptees: Findings from the Danish national sample. *Schizophrenia Bulletin*, 14: 217–22.

KIM, C.H., JAYATHILAKE, K. and MELTZER, H.Y. (2003) Hopelessness, neurocognitive function, and insight in schizophrenia: Relationship to suicidal behaviour. *Schizophrenia Research*, 60(1): 71–80.

KING, N.J., ELEONORA, G. and OLLENDICK, T.H. (1998) Etiology of childhood phobias: Current status of Rachman's three pathways. *Behaviour Research and Therapy*, 36: 297–306.

KLAR, A.J.S. (2003) Human handedness and scalp hair-whorl direction develop from a common genetic mechanism. *Genetics*, 165: 2027–30.

KOEGEL, R.L., SCHREIBMAN, L., O'NEILL, R.E. and BURKE, J.C. (1983) The personality and family interaction characteristics of parents of autistic children. *Journal of Consulting and Clinical Psychology*, 51: 683–92.

KOHLBERG, L. (1966) A cognitive-developmental analysis of children's sex-role concepts and attitudes. In E.E. Maccoby (ed.) *The Development of Sex Differences*, Stanford, CA: Stanford University Press.

KORDON, A. et al. (2005) Clinical outcome in patients with obsessive–compulsive disorder after discontinuation of SRI treatment: Results from a two-year follow-up. *European Archives of Psychiatry and Clinical Neuroscience*, 255: 48–50.

KRUPA, D.J., THOMPSON, J.K. and THOMPSON, R.F. (1993) Localisation of a memory trace in a mammalian brain. *Science*, 260: 989–91.

KUMAR, K., WYANT, G.M. and NATH, D. (1990) Deep brain stimulation for control of intractable pain in humans, present and future: A ten-year follow-up. *Neurosurgery*, 26: 774–82.

LA FRAMBOISE, T.D., HEYLE, A.M. and OZER, E.J. (1990) Gender and ethnicity: Perspectives on dual status. *Sex Roles*, 22: 455–76.

LANG, P.J. and LAZOVIK, A.D. (1963) Experimental desensitisation of a phobia. *Journal of Abnormal and Social Psychology*, 66: 519–25.

LA PIERE, R.T. (1934) Attitudes and actions. *Social Forces*, 13: 230–7.

LASHLEY, K.S. (1950) In search of the engram. In *Symposium for the Society of Experimental Biology*, vol. 4, New York: Cambridge University Press.

LATANE, B. and L'HERROU, T. (1996) Spatial clustering in the conformity game: Dynamic social impact of electronic groups. *Journal of Personality and Social Psychology*, 70: 1218–30.

LAZARUS, R.S. and MCCLEARY, R.A. (1951) Autonomic discrimination without awareness. *Psychological Review*, 58: 113.

LEBOYER, M., BOUVARD, M.P., LAUDAY, J.M. et al. (1992) Brief report: A double-blind study of naltrexone in infantile autism. *Journal of Autism and Developmental Disorders*, 22: 309–19.

LECKMAN, J.F. et al. (1997) Symptoms of obsessive–compulsive disorder. *American Journal of Psychiatry*, 154: 911–17.

LESLIE, A.M. (1987) Pretence and representation: The origins of 'theory of mind'. *Psychological Review*, 94: 412–26.

LEVINGER, G. and CLARK, J. (1961) Emotional factors in the forgetting of word association. *Journal of Abnormal and Social Psychology*, 62: 99–105.

LIEBERMAN, P. (1963) Some effects of semantic and grammatical context on the production and comprehension of speech. *Language and Speech*, 6, 172–87. Also in M.M. Smyth, P.E. Morris, P. Levy and A.W. Ellis (1987) *Cognition in Action*, London: Lawrence Erlbaum Associates.

LINTON, M. (1975) Memory for real-world events. In D.A. Norman and D. A. Rumelhart (eds) *Explorations in Cognition*, San Francisco, CA: Freeman.

LOCKHART, R.S. and CRAIK, F.I.M. (1990) Levels of processing: A retrospective commentary on a framework for memory research. *Canadian Journal of Psychology*, 44: 87–112.

LOGIE, R.H. (1999) Working memory. *The Psychologist*, 12: 174–8.

LOGIE, R.H., BADDELEY, A.D., MANE, A., DONCHIN, E. and SHEPTAK, R. (1989) Working memory and the analysis of a complex skill by secondary task methodology. *Acta Psychologica*, 71: 53–87.

LOVAAS, O.I. (1977) *The Autistic Child: Language Development through Behaviour Modification*, New York: Holsted Press.

LOVAAS, O.I. (1987) Behavioural treatment and normal educational and intellectual functioning in young autistic children. *Journal of Consulting and Clinical Psychology*, 55: 3–9.

LUCHINS, A.S. (1957) Primacy–recency in impression formation. In C. Hovland (ed.) *The Order of Presentation in Persuasion*, New Haven, CT: Yale University Press.

MACCOBY, E.E. and JACKLIN, C.N. (1974) *Psychology of Sex Difference*, Stanford, CA: Stanford University Press.

MacCRACKEN, M.J. and STADULIS, R.E. (1985) Social facilitation of young children's dynamic performance balance. *Journal of Sport Psychology*, 7: 150–65.

MARKUS, H. and NURIUS, P. (1986) Possible selves. *American Psychologist*, 41: 954–69.

MARTIN, C.L. (1989) Children's use of gender-related information in making social judgements. *Developmental Psychology*, 25: 80–8.

MARTIN, C.L. and HALVERSON, C. (1981) A schematic model of sex-typing and stereotyping in children. *Child Development*, 52: 1119–34.

MASLING, J. (1966) Role-related behaviour of the subject and psychologist and its effect upon psychological data. In D. Levine (ed.) *Nebraska Symposium on Motivation*, Lincoln, NE: University of Nebraska Press.

MASLOW, A.H. (1970) *Motivation and Personality*, 2nd edn, New York: Harper & Row.

MASSON, J.M. (1985) *The Complete Letters of Sigmund Freud to Wilhelm Fleiss, 1887–1904*, Cambridge, MA and London, Cambridge University Press.

MASTERS, J.C., FORD, M.E., AREND, R., GROTEVANT, H.D. and CLARK, L.V. (1979) Modeling and labelling as integrated determinants of children's sex-typed imitative behaviour. *Child Development*, 50: 364–71.

MATLIN, M. (2002) *Cognition*, 5th edn, Fort Worth, TX: Harcourt College Publishers.

McADOO, W.G. and De MYER, M.K. (1978) Personality characteristics of parents. In M. Rutter and E. Schopler (eds) *Autism: A Reappraisal of Concepts and Treatment*, New York: Plenum.

McCONAGHY, M.J. (1979) Gender permanence and the genital basis of gender: Stages in the development of constancy of gender identity. *Child Development*, 50: 1223–6.

McCRACKEN, J.T., McGEOGH, M.D., SHAH, B. et al. (2002) Risperidone in children with autism and serious behavioural problems. *New England Journal of Medicine*, 347: 314–21.

McGINNIES, E. (1949) Emotionality and perceptual defense. *Psychological Review*, 56: 244.

McKEON, P. and MURRAY, R. (1987) Familial aspects of obsessive–compulsive neurosis. *British Journal of Psychiatry*, 151: 528–34.

MEAD, M. (1935) *Sex and Temperament in Three Primitive Societies*, New York: Dell.

MEDIN, D.L., ROSS, B.H. and MARKHAM, A.B. (2001) *Cognitive Psychology*, 3rd edn, New York: Harcourt College Publishers.

MENZIES, R.G. and CLARKE, J.C. (1995) Danger expectancies and insight in acrophobia. *Behaviour Research and Therapy*, 33: 215–22.

MESSER, D. and MILLAR, S. (1999) *Exploring Developmental Psychology*, London: Hodder Education.

MEYER, V. (1966) Modification of expectations in cases with obsessive rituals. *Behaviour Research and Therapy*, 4: 273–80.

MICHAELS, J.W., BLOMMEL, J.M., BROCATO, R.M., LINKOUS, R.A. and ROWE, J.S. (1982) Social facilitation and inhibition in a natural setting. *Replications in Social Psychology*, 2: 21–4.

MIDGLEY, S.J., HEATON, N. and DAVID, J.B. (2001) Levels of aggression among a group of anabolic-steroid users. *Medicine, Science and the Law*, 41: 309–14.

MILGRAM, S. (1963) Behaviour study of obedience. *Journal of Abnormal and Social Psychology*, 67: 371–8.

MILGRAM, S. (1965) Some conditions of obedience and disobedience to authority. *Human Relations*, 18, 57–76.

MILGRAM, S. (1974) *Obedience to Authority*, New York: Harper.

MILLER, G.A. (1956) The magical number seven, plus or minus two: Some limits on our capacity for processing information. *Psychological Review*, 63: 81–97.

MILNER, B., CORKIN, S. and TEUBER, H.L. (1968) Further analysis of the hippocampal amnesic syndrome: 14-year follow-up study of HM. *Neuropsychologia*, 6: 215–34.

MINARD, R.D. (1952) Race relations in the Pocahontas coal field. *Journal of Social Issues*, 8: 29–44.

MISCHEL, W. (1966) A social-learning view of sex differences in behaviour. In E.E. Maccoby (ed.) *The Development of Sex Differences*, Stanford, CA: Stanford University Press.

MONEY, J. and ERHARDT, A.A. (1972) *Man and Woman, Boy and Girl*, Baltimore, MD: Johns Hopkins University Press.

MULLEN, B. (1991) Group composition, salience and cognitive representations: The phemenology of being in a group. *Journal of Experimental Social Psychology*, 27: 297–323.

MUNROE, R.H., SHIMMIN, H.L. and MUNROE, R.L. (1984) Gender understanding and sex-role preference in four cultures. *Development Psychology*, 20: 673–82.

MURIS, P. and MERCKELBACH, H. (2000) How serious are common childhood fears? The parent's point of view. *Behaviour Research and Therapy*, 38: 813–18.

MURREL, A.J., DIETZ-UHLER, B.L., DOVIDIO, J.F., GAERTNER, S.L. and DROUT C. (1994) Aversive racism and resistance to affirmative action: Perceptions of justice are not necessarily color blind. *Basic and Applied Social Psychology*, 15: 71–86.

NAESAR, M.A., PALUMBO, C.L., HELM-ESTABROOKS, N., STAISSY-EDER, D. and ALBERT, M.L. (1989) Severe non-fluency in aphasia. *Brain*, 112: 1–38.

NAIRNE, J.S. (1996) Short-term/working memory. In E.L. Bjork and R.A. Bjork (eds) *Memory*, San Diego, CA: Academic Press.

NAVON, D. (1977) Forest before trees: The precedence of global features in visual perception. *Cognitive Psychology*, 9: 353–83.

NEISSER, U. (1976) *Cognition and Reality*, San Francisco, CA: W.H. Freeman.

NEWCOMBE, N.S., DRUMMEY, A.B., FOX, N.A., LIE, E. and OTTINGER-ALBERTS, W. (2000) Remembering early childhood: How much, how, and why (or why not). *Current Directions in Psychological Science*, 9: 55–8.

NISBETT, R.E. CAPUTO, C., LEGANT, P. and MARACEK, J. (1973) Behaviour as seen by the actor and the observer. *Journal of Personality and Social Psychology*, 27: 154–64.

NISBETT, R.E. and WILSON, T.D. (1977) Telling more than we can know: verbal reports on mental processes. *Psychological Review*, 84: 231–59.

OETTINGEN, G. (1995) Explanatory style in the context of culture. In G.M. Buchanan and M.E.P Seligman (eds), *Explanatory Style*, Hillsdale, NJ: Lawrence Erlbaum Associates.

OHMAN, A., ERIXON, G. and LOFBERG, I. (1975) Phobias and preparedness: Phobic versus neutral pictures as continued stimuli for human autonomic responses. *Journal of Abnormal Psychology*, 84: 41–5.

OHNISHI, T., MATSUDA, H., HASHIMOTO, T. et al. (2000) Abnormal regional cerebral blood flow in childhood autism. *Brain*, 123: 1838–44.

O'KEARNEY, R.O. (1993) Additional considerations in cognitive-behavioural treatment of obsessive ruminations: A case study. *Journal of Behaviour Therapy and Experimental Psychiatry*, 24: 357–65.

OLSON, J.M. and ZANNA, M.P. (1993) Attitudes and attitude change. *Annual Review of Psychology*, 44: 117–54.

OST, L.G. (1992) Blood and injection phobia: Background and cognitive, physiological and behavioural variables. *Journal of Abnormal Psychology*, 101: 68–74.

PARKIN, A.J. (1993) *Memory: Phenomena, Experiment and Theory*, Oxford: Blackwell.

PAULESU, E., FRITH, C.D. and FRACKOWIACK, R.S.J. (1993) The neural correlates of the verbal component of working memory. *Nature*, 362: 342–5.

PENFIELD, W. and RASMUSSEN, T. (1950) *The Cerebral Cortex of Man: A Clinical Study of Localisation of Function*, Boston, MA: Little, Brown and Co.

PENFIELD W. and JASPER, H. (1954) *Epilepsy and the Functional Anatomy of the Human Brain*, Boston, MA: Little, Brown and Co.

PENNINGTON, D.C. (2002) *Social Psychology of Behaviour in Small Groups*, London: Routledge.

PENNINGTON, D.C. (2003) *Essential Personality*, London: Hodder Education.

PENNINGTON, D.C., GILLEN, K. and HILL, P. (1999) *Social Psychology*, London: Hodder Education.

PERNER, J., FRITH, U., LESLIE, A.M. and LEEKHAM, S.R. (1989) Exploration of the child's theory of mind: Knowledge belief and communication. *Child Development*, 60: 689–700.

PERRY, D.G. and BUSSEY, K. (1979) The social learning theory of sex difference: Imitation is alive and well. *Journal of Personality and Social Psychology*, 37: 1699–712.

PETERSEN, S.E., FOX, P.T., POSNER, M.I., MINTIN, M. and RAICHLE, M.E. (1988) Positron emission tomographic studies of the cortical anatomy of single word processing. *Nature*, 331: 585–9.

PETERSON, L.R. and PETERSON, M.J. (1959) Short-term retention of individual verbal items. *Journal of Experimental Psychology*, 58: 193–8.

PETTIGREW, T.F. and MEERTENS, R.W. (1995) Subtle and blatant prejudice in Western Europe. *Journal of European Social Psychology*, 25: 57–75.

PETTY, R.E. and CACIOPPO, J.T. (1986) *Communication and Persuasion: Central and Peripheral Routes to Attitude Change*, New York: Springer-Verlag.

PINEL, J.P.J. (1993) *Biopsychology*, Boston, MA: Allyn & Bacon.

PLOMIN, R. (1988) The nature and nurture of cognitive abilities. In R. Steinberg (ed.) *Advances in the Psychology of Human Intelligence*, Hillsdale, NJ: Lawrence Erlbaum Associates.

PLOMIN, R. and DEFRIES, J.C. (1998) The genetics of cognitive abilities and disabilities. *Scientific American*, May: 62–9.

POPPER, K. (1963) *Conjectures and Refutations: The Growth of Scientific Knowledge*, New York: Basic Books.

POSTMAN, L. and PHILLIPS, L.W. (1965) Short-term temporal changes in free recall. *Quarterly Journal of Experimental Psychology*, 17: 132–8.

PRIOR, M. and WHERRY, J.S. (1986) Autism, schizophrenia and allied disorders. In H.C. Quay and J.S. Wherry (eds) *Psychopathological Disorders of Childhood*, 3rd edn, New York: John Wiley and Sons.

RACHMAN, S. (1997) A cognitive theory of obsessions. *Behaviour Research and Therapy*, 35: 793–802.

RITVO, E.R., FREEMAN, B.J., MASON-BROTHERS, A., MO, A. and RITVO, A.M. (1985) Concordance of the syndrome of autism in 40 pairs of afflicted twins. *American Journal of Psychiatry*, 142: 74–7.

ROBBINS, T.W., ANDERSON, E.J., BARKER, D.R., BRADLEY, A.C., FEARNYHOUGH, C., HENSON, R., HUDSON, S.R. and BADDELEY, A.D. (1996) Working memory in chess. *Memory and Cognition*, 24(1): 83–93.

ROBINS, L.N. and REGIER, D.A. (1991) *Psychiatric Disorders in America: The Epidemiological Catchment Area*, New York: Free Press.

ROCHAT, F. and MODIGLIANI, A. (1995) The ordinary quality of resistance: From Milgram's laboratory to the village of Le Chambon. *Journal of Social Issues*, 5: 195–210.

RODER, P. (2000) The early origins of autism. *Scientific American*, 282(2): 56–63.

ROGERS, C. (1959) A theory of therapy, personality and interpersonal relationships, as developed in the client-centred frameworks. In S. Koch (ed.) *Psychology: A Study of Science*, vol. 3, Boston, MA: Houghton Mifflin.

ROGERS, C. (1961) *On Becoming a Person: A Therapist's View of Psychotherapy*, Boston, MA: Houghton Mifflin.

ROGERS, C. (1980) *A Way of Being*, Boston, MA: Houghton Mifflin.

ROKEACH, M. (1960) *The Open and Closed Mind*, New York: Basic Books.

ROSE, S. (1992) *The Making of Memory: From Molecule to Mind*, London: Bantam Books.

ROSS, L., AMABILE, T.M. and STEINMETZ, J.L. (1977) Social roles, social control and biases in social perception processes. *Journal of Personality and Social Psychology*, 35: 485–94.

ROSS, L., BIERBRAUER, G. and POLLY, M. (1974) Attribution of education outcomes by professional and non-professional instructors. *Journal of Experimental Social Psychology*, 29: 609–18.

RUBIN, D.C., WETZLER, S.E. and NEBES, R.D. (1986) Autobiographical memory across the lifespan. In D.C. Rubin (ed.) *Autobiographical Memory*, Cambridge: Cambridge University Press.

RUFER, M. et al. (2005) Long-term course and outcome of obsessive–compulsive patients after cognitive-behavioural therapy in combination with either fluvoxamine or placebo: A 7-year follow-up of a randomised double-blind trial. *European Archives of Psychiatry and Clinical Neuroscience*, 255: 212–28.

RUTTER, M., SILBERG, J., O'CONNOR, T. and SIMINOFF, E. (1999) Genetics and child psychiatry: Empirical research findings. *Journal of Child Psychology and Psychiatry*, 40: 19–55.

SAPOLSKY, R.M. (1992) *Stress, the Aging Brain and Mechanisms of Neuron Death*, Cambridge, MA: MIT Press.

SAUNDERS, G.G. (1983) An attentional process model of social facilitation. In A. Hare, H. Blumberg, V. Kent and M. Davies (eds) *Small Groups*, London: John Wiley and Sons.

SAUNDERS, G.S., BORAN, R.S. and MOORE, D.L. (1978) Distraction and social comparison as mediators of social facilitation effects. *Journal of Experimental Social Psychology*, 14: 291–303.

SCARR, S. and WEINBERG, R.A. (1978) The influence of 'family background' on intellectual attainment. *American Sociological Review*, 43: 674–92.

SCHER, C.D., STEIDTMANN, D., LUXTON, D. and INGRAM, R.E. (2006) Specific phobia: A common problem rarely treated. In T.G. Plante (ed.) *Mental Disorders of the New Millennium*, vol. 1, Westport, CT: Praeger Publishers.

SCHMIDT, H.G., PEECK, V.H., PAAS, F. and VAN BREUKELEN, G.J.P. (2000) Remembering the street names of one's childhood neighbourhood: A study of very long-term retention. *Memory*, 8: 37–49.

SCHMITT, B.H., GILOVICH, T., GOORE, N. and JOSEPH, L. (1986) Mere presence and socio-facilitation: One more time. *Journal of Experimental Social Psychology*, 22: 242–8.

SCHULKIND, M.D., HENNIS, L.K. and RUBIN, D.C. (1999) Music, emotion, and autobiographical memory: They're playing your song. *Memory and Cognition*, 27: 948–55.

SEAVEY, A.A., KATZ, P.A. and ZALK, S.R. (1975) Baby X: The effect of gender labels on adult responses to infants. *Sex Roles*, 1: 103–9.

SEGALL, M.H., CAMPBELL, D.T. and HERSKOVITS, M.J. (1963) Cultural differences in the perception of geometrical illusions. *Science*, 139: 769–71.

SHAH, A. and FRITH, U. (1993) Why do autistic individuals show superior performance in the block design task? *Journal of Child Psychology and Psychiatry*, 34: 1351–64.

SHALLICE, T. and WARRINGTON, E.K. (1970) Independent functioning of of verbal memory stores: A neuropsychological study. *Quarterly Journal of Experimental Psychology*, 22: 261–73.

SHARP, M.J. and GETZ, J.G. (1996) Substance use as impression management. *Personality and Social Psychology Bulletin*, 22: 60–7.

SHAVITT, S. and NELSON, M.R. (2000) The social identity function in person perception: Communicated meanings of product references. In G.R. Maio and J.M. Olson (eds) *Why We Evaluate: Functions of Attitudes*, Mahwah, NJ: Lawrence Erlbaum Associates.

SHERIF, M. (1936) *The Psychology of Social Norms*, New York: Harper & Row.

SHERIF, M., HARVEY, O.J., WHITE, B.J., HOOD, W.R. and SHERIF, C.W. (1961) *Inter-group Conflict and Co-operation: The Robber's Cave Experiment*, Norman, OK: University of Oklahoma.

SIDANIUS, J. and PRATTO, F. (1999) *Social Dominance: An Intergroup Theory of Social Hierarchy and Oppression*, New York: Cambridge University Press.

SIGMAN, M., MUNDY, P., SHERMAN, T. and UNGERER, J. (1986) Social interactions of autistic, mentally retarded, and normal children and their caregivers. *Journal of Child Psychology and Psychiatry*, 27: 657–69.

SILBER, K. and WAGNER, H. (2004) *Physiological Psychology*, Abingdon: BIOS Scientific Publishers.

SKINNER, B.F. (1953) *Science and Human Behaviour*, New York: Macmillan.

SKINNER, B.F. (1990) Can psychology be a science of mind? *American Psychologist*, 45: 1206–10.

SLABY, R.G. and FREY, K.S. (1975) Development of gender constancy and selective attention to same-sex models. *Child Development*, 46: 849–56.

SLOMAN, L. (1991) Use of medication in pervasive mental disorders. *Psychiatric Clinics of North America*, 14: 165–82.

SMITH, M.L. and GLASS, G.V. (1977) Meta-analysis of psychotherapeutic outcome studies. *American Psychologist*, 32: 752–60.

SMITH, P.B. and HARRIS BOND, M. (1998) *Social Psychology Across Cultures: Analysis and Perspective*, London: Prentice Hall.

SMITH, S.M. (1979) Remembering in and out of context. *Journal of Experimental Psychology: Human Learning and Memory*, 5: 460–71.

SNYDER, C.R. and DeBONO, K.R. (1985) Appeals to images and claims about quality: Understanding the psychology of advertising. *Journal of Personality and Social Psychology*, 49: 586–97.

SOLSO, R.L. (1995) *Cognitive Psychology*, 4th edn, Boston, MA: Allyn & Bacon.

SPERLING, G. (1960) The information available in brief visual presentations. *Psychological Monographs*, 74: 1–29.

SPERRY, R. (1984) Consciousness, personal identity and divided brain. *Neuropsychologica*, 22: 661–73.

STANG, D.J. (1973) Effects of interaction rate on ratings of leadership and liking. *Journal of Personality and Social Psychology*, 27: 405–8.

STERN, M. and KARRAKER, K.H. (1989) Sex stereotyping of infants: A review of gender labelling studies. *Sex Roles*, 20: 501–22.

STERNBERG, R.J. (2001) *Psychology: In Search of the Human Mind*, 3rd edn, Fort Worth, TX: Harcourt College Publishers.

STORMS, M.D. (1973) Videotape and the attribution process: Reversing actors' and observers' points of view. *Journal of Personality and Social Psychology*, 27: 165–75.

SUE, D., SUE, D.W. and SUE, S. (2003) *Understanding Abnormal Behaviour*, 7th edn, Boston, MA: Houghton Mifflin Company.

SURIN, J.K., ASKIN, K.J., HALL, W.S. and HUNTER, B.A. (1995) Sexism and racism: Old-fashioned and modern prejudices. *Journal of Personality and Social Psychology*, 68: 199–214.

TAJFEL, H. (1970) Experiments in inter-group discrimination. *Scientific American*, 223: 96–102.

TAJFEL, H. and TURNER, J.C. (1986) The social identity theory of intergroup behaviour. In S. Worschel and W.G. Austin (eds) *Psychology of Intergroup Relations*, 2nd edn, Monterey, CA: Brooks/Cole.

TAYLOR, S.E. and KOIVUMAKI, J.H. (1976) The perception of self and others: Acquaintanceship, affect and actor-observer differences. *Journal of Personality and Social Psychology*, 33: 403–8.

THORNDIKE, E.L. (1911) *Animal Intelligence*, New York: Macmillan.

TOCH, H.H. and SCHULTE, R. (1961) Readiness to perceive violence as a result of police training. *British Journal of Psychology*, 52: 389–93.

TRICKER, R., CASABURI, R., STORER, T.W. et al. (1996) The effects of supraphysiological doses of testosterone on anger behaviour in healthy eugonadal men – A clinical research centre study. *Journal of Clinical Endocrinology and Metabolism*, 81: 3754–8.

TRIPLETT, N. (1898) The dynomogenic factors in pacemaking and competition. *American Journal of Psychology*, 9: 507–33.

TULVING, E. (1972) Episodic and semantic memory. In E. Tulving and W. Donaldson (eds) *Organisation of Memory*, London: Academic Press.

TULVING, E. (1989) Memory: Performance, knowledge and experience. *European Journal of Cognitive Psychology*, 1: 3–26.

TULVING, E. and PEARLSTONE, Z. (1966) Availability versus accessibility of information in memory for words. *Journal of Verbal Learning and Verbal Behaviour*, 5: 381–91.

TULVING, E. and THOMPSON, D.M. (1973) Encoding specificity and retrieval processes in episodic memory. *Psychological Review*, 80: 352–73.

TURK, C.L., HEIMBERG, R.G. and HOPE, D.A. (2001) Social phobia and social anxiety. In D.H. Barlow (ed.) *Clinical Handbook of Psychological Disorders: A Step-by-Step Treatment Manual*, 3rd edn, New York: Guilford Press.

TURNBULL, C.M. (1961) *The Forest People*, New York: Simon and Schuster.

TURNER, M. (1999) Generating novel ideas: Fluency performance in high-functioning and learning-disabled individuals with autism. *Journal of Child Psychology and Psychiatry and Allied Disciplines*, 40: 189–201.

UNDERWOOD, B.J. and EKSTRAND, B.R. (1967) Word frequency and accumulative proactive inhibition. *Journal of Experimental Psychology*, 74: 193–8.

URBERG, K.A. (1982) The development of the concepts of masculinity and femininity in young children. *Sex Roles*, 8: 659–68.

Van de POLL, N.E., TAMINIAU, M.S., ENDERT, E. and LOUWERSE, A.L. (1988) Gonadal steroid influence upon sexual and aggressive behaviour of female rats. *International Journal of Neuroscience*, 41: 271–86.

VONK, R. (1998) The slime effect: Suspicion and dislike of likeable behaviour toward superiors. *Journal of Personality and Social Psychology*, 74: 849–864.

WADE, C. and TAVRIS, C. (1998) *Psychology*, 5th edn, New York: Addison-Wesley.

WARR, P.B. (1964) The relative importance of proactive inhibition and degree of learning in retention of paired associate items. *British Journal of Psychology*, 55: 19–30.

WARREN, R.M. and WARREN, R.P. (1970) Auditory illusions and confusions. *Scientific American*, 223: 30–6.

WASON, P.C. (1968) Reasoning about a rule. *Quarterly Journal of Experimental Psychology*, 20: 129–40.

WATSON, J.B. and RAYNER, R. (1920) Conditioning emotional reactions. *Journal of Experimental Psychology*, 3: 1–14.

WAUGH, N.C. and NORMAN, D.A. (1965) Primary memory. *Psychological Review*, 72: 89–104.

WAYNE, S.J. and LIDEN, R.C. (1995) Effects of impression management on performance ratings: A longitudinal study. *Academy of Management Journal*, 38: 232–60.

WEINER, B. (1985) Spontaneous causal thinking. *Psychological Bulletin*, 97: 74–84.

WESTEN, D. (1999) *Psychology: Mind, Brain and Culture*, 2nd edn, New York: John Wiley and Sons.

WHEELER, M.A., STUSS, D.T. and TULVING, E. (1997) Toward a theory of episodic memory: The frontal lobes and autonoetic consciousness. *Psychological Bulletin*, 121: 331–54.

WHITELY, B.E. (1983) Sex-role orientation and self-esteem: A critical meta-analytic review. *Journal of Personality and Social Psychology*, 44: 765–85.

WICKLUND, R.A. (1975) Objective self-awareness. In L. Berkowitz (ed.) *Advances in Experimental Social Psychology*, vol. 8, New York: Academic Press.

WILLIAMS, L.M. (1994) Recall of childhood trauma: A prospective study of women's memories of child sexual abuse. *Journal of Consulting and Clinical Psychology*, 62: 1167–76.

WING, L. and GOULD, J. (1979) Severe impairments of social interaction and associated abnormalities in children: Epidemiology and classification. *Journal of Autism and Developmental Disorders*, 9: 11–29.

WOLF, M., RISLEY, T. and MEES, H. (1964) Application of operant conditioning procedures to the behaviour problems of an autistic child. *Behaviour Research and Therapy*, 1: 305–12.

WOLPE, J. (1958) *Psychotherapy by Reciprocal Inhibition*, Stanford, CA: Stanford University Press.

YARNELL, P.R. and LYNCH, S. (1970) Retrograde memory immediately after concussion. *Lancet*, 1: 863–5.

ZAJONC, R.B. (1965) Social facilitation. *Science*, 149: 269–74.

ZAJONC, R.B. (1983) Validating the confluence model. *Psychological Bulletin*, 93: 457–80.

ZAJONC, R.B., HEINGARTNER, A. and HERMAN, E.M. (1969) Social enhancement and impairment of performance in the cockroach. *Journal of Personality and Social Psychology*, 13: 83–92.